1

For Christine, Riley, Chase and Georgia

Hopefully, this explains a few things... I love you.

Info@StephenGriffinAuthor.com

PROLOGUE

When my middle son Chase was twelve years old, he and his
teammates participated in an American rite of passage for little
league baseball players. They played on their town's twelve-year-old
all-star team. Unfortunately, they lost in the state finals. While they
were disappointed that they weren't heading to the Little League
World Series in Williamsport, Pennsylvania, a number of them were
already looking forward to another trip, one that had been scheduled
for their "travel team" over a year in advance – to Cooperstown
Dreams Park.

In 1996, outside of Cooperstown, NY, on 156 acres of farmland, a
gentleman named Lou Presutti built twenty-two baseball fields,
twenty batting cages, over one hundred Quonset hut-like barracks to
house the players, a cafeteria, concessions for the fans, and a
merchandise shop. Each summer nearly 20,000 children, and another
50,000 spectators, came to the facility to play in week-long
tournaments; more visitors than the Baseball Hall of Fame generates
annually.

While at the tournament, I witnessed first-hand a paradigm shift in
youth sports. Along with four other dads, we had rented a house
about fifteen minutes from the Park because all of the hotel rooms in
the area were booked. I watched parents eat non-stop at the
concessions stand; buy shirts, hats, hoodies, and photographs of their

children. The kids traded commemorative pins when they weren't practicing or playing games. They also pumped quarters into the video games at the arcade located a short walk from their barracks. The influx of these families had a significant impact on the local Cooperstown economy - estimated in excess of $75 million annually.

The tournament itself was a well-oiled machine. From the moment you arrived, there were greeters guiding you to a designated drop-off area, based on your team, so you could get your child moved into their barracks. The opening ceremonies included a parade with each team entering the main stadium filled with awaiting family members. Once the stadium was full, Lou Presutti delivered an impassioned speech about patriotism and sportsmanship, followed by a parachutist dropping in with a ball for him to throw the ceremonial first pitch to officially kick-off the tournament. Games started on time, umpires were always available, the fields were impeccably maintained, each field was even surrounded by deep green-painted plywood instead of chain link fencing which made the kids feel like they were playing within the confines of Fenway or Wrigley. Interestingly, the property was devoid of advertising or sponsorships from baseball-related and consumer product companies. Lou liked it that way – despite having been pursued for a number of years by the likes of Louisville Slugger, Wilson and Rawlings, Lou turned down sponsorship dollars. Instead, he wanted only the Dreams Park brand to be featured. To this day, I'm not sure he was trying to keep Dreams Park pure and devoid of more commercialization or if the brands simply weren't able to meet his lofty financial demands.

I met Lou while I was in attendance and took a ride with him around the complex in his golf cart. He was rightfully proud of what he had built. He would point out some kids trading pins and talk about how those "boys never would have met had they not come to Dreams Park". He was also a businessman, and on that day, he wasn't shy about sharing some key statistics with me. I must have shown interest because he kept sharing more information. By the end of our ride, I had a pretty good sense of the profitability of this venture. It was impressive to say the least.

My son had a great time at Cooperstown with his friends. By the end of the week, he was exhausted and slept the entire ride back to Rhode Island – I am sure he wasn't able to get much sleep in the barracks. Nonetheless, it was a once-in-a-lifetime experience that I still hear him mention occasionally when he and his friends get back together nearly ten years later. This was my first experience with a youth sports destination event, and I couldn't get it out of my mind.

The days of playing for your town team, be it baseball, soccer, basketball or lacrosse were quickly coming to an end. Across America, there would soon be an arms race – how do I get my child on the best travel team, which team had the best facilities, should I hire a personal trainer, which college showcases should my child attend, should I subscribe to a recruiting service, and so on. Youth sports had become big business.

Shortly after our Cooperstown experience, an opportunity presented itself to me to invest in a sports event business and, soon thereafter, a couple other opportunities followed. Over the next five years or so, I had developed a rather broad network of contacts and relationships in the industry, including executives at Nike, Adidas, Wilson, Under Armour and so on.

My view and approach to the youth sports market was pretty simple:

- First and foremost, operate events and programs that are values-based – sportsmanship, leadership, integrity, etc.;
- Exceed customer expectations;
- Deliver great experiences and value;
- Embed other forms of programming and curricula in the events, that include:
  - o Teaching and reinforcing values like positive coaching and sportsmanship
  - o Presenting relevant speakers when players, coaches and family members are engaged in games
  - o Presenting seminars for parents about setting appropriate expectations for their children, navigating the college recruiting process, and the like; and
- Capture, produce, and distribute free, short-form content

- Post the play of the day, interview the player of the game or highlight a player doing great things in their community.
- With the advent of social media, our customers became our marketers; moms, dads and kids were sharing branded content on Facebook, Twitter and Instagram, respectively.
- This excited our customers and, at the same time, marketed our events and brands.

Our marketing costs were virtually zero and our customers were spreading the word on our behalf. All we had to do was deliver high-quality customer experiences and instill the appropriate values in our athletes and coaches.

In the summer of 2017, I was contacted by Jamie Devlin, one of the founders and CEO of Epic World Sports ("Epic"). I hadn't heard of him or his company, which surprised me. I thought I knew of all significant players in the youth sports market, let alone one only a few hours north of where I lived. But then again, this was a highly fragmented and quickly changing market - perhaps I had missed one.

Devlin introduced himself, said that he had "heard good things about me" (I assumed it was from one of the consumer products companies, but he didn't name the source) and said he would like to get together and tell me about his company. He seemed to know a fair amount about my investments and activities in the sports space. He was a bit vague about why he was contacting me, however, it felt like a good networking opportunity and you never know where meeting like this could lead.

I had strong opinions about the youth sports market and a fully developed investment thesis - I was confident that there was tremendous opportunity both from an investment perspective and to provide customers with much better experiences. Perhaps Epic would prove to be a good opportunity, a multi-sport platform to execute the strategy.

I agreed to meet with him. Since I had never heard of Epic, I did a little research and made a few calls. No one else seemed to know much about the company. Its web presence was scattered and confusing. The company was based in Portland, Maine - a couple of hours north of Providence, Rhode Island.

I could never have imagined what the next two years of my life would be like.

"Laura, I never thought it would come to this, but it is time to release the memo to the attorneys".

February 2020

THE FIRST THREE MONTHS

CHAPTER 1

I would like to think my life is *relatively* simple. I married my college girlfriend, Christine; we have three children, two sons and a daughter; and two golden retrievers. We live on the East Side of Providence, Rhode Island - a couple of blocks from Brown University and the Moses Brown School; my children and I are graduates and my wife is a middle school teacher there.

While raising our children, sports played an important role at every age and stage of our lives. I coached my sons' little league teams; played tennis and squash with my daughter; enjoyed golf with friends and family and even ran the Boston Marathon with Christine. Pretty standard, normal stuff with a few bucket list items checked off along the way.

I am an accountant by training, a former CPA with one of the "Big Four" firms. I have a Master of Science in Accountancy - in short, I love numbers. In fact, I actually have a favorite financial statement - the cash flow statement. I recognize that sounds bizarre and nerdy, but trust me, the cash flow statement is a wonderful thing. If I had to choose, give me a cash flow statement over the income statement or balance sheet any day! More to come on that later.

My career hasn't been a straight line as I left public accounting to get operating experience, then ended up working as an operating partner with a couple of private equity firms, before investing my own capital. As an operating partner, I was the guy who got the call when something was going wrong at a portfolio company; either it wasn't performing as expected, the CFO wasn't cutting it, or something else was amiss. I had basically become a bit of a financial janitor. It is a great way to learn and deal with a variety of different business scenarios, management styles and industries, but not a great long-term career path. It can be exhausting.

I was fortunate enough to have made some money along the way and decided I wanted to invest my own capital, join the companies' boards and influence the growth and outcome of the investments. It was working as planned and I was enjoying it.

Like I said, there is nothing particularly special or unusual about me.

There is a lot special about my family - Christine, is the sweetest, most optimistic person I have ever met. She cares about (and wants to care *for*) everyone - I mean everyone. Her parents, sisters and grandmother are always on her mind. Her students and fellow teachers. The staff in the school cafeteria. The social workers, nurses and doctors at the hospitals she supports. Her friends. Hell, even the bagger at the grocery store feels special when Christine comes through the checkout line. It's all genuine and sincere.

One such example is a poignant, but, tragic one. When she lost her younger brother Michael to leukemia, she immediately created a foundation in his memory that supports other patients and families battling the same disease and facing similar challenges. Challenges like chemotherapy, bone marrow transplants, long periods of isolation and the financial burden that comes with it all. She had worked tirelessly to expand the scope and reach of the foundation throughout New England - she had literally changed the lives of strangers at the most critical times in their lives.

She does it with grace, the appearance of ease (even though I know how hard she works at it), and the inclusion of others. Even this is a gift - she knows that by including others in the process, they too will feel the pride of philanthropy and helping others in need.

She also seems to prohibit any form of negativity from entering her mind or leaving her mouth. If I only had a nickel for every time I heard her say, "if you can't say something nice, don't say anything at all".

She is remarkably disciplined - but not in annoying way. She eats well, exercises consistently, enjoys a good glass of wine or summer cocktail (in moderation) and is really low maintenance - not a big shopper. If I had to name a vice or two... she vacuums A LOT and can't go to bed with dirty dishes in the sink. I can think of worse vices.

With my work schedule and frequent travel, she has also been the driving force in raising three wonderful children. Her optimism, faith and unwavering value system have been infused in our kids' DNA.

Christine was a schoolteacher right out of college but took time off to raise our children. About three years ago, with our oldest in college and the other two approaching high school graduation, she returned to work. It was the perfect time and I think it diffused the anxiety and

9

sense of loss a devoted mom can feel as her children leave the nest. She now had a whole new group of little ones to care for and educate.

I too was anticipating the "empty nester" phase - actually dreading the thought of it. I was going to miss attending the high school sports, having the kids in the house, their friends, and the hectic schedules that come with three kids so close in age. But I was also looking for another challenge work-wise. I knew I would have more time on my hands, more flexibility and needed to make sure that I stayed active and engaged from a work perspective as I entered a new phase of my life. I was up for a challenge.

CHAPTER 2

Portland is a classic, quaint seaside city in southeast Maine, sitting on a peninsula surrounded by Casco Bay. Downtown Portland, with its winding streets, cobblestone alleyways and classic brick buildings, has witnessed a revival in recent years. While the city is still a thriving port, supporting commercial fishing and shipping, new industries are also thriving, resulting in some of the strongest employment statistics in the country. It's also a foodie town with acclaimed restaurants like Fore Street, The Honey Paw and Solo Italiano. Portland is particularly charming at 7:45am on a sunny and cool early June morning. Other than Starbuck's and a local competitor a few blocks to the east, the streets were quiet when I arrived.

My GPS guided me around a few one-way streets and cobblestone lanes until it told me that I had reached my destination on the right. A long brick building with shops and a couple of restaurants on the first floor and upper floors that either contained offices or apartments, gave me the impression that Epic was probably smaller than I expected. I shouldn't have pre-judged or jumped to this conclusion, but, based on the building, I expected to walk into a small second floor office with a couple of people operating a few youth sports tournaments. The skeptic in me was starting to wonder why this guy reached out to me, why I got out of bed at 5:00am to beat Boston traffic, only to be disappointed.

I took a quick look in the rear-view mirror to make sure I looked ok, grabbed my messenger bag and headed out. There was metered parking directly in front of what I thought was Epic's offices. Two hours would suffice. After all, this was just an introductory meeting. I slid the debit card and hit the max button. I noted the time and rotated the bezel on my watch.

There was no sign on the building confirming Epic's offices were inside. In fact, I couldn't even locate the street number on the building. After confirming the street numbers on either side of an unmarked entrance, I headed into a covered, but open-to-the-weather entry. It was dark inside, and it took a moment for my eyes to adjust as I walked towards the light at the end of the hallway. I came out the other side of the building and realized that I was directly on the waterfront. I also noticed the distinct smell of fried seafood - not the appetizing smell on a summer night on Cape Cod, but rather the morning-after smell. To my left was the entrance to a restaurant. I turned back and realized I walked past an elevator. A sign adjacent to an elevator indicated Epic was on the third floor.

The elevator opened directly into the office. There was a half-hearted attempt at a waiting area, a couple of chairs and a side table with a few magazines, but no sign of a receptionist. I picked up a magazine - it was a sports tourism publication. I thumbed through it and dropped it back on the table. I walked around the corner and saw a long hallway, lined intermittently with stacks of corrugated cardboard boxes. To my right was an office with a glass door closed, a guy standing up, wearing an earpiece and microphone, talking on the phone. He made eye contact with me and simply put up his index finger as if to tell me to wait a minute. I assumed this was Devlin. No smile, no indication of "oh hey, you're a guest, let me make you feel comfortable". I went back to the waiting area.

The walls were thin. I could hear his side of the conversation. It sounded like he was talking to a subordinate - providing strong encouragement to hit some sort of sales targets. He cited how many registrations for an event the person on the phone had at this time last year and that it should have been a "no-brainer" to beat that this year. He said "work the phones" several times. The conversation wasn't quite a *Glengarry Glen Ross* tongue lashing, but it was aggressive.

I flipped through all three of the industry magazines while I waited. After about 10 minutes, I could tell his call had ended. A couple more minutes passed - I looked at my watch, it was almost 8:20am. We agreed to meet at 8:00am. I was getting annoyed. His door opened, he turned the corner and greeted me.

"Steve?"

"Yes, Jamie?"

"Yea, nice to meet you" - he shook my hand. "Come on in." He turned and headed back into his office. I started to close the door behind me, but he asked me to keep it open.

No apology for making me wait. Hmmm. He seemed rushed, almost surprised that I was here - but he was the one who wanted to meet.

His office was modest in size. The windows behind his desk looked out over the water. His stand-up desk was organized, two screens, a wedding photo and photos of a couple of kids in hockey uniforms. Good signs. On the wall was a large framed hockey jersey with the number "1" on it and the words "ALL OR NOTHING" stitched across the shoulders. I didn't know it yet, but this would prove to be prophetic.

Also, on the wall was a certificate from Harvard Business School's division of continuing education for completion of a course on private equity and venture capital. I cringed a bit when I saw this, not a knock on HBS, but because I know a few people who have taken continuing education courses at HBS and act like they earned their

MBA there - painful. The same guy who wears a Harvard sweatshirt or Harvard-branded workout gear when he was really only in Cambridge for a cup of coffee. Give me a break.

There was also a small bookcase neatly organized with a couple of dozen recognizable business management books - *Good to Great* and the like. In the corner of the office were a couple of hockey sticks and a wooden baseball bat that appeared to be engraved with Epic's name and logo - it looked like a gift from a capital round or bank financing.

As you might have noticed, I take a lot in quickly when I meet with someone new. The due diligence process should be more than a quality of earnings exercise or checking a bunch of legal boxes, it needs to take in and consider the qualitative characteristics of a business and its management team as well. Recognizing I have certain biases, you can learn a lot just by observing.

Devlin was dressed casually, but a bit odd. He had on a pair of black loafers with a pair of grey pants (that may or may not have been jeans) that were a bit too short and an untucked black Epic polo shirt. He was about 6' tall, athletic, pale with black hair, and dark, rather cold eyes. He had a certain intensity and lack of emotion in his eyes.

As he walked behind his desk, he pushed a button to electronically lower his stand-up desk and told me to "take a seat".

"Thanks for coming up - did you hit any traffic?", he said.

I explained that I had left early to beat the Boston traffic, also implying that I had been waiting in the lobby for over 20 minutes hoping he may realize that he owed me an apology. No apology. Instead, he said, "remind me, where did you come up from?" Before I could remind him that I lived in Providence, someone walked into the office and interrupted us.

Without so much as acknowledging me, the intruder said, "Jamie, I need you now - we have to make a decision on these jerseys - we have to do it now". The guy seemed panicked and had no regard, whatsoever, for my presence.

Devlin stood up and said, "sorry, I'll be right back." He left me alone sitting in his office. I took out my phone and checked emails.

After five minutes or so, he returned and apologized for the interruption. He explained that he had to make a decision on some hockey jerseys for one of their upcoming tournaments. He suggested that we move down the hall to a conference room where we wouldn't be interrupted again. I followed him down the hall.

The conference room was small with a circular table, four chairs and a flat screen on the wall. The table was a little too big for the room which made it uncomfortable - I felt pressed against the table. As a courtesy, I jumped in and provided my background to kick off the conversation.

He reciprocated - told me he was from Canada originally, a hockey player. Came to the U.S. to play hockey at Boston University. I remembered this vividly because, 1) I went to Providence College, a rival Hockey East school; and 2) BU has always had an excellent program - I even asked if he knew a friend of mine who played hockey there. He said the name didn't ring a bell. Only months later, would I learn that he didn't play division I college hockey.

He told me he was an accounting major in college - "ah, me too", I said. This seemed like another good sign. A guy who likely lived by the numbers.

He told me that he had worked for a national home improvement company while in college which led to a sales job post-graduation. He seemed quite proud of how he moved up the ranks quickly within the company. He worked in sales. He said that he left the company to establish the predecessor to Angie's List, the home services website. I was impressed and asked a few questions about his start-up and how it turned out. He said he had raised "$25 million or so" in venture funding, but the dot com bubble burst and they sold the business / its remnants. I was a bit confused how that story correlated

14

to the Angie's List predecessor, but I let it go. In hindsight, I should have asked more questions about it.

After that, he said that he returned to his previous employer - that was when he founded Epic in Philadelphia as a "side gig", as he called it, about fifteen years ago. He said that the CEO of the home improvement business remained his "mentor" to this day, even serving as a board member of Epic.

Epic, he said, was founded by him and two friends who assembled and coached a youth travel hockey team to play in a tournament in Czechoslovakia, Sweden or Russia, I can't recall, basically a youth hockey tour to Europe. Their team had success, the players and parents had a great time, and this led to more teams and tours. He said that demand was driven by word-of-mouth and resulted in a stand-alone business. In addition, a satisfied parent and successful entrepreneur from Maine, a guy named Tom Gates, invested in the company. Shortly thereafter, they moved the operation here to Portland to share office space with Gates' other business.

My quick takeaways about this guy:
+ A former athlete, likely competitive;
+ A "grinder" as a hockey player - someone who gets things done;
+ Worked while in college (not sure how he did that as a division I athlete);
+ Proved himself to his employer in college and leveraged that into a post-graduation job;
+ The CEO of his former employer thought enough of him to still maintain a friendship / mentorship;
+ Had an accounting background - that's always a good sign;
+ Had an entrepreneurial desire (founded a couple of companies);
+ Launched Epic as a passion and side job (good sign);
+ The business sounded like it was growing organically by word-of-mouth (usually means high customer satisfaction and low customer acquisition costs);
+ A satisfied customer thought enough of his family's experience to invest in the business; and
+ Devlin was willing to relocate to NH to be closer to his investor.

These were all good signs.

Devlin asked what I thought of the youth sports market and why I found it so interesting. I told him that the industry fragmentation and unsophisticated nature of the incumbent operators indicated that the market was ripe for consolidation. I also believed that a more efficient, process-driven, customer-centric operator could take market share pretty quickly. I also told him that the business of operating youth sporting events and teams was "asset light" - meaning there was no required investment in real estate, machinery, equipment, etc. In fact, these businesses typically collect revenue from their customers long before actually delivering the service - in other words, these companies required little or no outside working capital to operate.

He was taking notes on a yellow legal pad.

I also told him that doing the right thing by the customer, in this case the athlete, parents and coaches, would result in clear market differentiation. He asked what I meant by that. I said, "treat them with respect, communicate consistently, deliver great experiences, push social media content about their teams, give them great value for their dollar and align with global brands to provide the customer with free or discounted products that they need to buy in order to participate."

He wanted to know what I meant by the last part - alignment with global brands. I explained that the family who participates in travel sports is one of the most attractive, compelling demographics in the world. These families are also the ultimate key influencers in their communities. They have raised their collective hands and self-selected as families who actively participate in sports, drive or fly to sports-driven vacations, choose hotels, book team dinners at restaurants, are active social media users, participate in recruiting and college placement programs, etc. I explained that I had accumulated market research data that broke down spend patterns, social media activity, by sport, age, gender, etc.

16

He put his hand up and said, "Stop. Don't go any further. I don't want you to say any more until I show you something." He left the room and quickly returned with his laptop. While connecting it to the flat screen on the wall, he said, "I should have had you sign a non-disclosure agreement, but since you just told me your strategy, I will return the favor. I don't want you thinking you gave me any ideas." I wasn't quite sure how to interpret this.

He then proceeded to display a PowerPoint presentation on the flat screen - it included some background about his company, some statistics about the number of events it operated and customers it served, his high-level strategy for Epic and some financial projections.

There was definitely some overlap with my view of the industry, but there were also some elements with which I didn't agree. For example, his presentation indicated that they were in the agency or representation space; meaning serving as agents for pro athletes. This was of no interest to me. They also had an apparel manufacturing facility in Puerto Rico. Not only is that a very difficult business, but it also undermined the company's ability to partner with global brands like Nike and Adidas. I didn't see where this fit strategically. Lastly, they were in the American football space - again, I disagreed with this strategically. Most people were running away from the sport, not towards it. Challenging demographics, declining participation, low tournament registration fees, and high risk from an injury liability perspective. I don't know why anyone would want to be operating in this sport unless you owned an NFL team.

I did, however like the characteristics of hockey, lacrosse and soccer. All three of these sports have compelling consumer spend patterns, strong socio-economic characteristics, good growth prospects (particularly lacrosse), and an aspirational college placement element that keeps the parents engaged and spending.

International sports tours were the DNA of the company and, if operated efficiently, should carry high dollar margins and provide great opportunities for content capture, social media marketing and word-of-mouth referrals. Lastly, the hotel bookings business was

17

particularly intriguing to me. One of the not-so-best kept secrets of the youth sports industry is how hotels are managed around tournaments and events. Typically, the event operator dictates in which hotels the players, coaches and families must stay. The hotels, in turn, pay a rebate to the event owner for putting heads in beds. There is also, usually, a middleman who coordinates the hotel room inventory sourcing and management of room bookings on behalf of the event operator and guests. This middleman receives a commission from the hotel. Most event operators generate the majority of their net profits from the hotel fees.

Epic had acquired a hotel booking "middle-man"; now, the company was not only collecting rebates but was also collecting the commissions for the hotel room nights it was generating with its own tournaments and showcases. I liked this integration, not only for financial reasons, but from customer service and quality perspective. To me, the ability to control more of the customer experience was critical to providing the consumers with a far better experience than they would receive elsewhere.

Devlin walked through the presentation with a blend of entrepreneurial passion and tactician's approach to execution. He came off a bit as a salesman, but he also spoke of organic growth and acquisition opportunities, emphasizing how great his team was at integrating acquisitions. He touted the company's home-grown "Platform", which, according to him, served as the customer registration platform, customer relationship management ("CRM") application, integrated seamlessly to the accounting system, and served as a data warehouse. If true, this was pretty cool stuff and would allow for really interesting customer data analytics and the development of customer-specific marketing strategies.

What I found most intriguing from the presentation was the customer statistics and financial projections. Devlin cited that the company served approximately 500,000 athletes per year and was on track to generate $100 million in revenue. If these statistics were accurate, this would make Epic likely the largest player in this fragmented market. I couldn't believe that I hadn't heard of this company and I told him so. He said that they were deliberately operating in stealth

18

mode because they didn't want the competition to know their strategy. He told me he was trying to decide whether to continue to "bootstrap" the growth or take on additional capital to drive "explosive growth", as he called it. He said he had set a ten-year plan and was halfway through it - $100 million in revenue in year five and $1 billion in year ten.

I liked his confidence, but I didn't see any way this company would grow 10X in five years without significant additional capital for infrastructure (systems and people) and acquisitions. I told him that I didn't know any members of his team, but I hoped he had great people to manage that type of planned growth - he replied, "we'll see. When I set a goal, I always achieve it." I wasn't sure if I just heard confidence from experience or blind arrogance.

Before I could respond, he was unplugging and closing his laptop. He said he was late for another meeting, shook my hand and said, "let's stay in touch, I like how you think". That was it, meeting over. I walked out, got in my car and drove back to Providence - I wasn't quite sure why he wanted to meet me or what had just happened.

CHAPTER 3

That evening, I sent an email to Devlin thanking him for taking the time to meet and complimenting him on his business. I was intrigued by the company. Elements of his strategy were consistent with my view of the opportunity. However, the number of athletes with whom they engaged and the scale of the business seemed to provide a substantial head start in the market. From what I could gather, the company felt like a start-up but had a certain degree of critical mass and scale with which you could potentially do some special things to differentiate it from its competitors. I didn't want to appear hungry so I ended the email with an open-ended closing... "let me know if I can be of any assistance going forward." I figured that was polite and vague enough to put the ball in his court.

Several days passed before I received a response. He eventually wrote back that he enjoyed meeting me as well and wanted to have a follow-up call the following week. We set a date and time.

In the interim, I did some more research on the company, both online and by making a few calls to industry friends. I was able to find a few articles in local newspapers about the company, but none that provided any more insight into the company than Devlin had provided. The company's social media presence was minimal and inconsistent both in terms of the quality of content and frequency of posts. I spent more time on the company's website which only further validated my opinion that it was confusing and poorly organized. Unless I had met with the founder and heard his pitch, I wouldn't know what the company did from a consumer's perspective. These were all areas of tremendous opportunity.

I also couldn't find anything online about the company's apparel operation in Puerto Rico. This didn't necessarily surprise me as Devlin had indicated that the operation was launched to provide its company-owned teams and events with apparel. I assumed it was simply a private label / non-branded operation that wasn't marketing or selling to third-party customers. Devlin had mentioned, however, that he planned to launch a brand to third party customers, but I couldn't find any evidence online of a separate brand. The idea of owning a cut and sew facility in a foreign country sounded like a nightmare. Years ago, I was a minority owner of an apparel facility outside of Guadalajara, Mexico. I knew first-hand the challenges of managing such a facility - these are not businesses for the faint of heart. The thought of launching an apparel brand to compete with the likes of Nike and adidas sounded absurd and like a financial black hole.

I was able to find a fair amount of information about the Company's entree into American football. It appeared that Epic had entered into a joint venture with an affiliate of the Pro Football Hall of Fame in Canton, Ohio. Piecing together several press releases and articles, I learned that the affiliate was planning to build a $800 million sports complex adjacent to the existing museum and stadium. The project would include a major renovation and upgrade of the existing stadium; the addition of a number of football fields that could also be used for soccer and lacrosse; hotels; retailers and restaurants; physical therapy and rehabilitation clinics; apartments for retired NFL players; an indoor water park and on and on. I didn't see this happening any time soon. I had seen this movie before.

The growth of the U.S. travel sports industry had been well documented - HBO, the Wall Street Journal, New York Times, Sports Illustrated had all covered this industry; both from economic and societal perspectives. The good, bad and the ugly. By all accounts, this had become a $15 billion domestic industry and was expected to continue to grow at over 7% per year for the foreseeable future. Some say that the industry preys upon obsessed, competitive parents living vicariously through their children, dreaming of college scholarships or, worse, a professional sports career. Parents often fail to consider that only between 3% and 5% of high school athletes go on to play at the college level. Regardless of their motivations, parents were spending on youth sports like never before. As a parent, I have seen, firsthand, the benefits of my children participating in youth sports – I simply believe that you can't lose sight of why we want our children to participate. We want them to learn to positive values that they will carry with them the rest of their lives.

The destination sports event had become the norm; from Lake Placid for hockey to Cooperstown for baseball to Myrtle Beach for softball to Atlanta for volleyball and San Diego for soccer. Hell, even the

21

town of Elizabethtown, Kentucky had made a $29.0 million investment in a baseball and softball complex in the hopes of attracting families and driving local economic impact by putting heads in beds. Every locale thought they could create the next Disney Wide World of Sports complex. Consulting firms had popped up providing economic feasibility studies to towns, municipalities and private investors pursuing the development of youth sports complexes. Other firms had launched focusing solely on provided outsourced management of these facilities. There was even a new conference and trade show sector that focused on youth sports tourism.

Unfortunately, often, it was the taxpayer that ended up footing the bill. Some municipalities would chase the dream of travel sports improving their local economy. Municipalities were concerned that they may miss the opportunity - the mayor, a few selectmen, or city counselors would attend a couple of conferences and return home with case studies and statistics that sparked flames of interest from their constituents and other elected officials. The municipality would then hire a consulting firm who would prepare a feasibility study in the form of a flashy PowerPoint presentation and then pour gasoline on the flames by letting politicians run with the dream. In short order, the municipality would pass legislation for a room night or hospitality tax, issue bonds and break ground on a youth sports complex.

It all sounds great, doesn't it? Unfortunately, many of these projects failed to properly consider the relative attractiveness of their location, identify the appropriate sport mix, include an accurate assessment of seasonality and likely capacity utilization in their financial models, and so on. Another problem is that kids go to school. Parents don't typically pull kids out of school, for extended periods of time, for their sports and there are plenty of weekends and vacation time to attend events. As a result, the volume of events, visitors and room nights doesn't exploit enough capacity, at and around the facilities, and the taxpayers often have to cover the bond payments.

So... call me skeptical, I didn't see an $800 million youth sports complex being developed in Canton, Ohio any time soon. The climate alone would limit its appeal to consumers. No offense to the residents of Canton, but if I had a choice of bringing my child to a lacrosse tournament in Florida in January or Canton, I think I would book a flight on Southwest and enjoy the sun and beaches. In addition, why would soccer or lacrosse families want to travel to a tournament at the Football Hall of Fame - for the most part, these families didn't have any interest in American football. Perhaps most importantly, being a financial partner in a sports complex was not in Epic's sweet spot – it should have been focusing on its core competencies.

I recognize the power of the NFL as a media property, however, youth participation in football had been on a steady and alarming decline. From 2016 to 2018, participation in tackle football had declined about 40%, not exactly a trend that would make one want to invest in this space. Even flag or touch football programming hadn't stemmed the decline in participation. While the NFL's viewership and engagement may not have wanes (thanks largely in part to the game's commitment to and alignment with fantasy football and gambling), this wouldn't put youth athletes on fields in Ohio.

There was also an excess supply of destination sports complexes, overly optimistic economic benefit assumptions and flawed thinking around capacity utilization. Regarding the latter, people simply didn't want to accept that youth athletes are in school more than two-thirds of the year and when you model out the likely capacity utilization, you quickly realize that these facilities sit empty most of the time. As a result, the planned hotels, restaurants and shops also cannot prosper.

I organized my thoughts, notes and hyperlinks from my research into one document and put it aside. To be clear, I found Epic's core business interesting, but if I didn't hear back from Devlin, I wasn't going to pursue it.

A couple of weeks passed, and I had a missed call and voicemail from Devlin. "Hey Steve, been thinking a lot about you - give me a call when you have a chance, I have an idea of how we can work together." I recall being a bit put off by this message. It seemed presumptuous that I would want to work with him. But, quite frankly, Christine was constantly telling me to not be quick to judge, misinterpret people's words, etc., so I took a deep breath and let it go. I returned his call.

He told me that his investor from Maine, Tom Gates, had been invested in Epic for about five years, was looking to monetize his investment and really wasn't adding much value as a board member or advisor since he didn't really know much about the industry. He went on to say that he had been impressed with my knowledge of the space and strategic thinking; it occurred to him that I would be a good replacement for Gates as either an investor or board member. He also said that Gates was very conservative and didn't seem to have the stomach or long-term perspective required to grow the business to $1 billion in annual revenue that Devlin had established as his goal.

I asked a few questions about Gates' ownership percentage, amount invested and valuation expectations. Devlin broad stroked his answers and said that it probably made more sense for me to meet with Gates and ask him about his interest to exit the investment. I agreed to the introduction.

Later that day, I received an email from Devlin introducing me to Gates. Shortly thereafter, Tom and I set up a time to meet in person. Again, I would be driving north. This time, to meet Tom in the Portland, Maine area where he lived. I met Tom at an indoor sports facility that he owned. I pulled in and parked next to a customized black Mercedes SUV with the license plate "ICEMAN". The facility was a former hockey rink converted to house batting cages, volleyball and basketball courts, a physical therapy office, some commercial office space, and a snack bar. It was a nice facility.

Once in the lobby, I met Tom - a tall gentleman with a thick mustache. He was dressed casually, but well. A pair of Cole Haan, white soled loafers, tan corduroys and a light blue cashmere sweater over a nice oxford. You could quickly tell he took pride in how he was put together. After a brief introduction, he offered to take me on a quick tour. He explained that he bought this facility a number of years ago when he owned the minor league hockey team in the area. This served as a training facility and home to his junior teams as well. He went on to say that minor league hockey teams are a money pit, as are rinks, and so he sold the team and converted this facility to what it was today. I found him to be friendly, open and sincere about his businesses and, at times, even self-deprecating. He was likable.

We went into an office area and sat at a conference table. I provided him with my background and spent more time on my activities in the sports industry knowing that he was an owner of Epic and why we were meeting. We had a nice back-and-forth about the industry and, as I did with Devlin, I shared my detailed views of the industry and opportunities. We seemed to have similar opinions about the business.

The conversation delved a bit deeper into Epic - specifically around the apparel and football divisions. He wanted my opinions and I provided unfiltered. He agreed with my views and expanded by indicating that he thought the company had spread itself too wide and thin and should have maintained its focus on the core businesses and not venture into apparel and football. I asked him how he thought about his role with the company and how long he planned to stay involved. He said he was a board member and that he preferred to focus more on culture than providing operational or financial guidance. To my surprise, he said that he was in no hurry to move on - he believed the company had a lot of growth ahead of it. Feeling a bit uncomfortable, I disclosed that Devlin mentioned that Tom may be looking to exit his investment. He backtracked a bit and said that he would consider "taking some money off the table, but only at the right valuation."

25

I was confused about why I was sitting there. In my mind, I retraced the steps that had brought me here. Devlin reached out to me, wanted to meet. We met, I provided my background and view of the market in which his company operated. He stopped me, showed me his company presentation with pride. The meeting ended abruptly. A couple weeks went by and he reached out again and indicated that Gates was looking to move on. Now, I met with Gates and I didn't get the impression he was looking to move on. WTF?

Before I could comment, Tom went on to say that he thought Devlin was "out over his skis", that he needed help operating the business. He continued to toggle between being professionally critical of some of Devlin's decision making and complimenting him as an ambitious entrepreneur. I asked what he thought of Devlin's goal of $1 billion in revenue in five years - he dismissed it as "typical Jamie hyperbole." Devlin's target was more than ambitious. Tom and I shared similar views on the size and growth characteristics of the market and settled on $500 million in annual revenue not being out of the question, but still a stretch goal. Additional capital and quality people would be required. Interestingly, he mentioned to me that he had concerns about the quality of the finance and accounting team at Epic. He said that they were not top tier and new talent needed to be brought in if the company was planning to drive aggressive organic growth and integrate acquisitions.

Before we parted ways, he mentioned that he would like me to take a look at another company in which he was considering investing and get my high-level opinion. I told him that I would be happy to do so. I felt that this was an indication that we had connected, and he valued my opinion. We walked outside to my car - as we continued talking, he pushed the button on his car key and the Mercedes parked next to me beeped and the doors unlock. If he wasn't so likable, I would have viewed this as a cheesy power move.

We agreed to stay in touch with no clear next steps; I hopped in my car and headed south... a bit less confused than when I left my meeting with Devlin in Portland, but confused, nonetheless.

The next day, I received an email from Devlin, "what did you think of Tom?" I wrote that he seemed like a very nice guy, enjoyed his company, and that he was bullish on Epic.

He wrote back, "are you available tomorrow at 11am for a call?" Before I could respond, I received a Google calendar invite for a dial-in call the next day.

On the call, Devlin was looking for a detailed download of my meeting with Gates - considering I had only met each of them once, it felt uncomfortable that I was being placed in between them when I didn't have any skin in the game. I couldn't put my finger on it, but there was something unusual going on here. My sense was that Devlin wanted Gates out more than Gates did. However, I didn't see Gates as a threat to Devlin as he, overall, was complimentary of what Devlin had built and the company's future prospects even if he disagreed with some of the strategic decisions and recognized that the company needed additional talent to support the growth. To me, this was to be expected considering the aggressive growth targets.

I told Devlin that it was a very positive meeting, that Gates was complimentary of him, excited about the future, but that he didn't seem particularly motivated to sell shares at this time. Devlin remarked, "that's typical Tom, he is just negotiating." I wasn't even sure how to respond, so I didn't. Again, I was just getting to know this company. He then continued, "hey, I think it would be great if you met two of our other board members from Revolution Capital." I didn't hesitate and asked, "Jamie, why do you want me to meet your board members?" I give him credit - he responded immediately with, "I'm really impressed by you, I need help taking the business to the next level, I want you to consider getting involved, but I also want you to have the opportunity to meet our investors and board members." That was the right answer. I agreed to connect with the guys from Revolution Capital ("RevCap").

Emails were exchanged and coordinating a call took some time. In the interim, I did my typical diligence. Revolution Capital is a Montreal-based family office. It manages the money for a multi-generational, billionaire family. Its CEO is Glenn Cobb, a former attorney, was a close advisor to the high net worth family. He was also a board member of one of the largest, most iconic American companies. By coincidence, although we have never met, we had a couple of mutual acquaintances because Cobb summers on Nantucket and is a member at Nantucket Golf Club, where I know a few members.

After a few weeks (by the way, we are now at late summer 2017), I connected with Jake Maddox, who worked for Cobb at Revolution Capital. The conversation felt easy and natural. I could tell immediately that Jake was a good guy, a true gentleman. He said that he appreciated me taking the time to connect, my patience in setting up a time that worked for both of us, and even apologized for Glenn not being available. I have learned over the years that these are not your typical statements from young private equity guys.

During our introductions, we learned that we have golf as a mutual hobby. We talked about my course, Rhode Island Country Club, as well as other southern New England Donald Ross courses. I quickly realized that Jake was not only a very good golfer, but a course design aficionado - he actually rated and wrote about courses for Golf magazine in his spare time. Some guys who talk golf, particularly course design, can be obnoxious - not the case with Jake. You could immediately tell that he loved the game, wasn't name dropping and was a really down-to-earth, good guy.

The conversation turned to Epic. He spoke in well-organized bullet points. "We really like the industry, the tailwinds, the financial model, even the sports that we are in now. Look, we are Canadian, we like the hockey business for sure. We see the value of the integrated hotel bookings business. We don't love the other stuff. We feel like there have been some decisions made that the board wasn't in favor of - kind of like we need another adult in the room. We have heard good things about you; would you have any interest in getting involved?"

Ok, now I had a much better sense of what was happening here. The founder had made some questionable strategic decisions, the investors and board believed in the business and opportunity but recognized that the company needed help. The founder / CEO was getting pressure and I could solve both of their problems.

The question was... did I want to get involved?

CHAPTER 4

A few more weeks pass until I received another email from Devlin - he wanted like to grab lunch. We scheduled to meet the following week, this time at a restaurant equidistant between Portland and Providence. In advance of the lunch meeting, I had some soul searching to do as I suspected that he was going to ask if I would consider investing in the business and / or taking an active role.

He chose Polcari's, an Italian restaurant on Route 1 north of Boston, for lunch - I was starting to really question this guy's judgement. I'm not knocking Polcari's, but a heavy Italian pasta dish at noon on a Tuesday didn't sound particularly appetizing to me. I entered the restaurant only to find that I was the first person to arrive for their lunch hour. The hostess seated me in a booth. It felt cold and damp in the restaurant; I assumed the heat hadn't come on yet after a cold night. Devlin was fifteen minutes late. Again! He arrived wearing a black Epic baseball cap and a black pullover with some sort of hockey logo on the chest. I was beginning to realize that this guy had no clue how to dress. At least this time, he apologized for being late.

He then cut right to the chase. He was immediately complimentary of me, my knowledge of the industry and evaluation of his strategy. He went on to say that Gates and Maddox really liked me and thought I would be a great partner. He was high energy and in sales mode. He continued, "so, what do you want to do?"

I shifted in my seat and said, "regarding what?"

29

He replied, "how can we get you involved in the business? I pride myself on knowing what I don't know and building great teams. You would be a great addition to this company. I am an entrepreneur, an operator, not a strategy guy or acquisitions guy. Would you consider making an investment and driving strategy and acquisitions?"

There, I finally had my answer. At least two of his board members were putting pressure on him to augment his team, particularly in the areas of overall strategy and executing on the industry consolidation opportunity. On the surface, this would be interesting to me, but I needed to learn more about the company, Devlin's operating style, his other team members, particularly his CFO, etc. I had a pretty good thing going - working from a home office, investing on my own terms, reporting to no one, setting my own schedule, and no staff to manage. The devil would be in the details.

I told him that I was interested, that I appreciated his interest in me, and that I thought the appropriate next step was a working session with him and any other team members he deemed appropriate. He wrinkled his brow and asked why I thought that was necessary. I could tell that he thought he was going to close the deal with me at that lunch. I was confused by his sudden sense of urgency when his communications with me had been so intermittent. I told him that I needed to meet his colleagues, have an iterative session with Devlin and his key team members to see if we had alignment of thought on overall strategy. I also wanted to meet the different personalities and see if this was a team with which I wanted to work. He *seemed* to agree.

I also told him that I would need to do my financial diligence on the company before considering an investment. Further, I had no sense of the company's valuation expectations or capital needs. He said, "that can wait - I would rather get you involved in the company first, then you can decide if you want to invest once you've dug in. I still haven't decided if we should bring in more capital or not." On the one hand, I liked having an option to invest, however, I also didn't want to get involved, drive up the valuation with my involvement and buy in at a higher price. I would have to sort this out.

I also told him that I needed to do some soul searching about taking an active operating role. He asked what I meant. I reminded him that I lived in Providence and that the company was two hours north and that I had two other investments in the sports space that I would need to divest if I were to get involved. To my surprise, he quickly replied that I wouldn't need to be in Portland very often and that I would not have to exit my other investments. I told him that I would expect that I needed to be in Portland often working with him, his CFO and others if I was driving strategy and acquisitions - the diligence, structuring and post-closing integration of acquisitions is incredibly time consuming and requires a good team working closely together. I also told him that I would have to exit the investments as I would not want to have any potential conflicts of interest. He said, "I don't see any potential conflicts of interest, but that's up to you." I found that odd since he didn't even know what companies I was referencing. If I were him, at a minimum, I would have asked what the nature of the companies were to see if they were direct competitors to Epic.

We finished our lunch and agreed to set up a time with him and his key team members for a working session ASAP. As I sat in my car and checked emails, Devlin drove out in a small black Mercedes SUV, a less expensive version of what Gates was driving when I met him in Maine. No vanity plates. Perhaps he was suffering from a little *Gates-envy*. Before I left, I sent Devlin an email thanking him for lunch and offering a couple of dates that worked for me for a working session in the coming weeks.

Two more weeks of silence and no response to my email - I found this very odd. His inconsistent communication style concerned me. It seemed inconsiderate at a minimum. He was the one pursuing me, yet he would go intermittently silent. This type of behavior invoked a couple of emotions for me - out of insecurity, I questioned whether I said or did something that caused him to have second thoughts; or did I misinterpret his level of interest in getting me involved; or was there something else happening behind the scenes? In hindsight, I should have dug in deeper on the third question and reached out to Gates or Maddox. Something was definitely happening behind the scenes.

I sent a follow-up email asking, "do you still want to get together for a working session?" Devlin responded quickly with, "sorry for the delay, a lot of great things going on - yes, how is next Tuesday at 9:00am in our new office?" He told me that they just moved into a new office and he provided the new address, only a few miles from the one I met him at before. I agreed.

My GPS guided me to the company's new offices - the building was located in an industrial park. I parked alongside a large metal building and noticed next to a side door an Epic sign alongside a couple of other company names. Epic's offices were located on the front side of the building with industrial businesses located in back two-thirds of the building. The new location and adjacent tenants struck me as an odd shift from the offices the company occupied during my last visit.

The waiting area, again, did not have a receptionist or means by which a visitor can let anyone know they have arrived. I walked around the corner and made eye contact with a woman in a glass office. She smiled and hurried out to greet me. She was friendly and introduced herself as Ashley. I introduced myself and before I could tell her why I was there, she said, "oh, yes, you are here to meet Jamie." She brought me to a conference room and asked if I needed anything, coffee, water, etc. I declined and she told me that she would let Jamie know that I had arrived.

Only a minute or two passed and Jamie came in with another gentleman, his CFO, Don Murray. Murray was about six feet tall, a solid looking guy in his mid-fifties with blue eyes and light-colored hair, parted down the middle. Yes, you read that correctly, he parted his hair down the middle. We shook hands, they both put note pads down on the conference table and Jamie offered to give me a tour of the new offices. Don excused himself, mumbling that he had to attend to something else and would come back when we finished the tour. Devlin took me around the corner to a large open concept workspace that included several rows of workstations. Everything appeared brand new and coordinated with Epic's color scheme. There were about twenty or so cubicles, with only about 50%

occupied. Around the perimeter of the space were about a dozen offices with glass walls facing the open area. He explained that they had the space customized for their needs and that they took occupancy only a few weeks ago. He seemed quite proud of the office.

"Accounting and finance is located in this area, our media division, here, and these folks work in our apparel division," he said he motioned with his hand. I told him that I was struck at how few people were in the office for a $100 million revenue business. He laughed (like I was an idiot) and said, "Oh no, we have people in 30 states and a dozen or so foreign countries. We have about 700 employees around the world."

I was shocked and said, "Wow, I had no idea you had that many employees."

He responded, "well, not all of them are full time."

I did some rough math in my head and said, "so, revenue generated per employee of about $140,000; I would imagine there is pretty good margin there knowing what salaries are typically like in this industry?"

Without a pause, he said, "exactly, you get it." Based on his response, I assumed he tracked revenue per employee as a key performance indicator. We kept moving. But because he didn't elaborate, I wondered if he actually understood what I said. To get a better sense, I asked what his margins were like. He asked me not to discuss financial aspects of the business in the open area. I looked around – no one could have possibly heard my question.

We kept moving. At the back of the space was a kitchen and dining area that also included a ping pong table. Two guys who appeared to be in their late twenties were playing when we arrived. They smiled in our direction but didn't seem at all distracted by their CEO's presence, despite playing ping pong at 9:00am on a Tuesday. Devlin saw me watching them and must have sensed that I found this unconventional. He proceeded to explain to me his "management style" and culture of allowing people flexibility in terms of work style and hours. "As long as people get their work done, I let them have their space - I don't micro-manage", he said. He also said that he had "assembled a unique and gifted team of high performers."

As we walked by a row of five empty offices, he mentioned that this office space was far less expensive than the previous lease and had more room to accommodate his growth plans. He also showed me a couple small rooms, only big enough for one, maybe two people, that he said he designed so that people could participate on conference calls in private.

As we returned to the conference room, we passed by Murray's office - he was at his desk looking at his laptop. There was nothing else in the office, literally nothing else. No papers on his desk, no artwork on the walls, nothing. Odd. Devlin told him that the tour was finished - he immediately stood up and followed us to the conference room.

Jamie then formally introduced Don as his new CFO who had only been with the company for a very short time - ah, that explained the empty office. He went on to say that Don worked with Tom Gates before Epic, so they knew each other a bit. This felt good to me that an investor and board member had dropped in a CFO with whom he had prior experience. It also was good to hear that Gates had followed through on his statement to me that the accounting and finance department needed a leadership upgrade. Devlin also mentioned that Don was a Brown University alum and had played hockey there. Ok, Ivy League educated, former athlete, that checked a few boxes. I had to say, in hindsight, that I should have found it odd that Devlin gave Murray's background rather than letting him introduce himself. Murray seemed oddly quiet - almost like he was sedated.

Murray did elaborate a bit about his prior work experience including being the CFO of a sporting goods manufacturer that was private equity owned; a few other good signs - he must have some baseline knowledge of the sports industry and had been the CFO in an institutional investor environment; one that typically had high expectations regarding timely and accurate financial reporting.

We made small talk for a while, then Devlin took the lead. "Let's talk about the industry and work our way down to what we do today and how we can drive explosive growth. If we are going to be a $1 billion company in five years, we need a good roadmap. Let's move some rocks," he said. I couldn't help but thing, "move some rock? What the hell was he talking about?"

One entire wall of the conference room, about fifteen feet long was covered with dry erase board - he stood up and grabbed a marker. He wrote a few headings that didn't align with my thinking or approach to having a strategic conversation. He must have noticed that the conversation wasn't gaining traction, so he offered me the marker and said, "do you want to drive?" "Sure" - I stood up, took the marker from him, grabbed the eraser from the table and erased the headings.

I proceeded to layout a comprehensive graphic of the youth sports ecosystem, its critical elements, opportunities and the key competitors that were relevant to each. I had spent a lot of time researching and working in this market - I was confident in my knowledge and the high probability of success of my strategies. I was in a flow - I grabbed other colored markers to highlight certain features of my graphic. I lost all concept of time and place.

I drew a continuum across the top of the white board that listed the key touch points between the youth sports consumers and a company like Epic - branding, messaging, word-of-mouth, social media, paid advertising, registration platforms, merchant service providers, CRM applications, team and event communication tools, performance improvement devices and applications, tournament management systems, event operations, partnership & sponsorship alignment and execution, merchandising, college placement and recruiting tools, customer surveys, and so on.

I then ranked the importance of each of these touch points for the consumer and their relative impact on a company's success. Using different colors, I flagged those processes and applications that I believed needed to be proprietary either due to the need to keep our data private and secure or building the tools internally would prove to be a competitive advantage. I also flagged those processes and applications that should be outsourced – either because they had become commoditized in the industry or were outside the of Epic's core competencies.

Next, I listed the key companies that delivered each of these tools and ranked them by market size and/or appeal of their offering. I drew a dotted line across the entire wall below this section. Below the dotted line, I moved left to right listing Epic's existing verticals (hockey, soccer, lacrosse, football, international tours, hotel bookings, and apparel). Devlin interrupted me - it was the first time either he or Murray said a word in at least thirty minutes; I had lost myself in the graphic as I was writing and providing a running commentary. He told me to add "media" as a vertical. He said that the company had a separate and distinct business that produced "world-class" content for company-owned events as well as third party customers. I wrote the word "media" after "apparel". I asked where the media division was located. He told me that the twins playing ping pong ran the media division.

I then listed several other sports that I believed were compelling and the company should consider pursuing down the road. I returned to the left side of the white board and proceeded to list bullet points under each sport - existing competitors, key characteristics like number of US participants, the sport's growth or contraction rate, average annual spend per family, estimated market size, and certain qualitative characteristics for each (socio-economic traits, college recruiting aspirations, key geographic markets, etc.). I applied modest market penetration targets to each and calculated target annual revenues - I excluded apparel, football and media. For international tours, I took a very modest percentage of the expected engaged customers from the sport verticals and applied a multiple for traveling family members and used a reasonable average price per traveler (both of which figures I confirmed with Devlin and Murray). I tallied up the numbers to arrive at an annual revenue of over $500 million and circled it in red.

I asked Devlin and Murray for the current revenues for each division. I expected the CFO to provide the answers, but, again, Devlin jumped in and provided run-rate revenues for each - I tallied them up and got close to $100 million. I asked how he defined run-rate. Devlin said, "those are the trends for each business unit by year end, including a couple of small acquisitions that will close ASAP." "Great," I replied. I was OK with how he thought about run rate, as long as the planned acquisitions weren't that material.

Lastly, I went to the lower-right corner of the whiteboard and wrote the words *data warehouse* and drew a three dimensional box around them - I drew a series of lines connecting the consumer touch point categories at the top of the board to data warehouse box and repeated the same exercise with the applications and tools I had identified. I then drew a long semi-circle line from the data warehouse box back to the first couple of consumer touch points (branding, messaging, etc.); along the line, I wrote the words *analytics and insights* above the line and *feedback loop* below.

I stopped, took a breath, put the cap on the marker and turned to look at my audience. They appeared speechless. They either thought that I really knew this market and had developed an interesting strategy, or they thought I was nuts. They both stared at the board. Devlin asked me to step aside as I was blocking the left side of the whiteboard. I assumed he was trying to evaluate my strategy, was going to ask a question, or challenge one or more of my assertions. Instead, he lifted his phone, focused the camera and photographed the whiteboard a couple of time. He placed his phone back on the table, looked at Murray and said, "well, there you have it - our business plan." They both laughed.

We used the whiteboard as an exhibit for the balance of our meeting, which lasted about two hours. I found Devlin engaging in the conversation. He was clearly passionate about the industry and was not shy about asking questions. However, it seemed that his knowledge of the industry and strategic thinking lacked depth. Nonetheless, he was quite opinionated. For example, when I challenged the football strategy, he ignored all of the statistics that indicated this was not an appealing opportunity and, instead, went

37

into salesman mode - hanging his hat on how powerful a partnership with the NFL was (I didn't think the NFL was actually all that involved), the developer was "world-renowned" and would partner with Epic in other sports complex opportunities. He even claimed that there could be a residential academy on the property that Epic would manage. I let it go - this wasn't the time to debate his decisions.

Murray was quiet throughout the meeting. Rarely did he speak and when he did, his contribution was not particularly insightful or additive. He had a notepad in front of him, but I noticed that he had only written a couple of lines on the page. I felt like he was holding back and evaluating me. But it was hard to tell - I also thought he may have been completely clueless.

I asked about the company's financial performance and current balance sheet - both Devlin and Murray participated in this conversation. I was told that the company was cash flow positive, not fully "optimized" yet from an operating perspective, but close. I again asked about operating margins and Devlin told me that the company was generating "almost 10% operating margins" which, in my opinion, would have been reasonable from an industry perspective, particularly if the company wasn't optimized yet.

Regarding the balance sheet, I was told that the company had some acquisition debt and used a seasonal working capital line of credit from a local bank with whom they had a *great relationship*. Devlin went on to say that they had decided to bring in additional capital - $20.0 million or so - to fund organic growth and acquisitions. He said that their existing investor, Revolution Capital, was going to participate and that he was already getting a lot of interest from private equity firms. I asked if I could get a copy of their offering memorandum, but he told me that he and Don were working on it and would get me a copy as soon as it was completed. He backtracked a bit and said that the conversations with new investors had been high-level, but there were a lot of people who "really wanted to invest in Epic."

The meeting wrapped up with Devlin telling me that he wanted me to join the company as Vice President and Director of Corporate Strategy and Acquisitions. He said he also wanted me to join the board of directors. He said that titles didn't mean anything to him and that he saw himself, Murray and me as three partners running the company. He paused and asked, "where is your head?" I told him that I was excited about the opportunity, very interested and would like to see what he was offering to get me on board. He said, "great, I will email you an offer in the next twenty-four hours." We wrapped up and I headed out.

The next day, I received an email from Devlin outlining a job specification, but no compensation details. Instead, he said he preferred to have one of his fellow board members handle the compensation elements with me - he explained that he didn't want the "sometimes uncomfortable conversations about compensation to undermine our ability to work as partners." Fine by me. He said that one of the guys from Revolution Capital will be in touch shortly.

A few days later, I bumped into Partner at a leading private equity firm. Our children were close friends of my daughter as were our wives. That's really the connection - he and I are not particularly close. We chatted for a bit and he suddenly remembered something, "hey, your name came up the other day," he said. "Epic World Sports - are you joining them?"

I was taken aback. I said, "I am looking at it - I think they are doing some interesting things. How did my name come up?" He said that his firm was also looking at the company, he had a friend who was already an investor (Glenn Cobb from Revolution Capital) and they too found it very interesting. I was confused. I was told by Devlin that they hadn't yet completed the offering memo, yet this guy's firm was looking at Epic. In our lingo, "looking at," means reviewing information, not just a conversation.

This guy's firm had tremendous success with investments in media, sports, live events, etc. They knew what they were doing. He said, "hey, we should get together and discuss it - if you are thinking of getting involved, we would be very interested too." I agreed to keep him in the loop. This brief conversation added more appeal to Epic and credibility to Devlin's claim that people were interested in investing.

At the same time, dollars were flowing into this industry - Blue Star took an investment from Jerry Jones, Providence Equity, the NFL, and Genstar to consolidate the space. They were making acquisitions at light speed. SportsEngine, TeamSnap and others in the youth sports registration space were seeing their valuations rise. There were rumors (which turned out to be true) that NBC Universal was in talks to acquire SportsEngine. Dick's Sporting Goods was making investments in the youth sports technology space. Steel Sports had invested in youth soccer and baseball assets. It felt like this was beginning to turn into a frothy market now that private equity was jumping in. The window may have been closing, and I didn't want to miss out.

Glenn Cobb, from Revolution Capital, reached out via email about getting together to nail down a deal to get me on board. We exchanged a few potential dates and realized that, by sheer coincidence, we were both going to be playing in a golf event at the Floridian, in Palm City, Florida, the following week. We agreed to carve out some time there to get together. He was an avid golfer and a member of numerous private clubs, including the Floridian.

The Floridian is the private club owned by Jim Crane, the billionaire owner of the Houston Astros. The property includes its own private marina, two helipads (I wondered how often one of the helipads is actually occupied), and a number of guest villas. I am not a member - I was there playing in a two-day member / guest; a business acquaintance is a member and invited me to be his partner. I am a single digit handicap golfer, but I don't play in a lot of these events - I prefer to play with a small group of friends or my sons. These events can be exhausting, both because of the amount of golf played and some of the guys who often play. Big egos, a lot of bullshit, storytelling, name-dropping, drinking, etc. It can get old really fast.

I will spare you most of the details about the event and the club and cut to the chase. I met with Cobb for breakfast on the second day - he talked fast and moved from topic-to-topic in a manner that made my head spin. He told me that they "needed an adult in the room" at Epic and that I was the right guy. I asked, "what does that mean, you need an adult in the room?". He replied, "Look, Jamie is a good guy. We invested in Jamie. But he doesn't always listen, doesn't realize the apparel thing is a stupid idea and he needs someone to keep him in check."

I wasn't sure what to make of his comments. Before I could respond and dig deeper, he grabbed a paper napkin, handed it to me, asked a passing waiter for a pen and told me to write down what it is going to take (meaning salary) for me to join the company. I nervously laughed and told him that I wasn't going to that. Instead, I asked him what he thought was appropriate for this position. He provided a salary range that was reasonable.

I then told him that, in addition to a base salary, I would need a meaningful bonus opportunity, incentive stock and the option to invest in the company at today's valuation for the next twelve months. He stood up, shook my hand, said "good, welcome aboard." He looked down at his phone and said, "I have to get loose on the range" and walked out. The entire meeting lasted about five minutes.

Cobb and I were not in the same tournament bracket, or "flight", as golfers call it, so I didn't play with him. However, after an exhausting thirty-six holes, I saw him again at the dinner that night. He clinked his drink against mine and told me that he was meeting some guys at his villa after dinner for drinks - he invited me over. Actually, he didn't so much "invite me over" as say, "I'll see you there." I felt like I had to go.

Throughout my life, I feel like there are these frequent, strange moments that seem to happen to me and only me. Here is a couple of them that happened that night. After dinner, I excused myself to head to the bathroom. I left the outdoor dining terrace and cut through a smaller bar / grille room. Besides the bartender, there were only two people dining. I said hello to the bartender and walked by the two gentlemen; they glanced up and said hello to me as I passed - it was the pro golfer Rickie Fowler and his legendary coach, Butch Harmon.

41

As I continued to the restroom, I was thinking, "that was pretty cool." I then opened the door to the men's room only to realize that someone was pushing the door towards me to exit. I stepped back and allowed the gentlemen through - He was a large man. He apologized, smiled and walked past as I held the door. It was Michael Jordan. I thought to myself, "just when I thought this couldn't get stranger."

I returned to my table and had a drink with my golf partner and a few other guys in our flight. They were starting to get after it pretty good. After about thirty minutes or so, I left the rear terrace of the clubhouse and walked along the marina, past the stand-alone fitness facility, towards the guest villas. The villas backed up to a lit walkway that lined the marina. The marina was a perfectly shaped rectangle that opened to the St. Lucie River. The clubhouse sat majestically above the marina, looking out over the eighteenth hole and the river. About a dozen villas back up to the marina along one side. If the marina had fifty or so slips, there were only about twenty occupied. A couple of sizable yachts, but mostly luxury fishing boats like tricked out Regulators and a few multi-million-dollar Vikings. They were all polished and pristine - they looked like they were rarely used. I noticed a couple of villas ahead that had lights on. I wasn't sure which villa was Cobb's, then I heard a number of voices, talking over each other and laughing. As I got closer, I could hear Cobb.

There were a number of guys on the back terrace sitting and standing around a fire pit. I walked up onto the terrace and, uncomfortably, tried to work my way into the conversation. It usually takes me a few minutes to settle into a setting like this - sometimes, I can't settle in at all. If there is a familiar face or two and they pull me in, I'm fine. If not, it is a heavy lift for me. Even in a non-business, social setting, I tend to stay close to my wife. She enjoys socializing; I, however, have to be in the right state of mind. I wasn't really feeling it this particular night.

There were eight or ten guys there - Cobb greeted me, did a quick round of introductions and pointed me in the direction of where a bar was set up inside. I recognized a few names from the Boston investment community - a couple of private equity and hedge fund guys. I didn't know who the others were. Following my introduction, everyone returned to their conversations, no one pulled me in. I was a spectator listening to conversations about who flew down with who on whose private jet; where they had dinner last night in Jupiter; what club they just joined in Ireland; and which of them just got an invite to play in the AT&T Pro-Am at Pebble Beach.... ugh.

I had found that the more successful and wealthy people become, the more they feel they have to tell stories. Not conversations about their families, or a book they just read, or even a new local restaurant. For some, it seems that their entire existence becomes centered around planning and engaging in activities designed so they can tell bigger and bigger stories. Joining another expensive country club, collecting over-priced wines, surfing school in Costa Rica, or a Ferrari driving school outside of Rome... blah, blah, blah. I don't get it. It seems like an awful lot of work. Whatever happened to working hard and going home to spend time with your family?

I went inside to grab a drink. Inside, I saw two guys that I met earlier at dinner. One was a pretty well-known Boston hedge fund manager who was also an owner of one of the city's professional sports franchises. Let's call him *Bob*. He talked incessantly. He never a heard a word anyone else spoke. He was telling the other guy about his whiskey collection and referenced how many bottles he had downstairs. I then realized this is not a guest villa, but *his* villa. He rambled on about how many bottles of a certain type of aged bourbon he bought ten years ago and how much they had appreciated in value since. The other guy didn't seem to be buying his story. Bob was trying to show him some app on his phone that showed the value of the bourbon. The other guy said, "I don't care what it's worth, 50-year-old Kentucky bourbon must taste like 50-year-old shit." Bob said, "fuck you," put his phone and drink down on the table and headed downstairs. Over his shoulder, he said, "I'm cracking one open, you will see how good this shit is."

Moments later Bob came up with a bottle in each hand, put them on the coffee table and headed into the kitchen. He came out with fingers full of shot glasses - I couldn't help but think, "who has ten shot glasses in their kitchen?"

"Grab those," he said to me motioning with his chin to the bourbon bottles and headed out onto the terrace. I followed with the bottles in hand. Bob announced his arrival to everyone on the terrace, interrupting their conversations and providing a profanity-laced, abridged version of the story I heard moments early about his bourbon investing prowess. I put the bottles on the table and stepped back.

I could smell something pungent and realized that one of the guys seated by the fire pit was smoking weed. He took a hit and shared the joint with the guy next to him. I recognized the guy taking the hit - he runs a multi-billion-dollar hedge fund in Boston. The banter back and forth was painful "ball-busting" as these guys refer to it. Maybe it is because I didn't know these guys, or I was tired, or I was simply not cut from the same cloth - I don't know what it was, but I certainly knew that I didn't fit in. As they were passing around the shot glasses, I quietly walked back into the living room, placed my drink down on the coffee table and walked out the front door.

ONBOARDING

"Things are not always what they seem; the first appearance deceives many; the intelligence of a few perceives what has been carefully hidden."

Phaedrus, 370BC

CHAPTER 5

September 2017 - we worked out the compensation details and I joined the company. I divested my only remaining interest in a software company that provided cognitive training to elite (division I college and professional) athletes. There was no overlap between the services that Epic provided and my portfolio company, however, I wanted to ensure that there was never any potential, or even perceived, conflict of interest as I would be responsible for setting Epic's overall strategy and execution of acquisitions. I was all in on Epic.

My first day, Jamie's assistant, Ashley, gave me another quick tour of the office, showed me the supply closet, and brought me to my new office. I would be a few offices down from Devlin, just after the CFO, Controller and assistant controller. There was also an empty office on either side of me. Via email, Ashley had told me the day before I started that the company didn't provide employees with computers; therefore, I brought my own laptop. I found that a bit odd, but she explained that Devlin felt that everyone already had a computer, so why spend the money if not necessary? I was more concerned about consistency of operating systems, applications, security, firewalls, anti-virus software, etc. than bringing my own laptop to the office.

Ashley told me that she would introduce me to the head of human resources when she arrived. She left me to get settled. I took out my laptop and charger, a note pad and a binder I had assembled of my so-called diligence materials on the company. As I was flipping through the binder, a young woman poked her head into my office - she introduced herself as Denise (literally, she did not say her last name), "head of HR." She seemed nervous, told me that she would email me the employee onboarding materials I would need. I wondered why I hadn't received these in advanced of my start date. I asked a few questions about enrolling in the company's health benefits and 401(k) plans, but she struggled to answer the most basic questions and defaulted to "most of that stuff will be in the email I send you."

Ashley returned with a Post-It note in hand - the WIFI network and password. "Oh, great, thanks," I said. She smiled and turned to leave. She quickly turned back and told me that the office was having its weekly "Kitchen Stand-Up," in about 20 minutes, at which time she planned to introduce me to everyone. "Awesome, looking forward to it," I told her.

A few people walked by over the next 15-20 minutes, each looking in at me, but no one stopped to introduce themselves. They were all pretty young and probably had no idea who I was or what I was doing in that office. The staff began migrating towards the kitchen, so I did the same. As I left my office and Devlin was walking towards me. He greeted me with a smile and handshake - "Hey, welcome aboard - we have a lot of rocks to move."

"Thanks, yeah, excited to be here and get started," I replied. I really hoped he would stop using the "move rocks" lingo.

There were about twenty-five people or so gathered in the kitchen and ping pong area - most stood around the perimeter of the room, a few leaned against the granite-topped island, and a few were seated. I stood against the wall just to the right of the doorway through which I had entered. Ashley kicked off the "Stand-Up" - she was high energy, big smiles and a bit loud for this room. She had notes in her hand and told everyone that she had a few "really exciting" topics to cover that morning.

Ashley opened with, "welcome everyone, I hope you all had a great weekend. A few topics to cover today before I hand it off to Jamie. First, our company online store will be live later today and open through the end of the week; so, if you want to buy apparel, hats, other really cool stuff and wear your Epic logo with pride, hurry up, because it won't last long." A young man spoke up and provided more color about the web store and gear - how to find the website, the type of products available. Devlin added that he wanted everyone to take advantage of the opportunity to buy the company-branded gear at cost and to remember that everyone should represent Epic even when they weren't at work. I was a bit confused, but I assumed that the company must periodically put up a web store of full of company-branded apparel and expect employees to buy the merchandise?

Ashley moved onto the next topic - the company's non-profit foundation, EpicCares. She provided a thorough overview of the foundation, its purpose, and how important it was that "we all give back". From what I gathered, the foundation provided financial support to families in need so that their children could participate in Epic events and programs. Devlin jumped in and emphasized how fortunate we all were, and that philanthropy, volunteerism, and servant leadership were core values at Epic - he encouraged everyone to consider having a portion of their compensation automatically deducted and contributed to the foundation each pay period. He asked Denise from HR to explain to everyone how *easy* it was to do this - he made sure to tell everyone that each pay period, a portion of his salary went directly to the foundation. Denise *tried* to explain the process.

Ashley reminded everyone that Epic's monthly "day of service" was coming up in a few weeks - everyone in the office would have the day off and be volunteering at the EpicCares annual golf tournament. She directed everyone to the website for more details and to sign-up for a specific role in a Google sheet. I needed to learn more about this foundation, it sounded really interesting - I loved the fact that the company's culture included community involvement and charitable giving.

Ashley then introduced me and two additional hires, one in the accounting department and one in marketing, to the rest of the team. We each provided brief backgrounds and what are roles would be in the company. I told everyone how excited I was to be part of such a unique opportunity. Ashley also asked each of us to tell three things about ourselves - two of which are were false, and one which would be true. I really don't enjoy these types of "ice breakers." I had to think on my feet - I chose, "I swam the English Channel, ran the Boston Marathon or climbed Mount Everest." A young lady guessed

Mount Everest another shouted out Boston Marathon, then an uncomfortable moment of silence. I shrugged and told everyone that I actually ran the Boston Marathon with my wife a few years ago. A few murmurs and mumbles from the group, capped off with Ashley's over-exuberant, "wow, that is great!".

She handed off to Devlin. He covered a number of broad ranging topics.... "people need to wash their own coffee cups rather than leave them in the sink.... the last person to leave at night needs to turn off the lights.... there will be a new system put in place to reserve conference rooms.... the company is in the running to be named one of the fastest growing companies in American by Inc. 500." He used the last comment to springboard into an overall update on the company's growth, performance and achievement of key initiatives. He was complimentary of the team and praised the work they had been doing. Quite frankly, he did a really nice job of making everyone feel like they were part of something special. Based on how he spoke, it felt like the company was operating on all cylinders.

The meeting adjourned and a few folks came over and introduced themselves to me. A young lady in accounting, a young man who served as a project manager, presently working in the apparel division, and the gentleman who led the apparel business. As I was walking out of the kitchen, I connected with was the VP of Finance, Matt Jackson.

Matt appeared to be in his mid-thirties with a neatly trimmed beard, short brown hair and glasses. He was wearing a Epic golf shirt and khakis. He told me that he came from public accounting and that he was excited to work with me on acquisitions. I asked if we could schedule a couple of hours to get to know each other and so I could get up to speed on the accounting functions. We walked down to his office so he could check his calendar. He had photos of his family on his desk and credenza. He also had a putting mat on the floor and a few putters leaning against the wall. I noticed a few photos of foursomes on the window ledge - we chatted about golf briefly, it was obvious that he loved the game. We set a time to meet and he said he was going to send me a calendar invite. I realized that I didn't have an email address yet. I asked him who would issue my email account. He told me to check with Jamie as he controlled the Google GSuite. "OK, will do. Look forward to meeting tomorrow," I said as I left his office. I couldn't help but think how ridiculous it seemed that the CEO was responsible for managing the email accounts.

I headed two offices over to Devlin's, but his glass door was closed, and I could see that he was already on a call. As I turned to walk back to my office, I heard Ashley ask, "Steve, do you need something from Jamie?" I turned back; her office was next to Jamie's - the front wall was all glass. I told her that I needed my email set up. She said she could take care of it and would be right down. A couple of minutes later, Ashley came into my office and guided me through using GSuite's email, calendar and file storage capabilities. She also provided me with a key to my office and an RFID fob that provided access to the building and main office door. Perfect, I was all set up.

I had booked a room at the Fairfield Inn in Portland for the week so that I could be in the office every day and get myself integrated. I had laid out a detailed plan to spend time with each of the key leaders to get to know them individually; get a clear understanding of each division, how they functioned, technologies they used, how they worked with each corporate function, etc. I also wanted to dig into the accounting and finance functions so that I could understand its strengths and weaknesses in order to know how much I could leverage its resources for acquisitions and post-closing integration work. I also expected to spend a fair amount of time with Devlin and Murray, getting alignment on strategy and a better understanding of the financial performance of each division so I could set baseline expectations for acquisitions and model out potential synergies. Once my email was set up, I spent most of the first day scheduling the rest of my week with meetings with a few of my new colleagues. Devlin also had scheduled me to participate in a number of meetings with him as well.

The week proved to be extremely productive. My days started early, out of the hotel by 6:30am, the office was only a couple of miles away from the hotel down Route 1. I would hit Starbucks on the way, grab a tall, dark roast, black and a yogurt. I noticed Matt was usually in even before me - he told me that he liked to get in early as it allowed him to get work done uninterrupted and wrap his day a bit early to play nine holes in the summer or spend extra time with his wife and kids.

I was able get my day planned before people arrived and found a good cadence between meetings, calls and time organizing my thoughts and notes. Every day, I met someone new and socialized a bit more with those I had already gotten to know. I was starting to feel like I was part of the team. Since I had no one to go home to at night when I was staying in the hotel, I usually stayed at the office until 7:00pm or 8:00pm, wrapping up each day by pulling together a more complete picture of the company and opportunities. I usually ate dinner alone - a couple of times at a restaurant called the Tuscan Kitchen close to my hotel and also at a few restaurants in downtown Portland. I was usually back in my hotel room around 9:00pm, would call or text Christine and then turn in for the night. To be clear, when I am on the road, I try to spend as little time as possible in the hotel, other than sleeping. As much as the hotel operators try to create a comfortable atmosphere, I find the chains to be sterile and depressing; not to mention, the clientele is usually an odd mix between a few families and a bunch of business travelers; some are good, hardworking people and others are living, breathing caricatures of alcoholic, traveling salesmen.

Around 3:00pm on Friday, Devlin poked his head in my office and asked if I had a few minutes. I did - he told me to head down to his office when I was ready. I grabbed my notebook and headed down. He was standing behind his stand-up desk (it made the move from the old office to here) and told me to shut the door and have a seat. He pushed the button to lower the desk - he loved that function. I sat across from him and he asked how I thought the week went. I told him I was pleased and provided a casual, but detailed breakdown of who I had gotten to know, what I covered, areas that needed more attention, etc. He nodded along in approval. He asked, "anything of concern?" I told him "no, everyone has been great to work with. I definitely need more time with Don and Matt to get a deeper understanding of the respective divisions' historical performance and budgets, but I feel good."

"Great," he said. "What's your plan for next week?" I told him that I would be back first thing Monday morning and planned to be in Portland all week. I also told Devlin that I had updated my 100-day plan to reflect what I had learned that week along with the acquisition pipeline. I wanted to present it to him on Monday. He proceeded to tell me that I didn't need to worry about being in the office that much. I was surprised by his response. Actually, I was disappointed - I expected him to be pleasantly surprised that I would have a detailed, 100-day Gantt chart prepared so quickly. I told him that I believed it was critical that I be in town as much as possible to build personal relationships and credibility with the team while getting to know the business. He said, "I get it, but I want to make sure this doesn't impact your family." I told him that I appreciated that, but that everything was fine. My family was accustomed to my travel schedule. He didn't seem convinced. He then told me to head out to beat the Boston traffic.

Over the next month, I became more integrated with the team in Portland and was able to spend time on calls with the leaders of the divisions who were not based in Portland. I was learning that the company was far more decentralized than I originally thought - Hockey was based outside of Chicago with a European office in Munich and part-time staff spread all over Europe; Lacrosse was in Baltimore with staff scattered from the Mid-Atlantic to Florida; Soccer was located in Dedham, Massachusetts with additional offices in a number of other states and parts of Europe; the hotel booking business had staff in Detroit, Albany, and Memphis; the football team was based in New York and operated most of its events in Canton, Ohio; and the apparel division was based outside of San Juan, Puerto Rico.

There were a lot of moving parts here and I was beginning to learn that the operations and financial reporting functions for these divisions were further complicated by their geographic dispersion. Fortunately, the company's systems, particularly in accounting and finance, were fully integrated - at least that's what I had been told.

While managing people remotely is not easy, making acquisitions and integrating them operationally, culturally and financially is even more challenging when teams are spread out. Consequently, I took extra time and care to get to know the leaders out in the field. Understanding their teams' strengths and weaknesses, how their businesses functioned, as well as their views of their respective marketplaces. I couldn't shove deals down their throats; it simply wouldn't work. They had to buy in, agree with each acquisition and own it. I also needed to know what they could handle, what they were good at, and where there were weaknesses. This became my primary focus - getting to know the people who operated the businesses in the field. I had to trust that what I was hearing from them and from the leadership team in Portland was honest, accurate and consistent.

Building a healthy acquisition pipeline takes time - this was also a priority while working with the divisional leaders to understand their businesses. Fortunately, a good industry network coupled with few other buyers in the market allowed me to quickly build momentum. In a matter of weeks, we had about a dozen interesting opportunities at various stages of diligence. And, we were having new conversations almost every week with potential targets. Getting proprietary deal flow was not going to be an issue. However, I needed to ensure that Devlin and the board of directors were supportive of our acquisition strategy and that the company had sufficient capital to close these deals. I had no interest in misleading potential acquisition targets. If we were sincerely interested in a company, we needed to get to a definitive answer quickly, and if it was *yes*, we should close a transaction efficiently. Having the available capital and alignment with the board of directors was critical.

When you get in early and stay late every day, you tend to observe repetitive behavior and see certain trends with staff, particularly in a small company with an open concept office. I pride myself on *not* being a parochial manager, instead I trust people to manage their own time, projects and getting their work done until they prove that they can't. Having said this, you can't let people take advantage of a flexible work environment. If you do, other staff will take notice and it will impact culture. Not to mention, everyone needs to put the time in to be successful – there are no shortcuts, no cutting corners or

52

bending the rules (*remember these expressions*). Of the thirty or so staff in the office, I noticed that there were only a few (three or four) staff members who seemed to consistently put in a full workday, even working longer hours than was expected of them. Most others arrived at a relatively reasonable hour in the morning and were gone between 4:00pm and 5:00pm each afternoon. There were a remaining handful, who I quickly questioned their commitment and work ethic.

For example, the head of HR often arrived late in the morning, was frequently out of the office for blocks of time during the day and was never there at 5:00pm. I didn't know where she went, but she seemed to disappear often. When she returned to the building, she looked like she was sneaking back into her office. It felt like she had another job somewhere else. I knew that others in the company noticed the same thing and were annoyed by it - not a good look for the head of HR. Odd.

Then there were the two guys who I saw playing ping pong the first time I was given a tour of the office. No joke, these guys played ping pong for hours every day. Even worse, they would leave the doors open to the kitchen / ping pong room, so you could hear every detail and play-by-play of their matches. They didn't have a clue. Occasionally, I would walk into the kitchen to grab a coffee while they were playing and make eye contact with one of them. I would quickly head right back out - one of them would always say "wassup?" to me as I would leave. To make matters worse, I would later learn that their division, that they managed, was under-performing.

Then there was Linda in accounts payable. Some days, she didn't come in at all. Other days, I would see her arrive at 6:00pm. 6:00pm! Other times, I saw her arrive in the morning, stand outside of the main entrance smoking a cigarette, only to never come into the office. Absolutely bizarre behavior. When she was in the office, she hardly interacted with anyone and seemed to spend more time in the restroom than at her desk. Everyone in the office saw the behavior - I noticed eyes rolling and heard inside jokes being made behind her back. Her hair was bleached blond, she wore an unusual amount of makeup (by any standard, not just mine), and always wore heels; the highest heels I have seen.   She struggled to walk in them and the clicking of the heels on the polished cement floor of the office was like fingernails on a chalkboard.

This situation was so odd that I actually felt comfortable mentioning it to Devlin during my first couple of weeks. I asked who she was, what her role was and why her hours seemed so peculiar. He explained that she had a young child, recently went through a divorce and needed flexible hours to care for her child. He went on to say that he put her in a "special projects" role in accounts payable that allowed her to work independent of the other accounting team members, "so it works out well for everyone." I asked if she was a full-time employee and he confirmed she was. I didn't feel like it was my place to push back, but there was no way she was putting in a full work week, not to mention the message it sent to her colleagues. Very strange to say the least.

I chalked these examples up to a young, growing company with a CEO who was trying to create a casual culture that he thought would attract millennials. I would bet that over time, those who were not putting in the work would be exposed, and that Devlin would come to his senses sooner than later. However, it drove me nuts when it was so obvious, and no one took action.

Here is the good news...

The team that managed the hockey division was passionate, dedicated, customer-focused, metrics driven, and willing to adopt new technologies and best practices. They seemed genuinely excited to have me on board to help them strategically and with potential new investments. In addition, the team and their events were known in the world of hockey and respected by the customers, rink owners, college recruiters, pro hockey clubs and, in many cases, their competition. The hockey division's leadership was conservative, so the challenge would be getting them to drive more organic growth and take some calculated risks with launching new events. This division operated tournaments and showcases for boys and girls from ten to eighteen years old. They also had a few acquisition targets they wanted to pursue. I could definitely work with this group.

The soccer business had some scale - it was the company's largest division, representing almost 50% of consolidated revenue. A heavy operational load and staff came with that scale. A lot of people to manage - at peak season, this division had upwards of 500 staff. It operated exclusively under the Back Bay Football Club ("BBFC") brand. The company was founded nearly fifteen years ago by two brothers from Northern Ireland, Patrick and Sean Baldwin. They came to the Boston area to play college soccer - Patrick Baldwin later launched the predecessor to BBFC, a non-profit club program called Back Bay Football. It was rebranded as BBFC in or about 2014 and converted to a for-profit limited liability company. Epic acquired a controlling interest in BBFC in 2016, its entree into the soccer market. I had met with the Baldwins several times after I joined Epic but had interacted more frequently with their COO, Jack Cahill, to get my arms around the business.

BBFC had several revenue streams. It operated travel soccer teams on a tuition basis - players would play for a BBFC team from September through the following May with parents making installment payments along the way. In addition, BBFC operated camps, clinics, tournaments and assembled all-star teams to compete in regional, national and international tournaments. The company also had a presence in parts of Europe in which it operated international academies. Under the academy model, players, from the U.S. and abroad alike, could choose to attend a residential academy in a place like London or Rome where they would complete their high school education while simultaneously focusing on soccer - most of these players hoped to play professionally or at the collegiate level, at a minimum.

I quickly learned that Patrick Baldwin seemed to have created a cult-like loyalty among his staff, mostly Irish, English and Scottish "lads" who had migrated to the U.S. to continue to be part of the sport they loved. It was early in my learning curve and I couldn't tell if his team respected him or feared him; based on some of my early observations, some of his staff could have been suffering from

Stockholm Syndrome. I knew I was going to have to work hard to get my arms around BBFC.

Epic's international tours division was the original vertical of the business; marketing hockey tournaments in Europe to North American families who wanted both competition and a cultural experience. The company operated tours in places like Chamonix, Prague, Stockholm, Bolzano, Moscow and the like. There was a baseline price to go on a tour with a number of potential upgrades for the parents and other guests including local tours, wine tasting, pub crawls, etc.

I learned that the company's tours staff worked closely with the hockey staff to identify North American players and then make introductions to the families in order to market the tours. The tours staff would then begin the process of selling the tours to these families and put together a competitive team. It was a lot of direct sales - it seemed like an extremely inefficient process. The company was not using any digital market tactics. Simultaneously, the tours staff coordinated the logistics supporting the tour - booking flights, coordinating ground transportation, reserving hotel rooms, planning team dinners and the like. In some cases, Epic owned and operated the tournaments in Europe and in other cases, teams attended third-party operated tournaments.

The tours business was all about economies of scale - maximizing the number of travelers per tour and making sure that the last available seat on the tour was occupied. There was margin to be realized at each step of the tour (mark-up on the tournament entry fee, flights, ground transportation, hotel room, local tour, wine tasting, and even the special uniforms and apparel the players wore). This was how Epic management currently viewed this business. I saw it differently - what I just described was the financial model, but not how we should have been thinking about it strategically. These were once-in-a-lifetime opportunities for players and families to experience a new place, a new culture wrapped around a sporting event. A chance to bond with your teammates, build new friendships, connect with players from around the world, for parents to watch their child compete and have a new cultural experience and so on. When you provided consumers with opportunities to travel together, the sky was the limit.

Families were spending a lot of money to participate in these tours and they deserved a best-in-class customer experience from the moment they expressed interest in one of our tours and at every touch point until they returned home. In fact, we should have continued to deliver value and lasting memories even when the tour wrapped up via content captured while they were on the tour. I knew that much of this was not happening - it spoke to the opportunity. The business was profitable, but there was a lot of upside. After meeting the tours leadership, I had serious concerns about their ability to take this business to the next level.

The lacrosse business was much smaller than I thought - Devlin had included potential acquisitions in his "run rate" financials and participant statistics, thereby overstating the size of the lacrosse division (along with a few others). In fact, the lacrosse business was dying on the vine. Its brands were old and tired.

Epic had acquired a couple of owner-operator lacrosse event businesses over the previous few years. The company was not in the travel club business yet but wanted to enter that market. They only operated a handful of events and this was the smallest of the sports divisions. My interactions with the lacrosse team caused me significant concerns. I had yet to meet anyone in the group who could express a clear view of their position in the marketplace, what the market was looking for, how we satisfied those needs, how we differed from our competition, what was compelling about our offerings, and so on. The other challenge was that the team was spread out all over the east coast without a centralized office. Their leader was Larry Fairchild, one of the owner-operators who sold to Epic. He was based in the Baltimore area and fancied himself as a lacrosse industry expert. Fairchild was likable at first but spoke in anecdotes about the industry and trends - he never supported his assertions with statistics or data. Everything was his personal opinion yet presented as fact. On top of that, when he visited the Portland office, he arrived without an agenda, was ill-prepared and spent most of his time chatting up the female members of the accounting and marketing staffs - all of whom were young enough to be his daughter. It was obvious to me that he was not going to make the cut.

The lacrosse market, however, presented a great opportunity. The sport continued to have strong growth trends at the youth level, particularly the girls' game. The girls' game had strong tailwinds and was in need of a provider that could deliver a high-quality product and great coaching for kids. The spend patterns of the families involved in the sport were compelling. These families enjoyed traveling to events, staying in hotels, buying apparel and gear. Lacrosse players and parents often see the game as a potential differentiator or "hook" to getting into a better college; Ivy League, NESCAC schools, etc. Consequently, there is a robust college showcase model in lacrosse and competitive element to the travel club side of the business. We saw an opportunity for Epic to enter the club business, like we operated in soccer with BBFC, and provide a comprehensive offering to the lacrosse market. We would have to acquire our way into this strategy, however, since we didn't have the internal lacrosse talent to grow organically. We would need a proven and respected lacrosse leader who was passionate about teaching the game to kids and developing them as well-rounded student athletes.

Our hotel bookings business, known as HTL, really intrigued me but also had its challenges. As I mentioned earlier, this business served the Epic events, third-party event operators as well as the consumers who attended the events. HTL sourced blocks of hotel rooms well in advance (six months to a year) of an event by committing to a certain volume of rooms to hotel operators. As the date of the event approached, HTL staff would assign hotel rooms to the event attendees - in turn, the hotels would remit a commission to HTL and a rebate to the event operator for driving room night demand.

Our research indicated that there was a sizable market opportunity here but a highly fragmented and competitive industry. In short, there were a lot of *mom & pop* hotel booking companies providing this service. However, the level of service provided to either the event operators or consumers was not high, therefore, I believed we could elevate the quality of service and devise a marketing and sales

58

strategy to take market share from our competition. I also saw an attractive financial model here. The amount of room night commissions required to cover the fix cost of sales, customer service and room procurement teams was low relative to the incremental capacity of a sales and service team. In other words, the break-even point on a new team was very low, but their upside was quite high. We could grow this business quickly while delivering more value to our customer. I liked the characteristics and wanted to continue to invest in this division.

Here is what I didn't like about HTL - like most of the rest of Epic, Devlin acquired his way into this business. Several years ago, he first acquired HTL, then another acquisition of similar business followed. The founders of those businesses were longtime friends who played college hockey together in Minnesota. They remained friends to this day and appeared to enjoy operating the business together. Shortly after I joined Epic, Devlin closed on the acquisition of another hotel bookings business called Travel Ball America ("TBA"). Apparently, the deal had been in the works for over a year - I'm not sure why it took so long to close. What I had learned, however, was that the two college teammates (and leaders off this division) were not involved in the due diligence or decision to acquire TBA. The directive to them, from Devlin, following the closing, was to integrate the businesses and management team. I was told it wasn't going well. While I wasn't responsible for operational matters such as this, I certainly was not yet comfortable pursuing an acquisition strategy for this business until they got their house in order. Stay tuned.

Here is the bad news about the other divisions...

The apparel division - how do I say this?... I absolutely, unequivocally, did not see a viable business here; it made no sense whatsoever.

1) Epic's management lacked any apparel manufacturing experience;

2) Epic was in an "asset light" business that should have required minimal working capital; apparel manufacturing was precisely the

opposite (machinery and equipment; raw materials and finished inventory; and floating customer receivables);

3) Alternative internal investment opportunities (like launching new events) would yield much higher probabilities of success and return on investment;

4) Building a consumer brand takes a long time, significant investment, expertise and, even with that, the likelihood of success is very low when the competition includes the likes of Nike and adidas (as an FYI, the brand prefers the "a" to be in lowercase);

5) Global brands want to sponsor and work with companies like Epic that have direct access to the youth sports consumers - trying to launch an Epic brand eliminated this opportunity. By the way, the per consumer profit opportunity was higher through a partnership with a global brand than if we built our own apparel business (and were successful at it, which was highly unlikely); and

6) The distraction and allocation of brain power internally took time and energy away from the core business.

Before I presented my opinion, I needed to see the facility in Puerto Rico so that I was fully informed. I flew into San Juan from Logan Airport, arriving on a sweltering, humid day. The gentleman from the factory who was scheduled to pick me up was over an hour late. He spoke broken English and I don't speak Spanish. A tough start to the trip. We went straight to the factory.

I entered the building and was greeted by Steve Lomax, a Portland-based team member who had been asked by Devlin to take on the apparel facility as a "project manager" and make it successful. How unfair. Steve was in his mid-to-late twenties, had his MBA and had interned at Epic while still in college. I had spent a fair amount of time with Steve in Portland - he was smart, ambitious, diligent, hard-working, humble and polite. In short, I found him to be a high-quality young man. He also didn't deserve to be handed the apparel project.

Steve gave me a tour of the facility and it was pretty much what I expected based on my prior experience with a *cut and sew* shop in Mexico. Set in an industrial park, the cinder block building appeared to be about 20,000 square feet, of which about half was being utilized. The empty space housed some obsolete rolled fabrics and cache of broken-down machinery and equipment; what appeared to be a sublimation printer, a cutter and some sewing machines.

The manufacturing floor had the finished goods area located towards the front of the building, adjacent to the single loading dock. There were stacks of cardboard boxes on pallets with product description and quantities written in black marker (no labels, UPC codes, etc.). Beyond the boxes were tables of stacked apparel that included hockey jerseys, socks, hoodies, and the like. I assumed this was the makeshift packaging area. Immediately beyond this area were rows of tables for the sewing operators.

There were about twenty sewing operators and two or three supervisors among them. They were sewing a variety of products similar to those in the packing area. The individual components they were stitching together were stacked next to them in tight quarters. I am not a manufacturing expert, but it was apparent that the operators didn't have enough room - in fact, as I walked along, I noticed components that had fallen on the floor and had been stepped on. Beyond the operators were the manual cutting tables and a separate walled-in area that contained the sublimation printers.

After the tour, we returned to the front office to meet the general manager, Ramon. Steve took me to a conference room connected to Ramon's office. Ramon was on his cell phone, gave me a wave followed by his index finger indicating he needed a minute. Steve and I took the time to catch up a bit. He had been spending almost every other week in Puerto Rico trying to implement policies and processes that would allow for more efficient management and oversight from the U.S. He said it was "going pretty well," but based on his tone and body language, I wasn't convinced. Steve was incredibly conscientious, but this project was taking a toll on him.

Ramon joined us and brought a couple of bottles of water with him. He was warm and welcoming and insisted on giving me another tour. We did another walk through of the facility - having had the benefit of the earlier tour, I took the opportunity to ask more focused questions around workflow, processes, controls, capacity, current utilization, utilization to break-even, etc. Ramon was able to answer some of the questions, Steve filled in when needed and was also open and honest enough to admit when he didn't have a good answer.

We returned to the conference room. Steve was an excellent project manager - he had prepared a Gantt chart of the improvements needed to be made at the facility and we walked through them with Ramon. He also provided me with a monthly key metrics report for the last several months that included indicators like units produced, labor per unit, cost of materials per unit, unit selling price, margin per unit, monthly gross margin, overhead expenses, etc. From this, I was able to quickly get my head around the monthly burn rate and whether the facility could *ever* be a profit center.

It could have been the travel, the heat & humidity, the facility, or a combination of them all, but I had a raging headache. On second thought, it definitely was the apparel operation that was causing the headache. I wouldn't know where to begin to improve it. As a contract manufacturer, your margins are relatively thin - so third-party customer business isn't that attractive compared to internal business. Customers are always shopping price, so it's a race to the bottom. Epic's internal needs didn't deliver sufficient volume to drive meaningful capacity utilization. As a result, we had a small cut and sew shop that couldn't generate enough volume to realize any manufacturing or process efficiencies. Layer on top of that a management team that lacked any domain or process experience and you had a doomed business model.

For the balance of the day, we moved back and forth between the conference room and the shop floor; working through processes that could make the operation more efficient and evaluated which products were more profitable than others and why. It was a productive session, but likely wouldn't have a lasting impact as I could not see us being in the business for long.

As the day was coming to a close, Ramon drove Steve and me to our hotel. It was a small, clean hotel on a busy road. Ramon offered to take us to dinner, but I respectfully punted to the next night as I was exhausted and simply not in the mood. Steve headed to his room and we agreed to grab a quick dinner in the lobby restaurant - we would meet back in the lobby in fifteen minutes. I walked to the check-in counter and slipped on the tile floor - the humidity outside coupled with the air conditioning had made the tile floors treacherous. Both feet flew out from under me and I landed my tailbone and then hit my head. It hurt like hell, but I was fine. I was embarrassed more than anything. I remained on the cold, damp tiles for a minute or so while I was trying to convince the receptionist that I was fine. For the first time since I had joined the Company, I was beginning to question my decision.

Steve and I met in the lobby and he suggested two restaurants connected to the hotel where he had eaten before. We went with the Mexican-themed restaurant over the steakhouse. We sat at the bar and ordered a local beer. Steve pointed out a casino adjacent to lobby that I hadn't even noticed. He said it was quite small, but included poker, blackjack, slot machines, and so on. I watched two men walk into the casino. This wasn't a tourist area. The casino clientele were locals and business travelers. I told Steve that I found it kind of depressing. He agreed and proceeded to tell me that when Devlin and Murray came to the DR, they liked to go to that casino. "Really?", I asked. He nervously laughed and said, "Yeah, Jamie loves to gamble." "Oh God", I mumbled.

I ordered something safe - a cheese and veggie quesadilla. Steve did the same. The food was fine. It was nice to have the time to talk with Steve. I enjoyed his company - he was respectful, but not afraid to express his opinions about the business; he also recognized the challenges of the apparel business and also thought that entering that space was a mistake, but he delivered the message in a way where he is trying to not be disrespectful to Devlin. He told me that Devlin was "persistent, but also stubborn" about acknowledging when things weren't working as planned. He attributed it to Jamie's confidence in "fixing things and making them work," but he said that he was

63

starting to realize that Devlin had some blind spots. We also talked about the other divisions at length. He validated my assessment of each - it was refreshing to hear his perspective since he had touched almost every element of the business from his internship to his current project manager position. He also shared my concerns about the football business.

In 2015, Jamie Devlin became acquainted with a gentleman named Mike Patterson. Patterson had been in the youth sports business for a number of years. He was the co-founder of a company that had operated a number of national events in a few different sports. He had parted ways with his co-founder a few years earlier and started a new business in the same industry. Although he hadn't held any significant events yet under his new company, he had developed a relationship with several executives at the Pro Football Hall of Fame. Patterson had learned that the Hall of Fame had been experiencing stagnant or declining visitor numbers over the previous several years and they had been exploring ways to make the Canton a more attractive destination.

Around the same time, a real estate developer, with a history of refurbishing distressed properties, came into the picture. The developer had carved out a niche buying distressed real estate, often abandoned mills, factories and even environmental superfund sites and converting them into offices and multi-use properties. I wasn't aware of him ever having developed a sports-related property. There were also some articles in the public domain that raised questions about his business practices.

The developer saw an opportunity in Canton. A strategy stared to take shape to leverage the appeal of the Hall of Fame (particularly its ties to the NFL), access to its members (the *gold jackets*), and the depressed local real estate market (particularly the single-family homes surrounding the Hall). An affiliate of the Hall of Fame would acquire the surrounding residential properties, raze the houses, construct multi-purpose athletic fields, add hotels, a water park, restaurants and retail shops in order to make this a youth sports destination. Those involved each had different but aligning motives. Certain executives at the non-profit Hall of Fame felt that they had limited financial upside as managers of a non-profit. They were looking to participate in the for-profit side of this potential development.

Another member of the Hall of Fame's management team fancied himself as a media and production expert. He would later look to claim the media rights associated with any and all content to be produced at the Hall of Fame's new sports complex. Lastly, the developer was looking to take advantage of the depressed Canton real estate market and leverage the Hall of Fame's relationship with the NFL to draw investors, lenders and sponsors while keeping a chunk of the equity in the development for himself.

They were all missing two things: capital and youth sports event programming. In stepped Mike Patterson. Patterson was a fast talker, but someone who passionately spoke of both the merits of sports participation for America's youth and his vision of a football version of the Little League World Series to be held in Canton. He had a network of high school and Pop Warner football coaches in every market who would promote local qualifiers and regional tournaments that would drive teams to a series of games held over a number of weeks in Canton. The media and production expert would produce the content and try to sell the rights to the likes of ESPN or CBS Sports. Sponsors and advertisers would be lining up at the door, or so they thought. Visitors to the museum would skyrocket. People would want to go Canton year-round just to visit the venue, stay in a hotel, swim at the water park, eat in the restaurants, etc. They all bought into each other's' pitch... hook, line and sinker.

One problem: since leaving his other company, Patterson lacked the infrastructure and staff to put on events - not exactly a small detail. He would need capital and to assemble a team. This would take some time, something he didn't have - he needed to get the deal done with the Hall before they chose another partner or decided to launch their own events. He needed to demonstrate to them that he could move fast - the Hall also needed its own pitch to investors that the youth sports events could be pulled off. Around the same time, Patterson found Epic.

He pitched Devlin on his concept of operating events in Canton. Devlin knew nothing about the football market, nor does it appear that he did any meaningful research. If he did, he didn't place any weight on the declining participation rates, the minimal or non-existent tournament registration fees and the grassroots nature of youth football - meaning it was typically local in nature, organized via Pop Warner or USA Football and there likely wasn't a need for a national event organizer. Instead, he liked the idea and potential publicity of being indirectly associated with the NFL and he had a particular interest in learning more about destination sports complexes and residential academies. He also liked the concept of simply aggregating more, more, more - this seemed to be his real strategy. Just grab a bunch of stuff and figure out the details later. Remember, he had set a goal of $1 billion in revenue in five years, consequently, he would acquire or partner with almost anyone who came knocking on his door.

There was yet one more twist - unbeknownst to any of us at the time, Devlin and one of his Epic co-founders, Scott Boyle, were working on a separate business, a youth sports complex and academy only a short drive from Epic's offices. This was *their* project; one in which Epic had no financial interest, however, they both appeared to spend considerable time and energy on it while using Epic's brand and credibility in the marketplace to give it momentum. In fact, I later spoke to several people who thought that the project was an Epic-owned business. Getting Epic involved with the Canton project would give them a front row seat to the intricacies of building a destination sports complex and residential academy. More to come on this later.

Patterson, if nothing else, was a good salesman. He actually convinced Devlin to have Epic acquire his new company (which had operated few if any events) based on a so-called exclusive arrangement Patterson had negotiated with the affiliate of the Hall of Fame. However, the arrangement between the Hall and Patterson had not even been finalized, therefore there wasn't even a binding contract in place when Epic acquired Patterson's business. The transaction included some cash at closing, a full-time job at Epic for

Patterson as well as future bonuses tied to the performance of Epic's new football division.

It took me months to get to the bottom of what I summarized above and that just scratched the surface. I didn't know all of this in the Fall of 2017, but I knew that the football business, like the apparel business, was going to be a drain of resources - time, human capital and money. I also feared that Epic's brand could suffer damage when the Hall's real estate development inevitably failed. I was not going to be an advocate of this particular initiative.

CHAPTER 6

Getting up to speed and understanding the individual divisions, their teams and processes took longer than I expected. People were located all over the place, they were busy running their businesses, prior acquisitions had not been integrated and I was careful to not make them think I was auditing what they did on a daily basis. It was important that I respected them, their time and what they had built. I quickly learned that there was no single, comprehensive documentation of the business, something as simple as a business plan that outlined the overarching business thesis, mission, values, individual divisional characteristics, financials, etc. Instead, I had to take pieces of what I could find and fill in the rest through phone calls and in-person meetings with divisional leaders and the staff in Portland. Thankfully, I had Steve Lomax a few doors down to help fill in the blanks. I would then circle back with Devlin, Murray or Jackson to confirm my findings. This was an iterative process and I quickly found that anytime I identified a process gap or performance improvement opportunity, Devlin would become defensive. He answers often lacked substance and fact; instead they were full of spin.

Initially, I dismissed his defensiveness as a combination of a few things: 1) he founded this company, built it, and managed it every day - I, too, might be defensive if a new guy was turning over stones and pointing out things I may have missed along the way; 2) I may simply be expecting too much from a young company growing fast - he probably thought the business would be optimized on the fly; and 3) it may simply have been his personality - what I intended as constructive criticism and performance improvement opportunities, he seemed to views as personal attacks.

However, I had also noticed that often he would either outright refute my assertions or spin his responses to my observations or recommendations. If I suggested that the hockey management team had expressed to me that they needed more timely monthly financial reporting from corporate accounting so that they could adjust discretionary spending, Devlin would say, "that's not the case - they are getting their monthly financial statements faster than ever. I will circle back with them and take care of it." Or, in one instance, an alarming instance, one of the junior accountants casually mentioned to me that the company was running at least three separate accounting systems depending on the division. Devlin had boasted, on a number of occasions, that one of the company's significant strengths was its centralized, standardized and integrated accounting system. He had gone so far as to say that closing the books at the end of the month was "as easy as tapping a few keys." I asked him about the separate accounting systems, and he was clearly angered. He wouldn't answer the question directly. He wanted to know who told me about the separate systems. He finally refuted it and said that the company's accounting functions were fully integrated. I realized pretty quickly that he would shut me out completely if I asked too many questions.

I needed to construct my own baseline understanding of the so-called integrated registration, expense management, general ledger, CRM system so that I could plan post-acquisition processes and expected synergies as well as articulate the benefits of such an integrated system to potential acquisition targets. I had found that many

68

potential targets in this space were looking to be part of something bigger. The appeal of getting back to what they loved, the sport itself... coaching kids and operating events was what they enjoyed - they wanted to do that, not the marketing, planning, accounting and other business stuff. We needed to take those functions off their plate, centralize and upgrade them.

I scheduled a time to meet with Devlin and Murray on this specific topic. We met in the main conference room. It felt uncomfortable from the moment I walked in. I said hello and didn't hear a response from either of them. They were already seated at the table. Devlin at the head of the table looking down the table towards the flat screen on the wall. He was trying to connect his laptop to the screen and seemed frustrated. He and Murray were talking about a workout they had just completed at Orange Theory down the street from the office. I had learned over the last couple of months that this was, quietly, one of their midday routines.

I watched the flat screen while Devlin was troubleshooting. He was complaining that other staff members never signed off the Apple TV application in this conference room when they left. He seemed particularly annoyed. Finally, he gathered himself, looked at me and said, "you had a question about our Platform?" I responded, "well, more than the Platform. I need to understand the integration of the budgeting, registration system, expense management... how that all feeds into the general ledger and financial reporting...." Before I finished, he said, "OK, OK, I get it. It's a lot easier if I walk you through it visually." His eyes never met mine during this exchange, he was fiddling with his mouse and looking at the flat screen the entire time. Murray, the CFO, the guy who should own all of this, never said a word.

Devlin proceeded to filibuster for the next hour. He toggled between PowerPoint presentations showing graphics of workflows, logging into the home-grown registration and flashing Google Sheets that apparently were monthly reporting packages. The concepts all made sense to me, but they appeared to be exactly that, concepts. He was using multiple systems and applications, all the while trying make a case that they were integrated. This was ridiculous.

I simply needed to know a couple of things:

1) If each division used our home-grown registration system and, if not, what other platforms they were using?;

2) In what general ledger packages were the financial activities of each of our divisions captured?;

3) How were financial statements generated for each division and the method by which we consolidated those financial statements?; and

4) Where was all of this data maintained and stored?

 I tried to ask these questions several times but couldn't get a straight answer. It was abundantly clear that my questions made him uncomfortable and he was getting annoyed. His standard response was that I didn't understand the full capabilities of the Platform. There comes a point in a meeting like this when you realize it isn't going anywhere and you have to avoid a fight. Murray, the CFO, contributed nothing, absolutely nothing, to the meeting. I knew then that he was an empty suit, a pawn under Devlin's thumb.

Before the meeting ended, Devlin let me know, again, that he had made the final decision to go to market and raise a minimum of twenty million dollars to execute our acquisition strategy. Great news but delivered in an odd manner considering I interacted with him multiple times a day, but he dropped this on me at the end of an uncomfortable meeting. In hindsight, I think he felt very uncomfortable that I may have been on to something fishy, so he threw me a bone that he thought was positive news and would divert my attention.

He told me that he and Murray had already begun to have conversations with potential investors and were still working on an offering memorandum. He had already told me this once before, a few months earlier when I was only considering getting involved. He said he would send it over to me in a couple of days for comments. This felt like a slap in the face. I was responsible for corporate strategy and acquisitions and I had the option to invest in the company, but I was not in the loop or contributing to the offering memo nor the fundraising conversations with potential investors. I found this both odd and annoying. I stayed calm, and told him... "that sounds great, I look forward to seeing the deck. Let me know who you have on your potential investor list, I may have a few to add." Devlin simply said "OK" and the meeting adjourned.

I continued to work with divisional leaders as well as managing the acquisition pipeline. The list continued to grow, but I had to manage expectations and workload in light of the fact that the company did not have the liquidity to close any transactions yet. While I still wasn't privy to the company's financials, I had been invited to a board meeting later in the month at Revolution Capital's ("RevCap") offices in Toronto. Devlin had asked me to provide draft strategy and acquisition slides to him, so I assumed that I would see a draft board presentation prior to the board meeting that would finally provide me with a clear view of the company's year-to-date performance vs. budget and its current balance sheet.

I provided the slides to Devlin and offered to help any way I could with the board package. No response. Instead, several days later, he sent me a copy of the confidential information memorandum (the "CIM") watermarked *DRAFT*. A CIM is the document used to attract potential investors. The document listed Devlin and Murray as the points of contact for further information about Epic. No mention of me. It was about sixty pages in length and appeared to include some of the slides he walked me through the first time I met him over six months ago. I noticed, however, there were a number of additions to the deck taken from materials that I had provided him regarding my industry research and strategic vision. There were other additions as well, including financial slides.

I did a detailed review of the slide deck, inserted comment callouts throughout. I am not typically shy with my comments and questions. The first thing I wondered was about Devlin's earlier start-up that he said he sold to HomeAdvisor.com. Devlin told me he had raised capital for his start-up that he later sold - I doubted that he was directly responsible for raising the capital since the slide deck he

71

provided me failed to include many of the necessary and most basic elements a sophisticated investor would expect. Second, if this was going out to potential investors and my name was going to be included as a member of the management team, I wanted it to be done right. Lastly, I believed strongly in this opportunity and wanted it to be successful.

I provided a lot of comments, but I gathered he didn't appreciate them - if I were in his shoes, I would have appreciated having someone challenge me and interested in making the document as accurate and attractive as possible. We met to review my comments and questions. Many of my comments were about formatting, grammar, suggestions for adding or deleting slides, but more importantly, I questioned some of his key assertions. For example, the document stated that Epic managed over 500 events with over 1.0 million participants and families. Those statistics were compelling to say the least – between registration fees, hotel commissions & rebates, affiliate revenue opportunities with brand partners and sponsorships, the average revenue would grow very quickly. With over 1.0 million customers, there was a tremendous opportunity here. I wanted to ensure that the company actually engaged with that many customers. I asked for the supporting data. I never received it.

Several of the divisions were called *leaders* in their respective markets. I wanted to make sure the company was careful using such language. Devlin had referred to Epic's media division as a leader in its industry. I'm not sure how he was defining "leader," but based on its nominal annual revenues, lack of a growth strategy while operating in a recruiting / highlight reel category that had been recently been dominated by several tech players, I didn't see how that business could survive, let alone be called a leader.

The document also referenced combines and training as key services provided by the company. The documents emphasized that Epic maximized its network of elite athletes, strong internal sports brands and big data to build youth teams in different regions that can participate and fuel Epic internal events. It also said that athlete development training programs were promoted to the company's customers from grassroots-age levels in an effort to develop strong lifetime relationships. I was not aware of a single combine that Epic offered. When I asked about it, the response was, "we provide those services at our events and for our teams at BBFC – we plan to expand it in 2018." I read the language a few times and assumed I didn't understand the offering, so I changed my question. I asked what the reference to big data meant? I was told that we were using customer data to feed our Platform and CRM activities. Devlin was short with his answer. I would later learn that none of this data was being used as described. Further, the CRM was a single function in the Platform that allowed email blasts... nothing else.

The CIM also highlighted an Epic Academy initiative including, existing partnerships with third-party, residential secondary schools for both girls and boys. It also explained the company was planning addition expansion to develop Epic Academies (similar to IMG Academy) - it would offer athletes an academy model for its current and future sport offerings. My questions here were related more to strategy. I asked about our commitment to the academy model and how much research had been done in this area. Devlin told me that he wanted to expand the hockey academy business across the country and around the world. He also said that he viewed Epic's acquisition of BBFC as critical to bringing their European soccer academy model to the U.S. as well. He told me that he had identified a hockey academy operator that he wanted to pursue as an acquisition as soon as possible. My sense was that he wanted to make a big push in the academy space but had yet to perform the necessary research and financial modeling.

I asked about the references to baseball and softball in the CIM as divisions – I knew that Epic was not operating in either of these sports. He told me that the apparel division produced baseball and softball uniforms, but that he intended to acquire or launch baseball and softball events in 2018. I knew the baseball space well and was surprised to hear his response. I asked what acquisition targets he had in mind; he couldn't name a single one. He pushed back and asked who I would like to acquire. As I started to answer, he interrupted and said, "maybe we should push that out to 2019" and he moved on.

The CIM also stated that Epic was the *lead sponsor* of over 450 events, operating in over 25 countries, access to over 100 athlete celebrities, and over 30 million social media followers. By the time, I got to this question, Devlin was fed up. He said, "look, the statistics are all accurate." Months later, I would learn these were grossly overstated.

I didn't bother asking about the logos of partners in the CIM that included a number of top global brands and sports franchises. I assumed they were all partners in some form or another - I could not imagine including the logos in they weren't actually partners. I was impressed that we had attracted such brands to work with Epic. Again, it would only be a matter of months before I would learn that Epic had no connection or business relationship with most to these brands.

The CIM also summarized Epic's proven track record of consolidating global sports organizations that provided both a short-term and long-term strategic fit to the organization. It also touted the company's ability to acquire businesses with creative financing strategies, along with the ability to shrink the acquisition multiples. He was implying that acquisitions had required minimal up-front capital but had performed well under Epic's control, effectively driving down the multiple of earnings paid to acquire the business. At the time I was reading the CIM, I wasn't yet convinced that the company's financial systems and processes were "best-in-class" as Devlin often professed. He emphasized that the company's process of integrating and realizing synergies from acquisitions was efficient and effective - from what I had heard internally, that didn't seem to be the case. I would need to dig in at some point and evaluate his acquisition history. I would need the company's consolidating financial statements, the purchase and sale agreements and diligence materials for each acquisition to determine if these had been good deals.

Devlin beamed with pride whenever he spoke of Epic's proprietary Platform. In the CIM, he listed the following features of the system: player & team registration, internal CRM and database administration, event launch and management tools, field accounting systems & controls, travel and marketing management, tour management system, event hotel bookings system, tournament management software, and full integration with accounting software. If these were truly functional elements of the Platform, he had built something special. Again, we would learn months later that most of these features did not exist and certainly weren't integrated.

I also had the benefit of having listened in on several monthly leadership calls and at least one company-wide call. On these calls, Devlin would provide updates on certain initiatives - always with a positive spin. He would also touch on the company's core values more than once on each call. The core values included things like *financial stability* and *integrity*. Devlin would usually transition into fundraising for the EpicCares Foundation and emphasize that all of us had a special opportunity to make a difference by contributing to the Foundation.

Although I couldn't put my finger on specific examples yet, likely since I didn't have access to the company's financial information, but I wasn't entirely comfortable with Devlin's representations and assertions on these leadership or company-wide calls. It felt like he was always embellishing. In addition, he would quickly become defensive when asked a question about his strategy or if someone was looking for additional information that supported his claim. Lastly, he would often interrupt and answer questions that were directed at others – particularly, his CFO and VP of Finance. Was he a micro-manager, a control freak, was his CFO incompetent... or, was he manipulating things?

NEW CAPITAL

CHAPTER 7

In December of 2017, Devlin had narrowed down the potential investors to two leading candidates, both family offices of high net worth individuals that made private equity-type investments. One was Chicago-based, and the family's wealth was largely built in the hospitality sector. The other was New York-based and the high net worth individual was one of the more prominent private equity executives in the world. He was still a top executive of one of the largest publicly traded financial service firms. I had introduced Epic to this firm – though I had never worked with them, I had recently met one of the partners through a mutual friend. I had met with and had numerous calls with both groups, among others. Quite frankly, I would have been comfortable working with either of them.

The group from Chicago had another youth sports event business in its sights that they wanted to acquire and roll into Epic. It was a business that I knew pretty well. The business didn't operate elite-level events, which Epic's typically did, and it also owned a large facility with fields, dormitories and concessions. I, and Epic's board, preferred an "asset light" model, not one that tied up capital in real estate. Even during my short tenure at Epic, I was already concerned about integrating acquisitions, so I didn't want to rush into a deal without being fully prepared. The Chicago group needed us to commit to a simultaneous closing of their deal with our financing. They viewed it as a package and wouldn't do one without the other.

We slow played it to see what was going to happen with the New York firm.

The New York firm, Canyon Ferry Capital ("CFC") was deep in due diligence, with Diligence Partners (an accounting advisory firm) and Perkins & Black (a prominent law firm) performing the financial and legal diligence, respectively. Devlin, of course, played point on all of it; he controlled the internal process of gathering information, the flow of information to the service providers as well as any information that was going directly to the CFC team. He created folders on Google drive to manage it all. I would have expected the CFO to carry most of the burden and manage the process.

I had been on a couple of calls with Diligence Partners and sensed their frustration with the process. It seemed that they were not getting information request responses as quickly as they liked and the information, they did receive, was inadequate. I was more of a spectator on the calls than an active participant since Devlin was controlling the process and I was still getting up to speed on the company. I was still trying to understand processes and systems, I certainly wasn't in any position to direct Diligence Partners to source data, and I simply wasn't included on many of the calls and meetings. The diligence felt like it was dragging on.

In the midst of this, I attended the Epic board meeting in Toronto at RevCap's offices. I was asked to attend so that I could present to the board my strategic plan and acquisition targets. The board meeting was more casual than I would have expected, and the materials provided by Epic management were light, to say the least. The attendees included Devlin, Murray, Jake Maddox & Glenn Cobb from RevCap, Tom Gates, and a representative from Elite Sports Group ("ESG"). ESG owned several sporting goods brands and had invested in Epic a couple of years ago. They held a rather small stake in the company. Quite frankly, I didn't understand why Devlin would have wanted ESG to own an interest in Epic - it limited partnership and sponsorship alternatives and they had provided minimal or no strategic value whatsoever.

My takeaways from the board meeting were that RevCap and Gates were not pleased with the flow or quality of information from Devlin and Murray, they shared my view that Epic should not be in the apparel or football businesses and that they were frustrated with the company's financial performance. The ESG representative seemed rather apathetic. For the first time, I was also able to get a clearer picture of the company's liquidity.

One of the main topics of the meeting involved bridge financing. Devlin and Murray told the board that they needed a capital infusion immediately. They claimed that their senior lender had required that Epic hold funds in escrow, totaling several million dollars, for principal payments due in early 2018 - these were payments to sellers who had sold their businesses to Epic. The notes payable were the result of Devlin's "creative financing" - it was a debt load the company simply couldn't support. It also sounded like there was tension between Epic and its senior lender, despite the fact that I had been told repeatedly that the relationship was amicable. Regardless, I was surprised to hear that there was a cash crunch - this was never shared with me.

Following the board meeting, I spent a few minutes alone with Jake Maddox. He confirmed my earlier impressions about the board's frustrations. There was no doubt in my mind now that bringing me in was intended to get someone inside the company to act as a check and balance to counter Devlin and provide some substance and backbone that Murray clearly lacked. Jake eased my concerns a bit regarding liquidity by reinforcing RevCap's continued support of the company by saying that they fully intended to participate in both a bridge financing and the planned financing with one of the other family offices.

The board was going to have dinner that night, but before that, Devlin had scheduled a meeting with colleagues of the developer of the proposed Canton, Ohio sports complex and related hospitality facilities. Only as we were walking to the meeting was I told what the meeting was about. I was told that the developer had recently launched a branding and marketing agency focused on sports sponsorships and partnerships. I asked, "let me get this straight, the real estate developer who focuses on distressed industrial properties, launched a marketing agency focused on the sports sector?" I told them that it didn't make any sense to me. They sounded like polar opposite worlds and skillsets... distressed industrial real estate and sports marketing. Devlin and Murray got very defensive. They were either naïve or, potentially, there was some other hidden benefit to this potential relationship. Their explanation was that the developer was a billionaire (highly doubtful), he recognized the opportunity in the youth sports space because of his work at the Hall and had brought in some of the "best minds" to build out the agency.

We met in a conference room at a nearby hotel. There were four men representing this new agency. It appeared that at least one of them had definitely met Devlin and Murray before based on their greetings and the fact that their lead guy asked how our board meeting went. Brief introductions and backgrounds were provided by all. Then, the lead guy started name dropping right away, telling Devlin that he had just hung up from a great call with Pepsi about Epic. He said, "Pepsi's marketing folks are dying to meet you, this is exactly what they are looking for." Even if this was true, why was this guy talking to Pepsi about Epic? I asked him. He looked at me like I had no right to ask. He then answered like I was a five-year-old, explaining to me how corporate sponsorships worked. I asked if his firm had already been engaged – partnerships and sponsorships were my responsibility and I hadn't even heard of these guys before today. He said, "well not officially, but you guys are late to the game and we have some catching up to do." Devlin joined in, suggesting that the agency guys provide me with more background about their firm and the "great things" they were doing at the Hall.

Their story was lame, that's the only way I know how to put it. The lead guy was a pushy salesman. I couldn't stand him right away – he took the concept of the presumptive sale to a whole new level. To his right was their "creative" guy – he was dressed like a cast off from a '70's rock band. When I asked what sort of creative work he would be doing for Epic, he said, "well, you know, branding, logo design, messaging, all that *stuff*." He seemed completely clueless. What the hell was going on here? The guy to my right was introduced as their director of analytics - the salesman said that he was their "secret sauce." He looked like they picked him up at a bus stop on the way to the meeting. I said, "great, can you provide me with some examples of how you use analytics to add value to your client relationships?" He paused and said, "well, that's proprietary information, but let's just say that I have created a number of algorithms that allow us to measure the effectiveness of our campaigns with sponsors." I called bullshit and asked for a real example. He couldn't provide one that made any sense and the salesman tried to bail him out. I was convinced that they did not have a functioning agency, instead they were assembled to try to wrangle the sponsorship opportunities away from Epic.

The salesman proceeded to explain that they had worked with the developer, their partner in this new agency, to secure a $150+ million sponsorship with a multi-national company for the proposed Canton development. I told them that I was aware of it and that it didn't make any sense to me. He asked why. I told him that the Hall hadn't secured the funding for the development; other than a couple of grass fields, nothing substantial had been done on the project; and, in my opinion, the project basically had stalled - why would a sponsor commit those kinds of dollars? He said, "that's where we come in. We created a story, a vision that our sponsor couldn't pass up." I thought to myself, give me a break.

Devlin and Murray would actually join the conversation at times, assisting the salesman. Comments like, "yea, I heard you guys did a great job on the pitch book" or *so-and-so*" said he was blown away; in all of his years in the business, he had never seen a sponsor so excited to be part of a project." I was starting to question again whether Devlin and Murray had Epic's interest in mind or something else was going on.

Murray asked a question of the analytics guy and while he was answering, I heard the salesman having a side conversation with Devlin. He had a big grin on his face when he said, "did you hear that we sold the sponsorship contract?" Devlin said that he "heard something about it but didn't know it was a done deal." The salesman then told him that the developer had sold the sponsorship contract to a global financial firm and generated almost $100 million in cash to use on the project. This sounded really sketchy. Devlin said, "He is good!".

I spoke up and reminded everyone at the table that I was responsible for partnerships and sponsorships, so it was great that we all met in person but that I had some catching up to do. I asked that they send me their proposal and some samples of prior work, client case stories, etc. The salesman said, "sure, I will do that tonight. But we really need to get started right away." He looked at Devlin and asked, "we have a deal, right?" Devlin looked at me and said, "Steve, we can get these guys started, right?" I explained that I just met them and didn't know anything about their work or proposed terms of our relationship. The salesman spoke up and said, "well we just told you that we secured a $150 million sponsor for our other client, do you have partnerships at Epic like that?" and he laughed. Literally, he laughed. I didn't trust these guys, something wasn't right, so I wasn't concerned about offending them. I'm not suggesting anyone at Epic

81

was getting a kickback (at least we haven't been able to confirm that yet), but rather these agency guys knew that most sponsors for a sports complex need the event operator locked up as well. You can't have Nike plastered all over the fencing at a soccer facility when the event operator works with adidas. You need alignment. If you have it, the sponsors are easier to secure. The agency wanted their take on both the facility and event operator (Epic) sponsors. We had more leverage than Devlin and Murray understood.

I said to the salesman, "when I was younger, my father would tell me that when someone puts pressure on you to make a decision, like a used car salesman, and they put a strict time limit on you, walk away." The room went silent. I added the "used car salesman" line because I thought it would annoy this guy. I continued, "if you guys are the right guys for us, my review of your prior work and proposal shouldn't be a problem, agree?" He had no choice but to agree. He said, "I don't want you to think I am pressuring you; we have a lot of other clients that need our time and attention." By the way, that meant they didn't have any other clients. He continued, "I just don't want you to miss any opportunities - we need to strike while the iron is hot." I said, "If we miss an opportunity, it will be on me, not you guys." I then asked, "Oh, how are your fees structured?"

The salesman told me that their philosophy is that their firm "only makes money if the client makes money." I told them that I liked that philosophy and then waited for him to provide me with details about their fees, not just a one sentence philosophy. I waited, nothing. So, I said, "how do you charge?" He said, "we charge a small retainer and then a success fee on sponsorship dollars." I asked him what he meant by a "small retainer" and he said, "something in the twenty-five to fifty thousand dollars a month range." Without missing a beat, I said, "what happened to 'only making money when the client makes money?'" He told me that his creative and analytics team needed to be compensated for their time and talent - he said the retainer wouldn't "even keep the lights on." I asked about the success fee and he told me that they take a 50% commission. That was it, conversation was over. I didn't let them see it, but I was aggravated.

This was a complete waste of my time. I said, "well, great. I look forward to seeing your pitch book and any client case studies you think are relevant."

On the walk back to our hotel (we had a little time before our board dinner), both Devlin and Murray sang the praises of the guys we just left. Devlin asked what I thought of them. I didn't hold back - I told them that I thought they were clowns, probably had little or no experience in this industry and that their fee expectations were ridiculous. I told him that our board would never support such a fee arrangement. He pushed back, referenced the developer's successes (which I am confident he knew nothing of) and that "he only works with winners." I let it go but I would never do business with those guys.

Our board dinner was at a small Italian restaurant, Trattoria Nervosa. The restaurant was only a few blocks from our hotel and the weather was unusually mild, so I walked... alone. When I arrived, Jake and Glenn Cobb were the only ones there, having a drink at the small bar. I joined them and they immediately asked about my meeting with the sponsorship agency. I gave them my unfiltered opinion. They didn't seem surprised. Cobb was shaking his head; I could tell he was not in a good mood. He said that Epic couldn't continue to make dumb decisions that have long term consequences. He went on to say that the board had repeatedly told Devlin to stay away from the apparel business and was skeptical of the football initiative. He said the company would not be facing a liquidity crisis if Devlin had listened. He also told me that today's board meeting was a waste of time. He felt like he learned nothing about Epic's current operational or financial performance - he went on to say that every time he saw Devlin, he was asking for more money. Just then, Devlin and Murray arrived. I felt like I had been caught in the act, meeting with board members without the CEO when, in fact, I had arrived on time for dinner and the CEO and CFO were late. Cobb asked the hostess to take us to our table rather than ask our new arrivals if they wanted a drink at the bar. Tom and the ESG representative also joined while we were getting seated.

Dinner was fine - most of the time there was more than one conversation happening. Occasionally, Glenn would carry the conversation, but not like I had expected. He was looking at his phone often. From the time I was with him at the golf event at the Floridian, I knew he was usually the most vocal person at probably most tables in the world. That's not a criticism, it's just who he is. At this dinner, he clearly wasn't himself. In fact, right after we finished our meal, he apologized and said that he had to take off. After he left, Jake reminded everyone that Glenn had a lot going on - he was on the board of directors of a public company at a tumultuous time, to say the least. In addition, there were California wildfires that were threatening certain real estate holdings of RevCap. And, if that wasn't enough, he was in the midst of planning his wedding. It was an early night for all of us. I flew back to Boston in the morning.

Over the next week, I learned how tight the company's cash position really was - it needed capital immediately, otherwise payroll would be at risk. I found it irresponsible of management to not forecast this well in advance and emphasize the need and urgency to its board. I was also aggravated that I hadn't been told about the company's financial position. This is precisely why timely and accurate reporting is so critical. The board also should have been pushing management for better reporting. Also, a cash crunch like this doesn't happen overnight unless there is some extraordinary event. In this case, nothing unusual had happened. Instead, the company had been undercapitalized for a long time and it clearly was continuing to burn cash. What happened to the 10% operating margins Devlin had cited to me? Remember, this was an asset-light business, meaning no significant capital expenditures. Further, the company carried minimal accounts receivable; instead, the customers paid well in advance of the events. The company should have been swimming in cash. It just didn't add up.

A few days after the board meeting, Devlin asked me if I was going to participate in the bridge financing. I hadn't received any financial information nor details about the bridge financing itself. What a question to ask - I was starting to get really annoyed. Instead of getting into it, I told him that I wasn't sure. His response was interesting. He said, "don't you believe in our model?" I told him that I did. I knew the youth sports business as well as anyone and I believed we could operate a good business in this industry and *do* good at the same time. He then said, "well, then, do you believe in our team?" Now he was putting me on the spot. I felt uncomfortable so I said, "what are the terms of the bridge financing?" He told me that he had negotiated financing terms with RevCap and Gates - in short, it would be a preferred instrument that would convert, at a discount, to common equity at the time of the next financing.

I felt confident that capital would not be an issue for this company - this was an attractive industry and, if operated effectively, this business would attract investors. It was pretty clear that a financing was imminent. Why wouldn't I invest? It would demonstrate my commitment and the terms were attractive. If any of my doubts about Epic's management team were accurate, the board would make the necessary changes. I was more focused on the market opportunity. A couple of days later, I committed to participating in the financing. I made a mistake - I let someone pressure me and guilt me into investing. I didn't adhere to my own basic rules of performing the appropriate due diligence.

We were now into January 2018 and the New York firm continued their diligence efforts. From what I could gather, Perkins & Black seemed to be wrapped up on the legal side. It was Diligence Partners that was struggling with the financial diligence. I was on a couple of calls that made the picture clearer for me. The information provided to Diligence Partners about BBFC (Epic's soccer division), in particular, sounded really scattered. The manager from Diligence Partners did a walk-through of the data collection with Murray, Matt Jackson and I. To my surprise, Murray had asked that I join the call.

Diligence Partners explained that they were having difficulty reconciling the 2017 BBFC revenues for a couple of reasons. First, most of BBFC regions were still being accounted for on a cash basis - this was news to me. I had been told, and heard others being told, that all of BBFC was on accrual basis. If this was true, then Diligence Partners must have been reviewing and testing Epic's conversion of BBFC's books from cash to accrual. That analysis would be critical. Diligence Partners was unable to get a clear picture of that conversion from Epic's accounting team. Whether a company used cash-based versus accrual-based accounting methods can mean a world of difference in a given year. Under cash-based accounting, you record revenue when the cash is collected and expenses when they are paid. So, you could accelerate collecting cash and push out vendor payments and make your company appear more profitable in a given year. Company's that use accrual-based accounting recognize revenue and expenses when they are earned and incurred, respectively. It provides a far more accurate portrayal of a company's actual financial performance.

The second issue, also tied to accrual-based revenue, was that Epic was using a Google sheet (like an Excel workbook) to calculate the BBFC earned revenue each month for each region. Apparently, the sheet was riddled with formula errors and was not linked directly to the registration system. Why does this matter? Because, the underlying data in the Google sheet may have been wrong due to formula errors, because the person who input the data made a mistake or deliberately inflated the registrations or selling price. Performing detailed testing of this data across all of the regions would be a daunting task even if the registration system provided appropriate reporting. However, Murray advised Diligence Partners that the company's outside accounting firm, who performed an annual review, had signed off on Epic's process of recognizing BBFC revenue.

To this day, I don't know if Diligence Partners ever spoke directly to the auditors or reviewed their workpapers; I simply wasn't in the loop. But I do know a couple of things: 1) the outside accounting firm had only conducted a review, not an audit, of the prior year financial statements and had yet to perform any procedures on the 2017 financials when Diligence Partners was performing their diligence; and 2) Diligence Partners expressed their concerns to their client. I was told by one of the partners at CFC that the manager at Diligence Partners advised them that he could not provide a final diligence report due to the challenges they were dealing with at Epic; specifically, systems and processes. Effectively, Diligence Partners was telling its client that it could not get comfortable with Epic's financial statements, as presented in the CIM. Many investors would put their pencils down and walk away based on feedback like this.

Instead, Diligence Partners 'client, CFC, decided that the lack of systems and processes may have actually presented an opportunity. They had come to expect gaps in systems and processes in companies of this size. They believed that's where they added value as investors - upgrading systems, processes and people. The senior partner decided he and his team needed to go to Portland to spend more time with Devlin to get comfortable with the systems and processes.

I had started attending the monthly financial statement closing calls, in which Devlin, Murray and Jackson reviewed divisional performance with the respective leaders. There was never a complete set of financial statements provided on these calls - never a cash flow statement and, maybe, certain balance sheet items, but never a complete balance sheet. I asked about this several times. Jackson's answer was that the accounting department cleaned up its inter-company eliminations as part of the consolidation, so the balance sheets couldn't be prepared in advance of the divisional closing calls. This didn't make any sense to me - I didn't care if I saw a balance sheet that still had inter-company accounts on it. I could do my own rough intercompany eliminations. Devlin provided a different answer. He said that the divisional leaders wouldn't understand a cash flow statement and the only thing he cared about on the balance sheet was that accounts receivable were getting collected in a timely manner. This was a pathetic answer. Every item on the balance sheet needs to be evaluated on a monthly basis. In addition, you must review a statement of cash flows to actually understand the performance of a company. The income statement can indicate significant profitability, but, for example, if accounts receivable were aging (meaning, not getting collected), inventories increasing, recurring investment in long term assets was required, vendors needed to be paid on time, and debt payments were being made, a profitable company would be burning a ton of cash.

Devlin also had a way of delivering an answer that made you feel like you had no right to be asking the question. Further, he could make you feel that if you asked again, it would create an uncomfortable situation. I pushed back and told him that incomplete financial statements were useless and, if his divisional leaders lacked an understanding of financials, this would be a great opportunity to train his team.

I like to think that I am professionally skeptical and don't typically see ghosts - but, in hindsight, I should have been concerned that the absence of balance sheets and cash flow statements was because certain expenses were being capitalized as prepaids. In other words, instead of the expenses flowing through the income statement, they were building up as prepaid expenses (an asset) on the balance sheet. A consistent review of monthly balance sheets or, simply, a cash flow statement, would have revealed this. In addition, the sudden cash crunch made me feel like management had been reporting inflated profits but there simply wasn't any cash - which there wouldn't be if you were inflating revenues and receivables were building, or you were burying expenses on the balance sheet. I couldn't get my hands on the necessary financial information to create a consolidated balance sheet. In hindsight, this was one of those moments that I think about often. Had I pushed harder on this topic, perhaps things would have turned out different.

The New York firm brought most of their team, six of them, to Portland. It was a cold, blustery day when they landed at private airport a few miles away. They had chartered a twin prop for the day. When they arrived at the office, a couple of them looked pale - they were still talking about how nauseating the flight had been; one of the younger guys said it was the worst roller coaster ride he had ever been on. I couldn't imagine taking a twin prop from NY to NH in a New England winter storm blowing 30 knots.

We met in the main conference room and, of course, Devlin sat at the head of the table. There were menus on the table from which people could choose their lunch orders to be brought in around midday. Everyone settled in, made their pleasantries and the senior partner, Dan Atwater, didn't waste any time. Atwater was a seasoned private equity investor and President of CFC. He had put his time in at one of the larger PE firms and recently founded CFC along with his former colleague, the lead investor. Atwater was about 6 '2" with a lean build and grey hair parted on the side. He wore clear, round glasses and was dressed casually in a light blue Peter Millar 1/4 zip sweater over a white button-down shirt and dark blue plain front trousers. He also wore a pair of "dress sneakers," mostly dark blue with a white sole and not-so-subtle red stripe on the heal to remind everyone that they were Prada. If nothing else, Atwater was usually extremely attentive - unfortunately, he usually squinted and wrinkled his brow trying to understand the details being presented to him. As a result, he often looked confused when, in reality, he was just focused and processing everything.

Atwater said, "Jamie, we are here today, mainly, to understand your systems. The Diligence Partners guys have found it challenging to understand the way transactions flow through your systems and processes." He was being kind and diplomatic. Devlin was nodding

89

along. Atwater continued, "we like your industry, the business you have built and the team members that we have met. We really want to be partners in your business. We just need to understand your systems in order to move forward. We know they are not perfect; we can even help refine these things post-closing, we just need to get a better understanding. Make sense?"

Devlin finished writing something on the notepad in front of him, looked up and said, "absolutely - makes perfect sense. By the way, the Diligence Partners 'guys have been great, but I was afraid they were getting bogged down in the numbers before they were able to get a full understanding of our Platform." Atwater interrupted, "I've heard you use that term, 'Platform 'before - can you explain what that is exactly?" Devlin explained the customer registration process. He emphasized that it's the best opportunity the company had to collect information about its customer. He explained how valuable customer information is and how the way it is collected impacts how and where it was stored. These were my insights he was sharing - I didn't believe he thought this way when they were building the Platform. He then paused and said, "maybe it will be better if I explain it while actually walking you through a transaction - would that be helpful?" Everyone agreed.

He took the mouse and keyboard in front of him and logged onto the large screen in the conference room. Over the next two hours, using a customer (a fictitious customer) example he walked everyone through a typical transaction. He demonstrated how event managers could set up a new tournament or showcase in the system and build a detailed budget for the event. He showed how the event manager could send mass emails to past customers inviting them to the new event. He even demonstrated how expenses could be coded to the same event so the event manager could see budget variances in real time. He walked through a screen where the event manager could see his or her progress towards registration targets. As he toggled between screens, he often would revert back to the main screen for

90

the Platform. At one point, the senior partner from New York asked Devlin to pause on that screen - it showed a series of statistics and trend lines. The partner asked what this was. Devlin told him it was the daily flash report or dashboard - he explained that it showed orders booked for the day, average revenue per order, cash collected for the day, and so on. The partner was impressed. Months later, I learned that the data on the flash report was static... it never changed and did not represent actual activity.

The guys from CFC were paying close attention. One of younger partners asked if all of this information, particularly the budget data, actual registrations and expenses were tied to the general ledger.

Devlin smiled, paused for effect and said, "it's all integrated." One of the analysts asked, "does the system calculate monthly revenue recognition?" Devlin displayed a sly grin, paused for effect, and said it did - he even provided more detail - he said that the system took the start and end dates of team programs and the actual event dates for a tournament or showcase and spread the revenue over the period it was earned. Everyone in the room seemed impressed and relieved.

You could tell that they were thinking, why hadn't Diligence Partners gone through this exercise?

Devlin was on a roll - he even explained the further enhancements of the Platform that were in-process. He said, the next version of this would have "more robust and dynamic" customer analytics. Atwater asked what he meant by that. Devlin explained that this Platform was, effectively, a data warehouse. A repository of customer information. He explained the value of the consumer and transaction information, even quoting Kevin Plank from Under Armour who had recently said that "data is the new oil." He said that he was creating a user interface that would allow our marketing team to gain valuable insights about each customer's characteristics and behavior - when they first became a customer, how many events they attended, when was the last time they came to an event, do they have multiple kids who are customers, what's their lifetime revenue, have they purchased apparel from us, have they referred a friend to become a customer, what hotel brand do they prefer, and so on. Devlin said, "imagine the fun our marketing team will have with these insights."

Atwater said, "have you considered licensing this software?" Devlin smiled and said that he "planned to keep the Platform proprietary for a while to get a head start on the marketplace, but then we will roll it out as a stand-alone SAAS model." Atwater said, "you may find that you can make more money licensing this software than you can in your core business." Devlin said that he agreed and that was always his plan - build the youth sports live event business then roll out the software model later. I was confused - this was the first I had heard of this. Not to mention, there would be little or no market for a product like this since there were virtually no enterprise-level operators in the industry. This was a fragmented, mom & pop industry; there wasn't a scalable market for such a product. Devlin said that he wanted to make sure that the analytics "engine" and the CRM tools were world-class before he launched the product.

Lunch had arrived so everyone took a quick restroom / email break. I went to my office briefly to check emails. When I was heading back to the conference room, several of the New York guys were huddled in the lobby. Atwater made eye contact with me and called me over. He was clearly excited. He told me that he thought they had underestimated the power of the Platform. He said that he was confident that Epic's competitors didn't have such a system, that it would prove to be a competitive advantage near term and, likely, a stand-alone product long term. I said, "perhaps, but I'm not so sure the Platform is as integrated as Jamie is saying. I think there is some manual work getting the financial information out of the Platform and into the general ledger." One analyst spoke up and said, "no, I don't think so - he said it's seamless." I suggested that we get some clarity on that topic when we resumed.

We all returned to the conference room and continued the conversation over lunch with Devlin moving the mouse around the screen, clicking on links and changing screens so quickly, people were in awe of the system. He not only had an immediate answer for every question, but as he was answering he would show you tangible support on the screen with only a few clicks of the mouse. At times, someone would ask him to "slow down" or "do that again" and he would back up and retrace his steps - he was like David Blaine performing magic on a street corner. "Do that again... wow, that is awesome." I noticed at times, however, that Devlin had multiple browsers and applications opened simultaneously. They were layered on the screen so that when he would click his mouse, he would actually leave the so-called Platform and move to a Google Sheet - others didn't seem to notice. For example, he would be showing us an event budget in the Platform, clicking on individual registrations and call out the name of the event (something like, the Chicago Hockey Classic event); then, with a few clicks, he would show us the income statement for that event and how it rolled up into the hockey divisions 'income statement. The problem was that he had jumped from the Platform to a bunch of spreadsheets and no one noticed. A smooth sleight of hand.

A few other topics were covered in the meeting, but everything else paled in comparison to the demonstration we had just witnessed. The potential investors were wowed by the Platform. My thoughts drifted at one point and I wondered why the New York firm hadn't brought in an IT consultant to evaluate the bank-end. As the group was preparing to head back to their twin prop rollercoaster ride, one of the partners shook my hand, winked and said, "we are going to get this done."

After they left, I returned to the conference room. Devlin and Murray were seated at the table and Jackson was standing in the doorway. I slid by Jackson and started to clean up some of the remaining lunch mess from the table. Jackson, who hadn't attended the session, was asking how the meeting went. Murray was praising Devlin's walk through of the Platform. Devlin asked me what I thought of the meeting - I told him about the partner's comment to me in the lobby. He said, "that's good news, but what did *you* think of the meeting?" I told him that I thought it went well; I said, "if the meeting wrapped up with one of the partners saying they will get this done, then I think it went well." He wouldn't accept that answer - he said, "but, again, what did *you* think?" He emphasized the word "you." Again, I said that I thought it went well. But I also added, "I think they came away with the impression that the Platform is more than it really is, particularly, that it is fully integrated with the general ledger." He said, "it is integrated with the GL." I looked at Jackson, the VP of Finance who was responsible for the general ledger, with my hands outstretched and head titled to the side, implying, "is it?" I could tell he did not want to answer the question; finally, he said, "it depends what you mean by integrated." I laughed and said, "that is great, depends on what you mean by integrated." Devlin didn't like it and said, "you are unbelievable. We have a great meeting with potential investors, and you take the air right out of the balloon." I pushed back and said, "that's not the case at all - my point is that they think that the data from the Platform flows seamless and automatically into the general ledger." Devlin looked at me and said, "it does. You don't understand the systems."

Back in New York, CFC had another call with the manager from Diligence Partners. They told him about their meeting in Portland and the systems demonstration. He told the manager that they were planning to move forward with the investment. The Diligence Partners manager pushed back again, emphasizing that he was not comfortable with the systems, controls, processes, nor the accuracy of the resulting financial reporting. The CFC team told the manager that they didn't need a final report if they couldn't get comfortable with the systems and wrapped up the call. Diligence Partners never issued a final diligence report. The senior partner told his team, "even if Epic's profits are off by 20%, this is still a good deal for us." They were moving forward with the investment.

Over the next several weeks, and during the final negotiations of investment terms and valuation between Epic and CFC, there were moments when it looked like a deal may not get done. In my opinion, and since confirmed by a senior partner at the New York firm, there was a single moment that sealed the transaction. Devlin was arguing for a higher valuation than CFC wasn't willing to accept. Finally, Devlin said, "I will put my money where my mouth is." He told Atwater and other CFC team members that he would personally invest a seven-figure amount in Epic at the higher valuation. That was it - the partner agreed. The partner later told me that was the precise moment when he felt the most comfortable with the investment - "if the founder and CEO is investing alongside us, I feel really good," he said.

A few weeks later, days before the closing, Devlin advised CFC and RevCap that he could only invest a portion of his commitment at closing but would make the rest of the investment within twelve months. CFC agreed - I think it was too late to pull the plug. Devlin never invested again.

FOR THE HONOR OF TRUTH

"If you tell the truth, you don't have to remember anything."

Mark Twain

CHAPTER 8

The first formal board meeting was held at CFC's offices in New York in July 2018, about two months after the financing. One of the CFC partners had provided Devlin with a suggested outline and template for the board package. He copied me on the email, and I agreed with the requested content and format. I emailed Devlin letting him know that I was more than happy to help put together the board package. I told him that I knew what the guys were looking for and that we should plan to have the package to them about three days in advance of the meeting. I told him, that in my experience, board meetings are far more productive and board members far more prepared and engaged if they receive the package a couple of days in advance. If you send it over the night before, tensions will run high. I don't recall getting a response to my email.

A few days later, Devlin asked if I could provide some updated strategy and acquisition slides for the board package. I had already assembled them before he asked. I sent them over with a note letting him know again that I was available to help with the rest of the package. He replied that he would let me know if he needed any assistance. Two days before the board meeting, I sent a note suggesting that he circulate the package to the board (including me since I was now a board member) as soon as possible. He replied that he would send it over shortly.

The board agenda included having dinner the night before at Ocean Prime, just around the corner from CFC's office. That afternoon, I boarded the Amtrak Acela in Providence, still having not received the board package. I was sick to my stomach over it - this looked really bad. It was embarrassing and a terrible way to kick off the new relationship. I had received several emails from CFC and RevCap looking for the package – I told them that Devlin was preparing it and had assured me he would be distributing it shortly. I was meeting Devlin and Tom Gates on the train; both had boarded in Boston. Tom texted me the car number in which they were seated. I knew as soon as I walked into the car... I knew that something was wrong. Gates and Devlin were seated at a table – Gates was reading on an iPad and Devlin was typing away on his laptop with headphones on. Gates greeted me politely and moved over to give me the aisle seat. Devlin nodded at me without saying a word and barely made eye contact. I chatted with Tom for a bit when I realized Devlin was on a call. He picked up his laptop and left the table. I found it odd that he didn't want to have his call in front of us.

I said to Tom, "What is going on with Jamie?" He said that he didn't know but gathered he was still working on the board package. He said he was on the phone with Matt Jackson, the VP of Finance. We discussed Devlin not having the board deck distributed; Tom recognized that it wasn't acceptable but didn't seem nearly as concerned as me. While I didn't know the board members particularly well, I knew what typical private equity investors expected – they would not be pleased with this. Devlin returned to his seat and continued working on his laptop, headphones on, for the next two hours. I had my own work to do involving preliminary diligence I was performing on a hockey academy business. Finally, about a half hour from Penn Station, Devlin took out his headphones and said that he just sent the board package. He was clearly stressed.

97

We checked into the Hilton Midtown and agreed to meet in the lobby in about thirty minutes. As I was walking to my room, one of the board members called me. I said "hello" and was greeted with, "have you seen this board package? What the fuck?" I explained that I had offered, even pushed, several times to help put the materials together, but to no avail. He said, "ok, fine, but have you looked at it?" I told him I quickly reviewed it before I got off the train and, at first glance, it looked like a disaster. He agreed and said "tomorrow's meeting is not going to go well. I don't even know how we are going to have dinner tonight." There was a pause and he said, "I guess I will see you at the restaurant" and hung up. This was a bad start.

Dinner was exactly what I expected – about a dozen of us, including several non-board members from CFC, at an over-priced midtown restaurant. The good news was that this group did not drink at dinners like this; maybe a glass of wine, but this was not a party crowd. The restaurant, however, was loud – the place was virtually all male, except for some of the waitstaff. It served a business clientele for sure – every tab was being paid on a corporate credit card. There was a small group of younger men at the bar to my right who were loud and distracting. The ringleader was a large, bloated guy in a suit, necktie loosened and holding what looked like a scotch. He was holding court and had decided that his story couldn't be told effectively without using the world "fuck" every three or four words. The minions with him had no sense of anyone else in the room – they were laughing hysterically. Painful.

Someone at our table ordered two shellfish appetizer towers. I sensed that most of the people at the table had not even looked at the board package since only the board member I had spoken to earlier seemed particularly anxious. Although, right after the toast, one of the partners, still with his glass raised, said, "let's be sure to get the board package out a few days earlier in the future." Devlin was smiling and said, "for sure." He must have thought he got off easy.

Throughout dinner, there were always three or four separate conversations going on and most had nothing to do with the company. Instead, the conversations covered topics like golf, the Yankees v. Red Sox, the stock market, Amtrak Acela first class

98

instead of coach, etc. However, my ears perked up when I heard Devlin mention the plan for the company to have an audit of its 2018 financials. He was seated across from me and talking to the CFC board member to his right. I don't know how the topic came up, but he was suggesting that we shouldn't have an audit because of the expense and distraction to the accounting team. I thought this was odd, to say the least. Who in their right mind would try to convince a new investor to forgo a first-year audit, required in both the investment and bank loan documents, at the very first board meeting? The board member was polite but responded by explaining the value of going through the audit process. He said that the audit "is a great, rigorous exercise that requires a company to ensure that its processes and controls are tight as a drum." This seemed to end the audit discussion. However, a moment later, Devlin spoke up again, saying, "I do feel pretty strongly about converting the entire company to cash-based accounting from accrual." While he was making his case, which was ridiculous, the board member's eyes were fixed on mine. I knew he was thinking the same as me.

I often find a person's stream of consciousness, the sequence of their conversation topics, so interesting. This was one of those moments. This was our first board dinner with the newly constituted board and investors. The board package, which should have been delivered days ago, was just delivered about an hour ago. The founder and CEO, who prepared the board package, declined any assistance and was clearly a bundle of stress on the train ride down, was now raising the concept of not having a first-year audit. When that idea was swiftly and appropriately shot down, his next topic was switching the company's accounting method from accrual to cash-based. It was at this very moment, when I knew that there was something terribly wrong with the company's books. He was trying to dodge the audit and when that didn't work, he wanted to switch accounting methods. In his unsophisticated accounting mind, Devlin thought that a change in accounting methods would provide enough "messiness" and eliminate meaningful year-over-year comparisons to conceal whatever inappropriate things had been done. I could see what he was trying to do - it was not good.

When I returned to my hotel room after dinner, I reviewed the board package in detail. It was terrible. The first few slides were all hyperbole and misrepresentations… "each division is at or above plan" – how could he put that in writing? We knew that the apparel and football divisions were way off budget. The financial section included only income statements, no balance sheets or cash flow statements. I knew this was going to anger the board. An incomplete set of financial statements is useless to an investor. Then I noticed something else – each division's individual income statement was presented, except for BBFC. BBFC represented about 50% of the company's revenue - how could this income statement be omitted? I looked through the materials several times to make sure I hadn't missed it. Knowing Devlin was stressed and had barely spoken to me on the train, I decided to email Jackson and ask why the BBFC financials weren't included.

The next morning, Jackson emailed me apologizing for not seeing the email earlier and telling me he was available if I had a question. I called him and asked why the BBFC financials were not included in the board materials. He told me that he hadn't closed the BBFC financials yet. I told him that I was confused – the board deck indicated that all divisions were at or ahead of plan. How could we know that if we haven't even closed the BBFC financials yet? He agreed with me. I pushed harder, asking "so how does Jamie make that statement?" He paused and said, "I have no idea."

Jackson was still on the line while I was staring at the board presentation. He said, "are you still there?" I said that I was, but I was reading through the materials again. I asked him to hang on for a moment. I asked him if he had the board deck – he said, "no." I emailed it to him and asked him to open the file. I directed him to the consolidated income statement, and I walked him through it; it showed that the company was pretty much on plan, if you accepted Devlin's "add-backs" line item. I then did a back of the envelope exercise of adding up the individual divisions' income statements on the subsequent pages. He followed along. Then I asked him, "the difference between the consolidated revenue and profits and my calculations is attributable to BBFC, right?" He agreed. I opened a budget file and looked at the BBFC tab. Devlin was using BBFC's *budget*. He plugged in the BBFC budgeted numbers and was going to tell the board that they were on plan. What a joke.

Jackson confirmed it. BBFC's financials were not closed yet, so Devlin used their budget as actuals in the board package. Jackson confirmed that he hadn't helped Devlin prepare the board deck either. Devlin had been calling him from the train with a few questions, but that was it. It appeared that the CEO had *created* his own consolidated income statement that creatively blended the actual financial performance of most divisions and the budget for another division that represented nearly 50% of the company's revenue – how could he possibly think it was appropriate to do this? This also put me in one hell of a spot. Do I raise the issue with Devlin, with a board member? If I raise it with a board member, do I go to one of the incumbent members who knows Devlin well or one of the new members. A new member will flip their lid. I decided to leave it alone, at least for now. I would let him run his board meeting and see how it goes. My role today was to walk the board through the market, competition, our strategy and our acquisition pipeline. I would stick to that.

I walked to CFC's offices for the board meeting. They had bagels, muffins, fruit and the like set up in one conference room and a larger conference room was set up for the board meeting. I made small talk with the same people I was with ten hours earlier and took a seat at the middle of the conference room table. Devlin was already there and was trying to get his computer to connect to the screen in the conference room. He was frustrated. One of the CFC partners came in and asked how it was going. Devlin barely answered, saying, "I don't know…" The partner looked at me, shrugged and said, "I'm not sure I have ever seen anyone use that screen," and walked away. After a few more minutes, Devlin gave up and asked the young assistant at the front desk if she could print a bunch of copies of the presentation. Devlin was rattled.

Devlin situated himself at the head of the table, as he always did. I recognize that everyone has their own style and preference, but I never sit at the head of the table. I certainly wouldn't sit at the head of someone else's table. The meeting started in a more informal fashion than I would have expected. Devlin said, "should we get started?", a few folks said, "yes" and the meeting began. I was on the board, so I spoke up and asked if we had appointed a clerk. The answer was no, and I knew that. I volunteered to be the clerk – I had been the clerk on several other boards, and I didn't mind it. I actually found it helpful to keep me focused and engaged during some long board meetings.

Devlin began to walk through the slides, when the senior partner at CFC interrupted and reminded him that, going forward, the board materials needed to be provided several days in advance. He said that receiving them the night before was unacceptable. His tone was professional, but entirely different from the social tone at dinner the night before. Devlin simply nodded. The partner looked at him, then around the table and said, "so we all agree this won't happen again, right?" His eyes returned to Devlin who apologized and said that he had been waiting on information from accounting." Unbelievable, it took him all of two minutes to throw his accounting staff under the bus.

Typically, in a board meeting, we would officially call the meeting to order, approve the prior meeting's minutes, walk through the proposed agenda and ask if anyone had anything to add to the agenda, hold the meeting, hear any motions, take any votes, ask if there were any additional matters to be covered, confirm the date, time and location for the next meeting, and adjourn. In this case, the meeting started informally, there were no minutes to be reviewed and Devlin did not present an agenda. Instead, he went right to his opening slide, saying, "all divisions are achieving or exceeding plan." One of the board members and two of the CFC analysts looked at each other, around the table, then at me. They were already on to his salesmanship. It wasn't going to work in this room. He continued to speak in qualitative, soft terms. In no time at all, I could see board members flipping through the presentation. They wanted facts, financial statements, and key metrics. They wanted to see favorable variances on the actual-to-budget slides. They wanted to know that the company was beating plan, growing organically and that cash was sticking to the ribs. That's it – they didn't want to hear spin; they didn't want to hear bullshit.

After about a half an hour, the younger board member who called me the night before interrupted Devlin. He asked if Devlin had received the board package template, he had emailed him a couple of weeks earlier. Devlin said he had and that he thought this package followed that template. The board member told him that Devlin's board deck didn't mirror his template and that the board packages in the future must follow the template. He also offered to provide any assistance necessary in advance of the next board meeting. The exchange was uncomfortable to say the least.

Next, Devlin walked through the company's financials - it was a disaster. The formatting and terminology were inconsistent between the divisions; there were add-backs and adjustments reflected in the income statements in some cases, not in others; there was no detailed explanation nor corrective action for unfavorable variances; and there was no BBFC income statement. He didn't even include year-over-year comparisons. It didn't take long for someone to ask on which page of the package they could find the BBFC income statement. I watched Devlin turn the pages of his deck as if he was trying to find the BBFC income statement. He knew it wasn't in there – what was he doing? I had spoken to Jackson earlier, there wasn't a BBFC income statement, the books hadn't even been closed yet. I watched him closely while he and others were flipping through their materials. Devlin then said, "oh man, I'm sorry – it looks like our guys forgot to include it. But BBFC is included in the consolidated income statement on page six." He knew it wasn't in there. I couldn't believe what I just witnessed.

One of the CFC analysts at the table was working away on his laptop – I knew exactly what he was doing... what I did earlier this morning. He was backing out the other divisions' revenue and key expense items from the consolidation to arrive at a BBFC stand-alone income statement. He did it even quicker than I did. After one of the board members had made it clear that we needed complete financial statements, including balance sheets and cash flow statements, for each division, the analyst spoke up. He said, "so, BBFC looks like it is right on plan." Another board member said, "great" and Devlin said, "yea, that's what I said, it's right on plan." The analyst was looking back and forth between his laptop and one of his colleagues and then said, "it's exactly on plan – like to the dollar." There was silence. I had no choice, I had to speak up. I said, "well, I spoke with Matt Jackson this morning…" Someone interrupted and asked who Matt was – I told them he was VP of Finance. I continued, "he told me that the BBFC financials weren't ready yet, so what you are looking at is budget, not actual."

Gates repeated what I said as a question. I said, "yes." He said, "well, these financials are meaningless." Atwater CFC piled on. He was not happy. He sat back in his chair and seemed to address the entire room, not just Devlin, "look, if we can't provide accurate financial statements along with the key metrics for this business, we are going to be in trouble. The plan is to grow organically and through acquisitions. We need to know how each division is performing and we need to know in a timely manner. If something isn't working, you need to know early enough to make the necessary changes to correct it. I'm not going to be comfortable writing checks for acquisitions until we get our house in order. Got it?" Everyone nodded. He then said, "it's not worth going through these financials, let move on to the next topic."

We walked through a variety of industry statistics – all of which were presented during diligence and research; however, I had narrowed everything down to the key statistics that were relevant to Epic. We were focused on hockey, soccer and lacrosse. Based on projected participation growth rates, the social-economic characteristics of our target consumers, and annual spend patterns, we were going to focus heavily on lacrosse. We had a number of lacrosse acquisition targets in process and I walked the board through each company; where it fit in the market, why it was attractive to us; revenues and EBITDA; expected valuation ranges; likely structures; diligence stages; and potential timing to close each. I repeated the exercise for a couple of hockey, soccer and tours opportunities as well. On a legal pad, one of the partners from CFC assigned probabilities of closing each acquisition target, calculated the total revenue and EBITDA as well as the equity and debt we would need to get the deals done. He then added the revenue and EBITDA to Epic's run rates, applied a rich multiple and came up with a valuation for Epic north of $100 million.

He looked at me and said, "Go!" The investment premise was that we could acquire businesses at relatively low valuations, integrate them, realize some financial and strategic synergies and the increased EBITDA would be valued at a higher multiple.

The meeting was taking on a much more positive, optimistic tone. The next topic was the current org chart and Devlin's proposed future chart. Devlin had included both graphics in the board materials. In both cases, the organizational structures were incredibly flat. Each division, marketing, sales, finance, acquisitions, IT, human resources, etc. all reported directly to Devlin. Oh, and by the way, Devlin *was* Information Technology. Not only was this impossible for one person to handle, it would limit the company's ability to scale and presented serious segregation of duties issues. His hands were in everything.

Atwater cut right through it – he spoke up and said, "neither of these org charts work." Devlin pushed back and said that he was comfortable with them. The partner told him that it was impossible for one person to have all of these people reporting to him, he said, "you are going to kill yourself. I've invested in a lot of companies, trust me, these org charts are not scalable." Another CFC partner looked at me and said, "do you have any personal bandwidth?" I told him that I did. He said, "OK, let's have finance and accounting report to Steve," while he circled those functions on the org chart in front of him. He was still looking at the org chart and seemed he was about to make another recommendation when Devlin pushed back – he said, "that won't work, finance and accounting have to report to me."

Atwater tilted his head, wrinkled his brow and then looked up from the org chart – "why?", he asked. Devlin proceeded to stumble through a half-baked explanation that a CEO needed to have finance report to him in order to operate the business effectively. He seemed panicked. He said that if he didn't have "control" over finance and accounting, he couldn't take the timely corrective actions the CFC partner had referenced earlier. Atwater pushed back, "you don't have timely financial reporting now under your current org structure." Devlin continued to debate him; it was uncomfortable for everyone in

105

the room. Atwater said, "Steve is a former CPA, has a lot more accounting experience than anyone else in the company; this will free you up to focus on your strengths." Devlin pushed back one last time. He said, "let me tell you why this won't work..." Atwater cut him off and said, "look, I've made my decision. I was going to have Steve report to you, but based on how hard you are fighting this, I am going to suggest that he report directly to the board." I felt like I had just watched a video case study for the ethics portion of the CPA exam; fraud red flags.

The board meeting continued, albeit very subdued. CFC, RevCap and Gates all wanted to form audit, finance and compensation committees of the board. As we were discussing who should sit on each committee based on each person's strengths and prior experiences, Devlin asked why we needed a compensation committee. Gates and one of the CFC partners both expressed their views. They covered most of the appropriate reasons: to ensure that the company offers market competitive salaries, to structure performance-driven bonus plans; to implement an incentive stock plan and determine the appropriate executive grants; all with a focus on attracting, developing and retaining talent.

Devlin listened and pushed back again. He thought the board should work with him to make those decisions, not "some committee removed from the people operating the business everyday." Again, board members tried to explain to him that he would provide insights and recommendations to the compensation committee, but he would not be on the committee. He clearly did not like this. When Gates and Maddox offered to be on the committee with one of the CFC partners, Devlin lost it – he said, "oh great, so the two guys who have been promising me an incentive stock plan for two years are now on the compensation committee." One of the CFC partners put an end to the conversation and said that we could form the committees and determine the committee members by email. This was shaping up to be a horrible first board meeting.

We set a date for the next board meeting and agreed to hold it in Portland at Epic's offices. We adjourned. As people were packing up, Devlin went to the restroom. Atwater asked Jake and me to step

106

into his office. He closed the door and said, "what the hell was that?" Before either of us could comment, he said, "let me tell you what it was. The financials were a mess. He tried passing off budgeted numbers as actuals and he is trying to spin everything. When he fought me about taking finance and accounting away from him, red flags popped up all over the place. I hope I am wrong, but I don't have a good feeling about this." Jake spoke up and told us that Devlin had demonstrated defensive behavior in the past when RevCap pushed him on better financial reporting and not pursuing certain initiatives. Jake thought it was ego driven. Atwater looked at me and said, "straighten this out."

Devlin, Gates and I headed to Penn Station. Rush hour traffic had begun, so I suggested we walk – it was only about a mile and the train runs frequently; either Acela or the Northeast Regional. There was virtually no conversation during the walk. When we arrived, we realized we could make an earlier train than we had expected, one that would be boarding shortly. I hadn't booked a return ticket yet and I had the Amtrak app on my phone, so I stood under the departures sign and booked my ticket. Devlin and Gates headed over to the kiosks to change their tickets. Devlin returned to where I was standing a few minutes later just as boarding was announced on track 10 East. The crowd hustled to the escalator that leads down to the tracks. Boarding at Penn Station remains an archaic, disorganized, mad rush of humanity. It is a total shitshow. I looked towards the kiosks to my right trying to locate Tom. Devlin started to head to the tracks, turned and said, "c'mon, Tom said he would meet us on the train." I assumed that was the case, so I followed. Waiting to board, I looked around for Tom a couple of times. I didn't see him. We boarded and grabbed seats with a table. I tried texting Tom our car number, but I didn't have service down on the tracks. I tried calling him too, but no luck. Devlin already had his laptop opened and didn't seem concerned about Tom. The train left the station.

As soon as we emerged from the tunnel, I had texts. Devlin's phone went off a couple of times too. My texts were from Tom – he had been trying to find us when we boarded. He wasn't on the train. I told Devlin that Tom had missed the train and he dismissed it by saying, "he can take the next one." What a jerk, I thought. We were traveling together; you don't leave a colleague behind like that. I said, "I felt bad", as I got up and went to the back of the car. I called Tom and apologized. He asked why we didn't wait for him. I told him I had been looking for him, but Devlin said that Tom told him he would see us on the train. Tom told me that he never said such a thing. Devlin did not want Tom on the train with him. I returned to my seat. Devlin had headphones on the entire ride. There was no conversation until we said goodbye when I got off in Providence about three hours later. Based on how the board meeting had gone, how could this guy not want to discuss it?

CHAPTER 9

The Monday after the board meeting, Devlin scheduled a meeting with Murray, Jackson and me to let us know that finance would report to me going forward. Instead of messaging it in a positive way for the company, he was cold and sterile in his delivery and simply said that "the board decided to do this" – not exactly the best way to infuse energy and commitment into the new reporting structure. Murray and Jackson just nodded along, then looked at me. I told them that I didn't expect much to change on a daily basis, that I was here to help (particularly on day-to-day technical accounting questions, if any, and monthly reporting). I suggested that we keep their current processes as usual for the next thirty days or so in order for us to get accustomed to working together. I said, "after thirty days, let's see what we have come up with to make things better." A pretty reasonable approach, in my opinion.

Matt had a few questions about our banking, audit firm and insurance relationships – apparently, Jamie had run point on those, and he wanted to know if I would take on those relationships. I found it odd that the CEO was the point person for those relationships – the CFO or VP of Finance should be managing lender, audit and insurance relationships. I said as much. Matt nodded in agreement. I then asked Don and Matt to change all of their recurring weekly meetings or calls with Jamie to be with me instead. Devlin, who had been quiet, immediately perked up. He said, "let's keep me on those invites for the near term until we feel like the transition is going well." I wanted to say the idea is to get you away from finance and accounting, not keep you involved and simply add me to the mix, but I bit my tongue. I let it go and assumed that after a week or two, he would trust that the finance and accounting function was in safe hands and he could find a way to let go. At this point, I was still operating under the premise that he was just an entrepreneur who micro-managed and found it difficult to delegate. Boy was I wrong.

The same day we had the meeting with Murray and Jackson, I asked Matt if he and I could get together and walk through how the accounting functions worked, in detail, for each division. From a distance, I had been struggling to understand what accounting activities were occurring at the divisional level, off-site, and what was being handled at corporate. Instead of scheduling a time that worked for the two of us, Matt jumped right into an explanation of each division's accounting – at least he was willing to provide the information, but I didn't expect it to be delivered casually standing in his office. He jumped right in and blew my mind. There were certain accounting functions occurring at each division - employees coding their expenses themselves in the Platform, but not the BBFC staff; most of BBFC was still on a cash-based accounting method, not accrual-based; apparel's transactions were not recorded in the general ledger, but rather off-line and then entered into the general ledger later; Epic's accounting staff was handling the accounting for the football joint venture. But our football division, I was told, was incurring expenses and entering into agreements constantly without notifying accounting in advance. There wasn't even a purchase requisition or purchase order function. The company was using a number of different registration systems and credit card processors. It sounded like a nightmare. In fifteen minutes, I learned more details, all deeply concerning, about the accounting function than I had been privy to over the last nine months.

It seemed like Matt was thrilled to actually have someone to talk to who was genuinely interested and wanted to make things better. I asked about the monthly closing process and resulting financial reporting packages. In particular, I wanted to know if it was as integrated and efficient as Devlin had repeatedly indicated. He had portrayed this as one of the company's strengths – the ability to efficiently produce timely and accurate financial reporting. Further, he had touted the strength of the company's financial systems and staff as a differentiator in on-boarding acquisitions, like BBFC. Matt started to walk me through the closing process and Devlin walked by Matt's office. I made eye contact with him. He stopped and said, "anything I can help you guys with?" I said, "no, just chatting." He walked away but quickly came back – "hey if you guys aren't working on something important, can I steal Matt for a minute", he said. "Of course,", I said. Matt told me he would send me some potential time slots for us to meet in the next day or so. I returned to my office. On my white board, I started mapping out the accounting processes I had just heard from Matt when I noticed Jamie's car pulling out the parking lot with Matt in the passenger's seat.

About an hour later, Devlin walked into my office and closed the door. I was still working on the whiteboard. As much as I leverage technology, I find that using a whiteboard, at times, can be very productive. It gets you up and away from your desk (something as simple as standing for a while is a good change and even better for your back and posture); you can write and erase so you tend to think more freely (there is something very deliberate about typing that can limit your willingness to make mistakes); and obviously, a whiteboard is more collaborative with others in the room. In addition, I like to leave a graphic on my whiteboard for others to see and challenge or validate. Devlin noticed the whiteboard and stopped in his tracks. "What is this?", he asked. I told him it was just some rough notes and my flowchart of the company's accounting processes. He walked closer to the board and surveyed it – he pointed at several items and said, "that's not right, that's wrong, no, that's not how that works…" He had his back to me. I found his tone and response disrespectful, but I had to bite my lip. I sat down

110

and said, "like I said, it's rough", even though I knew it was consistent with what I had heard from Matt. He turned and looked at me – he appeared aggravated and said, "this is exactly why I said I need to be in any meetings with Matt or Don." They don't understand the accounting function and systems as well as I do." I couldn't help myself and I said, "well that's a bit frightening." He asked what I meant. I explained that we may have serious issues if our CFO and VP of Finance don't understand how our accounting systems and processes work. He backpedaled and changed his story, "that's not what I said. I said that they don't know them as well as I do. Don is still new; he is really more of a guy who manages our banking relationship than a full-blown CFO. Matt is young and I am mentoring him – he will get there eventually. All I am suggesting is that we all need to work together."

I couldn't completely cave on this one. The board wanted Devlin to stay away from finance and accounting and I needed to own the function. I would look inept if I didn't take it over. I was also concerned from what I had heard from Matt. Things needed to change, and I could tell that Devlin resisted change if it wasn't his idea. So, I said, "Jamie, let's be clear about something, the board wants to free you up to focus on sales and operations, let me handle finance and accounting." As calm as could be, he said, "let me be clear about something – I need to be in every meeting you have with Don or Matt, got it?" I didn't answer. He paused and then left my office.

We implemented a monthly closing process in which our accounting staff would do a preliminary closing for each division. The lead staff accountant would then prepare actual-to-budget and year over-year analyses, key performance metrics and a draft management discussion memo. This package would then be distributed to the divisional leadership, VP of Finance, CFO, Devlin and me. Then, the group, including the lead accountant, would do a video call with the divisional management and senior leadership in Portland. This process was intended to serve a number of purposes besides simply closing the books. It would also provide professional development for our lead accountants by having them prepare the analyses, write the management discussion and analysis and present to the group. It

111

also was intended to educate the divisional leadership on accounting, finance and financial analysis. Lastly, it was a forum in which we, as a group, could drill down into each division's financial performance to instill fiscal discipline and budget compliance when necessary, encourage growth and risk-taking when a division was outperforming budget, and provide all of us with a more thorough understanding of each division's operations. Based on feedback from the divisional leadership on topics like accruals or reserves against accounts receivable, we would then do a final closing of the financials.

Unfortunately, a couple of things were happening. Instead of allowing the CFO or myself to drive the process and the video conferences, Devlin embedded himself in the exercise. He simply couldn't let go. If a division's revenues were below budget, he would jump in and find ways to justify that accounting had somehow missed some registrations that had actually come in but not found their way into the system yet. If expenses were unfavorable to budget, he would challenge that some of the items included in expenses should be capitalized because they were related to future events. He would also simultaneously beat up the divisional leaders about any outstanding receivables and fight the lead accountant that the allowance for doubtful accounts was excessive. There was very little discussion of strategy and growth opportunities, but rather a myopic view of how to hit the budgeted profit for that particular month. I now knew in my heart that the books were being manipulated.

After a couple of months, I was seeing behavioral trends - one alarming trend was that the preliminary financials often changed when the final closing was complete; and I couldn't reconcile the changes. In addition, consolidating the financials was performed in a black box. I had finally confirmed that there was virtually no integration of systems. Registration data which drove a significant percentage of our revenues was coming from multiple sources, none of which were integrated with our general ledger. Accountants would gather this information from the disparate sources and, literally, key it into a Google Doc like Excel. BBFC team revenue was calculated on a monthly basis in Google Sheets using assumptions provided by a BBFC employee whose bonus was tied to hitting revenue targets. BBFC also provided coaching services to towns and municipalities who chose to outsource their recreational clubs' coaching to our coaches instead of parents. I learned that the towns and municipalities were invoiced by the coaches themselves using Microsoft Word. Only if the coach remembered to send a copy of the invoice to accounting did this revenue get recorded. There was also no way of tracking the collection of this revenue stream; no accounts receivable aging whatsoever. On the expense side, there were over one hundred company-issued credit cards. Soccer coaches charged gasoline, rented cars, booked flights and hotel rooms. They also reserved and paid for soccer fields months in advance of actually needing them. There were no front-end controls over their spending. Furthermore, the expense coding at the end of each month was a monstrous task that delayed the closing process and preparation of an accurate financial package.

The hotel bookings business maintained a separate accounting system all together. Corporate handled their accounts payable and payroll, but everything else was handled in the hotels booking's office. At the end of the month, the hotel bookings' team would provide revenue and certain balance sheet items to the corporate accounting staff. It was a mess. The apparel division based in Puerto Rico maintained its books in a project management software application, it wasn't even an accounting package. At the end of the month, the apparel manager would meet with accounting and work together to pull together makeshift financial statements. This exercise included trying to figure out how much labor to capitalize in finished goods, transfer pricing between divisions, and so on. It was a total joke.

Once accounting had all of these individual elements, they would prepare consolidated financial statements in Google Docs. This involved intercompany activity and eliminations as well – the apparel division was selling product to hockey and lacrosse which in turn were selling product to its customers or including the product in the tournament fee – there was no way of knowing if the intercompany activity was being eliminated completely or appropriately. I'd never seen anything like this. I walked Murray and Jackson through my concerns – Murray was remarkably passive; I am convinced he didn't even understand what I was explaining. I would later learn his accounting skills were poor, to say the least. I don't think he

113

understood debits and credits. Jackson agreed with my assessment and concerns. He confided in me that he was overworked and out over his skis. He said that he had been pushing Devlin for some time for more staff in order to manage the existing processes and put better controls and systems in place. He even told me that they had started a migration to a single enterprise reporting package over a year ago, even bringing in a consultant to lead the implementation, but abandoned the project just before I had come on board. They abandoned it because the company lacked documented processes and controls.

During the August 2018 monthly closing process, we were having our preliminary closing call for the apparel division. The call had immediately followed the hockey call during which Devlin had been rather aggressive with the hockey leadership group about collecting some aged accounts receivable. I found his tone overly aggressive in light of the amounts of the receivables in question and the consistent performance of the hockey group. It was fresh in my mind, when we began discussing the apparel division's accounts receivable.

I am a bit particular about financial analysis, so when it comes to accounts receivable, I always tie out the amount on the balance sheet to the accounts receivable aging (which is the detail that makes up the amount on the balance sheet). On this call, the accounts receivable aging being discussed was significantly less than the balance sheet amount. Still acting like he was the de facto leader of these calls, Devlin said that we didn't need to discuss apparel's accounts receivable since most of the accounts receivable in the aging were intercompany, so the aging was irrelevant. I said, "hang on guys – not a big deal right now, but why doesn't the aging tie out to the balance sheet?" Instead of the lead accountant answering, Devlin jumped in and provided an answer that didn't make any sense to me. I noted it and let it go – I didn't want to press or embarrass him in front of the broader audience.

After the call, I bumped into the gentleman who led the apparel division in the kitchen area (he was based in Portland). We talked about how challenging the apparel division was – it was bleeding cash with no clear path to profitability. As we were about to go back to our offices, I asked about the accounts receivable discrepancy. He seemed a little uncomfortable about it and asked me to come into his office. He let me walk in first, followed me and closed the door behind us. He sat at his computer and brought up the closing documents we had just reviewed. He clicked on the accounts receivable tab – I leaned over and pointed out the total of the accounts receivable aging and asked him to click on the balance sheet tab. I then pointed to the accounts receivable balance and called out the difference. He said, "I know, look", and clicked on another tab at the end of the workbook. It was a schedule of invoices that totaled the difference. I said, "ok, what is this schedule?' He looked at me and said, "these are invoices due from Jamie's teams and his rink." I said, "what?"

He proceeded to tell me that Devlin was an owner, along with the leader of our tours division, of a hockey program and rink located not too far from our office. He told me that both the hockey program and the rink purchased apparel from Epic, often stretching the receivables up to a year before paying the balances due. He also told me that Epic rented ice from the rink. He seemed relieved to tell me this. He continued and told me that the hockey program used Epic's registration system and our accounting team processed the registrations and collected the credit card receipts on behalf of hockey program. He also told me that the hockey program sent teams on Epic tours and rumors had been out there that they were given discounted pricing that wasn't passed on to the families. Lastly, he told me I should look into Epic's non-profit foundation, EpicCares. He believed that most of the foundation's grants were going to Devlin's for-profit hockey program. I wanted to throw up.

Here I was, away from my family, working ungodly hours, trying to fix the accounting processes in this company while worrying about stepping on the founder's ego, only to learn that there may be more going on here than meets the eye. Now that I had been told these things, I had an obligation to get to the bottom of them. I went back to my office and opened up the apparel closing file again. I retraced the steps we had just walked through and reviewed the related party receivables. I found it so hypocritical that Devlin would beat up the hockey guys about collecting their accounts receivable while his separate company owed Epic money and it was so far past due. Some of the invoices were almost a year past due.

I Googled the name of the hockey program and found its website. I immediately recognized the logo from the uniforms in the photos on Devlin's office wall. It didn't take long to find Devlin and Boyle's names associated with the hockey program and the rink. The hockey program wasn't just one team, it appeared to have a number of teams across different age groups. In addition, the website was also marketing a hockey academy. It appeared that they were operating a full-time hockey academy at the rink as well; meaning players were paying tuition to attend school there. This would be a real conflict and issue since Epic already had a partnership with a third-party residential secondary school to operate a residential hockey academy there and we were considering expanding the academy model. In fact, I was in the midst of conducting diligence on a hockey academy business – I wasn't a big fan of the target company, but Devlin kept pressing me to conduct more diligence and even asked that I construct my own financial model that I *would* find compelling for a hockey academy.

A couple of searches of the Maine Secretary of State's database and I found the entities that owned the hockey program and the rink. I looked up the hockey rink's legal name in our system and, sure enough, it was listed as a vendor. We were making payments to the rink for ice time. On a hunch, I looked up the name of the hockey program in Epic's vendor file – sure enough, it was listed as a vendor. Payments were being made to the hockey program as well. How could he not have disclosed these related parties?

I had recently been provided access to Jackson's finance and accounting folders on the Google drive, so I logged in. I browsed the folders and opened several of the last few years' financial statements that had been reviewed by the outside accounting firm. In all of the financial statements, the related party footnote indicated that there hadn't been any related party transactions that required disclosure. Ok, why does this matter? First, under generally accepted accounting principles, officers and directors are required to disclose related party transactions – meaning if they, a family member or another company in which they have an interest conducts business with the company in which they are an officer or director, the nature of the relationship and the total value of the transactions, if material, must be disclosed in the financial statements' footnotes. This is an important disclosure to ensure that the readers of the financial statements are aware of any such relationships and transactions. Failing to disclose related party transactions raises red flags and credibility issues. For example, before I took the position and invested in the company, I certainly would have liked to know that the CEO owned businesses that were doing business with Epic. I may have made a different decision had I known this. Furthermore, had I known that he engaged in related party transactions and failed to disclose them, I definitely would not have gotten involved with Epic.

I stewed on this overnight back at the Hotel Portland. I usually stayed there because it was more of a bed & breakfast than a hotel. I find that typical corporate hotels can quickly become depressing when you are there frequently and for long stretches. Plus, this hotel was usually less expensive than the other branded hotels. The rooms were small by most standards, but totally functional. If I got back to the hotel at a reasonable hour, I would often set up in one of the two front sitting rooms on the first floor. Both had fireplaces, leather chairs, a couch and were quite comfortable. This particular night, I set up in the right-hand room and sat in one of the leather winged-back chairs in front of the fireplace. It was a cool, crisp fall night and the fireplace was lit. The walls were painted a slate gray and an American flag was mounted above the fireplace. It was a nice space - I felt like I was working from home. I doubt, however, it was designed to be a working space for a forensic auditor.

I signed into the hotel's WIFI network and then my Epic Google account. This allowed me access to any files or folders that were shared with me by other Epic employees, like Matt Jackson. I also signed into Epic's Platform. This would allow me to search vendors and their payment or credit activity. It would also allow me to see customer accounts. This would become my nightly ritual for next month plus when I wasn't in the office.

This particular evening, I focused on the transactions between Devlin and Boyle's hockey programs, rink and Epic. The process was time consuming as I had to open each transaction and review them individually; meaning each invoice and line item. Then, I had to review the payment activity for each line item. I confirmed that their hockey programs had been purchasing apparel from Epic for a couple of years – it also looked like the programs often took an unusually long time to pay their invoices, sometimes they didn't pay at all. There were also transactions between the rink and Epic that included apparel and some equipment from Epic's Puerto Rico facility. In reviewing the vendor records, I analyzed the payment history *from* Epic *to* the hockey programs and the rink. The payments were relatively large amounts and were often accompanied by notes that indicated that Epic was collecting payments from customers on behalf of the hockey programs and then remitting them to the programs. This would be consistent with the statement that was made to me earlier that the programs were using our registration system and our accounting staff was managing the programs' cash receipts. This was ridiculous - executives of Epic had blurred, or erased, the lines between Epic and their other business interests. They were using Epic's resources for their personal benefit.

It was impossible for me to trace back from the payments Epic made to the hockey programs to the actual customer payments that Epic would have received. In other words, I wasn't able to confirm that the hockey programs were only receiving funds that had actually been paid by their customers. I made a note to dig into that another time.

I then turned my attention to our customer files. I needed to know if the hockey programs, or Devlin and Boyle, individually, were customers of Epic. I was sure the hockey programs were - in fact, I had already been told by an employee and parent of a player on a team that the programs and Devlin were customers of the company. If they were paying fair market value, it wouldn't be an issue. I could see that the programs had attended a number of events and I made a note to review those invoices in detail later. But when I typed in Devlin and Boyle, separately, in the search box, I really hoped I was going to come up empty. Sure enough, they, along with their

118

children, were in the customer ledger in the Epic system. They attended a number of Epic's individual camps, clinics and international tours. The tours caught my attention, knowing how expensive these were, so I decided to focus there and, specifically, on Devlin.

I found that he had attended tours in Europe, along with his wife, children and even another relative, over the previous summer. As background, each element of a tour has options or a la carte items. In many cases, Devlin had elected upgrades (flights and room type) and add-ons (like ground excursions, wine tastings, etc.). The value of these tours, in total, were in the high tens of thousands of dollars. I thought, "wow, at least he is a good customer". Then I noticed something odd – most of the line items had payment adjustments credited to them. Under normal circumstances, you would see that the item had been marked paid, but not in this case. Instead, there were credits and discounts issued against the invoices. In reviewing the credits, the notes indicated things such as: coach credit, spouse credit, second child credit, scholarship player, team manager credit, team organizer credit, coach discount, etc. Most of these were unusual. I reviewed other customers and did not see similar credits being applied.

As an accountant, we are trained to be professionally skeptical, but I'm not sure these would have passed the smile test for even a casual reader. I copied the information from the system and was able to paste it in an Excel spreadsheet and clean up the formatting. After all of the credits, discounts and coaching per diems were applied, Epic actually had to issue Devlin a check for the tours. Seriously, we owed *him* money for attending our tours with his family. I checked my work again and slammed my laptop shut. It was after 3:00am.

Hoping to grab some sleep after that exercise proved fruitless. My head was spinning. I sat in bed and caught up on news on my laptop. Around 5:00am, I got up and went down to the hotel's kitchen area off the main lobby to grab a coffee. My routine was one cup of coffee while I watched morning news, usually First Look before Morning Joe on MSNBC – don't jump to any conclusions about my political views as I am pretty much non-partisan. Fresh coffee hadn't been prepared yet, but the thermos was still sort of warm. I pumped out a cup and returned upstairs. Walking up the stairs to my second-floor room, I noticed that I was having some difficulty. My lower back was killing me, and my right leg, down through my foot, felt like it was asleep. I dismissed it as too much time sitting down with bad posture.

I arrived in the office early and updated my list for the day. My day was stacked up with meetings and calls, but I also had two unusual bookends for the day – I would review the recent financing due diligence files on Google drive that had been provided to CFC and RevCap to see if any of the related party stuff had been disclosed and then meet with Devlin at the end of the day to discuss his hockey programs. I expected it would be quite a day.

I looked everywhere in the diligence folders but found no mention of the hockey programs, rink or officers receiving discounts for international tours. I was able to find management representation letters, signed by Devlin, provided to the outside accounting firm that made the assertion that there *weren't* any related party transactions. A management representation letter must be signed by an officer of a company, usually the CFO or CEO, or both, that has been reviewed or audited by an outside accounting firm. In an attempt to bore the hell out of you... per Auditing Standard No. 18, *Related Parties*, "the auditor should obtain a written representation that management has no knowledge of any relationships or transactions with related parties that have not been properly accounted for and adequately disclosed. The auditor should obtain this written representation even if the results of those procedures indicate that relationships and transactions with related parties have been properly accounted for and adequately disclosed".

My day had been straight-out busy and productive. I looked at my phone and realized it was almost 5:00pm. It was pretty rare for Devlin to be in the office much past 5:00pm; on a number of occasions, I had heard him say that he had to take off because his kids had hockey practice. I didn't know if he coached the team or was simply the parent responsible for bringing them to practice. I certainly never suspected that he owned the teams.

I walked down to his office, he was still at his desk typing away and looking at his monitors. He looked up while still typing and told me to come in – he seemed to be in a good mood. I sat across from him and he said, while still typing, "one second." He finished, put both palms down on his desk and said, "what can I do for you?" I told him that I had a quick question and cut right to it – "Jamie, do you own your kids' hockey program?" He wrinkled his brow and said, "who told you that?" I wasn't sure how to answer that question or if I should answer it. The person who told me was clearly nervous about telling me – I wasn't about to put him in a bad spot. I said, "it doesn't matter who told me, I just need to know. Here's why – if you are an owner and we do business with the hockey program, then that is a related party transaction. We are required to disclose those types of things in the financial statements. I don't think it should be a big deal, but we would want to get that out in the open right away."

His facial expression changed instantly. He went from appearing relaxed and cordial to looking anxious and confrontational. He didn't even pause, but instead responded immediately, "I coach my kid's team, that's it – is that ok with you? Did you ever coach your kids Little League team, did anyone ever tell you that was a problem?" I tried to diffuse the situation by saying, "relax, I am trying help here." I knew he was an owner of both the rink and the teams, I had documentation to prove it. He was lying to me and getting aggressive about it thinking I would just walk away.

What I was about to experience with Devlin would happen several more times over the next several months - not just with him, but with other Epic employees as well. I would ask a question and get an answer, but it would be a lie. I would then ask the question again, revealing that I had more pertinent information, and I would get a slightly different, twisted version of the first response, but still not the truth. Finally, I would ask a third question and reveal that I already knew the truth, usually because I shared supporting documentation at this point. Only then would I would finally get the truth. But in every instance, the person across from me, the person who was lying to me, acted like they had done nothing wrong. Bizarre. They subscribed to their own revisionist history, even though they were revising it through their lies in real time. Some of these characters were creating their own alternative reality.

I said to Devlin "so, to be clear, you are not an owner of a hockey program that does business with Epic?" He said, "no, I just told you that I coach the team." I replied, "and you are not an owner of the rink?" Again, he said, "no". But then, he quickly back peddled. He must have sensed that I had more information if I mentioned the rink. He said, "well hang on – I own a piece of the rink. The rink was going out of business and it was going to be bad for the community so I, along with a few other guys, stepped up and bought it. But it's not a business, it just more of a charitable thing for the community." I asked if it was a non-profit and he said he didn't know. I then explained why it was important to disclose to the board his ownership in the rink and provide detail and support for any transactions between the rink and Epic to show that they were at fair market value. He said he had no idea that you were required to disclose those types of things and that he hadn't done anything wrong. I was giving him the benefit of the doubt. I told him that as long as we disclosed it soon and there weren't other things like this that came up later, everything should be fine. I asked again about the hockey program and he said, "you know, let me check on that – I'm not sure who owns the program. I want to make sure the rink doesn't own it."

The next morning, I had a catch-up call with Jake Maddox. Jake had been on the board of Epic for a couple of years, but I sensed that he was a relatively hands-off, trusting type of board member, despite the frustrations he had expressed to me. Under normal circumstances, I prefer passive board member traits over "helicopter" board members who hover around, never really have a full understanding of the business, but think they do, and periodically swoop in and try to make operational decisions.

I knew that Jake was quite frustrated with the company's performance and Devlin's defensiveness whenever questioned on a sensitive topic, like the apparel division's burn rate. On our call, Jake asked my latest thoughts about the apparel division, so I provided them – they weren't pretty. I also told him about my conversation with Devlin regarding related party transactions and asked if he knew about Devlin's ownership in the rink or the hockey programs. He had no idea and was pissed. He said he knew Devlin coached a team but had no idea that he was an owner of the programs. He said he certainly didn't know that the programs were purchasing apparel from Epic. I didn't raise the other concerns I had – like the tours.

Jake went on to say that he felt like he couldn't trust Devlin. He said that his behavior at the board meeting in New York was really alarming, specifically, Devlin's reluctance to give up control of finance and accounting. I agreed with him and told him it felt like a segment out of a CPA continuing education video on ethics or potential fraud. He agreed and then asked if I had performed a detailed review of Epic's previous acquisitions. I hadn't. I asked him why he wanted to know. He told me that he couldn't put his finger on it, but the way Devlin had presented certain acquisitions to the board and pushed for them had made Jake uncomfortable. He was careful to say that he didn't want to come across as accusing Devlin of anything, but something just didn't feel right. He asked me to dig into the transactions and related accounting. I added near the top of my to-do list.

CHAPTER 10

I felt like I gotten up to speed with every division, except for one, tours. I had a couple of one-on-one calls with Scott Boyle, the head of tours. I had also been on several monthly closing calls with him along with the tours' lead accountant. The preliminary monthly closing calls for tours, which were just that, *preliminary*. One of the biggest challenges with closing the tours financials was that Boyle's staff was notoriously slow to code their credit card expenses and input vendor invoices into the system. Consequently, the accounting team was trying to prepare financial statements with one arm tied behind their back. Instead of acknowledging this and trying to correct it, he would direct his frustration and anger at the accountant, often using a demeaning tone and profanity. On more than one occasion, I had to reprimand Boyle about how he spoke to the accountant. I found him consistently rude and belligerent. His tone on the calls was completely inappropriate. I have no tolerance for bullies.

I had tried on several occasions to schedule an in-person working-session with Boyle, to better understand their operations and team structure. I also wanted to help refine the division's longer-term strategy and to address the uncomfortable monthly closing calls. Getting a meeting on the calendar had been impossible. Boyle was always traveling or had some other conflict. We finally locked down a date and he said he would send the calendar invite. The morning of the meeting, I noticed that the calendar invite included our Portland office as the location of the meeting. I had wanted to meet in the tours' office about fifteen minutes away. We had plenty of room in Portland for the tours staff and I couldn't understand, or get a straight answer from Devlin, why tours had their own office. I couldn't change the invite since he had initiated it, so I sent him an email suggesting that we meet at his office, that I was happy to drive over. He wrote back almost instantly, "I prefer to meet in Portland let's keep the location the same, see you at 1:00pm."

I read the email several times and even started to respond but stopped. I couldn't help but think that he didn't want to meet with me at all, and he certainly didn't want me to come to his office. So, knowing that his office was about fifteen minutes away, I left my office at about noon for the 1:00pm meeting that Boyle still thought was going to be held in Portland. The address of the tours office wouldn't come up in my GPS, but I was able to get the general neighborhood to work.

As I pulled off the main road into where I thought the office was located, I looked to my left and saw a large metal building. It was the rink that Boyle and Devlin owned. Oh my God. Several hundred yards up the hill on the right was what I gathered to be the tours office, located among other office condominiums. There was no sign indicating that this was their office, but I thought I had found the right building and believed the office was on the second floor. It was just shy of 12:30pm – early enough, I assumed, that Boyle hadn't left yet for Portland. I had decided earlier, that even if we missed each other, I still would be able to get a look at the tours operation and claim it was just a mix-up because of the calendar invite.

The office condo development was not particularly well maintained on the exterior. When I entered the building, I realized the exterior was its best side. Inside the entryway, there was a stairway to my left and door directly in front of me – no signage. I opened the door in front of me to an unfinished space. I could see straight through to the back of the building that had an open garage door. I heard voices and entered. There were boxes stacked up and other stuff around, but I was paying more attention to finding my way to the voices. A guy came around the corner, I startled him a bit, and he asked if he could help me. I said I was looking for Epic – he didn't answer me, instead, he simply pointed straight up and turned around. I said, "OK, upstairs? Thanks." Another happy character... must be something in the water. I turned to walk out to the entryway and realized there were hockey sticks in the partially opened boxes. Hmmm.

I walked up the stairs and opened the door. It opened into a hallway that led to my right. Directly in front of me was an office with its door closed. I turned right and walked to the back of the building. I walked past about six offices, a restroom and a small kitchen area. I didn't see anyone until I reached the back room. I heard laughter as I approached the end of the hallway. I walked through the open door into what looked like a fraternity beer pong room. Several dart boards on the wall; a poorly constructed bar to the right equipped with its own beer tap; jerseys and other sports banners tacked on the walls; several flat screen televisions mounted on the walls playing European Soccer games. To the left was a large table with about six men sitting around it, several of whom were playing cards. I recognized them – this was most of our tours staff. Jesus Christ, I thought. No wonder he didn't want me to come here.

Boyle was not at the table. What I found really interesting was that the guys at the table didn't seem at all uncomfortable with me walking in and seeing them playing cards. One of them said, "hey Steve, you looking for Scott? I think he thought he was meeting you in Portland, let me make sure he hasn't left yet." He got up and walked down the hall. I stood my ground, looked around the room to take it all in. The room was a mess. They must have just had lunch because there were empty food cartons and balled up sandwich wrappers and napkins on the bar. I turned and looked down the hall to see Matt walking towards me. He motioned over his shoulder with his thumb and said, "Scott is in his office." He walked by me and sat back down at the table and picked up the hand that had been dealt to him. I thanked him and headed down the hall. As I passed the kitchen area, I looked in and noticed the counter had dirty dishes on it – there was also a variety of beer mugs and pilsner glasses. I was beside myself.

I walked into Boyle's office – he was seated at a desk. I tried to act casual and comfortable, but it was difficult. He said, "what are you doing here? I told you we were meeting in Portland?" He was clearly not happy. I said, "oh, sorry, must have gotten our wires crossed. So, how are you?" He said he was fine, but, clearly, he wasn't. I looked around his office and asked how long they had been in this space – there was literally nothing in his office other than a desk and chair. Nothing on the walls, not even a computer or monitor on the desk. I felt like I was in some sort of boiler room operation where these clowns were pushing penny stocks to retirees and widows. He said they had been in the office for about a year and a half. I said, jokingly, "I really like what you've done with the place... the whole 1970's Animal House theme", while motioning to the playroom down the hall. He didn't laugh.

Instead, he gave me a lesson in culture. He told me how hard his team worked, that they didn't need anyone looking over their shoulder, that they needed to blow off some steam from time to time, how much they are on the road away from their girlfriends and wives....He told me he ran his division like a hockey team, he was the coach and they were his players. He said he actually had coached a couple of these guys when he coached a high school team a few years back. "I work my guys hard, but I also hang with them – golf with them and drink with them", he said. Sounded like great leadership to me. He then looked at me and said, "I know what I am doing here, and it works. I don't need your help; you need to stay away." I thought to myself, what a warm welcome. I told him, that I simply wanted to help strategically and with any potential acquisitions. Now that finance and accounting was my responsibility, I needed to understand every element of the business in order to drive the financial model and performance. Again, he pushed back – he told me that he was a CPA, had been the first CFO of Epic and that he knew the business better than anyone. This guy was a real pleasure to be around.

He went on to criticize the tours' accountant based in Portland who, in my opinion, was a well-intentioned and hard-working young man. I listened, then pushed back, explaining that his tours staff needed to get their expenses in on a timelier basis in order to facilitate the monthly closings. He didn't want to hear it. I then told him that he could not use profanity on the calls nor be rude to my team. He said he "would talk to whoever he wanted, however he wanted." I said, "ok, it seems like we aren't making any progress." He agreed. I started to put my notepad back into my bag and I couldn't help myself... I said, "can you explain to me your relationship with the rink over there (motioning with my hand to the right) and the hockey programs?" He asked, "why?" I explained the concept of related party transactions and that we needed to understand them and disclose them - I said, "oh, I forgot, you're a CPA, you don't need me to explain the disclosure requirements to you." He looked at me and said, "my relationship to the rink or the programs are none of your business. I don't trust you. This conversation is over." I said, "thanks for your time" and walked out. I walked down the hallway to the playroom and said goodbye to the frat boys.

I arrived back at Portland office about fifteen minutes later only to be greeted by Devlin. He was not in good spirits, to say the least. We sat down in his office – he asked why I met with Boyle. I told him that it was long overdue, that I needed time with him to understand and help drive growth in tours. He interrupted me before I could compare and contrast what I was doing with the other divisions. He told me that Boyle is "a different animal", that "he doesn't play well with others", and so on. He told me that tours moved out of Epic's office because Boyle couldn't get along with people in the office. He then tried imparting a bunch of new age management bullshit on me. He knew I wasn't buying it. I was finally comfortable here at the company and knew that the board would hold me accountable. I wasn't planning to fail because people weren't cooperating. Little did I know how destructive these people could be. Devlin said he would "personally mentor me" and "coach me" on how to manage and work with Boyle.

I returned to my office and looked at my note pad. My notes from my earlier call with Jake were staring back at me…. *look at previous acquisitions*. I emailed Matt Jackson asking if he had a schedule that detailed all of the company's acquisitions. Almost immediately, he sent me two links: one to a file on Google Drive and another for a folder entitled *Acquisitions*, also on Google Drive. The file was a spreadsheet and it was exactly what I was looking for – in chronological order, the name of each acquired company, the acquisition date, purchase price, transaction terms, any post-closing purchase price adjustments, and so on. The Acquisitions folder included sub-folders for each acquisition that included due diligence information, if any was available, and closing documents. I then pulled Epic's reviewed financial statements for the past five years.

My plan was to proceed chronologically, review the diligence for each transaction, perform a detailed walk through of the closing documents and tick and tie the financial elements of each transaction to the financial statements' footnotes for that particular year. I would then evaluate the post-transaction performance of each acquisition to determine if these were actually accretive deals. This exercise would really inform me about the acquisitions, the way Epic's management evaluated them, whether or not we were seeing post-closing benefits, and ease Jake's mind that something may be amiss.

First, I created my own simple summary of the individual transactions that included purchase price, cash paid and seller debt at the time of the closing, and an estimate of each company's profitability at the time of the acquisition. What I found was alarming - these aren't the actual numbers, but you will get the point. Over the previous five years or so, Epic, under Devlin's direction, had purchased approximately $25.0 million dollars' worth of companies (purchase price). Yet, Epic had, at the time of the April 2018 financing, approximately $22.0 million in debt (bank and sellers' notes, associated with the acquisitions and a working capital line of credit). Not only had he overly leveraged the business, but it was pretty obvious that the business was not generating any meaningful operating cash flow to pay down the debt. In valuing the business, we had added-back non-recurring items and the losses associated with the apparel and football divisions because we were planning to divest those, but when you cut through it all, this business was losing money and drowning in debt.

The first couple of transactions I reviewed were quite small and straight forward. The next was difficult to understand. It was a Swedish company that appeared to operate hockey events in Europe. There were no diligence materials in the diligence folder whatsoever. Nothing. At the time of the transaction, Epic acquired a 50% stake in the business for which it owed the seller a promissory note. Later on, under questionable circumstance, Epic somehow acquired the remaining 50% and a portion of the seller note was forgiven. I looked everywhere but couldn't locate stand-alone financial statements for this business. Very strange – add it to the list.

The next company was called Youth Hockey Invitationals ("YHI"). This appeared to be an operator of hockey tournaments primarily in Minnesota. Again, there were minimal financial diligence materials in the folder. No tax returns, financial statements, nothing that would provide detailed support for the Epic's valuation of the business. I don't know how Devlin was assigning values to these businesses. The purchase and sale agreement was pretty straight forward and the structure was like his other deals; minimal cash was paid to the seller at closing but rather a hefty percentage of the purchase price was to be paid over time in the form of a seller's note – a promissory note from Epic to the seller. Based on the recurring transaction structure theme, my gut told me that Epic had always been always under-capitalized (simply put, there wasn't enough cash on the company's balance sheet) and he was trying to buy earnings. If this was the

129

case, he had created circumstances that usually kill a company – too much debt and no liquidity. On top of it all, he was adding costs at the corporate level, so the consolidation of these acquisitions was resulting in even greater consolidated losses.

I saw something particularly odd about the YHI transaction. Months following the transaction, there was a significant purchase price adjustment, a reduction of the seller's note. The next day, I asked Jackson about the transaction. He told me that YHI had a sizable receivable outstanding at the time of the transaction. Money that was due to YHI for hotel commissions for events they had been held before the transaction closed. The parties had agreed that Epic would collect, and keep, the receivable after the closing. After Epic took over, it was unable to collect the outstanding receivable and the purchase price was adjusted downward as a result - failure to collect this receivable meant that the associated revenue actually wasn't earned, and the company was not as profitable as expected at the time of the transaction. Again, I could not determine the profitability of YHI today because it was absorbed into the hockey division.

Jackson said that he wasn't involved in the purchase price adjustment negotiations with the former YHI owners, but that he knew it was quite contentious. Attorneys had to get involved. Devlin had handled it all, finance wasn't involved. Jackson said that the former owners couldn't understand how the receivable wasn't collectible. It seemed like every stone I turned over, every question I asked, every meeting I took at Epic revealed something unusual or messy. I would have to look into the YHI transaction further and probably contact the sellers to get to this bottom of this one – add it to the list.

The next transaction that had strange elements to it was the 2017 acquisition of a hotel bookings company called Travel Ball America ("TBA"). TBA provided the same services as our existing hotel bookings business – they procured blocks of hotel rooms and provided them to attendees of events, taking a commission for their services and providing a rebate to the event operator. Again, I was unable to find any meaningful diligence materials or historical financial statements in the TBA acquisition folder. There were income statements in an exhibit of the purchase and sale agreement -

130

the last two years of income statements were *identical*. Like a true cut and paste job.

I also would learn that Devlin didn't include our existing hotel bookings leadership in the due diligence process or structuring of the TBA transaction. Wouldn't you want your divisional leaders to evaluate the target, compare the business to your own benchmark data, determine potential post-closing synergies, plan integration workflows and make sure the personalities fit? None of this happened. Instead, Devlin negotiated the deal alone with the seller, April Nash.

Epic's outside counsel had drafted the necessary closing documents, including the purchase and sale agreement. A draft of the agreement was provided to Epic's senior lender, a local bank. The bank approved the transaction and allowed Epic to draw funds from a line of credit that was in place solely for acquisitions, not working capital needs. Banks often separate the two – a working capital line that has a cap on it, usually secured by collateral like accounts receivable and inventory, based on the bank's risk tolerance. A separate acquisition line of credit was also in place for which the bank had to approve any transaction prior to the company drawing down any funds.

By the time I reviewed the TBA purchase agreement, it was after 9:00pm and I was still in the office. I decided I would get through this one, check it off the list and call it a day. The document read like most others and I was about to skip the boiler plate stuff when I noticed a paragraph with the wrong indentation. No joke, when you read enough of these, you know what the formatting should look like and rarely does a good attorney let a final document go out with poor formatting. Only because of the poor formatting did I read a particular paragraph. As I read the paragraph, I knew immediately that it hadn't been written by an attorney. The grammar was poor, terms were capitalized that should have been in lower case and it was difficult to understand the intent of the paragraph.

I could not understand what the language was trying to achieve – in summary, it was stating that the seller would return a specific portion of the purchase price in two unequal installments in the weeks following the closing. I couldn't get my head around this. Most purchase agreements have some form of post-closing purchase price adjustment language in them – this usually relates to working capital, because you don't know with certainty the exact amounts of cash, receivables, accounts payable and other current assets and liabilities in advance of the closing. Therefore, there is usually a window of time after the closing when both parties settle on what the amounts actually were and the net number either goes back to the seller or the seller owes the buyer more cash. As I am sure you can gather, it is impossible to know what a purchase price adjustment would be *before* a transaction closes. There was another thing about the paragraph that was unsettling – the payment back to the buyer was to be broken in two unequal installments. Why in the world would you do that? Right away, I thought that one reason would be to disguise the payments.

I sent an email to outside counsel – I wrote, "you must have really been off your game when you drafted paragraph 8(b) of the TBA purchase agreement." I closed my laptop, packed my bag and headed to the hotel. On the way to the hotel, my phone rang – it was outside counsel. He told me he was still at his desk and saw my email. He asked what I was referencing in my email – I told him I was trying to understand the details of this particular transaction and I couldn't get my head around that paragraph. He told me that he had the document open on his screen and that there wasn't a paragraph 8(b). I told him I may have typed the wrong subsection, but it was definitely in paragraph 8 – I was doing this from memory as I was still driving. I described the language and, again, he said he didn't see anything like it in his document. He even read me the working capital adjustment language that I didn't recall seeing in the agreement I had just reviewed. I knew it was late, but I asked if I could call him back in a couple of minutes when I arrived at the hotel.

I went straight to the right-hand sitting room in the hotel – no one was in there. I opened my laptop, the WIFI connected automatically since I was basically living here, and the agreement was still there on my browser connected to Google drive. I scrolled down and there it was paragraph 8(b). I emailed it to counsel and called him. He picked right up and said, "I am opening it now." About thirty

132

seconds of silence and then I heard, "this is not my agreement." I asked him what he meant, and he repeated it, "this is not my document." He then said, "I just sent you the final agreement I sent Devlin for the closing." As I was waiting for the email to arrive, I could hear him reading the paragraph aloud in a whisper. I could tell he was trying to understand its intent as well. I received and read his version of agreement and the paragraph wasn't there. Instead, there was standard working capital adjustment language.

He asked me if I had reviewed this with Devlin – "not yet, I just found it tonight", I said. I told him that I was simply "ticking and tying out" all of the transactions when I came across this, that I was planning to aggregate all of my questions and go over them with Devlin in the next couple of days. The more we tried to understand the changes, the more counsel was getting annoyed. He said, "I can't believe someone would make these changes without letting their attorney know." He also raised the issue of the bank. He said, "I wonder which version the bank received?"

When I arrived in the office in the morning, Jackson was the only one there. I printed two copies of the TBA purchase agreement, stepped into Jackson's office, made small talk and then handed him one of the agreements. I asked if he was familiar with it. It was starting to seem that every time I asked him a question, he was beginning to get more uncomfortable. Be it about accounting processes or acquisitions, he always seemed defensive. I tried to ease his insecurity by telling him that the company seemed to have been moving quickly, kind of building the airplane while flying it so he wouldn't feel like it was all on him.

He took his time and flipped through the document. "Yea, I've seen this before," he said. I told him to read the paragraph in question. He read it to himself and said, "ok, I think I understand it – what's the question?" The way he responded, he acted like he hadn't been involved in crafting the paragraph. I told him that it didn't make any sense, that you can't peg the amount of a purchase price adjustment before the closing. He read it again. I was also reading my copy as well. He took his time – he was really trying to understand it. He then shook his head and said, "I don't get it either." I asked him if he

133

was involved and he said that he wasn't, that Devlin handled it all. I asked why the CFO wasn't handling these matters and he said sarcastically, "have you met Jamie?" I replied, "I think I know what you mean, but why don't you tell me?" He went on to tell me that Devlin was a control freak, that he had to have his hand in everything in the company. I agreed wholeheartedly, but it was nice to finally hear someone else say it out loud. Maybe Jackson was cutting down on Devlin's Kool-Aid.

There was a pause and Jackson went back to the first page of the agreement and was reading through it again in more detail. I sat across from his desk in silence. I had been through the document a number of times but had been focused mostly on that one paragraph. I turned to the first page as well and the transaction date jumped out at me – January 1, 2017. How did I miss this? No one closes a transaction on January 1st. It's a holiday, no one is working and what are the chances of everything coming together to close on that day? I turned to the signature pages, no dates. But then, I noticed the document had been notarized. The notary dated the document November 2017. My mind raced – had someone actually backdated this transaction? Why would you do that? To get a full year's worth of the target company's profits - that would be the only reason. In the U.S., Generally Accepted Accounting Principles ("GAAP") are the governing rules provided by the Financial Accounting Standard Board. These rules ensure, among other things, that financial statements are prepared in a consistent manner, so the reader has confidence in the integrity of the information provided. There are very strict rules about accounting for acquisitions. One simple element is that you can only consolidate the financial activity for an acquisition from the date on which you took control of the company. You can't arbitrarily decide to backdate the transaction and take credit for prior period activity. This was ridiculous.

I asked Jackson to turn back to page one and look at the date. He read it and didn't respond the way I did. He said, OK?" I told him to turn to the last page and look at the notary's date. He read it aloud and then said, "yea, that's when we closed." I asked why the document was dated January 1st and he said, "that's when Jamie wanted the transaction recorded." This led to a fifteen-minute lesson in accounting standards. I then realized Jackson was either light on his technical accounting skills or had been brainwashed – perhaps a little of both. By end of the tutorial, he realized this was wrong and he looked like he might throw up. Then, looking like the Pepto Bismol finally kicked in, he said "well the lawyers approved this." I smiled and told him about my call with outside counsel.

It was my birthday and wedding anniversary and I had completely forgotten both. After my meeting, I returned to my office to hear my phone vibrating on the desk. A missed call from my wife and a number of text messages from my wife and kids. I called my wife back and wished her a happy anniversary. We talked for a bit, mostly about the kids. I told her I would see her tomorrow night when I got home. I hung up and called my local florist on Hope Street in Providence and ordered a bouquet to be delivered. I missed my wife and kids so much when I was away, that I threw myself into working day and night in order to not have the time to think about them. This wasn't healthy. On top of being away from home, work stress was building to an all-time high. I was starting to think that some bad things may have gone on in this company – the related party stuff was bad enough, but accounting shenanigans would take it to another level.

I assumed it was the stress, but I was starting to feel like I was in somebody else's body. I don't know how else to describe it. I found myself walking slower and my posture was poor. I had constant back pain and my coordination had declined significantly. The strangest thing of all was that I often felt like parts of my body were vibrating. It was a very strange sensation – it felt like I had a cell phone in my pocket, and it was vibrating. The first couple of times it happened, that's exactly what I thought it was. The vibrations had started around my hips and midsection. Recently, they had started to show themselves in my legs and feet. These vibrations, or tremors, were becoming a distraction, but I dismissed them, and the other symptoms, as caused by stress and lack of exercise.

I organized my notes from the review of the acquisitions; I had a lot of questions. I decided to meet with Murray, the CFO, and get his answers. If he couldn't answer them, then I would have to go to

Devlin. I walked down the hall to see if Murray had time today only to learn that he was in Puerto Rico at the apparel facility. I saw Devlin in the next office on his phone. I sent Devlin a note asking if he had time later in the day.

We met at 3:00pm. Knowing how defensive Devlin could get and what we had been through with the related party matters, I decided I would focus mostly on the TBA transaction. I walked into his office and asked if he was ready, he just waved me in with his right hand without taking his eyes off his monitors. He was standing up. I took a seat on the barstool height chairs across from his stand-up desk. I put my notepad on the desk – it had a series of neatly printed bullet pointed questions on it, covering almost the entire page. I noticed Devlin glanced down at it from his gaze that was still fixed on his monitor. To be honest, this kind of annoyed me – he was a stickler for telling staff to be on time and to give people your full attention. Yet, it seemed that every time I met with him, he made me sit there like a clown. The more I was around him, the more I started think it some sort of power play on his part.

He finally wrapped up whatever he was working on and looked at me – "how are we today?", he said. I told him I was doing great and that I had some questions about prior acquisitions that I needed to understand from strategic, financial and, potentially, an audit perspective. He asked what I meant by an *audit perspective*. 2018 was the first year the company was having its financial statements audited by our outside accounting firm. In prior years, the company had only had its financial statements reviewed – which I still don't understand as Epic's credit agreement with its bank required an audit in 2017. I had assumed he understood the difference between a review and an audit, but I explained it nonetheless with emphasis on making sure that our acquisition footnotes were accurate and complete. I walked him through my understanding of the individual acquisitions.

I was unable to get any real clarity on the Lund Sports business in Sweden – he told me that it had been absorbed into the hockey *and* tours divisions. I tried to get clarity on how it could be absorbed into both, but his explanation made no sense. I also asked where I could find Lund Sports' historical financials and he snapped at me – "I just told you three times that it doesn't exist anymore." I asked how that was possible since this entity still shows up as a legal subsidiary and has an office and staff in Stockholm. I said, "clearly the legal entity exists and must file financial statements in Sweden, therefore, we must be maintaining books and records." Frustrated, he said that he would have Murray explain it to me when he got back from his trip – he said that Murray had been "running point on Lund Sports." He clearly wanted nothing to do with this topic.

I had dug into Lund Sports and learned that Epic had acquired a 50% interest in the business a few years earlier - again, there was no evidence of any financial due diligence. I was told by Jackson that shortly after the acquisition, their partner in Sweden was failing to provide financial statements and there were rumors that he was misappropriating funds. In my discussions with our staff in Sweden, they also claimed that the partner had inappropriate text communications with a minor girl as well. He was pushed out. Good stuff.

At some point, Epic convinced the partner to relinquish his interest in Lund Sports and Epic became the 100% owner of the company. Unfortunately, Lund Sports had failed to file tax returns and financial statements with the Swedish government for the last several years. In addition, I could not find where the financial activities of Lund Sports were consolidated in Epic's financial statements - this was a complete cluster!

I then moved on to YHI – before I could even finish with my overview of what I understood, he said – "same thing, YHI was absorbed into hockey." I said, "ok, understood. Can you explain the purchase price adjustment?" He asked why. Who does that? When someone asks you a question, a reasonable, relevant question… don't you just do your best to answer the question? He clearly didn't want to answer the question. I told him that I needed to understand the substance of the purchase price adjustment to make sure we accounted for it properly. He said, "that's almost two years ago, why are you *wasting* your time on this?" Again, I explained the audit requirements and disclosures. He gave in and provided me with an explanation similar to what Jackson had given me. I asked why the receivable was never collected. He said that the sellers had misrepresented that they were due rebates for which they actually weren't entitled. I said, "wow, that's not good." He said, "no not good at all, we had to get attorneys involved, it almost got really ugly."

Next was TBA. As soon as I brought up the topic, he looked at his monitor and said, "just so you know, I only have a couple more minutes, I have a hard stop." I told him I would be quick. He was still looking at his monitor when I pulled out a copy of the purchase agreement from under the first page of my notebook – it caught his attention. I turned to the infamous paragraph and put the document in front of him and asked what it meant. He read it, said, "that is the working capital section," and looked back at his monitor. He clearly did not want to look me in the eye or have this conversation. I asked how he pegged the adjustment *before* the transaction. His explanation was complete nonsense. I let it go, but I asked why the seller returned the money in two installments. He said he wasn't sure if that was actually what happened as he was using his mouse and looking at the monitor. He then took the document back from me, flipped through it and said, "I don't think you have the final agreement. Let me find it and email it to you." I said, "ok" and took the document back. He said he had to "hop on a call." I then flipped to the last page and showed him the notary stamp and signature – I said, "I think this *is* the final document." He said, with obvious annoyance in his tone, "I have to get on this call" and put his headphones on. I left the office.

THE DARK SIDE

"'You certainly will not die', the serpent said to the woman."

Genesis 3:4

CHAPTER 11

The next month involved working seven days a week and every waking hour. It would prove to be one of the more eventful periods of my tenure with Epic. The board had been updated on the related party matters as well as questionable accounting practices. I was asked to conduct an internal investigation. CFC also dropped one of their partners into the company to serve as interim CFO. The board felt that Murray wasn't qualified for the position – instead of terminating him, Devlin put him in charge of special projects and focused him on apparel, football and lacrosse.

The main objectives for our interim CFO were to standardize accounting processes, consolidate to a single general ledger package, improve internal controls, ensure timely and accurate financial reporting, manage the audit and assist with our internal investigation. Unfortunately, his execution was not great. I voiced my concerns to CFC partners several times, which was not easy to do, but it fell on deaf ears.

The presence of the interim CFO (who Devlin despised) coupled with the internal investigation made for tension-filled days. Devlin clearly knew that the board had lost faith and trust in him; he was walking on eggshells. Most of the staff in Maine were loyal to Devlin, had enjoyed a pretty relaxed culture under his leadership and they were now being held to higher standards – some were good with the new expectations, most weren't. The tours division, I would later learn, was actively being poisoned by Boyle – he was telling his staff that I was going to cut their salaries, eliminate bonus opportunities and so on. All fabricated bullshit. The hockey, lacrosse and hotel divisions seemed to be working pretty well with me. We had made the decision to exit the apparel business and were in the process of selling the assets to the general manager, Ramon. We also made a similar decision regarding our football division; however, it would take some time to unwind Epic's football joint venture.

BBFC, the soccer division, was a whole other matter. Despite repeated efforts, it was impossible to get Patrick Baldwin to engage with me in a productive manner. I was trying to focus on two areas - the BBFC financial model and the division's strategic plan. I could not reconcile, or bridge, the 2016 (the year Epic acquired its stake) BBFC financial performance to the 2018 plan. Top line revenue had nearly doubled, but profitability was declining. For even the most unsophisticated businessperson, this should be alarming. The product mix hadn't changed, pricing was consistent, the way they staffed their clubs and events hadn't changed materially, etc. When I tried to get answers from BBFC management, the explanations were scattered and vague. The best I could get was that the cost to rent fields had increased and labor was getting more expensive. When I analyzed these two-line items, their assertions were accurate, but these expenses didn't represent enough to consume the operating scale that should have been achieved by doubling revenue.

It was also clear to me that I, and the interim CFO, were the only people in the company who were so concerned about the performance of BBFC. How could this be? BBFC represented nearly 50% of our consolidated business, its profitability was declining, and no one was making this a high priority. To the contrary – I was told by Devlin to "back off and not put so much pressure on the BBFC guys." Something wasn't right.

I had two experiences earlier in my career where we had found accounting irregularities that turned out to be fraud. In both

140

instances, I realized something so basic, but simultaneously profound. The vast majority of people operate every day from a foundation of trust. What do I mean by that? It's simple - I trust you... I believe that you are honest. And, I certainly don't think that you are trying to deceive me. I may not agree with what you assert, your position on a matter or your decision making, but I believe that your intentions are pure. This puts the person who is trusting at a distinct disadvantage – it allows the person with inappropriate intentions extended time to deceive and to cover up their actions. In addition, we are reluctant to push too hard, to ask too many questions, for fear of making the other person feel like we don't trust them. This buys them even more time. Keep in mind, a liar will never tell you they are lying. If something doesn't feel right, you should be comfortable asking the appropriate and, sometimes, difficult questions.

In 2005, I was asked by a partner at a private equity firm to attend a meeting with him at one of his portfolio companies. He was not only a co-worker of mine, but I considered him a friend. Both his undergraduate degree and MBA were from Harvard. He also had a law degree and had previously practiced at a top tier firm. Clearly, a very smart guy. His accounting skills, however, weren't the best. He had received a call from the controller of his portfolio company indicating that she had concerns about the accounting practices at the company. For the record, you never want to receive a call like that.

I hadn't worked on the deal, so I only had high level knowledge of the company. He sent me additional materials which I reviewed on the flight down to Atlanta, where the company was headquartered. We met in the lobby of a hotel across the street from the company's headquarters and he provided more color. He recounted the call he received from the controller – she told him that she was declaring herself a "whistleblower" and wanted the board's protection from any potential retaliation by management. She told him that she believed the CEO and CFO were overstating revenues and understating expenses. Ugh. She didn't provide any more detail than that. It was our job to meet with her and determine if her claims had merit.

We walked across the street to the company's offices. My colleague decided, out of respect for the CEO, that we should meet with him first. I disagreed – why aren't we meeting with the whistleblower to ask more questions. He argued that the CEO deserved the right to defend himself – innocent 'til proven guilty. We told the receptionist we were there to meet with the CEO. My colleague gave his name. Within a minute or two, the CEO came down to get us. He was obviously surprised to see my colleague and to meet me. We met in his office – a model of a private jet perched on his desk – I learned later that he had purchased a share of a jet after selling his company. His office was large and immaculately decorated. We told him why we were there. He was visibly angered and immediately discredited his controller. He said that this was clearly a ploy to keep her job, because her performance had been poor, and his CFO was considering terminating her. Because we hadn't met with the controller yet, we simply listened. In addition, this guy, apparently, was an accomplished entrepreneur who had built and sold his company for over $100 million dollars. We had to operate from a position of trust. Also, my colleague did not want to believe there could be fraud - it wasn't in his best interest either. I came in unbiased - completely objective since I had no prior history or financial interest in the company.

I was pointed in the direction of the controller's office, while my colleague stayed behind with the CEO – her door was open, I introduced myself, closed her office door and took a seat across from her desk. She was clearly nervous. I did my best to make her feel comfortable. We met for almost two hours. I learned about both her professional background and a few things about her personally. She had just been through a tragedy, the sudden loss of her fiancé. I had sympathy for her. I couldn't imagine suffering a personal loss like that and, shortly thereafter, finding potential fraud in your company. The CEO would later make assertions that she was "mentally unstable". I didn't think so.

She told me why she called my colleague and I asked the accounting questions that needed to be asked. She was confident that the CFO was not accruing for advertising expenses (which were material in this company) at the end of each quarter in order to make sure that the company was compliant with its bank covenants. I thought, this will be easy to prove or disprove. I asked about the overstatement of revenues. She didn't sound as confident. She only knew that customer enrollments (this was a for-profit education company) had spiked while the company was in negotiations to be sold. She didn't believe the increases were legitimate. Ok, I could see why someone would do that – they would want to show the buyer that more customers were signing up for classes and future revenues would be higher – thereby making the company appear more valuable today.

I told her that I was here to get to the bottom of it all, that we appreciated her reaching out to us and that I would make sure that no one retaliated against her. She was appreciative and seemed much more at ease when I left her office. I returned to the CEO's office, provided only a very brief summary of the meeting, deliberately leaving out her assertions and details, despite the CEO's efforts to get me to provide him with her claims. My colleague and I met privately in a nearby conference room. I gave him the full download. He asked what I thought. I told him that she seemed credible and that it would take very little time to prove or disprove the expense issue. I asked more about the spike in enrollments during his negotiations to acquire the company. He confirmed that in the months leading up to the transaction, the company was showing strong growth – he attributed it to the quality of new curricula and programs that management had rolled out. He also said that the marketing folks had "cracked the code" with the right mix of television and web-based advertising. He didn't believe that the CEO and CFO were capable of doing anything inappropriate. He told me that the CEO, while I was meeting with the controller, had told him that he had heard number of horror stories about the controller. He didn't provide any examples or details.

We then walked down the hall and met with the CFO – he greeted my colleague in a surprised manner. It didn't seem like the CEO had tipped him off that we were in town. During the short meeting, I found him to be extremely friendly, genuine and a pleasure to be with. We didn't tell him why were there, only that we had a meeting earlier with the CEO and wanted to come by and say hello. I would deliver the news later in the afternoon when I would meet again, alone, with the CFO.

In the days and weeks that followed, we confirmed that advertising expenses were not recognized when incurred in order to avoid violating bank debt covenants. Management had committed accounting fraud. We also learned that the company had changed its call center marketing tactics in the months leading up to the sale of the company to include offering potential students a "no money down" option along with a fifty-dollar gas card if they enrolled on the spot. The call center representatives would also tell the prospective student that they could drop out whenever they wanted. This change in marketing and recruiting tactics was never disclosed to my colleague. This drove a spike in registrations that only months later would result in an identical spike in dropouts. Nonetheless, these two acts simultaneously avoided the company being in default with its bank and made the company more attractive to a buyer. It also put millions of dollars in the CEO and CFO's bank accounts from the sale proceeds.

I joined the company's board of directors almost immediately and we terminated the CEO, COO and CFO. The private equity firm never sought to recover the portion of the purchase price that was excessive due to the inflated earnings. I was shocked. I later learned that the private equity firm's partners didn't want to deal with the negative press or the distraction and expense of litigation. More specifically, they didn't want their investors, pension funds and endowments, to know that they had been fooled. It took several years for the business to recover and grow into the transaction valuation.

Another fraud I encountered was even more bizarre. On Halloween 2009, I received a call from another private equity colleague. I remember the call vividly because I was dressed as a clown, full make-up, wig and red nose. Yup, a real clown. I had created a tradition of dressing up for Halloween with my kids and the clown had been a hit the prior year, so I went with it again. The image of me having a serious conversation with a partner at a well-respected Boston-based private equity firm while dressed as a clown will never leave my memory. He told me that he had a portfolio company in

Chicago that had been audited by KPMG – he asked if I would mind taking a look at the financial statements. I said, "sure, why?" He said he was starting to have concerns about the founders, and something was *off*. He couldn't put his finger on it, but it didn't feel right. He also told me that someone raised concerns about the financial statements. I told him to send me the financials.

While my wife was getting our youngest ready to go trick-or-treating, I checked my email and opened the attachment. It took no time at all to see that something was wrong. I called my colleague back and told him that these financial statements were not audited by KPMG. There were several formatting errors that would never get through partner review at KPMG. He asked if I could go to Chicago, to the portfolio company, with him the next day.

I met him at Logan Airport early the next morning – he provided me with the necessary background on the company during the flight. The company was Canopy Financial, a healthcare transaction software company that had raised over $75million in capital. The company had won a number of awards and provided software for health savings accounts, flexible spending accounts and healthcare cost reimbursements. My colleague was on the board along with other well-respected investors, including, among others, the head of Stanford University's endowment at the time.

I had a printed copy of the financial statements with me on the flight and walked my colleague through my concerns. I had reviewed them further after putting the kids to bed and removing my clown make-up the night before. I had found issues with them including a cash flow statement that didn't foot (in accounting terms, it didn't add up). These were basic things that would never slip through the cracks at a Big Four accounting firm. He was particularly concerned, but I tried to ease his concerns by saying that "there has to be an explanation, there are too many eyes on this company". He went on to tell me that there were several influential people from Chicago, even one guy from Obama's inner circle, who were associated with this company. This could turn into a big PR mess. I was starting to worry that I may have inappropriately raised a red flag. Again, I was questioning myself because of the people involved, instead of focusing on the facts.

On the way to the company's offices, I called a friend at KPMG - he was kind enough to confirm that the company was not an audit client. I now knew for certain that the financial statements were fraudulent. I didn't break the news to my colleague yet. We arrived at the company's offices in downtown Chicago in a high-priced officer tower just off South Wacker Drive. We checked in with security and took the elevator to the sixth floor. Like my first visit to the company in Atlanta, we had not tipped off management that we were coming. We walked into the reception area, but there was not a receptionist. We waited a minute or two and then decided to walk into the main office area. The office was massive, it occupied the entire floor. We passed row after row of empty cubicles. Finally, we saw a young lady in a cubicle and asked if she could point us to either of the founders. My colleague told her who he was. She walked us back to a conference room adjacent to the reception area, and told us we could wait there, and she would let the founders know that we were there. The conference room had a glass interior wall and I was seated facing the reception area and elevators beyond.

The young lady returned to the office from the other side of the elevator bay, stuck her head in the conference room and said Jeremy would be right with us. Moments later, I saw a gentleman come out of the same doors, walking towards us – I said, "here he comes." He stopped at the glass reception doors, looked at us for a moment. My colleague turned, looked at him, waved and said, "yup, that's Jeremy." In that brief moment, I was surprised at how casually he was dressed (jeans and a t-shirt) and that tattoos covered his forearms. I am not judging anyone with tattoos, it just stood out as a feature I had not expected. My colleague had turned back to face me. I continued to make eye contact with the founder. It was surreal - he was just staring at me, motionless. He then turned away and walked to the elevators. He pushed one of the elevator buttons and stood with his head down. I said, "what is he doing?" My colleague turned and we both watched him get on the elevator. He was gone.

The other founder was not in the office that particular day. He would never return to the office. I went back and forth to Chicago for the next three months. About a year later, both founders pleaded guilty to a massive fraud and received thirteen and fifteen-year prison sentences, respectively, for their crimes. One of them committed suicide while out on bail.

They had devised and executed a fraud in which investors, sophisticated investors, had been cheated out of $75 million and clients' healthcare accounts had been pilfered to the tune of nearly $20 million. I had no previous knowledge of this company; I came in clean with no preconceived notions. In the days after the founder got on the elevator, I interviewed countless staff members, reconciled bank accounts, reviewed canceled checks, traced wire transfers and tied out transactions to the company's financial statements. I reviewed investment materials and board presentations that overstated partnerships, business development successes and the number of customers on the platform. We quickly realized something bad had gone on – no one could contact the founders.

I will never forget the day I was in one of the founders' offices going through his desk and filing cabinet. I had only been there for a day or two and we were still trying to understand what had gone on. It was late at night and I was about to wrap up for the day and head to my hotel. I was sitting at his desk and I noticed the vague remains of a footprint on his desk blotter. I looked closer and noticed some white powder on the desk as well. I looked up and realized one of the ceiling tiles was slightly out of place. I climbed up on the desk and pushed up the ceiling tile. There were two things up there: a syringe with a hypodermic needle and a DVD, although I'm sure the footprints indicated that he had removed other items the day he left. The DVD was a video of the founders partying with a group of young women at a private event at the Coyote Ugly Bar in Chicago. In the days that followed, I found transactions that included massive purchases of Chicago Cubs tickets, unusually large payments to several Chicago nightclubs, massive cash withdrawals, a NetJets share and payments for Ferraris, Lamborghinis, Arabian horses and even a house is Malibu. I couldn't believe what we had found. I was now working day and night along with FBI agents and forensic accountants.

There wasn't a legitimate business here, yet sophisticated successful investors had been fooled. How could this happen? People trusted what they were being told. They wanted to believe, they wanted to invest, they wanted the company to be successful. Were a number of important elements were missed in due diligence? Absolutely. But it is very difficult to find fraud if the perpetrator is lying, forging documents, providing you with bogus information and attracting powerful and influential people to their company. Hooking credible, influential people to their company is the icing on the cake for the fraudster - don't forget what went on at Theranos - Elizabeth Holmes managed to attract the likes of Henry Kissinger, James Mattis, George Shultz, Sam Nunn and others to her massive, $750 million-dollar scam. The honest, trusting person is almost always at a distinct disadvantage.

These two prior experiences were coming to mind frequently in the fall of 2018. I wasn't deliberately trying to recall them, but I would have dreams that brought me back to the very details of those days in Atlanta and Chicago. I am convinced that my subconscious mind was correlating what was happing at Epic to these prior experiences even if we didn't identify actual fraud here.

As my internal investigation continued, we found misrepresentations (both financial and non-financial) in the confidential information memorandum that had been provided to prospective investors; a misrepresentation to the outside accounting firm that the company had obtained a waiver of default from Epic's bank regarding its debt covenants; the budget column in a board package had been changed to make it look like the company was achieving its targets when in fact it wasn't; a $1.0 million accounting entry had been recorded to reverse expenses and book them as an asset in order to reduce losses at BBFC; management even tried recording a material transaction that hadn't even occurred – fortunately, the outside accounting firm caught it; and we finally understood the substance of the TBA transaction.

With the help of Jill, the accountant, we were able to pull the TBA journal entries recorded in the general ledger. I also pulled bank activity for the same period. I learned that the company was basically out of cash, insolvent, in late 2017. It had maxed out its working capital line of credit with its bank. We also learned that Devlin had been repeatedly warned by RevCap that if he went back to them for additional capital, it would be highly dilutive and that they likely would replace him. They were frustrated with his apparel and football initiatives and his inability to hit a budget. This likely explained why he brought me in – he likely thought that I would appease the board – they would have "an adult in the room" and he would keep his job. He probably never imagined that I was going to be so inquisitive, principled and persistent.

Nonetheless, Devlin could not ask for bridge financing while trying to close another acquisition *and* missing budget. So, I believe this is what they did. They increased the purchase price for TBA and inserted the language that the seller would have to return the excess funds a few weeks after the transaction closed. They were able to draw the funds from the company's acquisition line of credit (not from the working capital line of credit that was maxed out), pay the funds to the seller and then get the funds back from the seller shortly thereafter. By doing so, they created liquidity. As they say in late night infomercials, "but wait there's more." When the funds were returned by the seller, in two separate, unequal installments, Epic recorded the cash receipts as *revenue*. By doing so, they fabricated revenue and profits while also increasing the company's profit margin. Unbelievable.

The company continued to hold monthly leadership and quarterly company-wide calls. I remember one call in particular – it was an over-the-top pep rally of how great Epic was performing. Devlin said that Epic had achieved all initiatives over the last quarter, the company was "cranking on all cylinders" and had won a number of awards as a fast-growing company and great place to work. He also said that the company had a net promoter score higher than the likes of Apple and cited a score that was virtually, mathematically impossible. In all the forensic work we did, we never found any evidence that a survey was ever conducted to calculate the company's net promoter score. On the call, he also mentioned that he had just given a speech at a local University to students and business leaders about Epic.

I was curious about the speech, but it didn't take long to learn more about it. I received a voicemail from a friend of mine congratulating me on my investment in Epic. I returned the call and asked what he was talking about. He told me that he saw an article about the CEO's recent speech. He said that he had no idea how big the business was or its high valuation. I asked him to send me the article. Devlin had told the audience, which included journalists, that the company operated in over twenty-five countries, generated over $100 million in annual revenues and was valued at about $1.0 billion. All three statements were significant exaggerations. The valuation statement was absolutely ridiculous – six months earlier, the company was valued at a mere fraction of that amount. Things had only gotten worse since the funding. I looked at the date of the presentation, it had been only a couple of days earlier, and recalled that day vividly. Devlin had been out of the office most of the day, only to arrive mid-afternoon wearing a jacket and tie - unusual as he was always casual. He was in an unusually good mood that afternoon – apparently still riding the high of his presentation. His ego had been massaged.

After I read the article, I printed a copy and went to Devlin's office. He was available. I had the hard copy of the article in my hand. I had learned, all too well, that if you don't bring hard evidence to these meetings, you will be put through his spin cycle. I told him I had received the call from my friend and showed him the article. He read it and just looked at me. I told him that you can't make those statements. He pushed back and said that he was misquoted. He claimed that he said the company was "on track to do $100 million in revenue and to be worth $1.0 billion." I told him that I doubted the journalist misquoted him, that I had heard him make similar exaggerated statements on internal company calls. He did not like when people called him out. He said, "well, how was I supposed to know that there was a journalist in the room?" I couldn't believe that was his new defense. He said, "they should have told me there were journalists in the room." I said, "so it's ok to lie if no one writes an article about it?"

I figured while the tensions were high, I may as well ask about the accounting for the TBA transaction. At first, he disputed the transaction structure and revised purchase and sale language. He also denied needing the cash. Then he changed his story and said that the accounting treatment was appropriate (remember, he claimed he was an accounting major in college) and that the returned funds represented TBA's full year profits. I explained the accounting guidance and that backdating the transaction doesn't fly. Even if the transaction had occurred earlier, you needed to record all of the operating activity of the business not just the net profit. He then said, "well, I'm not an accountant and I don't have access to the general ledger. Maybe you should be talking to Matt, he booked the entries." At this point, I knew this was not going to end well.

Danny Finch, the interim CFO, and I had to meet with Devlin to walk him through our findings from the internal investigation of the undisclosed related party matters. We met beforehand and prepared a memo that summarized the findings, included additional questions, but did not include certain additional evidence we had found.

There were four additional items that we had discovered and needed to discuss with Devlin. Devlin and Boyle's names were associated with a proposed sports complex development not too far from Epic's office – we needed to understand their involvement and the status of the development since it appeared to be competitive with several of Epic's existing and planned product offerings.

The second item was the EpicCares non-profit that was associated with Epic. We had confirmed that it did not have formal, legal ties to Epic, but it was clearly driven by Devlin; its board members were almost all Epic employees, one of Epic' staff accountants maintained the books, Devlin used other Epic employees to work at fundraising events, and Devlin frequently encouraged employees to contribute to the charity. We had learned that a significant percentage of the funds raised by the charity were being directed to the Devlin and Boyle's hockey programs.

The third item was the use of company credit cards – we had performed a detailed review of the charges incurred on executives' cards and did not find any material misuse. However, the annual spend volume on the cards was massive. The charges included all company travel, rental car charges and gasoline for the BBFC coaches, most facility rentals across hockey, lacrosse and soccer, as well as the activity for the tours division. All of the airfare, ground transportation, meals and hotels for the tours division ran through the company's American Express Card... or so we thought. In reviewing the cards, we couldn't find where the earned points resided. We found that Devlin was being awarded the points for many of the company's credit cards and, apparently, using these for personal benefit. We also found that one of the American Express cards did not fall under the corporate cards' account, it was a separate stand-alone account. Matt Jackson explained to us that the card was Scott Boyle's personal card that Epic paid. I reviewed the card's annual spend volume and was blown away – millions of dollars! Jackson explained that the charges were for the tours. I asked why he would put his personal credit at risk for the company, why not use a company issued card (one of which he had)? Jackson paused and said, "because he gets all of the points." Those points were substantial and should have been an asset of the company.

The fourth item was related to a company incorporated in New York. Epic's logo was used on the company's website. In addition, Devlin was listed as the President of the company on filings with the New York Secretary of State – he had executed an annual report filing only months earlier.

We met with Devlin in his office and walked through each of the related party items and our findings. We told him that the hockey programs could no longer use Epic's registration system and accounting staff unless it paid a fair market fee for those services. He told us that he had already decided to move the programs to a new registration application. We also told him that we were in the process of quantifying the value of the related party transactions and that we would have to disclose the existence of transactions and respective values in the financial statement footnotes. The company's outside accountants would require it.

152

We then asked about the proposed real estate development. At first, he said he didn't know what we were talking about. When I pulled a copy of an article, written in a local newspaper, about the project, he back peddled. He said, "oh, that. I'm not involved in that – that was just an idea that Boyle and a couple of other guys had a few years ago. That didn't go anywhere." We had evidence that capital raising efforts were actively ongoing at that time. We didn't push back or share with him what we knew.

We moved on to the EpicCares charity – he dug in and said that the charity maintained a detailed record of where the funds came from and then allocated the grants accordingly. I told him that I didn't understand. He explained that if a donation came from someone associated with the hockey program, then grants in that amount would be provided to the for-profit hockey program to provide a scholarship to a family in need. I don't believe they tracked or allocated the donations and grants in that manner. We told him that the board was not comfortable with a non-profit associating with the company and that it would have to discontinue using company resources and staff and refrain from encouraging employees to contribute to the charity. We had heard from a few employees that they felt pressured to contribute and, if they didn't, it could have a negative impact on their career trajectory at Epic. Only a few months later, the non-profit changed its name and continued to work with Devlin and Boyle's for-profit hockey programs.

The next topic was the credit cards. At first, he claimed he didn't know anything about the rewards points. Then we provided him with more information – he was starting to realize that we knew the whole story. At that point, he said that he only used his points for company purposes. We knew this was not the case. We asked about Boyle. His first response was that he had no idea that Boyle was using rewards points. We then explained the separate, personal credit card and the volume of points earned through the company's spend but were provided to Boyle for his personal use. We even quantified the value of the points. He then said that he remembered why Boyle used his own card. He said that when the company was in its infancy and couldn't establish credit, Boyle had been "nice enough" to get an

153

Amex card for the company in his name. As the company grew, Devlin let him continue to use his personal card and keep the points as a "thank you." We told him those days were over.

We started to wrap up the meeting telling him that we would provide the board with a final memo and that a board member would be in touch with him to bring this all to a conclusion. He didn't ask what we thought the "conclusion" would be, but he seemed relieved. Then I realized that I had one more item in my folder, the company in New York. Like it was a second thought, I said, "oh, we came across a company using Epic's logo (I passed him a printout of the company's home page); have you heard of it?" He looked at the paper, paused, and said, "no." I couldn't believe he said "no." I said, "so, you have never heard of this company?" He said no again. I said, "then we have a real problem – they are using our logo" and I pulled out more screenshots from the website and handed them to him. While he was looking at it, I said, "and *you* have a problem… someone forged your name on their annual report," and I handed him a copy of the filing with the New York Secretary of State.

He nervously laughed and said, "oh, this, uh, this is an old company. I don't have anything to do with it anymore." I said, "Jamie, are you sure? Look at the date of that filing, it was only a couple of months ago." He looked at it and said, "well, I'm on the board, but that's it, I don't have anything to do with it." This was the perfect example of how I would ask a question and get one answer; reveal a little more information and get a spun answer; and then present more information and get a different answer. He actually said that he had never heard of the company. We had been told that he was quite active with the company; in fact, he had learned that Devlin was actively negotiating an acquisition on the company's behalf at that time. We were in total disbelief of what we had seen and heard. We felt like we couldn't trust anything he said. We submitted a memo to the board with our findings, the rest was up to the non-executive members of the board.

A few days later, my week was about to end on a real high note. I was in a meeting in the main conference room, around 3:00pm on a Friday, when I received a text from Jill, the accountant. It was the first and only time she ever texted me. The text read, "can you please meet me in the small conference room with the round table?" I thought, "this can't be good." I wrapped up the meeting and went to the smaller conference room – the door was closed. I opened the door and saw Jill and another staff accountant seated at the table. Jill was in tears. I sat down and said, "is everything ok, what is wrong?" Neither answered. I asked again. The staff accountant handed me a folder. I sat down.

In the folder were copies of canceled checks and screenshots from our accounts payable system. Neither of the women offered to explain or walk me through what I had in front of me. I took the first canceled check and reviewed it. I took the screenshot that was under it and noted that the dollar amounts were the same, but the payee was different. I looked at the second and found the same characteristics.

I said, "OK, I think I get it – someone is cutting checks to one party but recording in our accounting system that the checks are going to another party, right?" They both nodded yes. Because she was in tears, I thought it must be Jill – this would be so disappointing since she had seemed so honest and had been so helpful to me. I said, "who is doing this?" The staff accountant said, "we think it is Linda." I was actually relieved. I looked at Jill and said, "why are you crying?" She said she felt bad. She felt horrible for the company and that Linda would do something like this. I told her to take a deep breath, that everything would be fine. It took us about five minutes to figure out the scheme. In a normal company this would have been shocking, but not here at Epic. I was starting to become desensitized to crap like this.

Linda, you may recall, was the accountant who was allowed to work bizarre, flexible hours. That didn't work out so well, did it? She also had been given access, by the assistant controller, to a stack of blank checks. Mistake number one (and internal controls 101) – the accounts payable clerk should not have access to blank check stock. The assistant controller should have controlled those checks. Linda had figured out that she could open a vendor file in the vendor management module of the accounting system, prepare a pending payment to be processed and, before actually hitting print, she could change the name of the vendor. She would then print the check and change the vendor name back to the original name in the system. Therefore, the payee on the check would be someone connected to her but there would be no record of that individual in the system. It appeared in the system that the check went to the appropriate vendor.

Lori would find checks in the system that had been sent to vendors, but the vendor never cashed them. She would cancel the check in the system and re-issue the check to a family member. If and when the vendor called looking for payment, they would reach her – it rarely happened but when it did, she would delay and tell the vendor she would research the matter. If they called a second time, she would issue another check. Clearly a lack of internal controls - lack of segregation of duties, failure to safeguard the blank check stock, and so on.

But then I realized these checks had Matt Jackson's stamped signature on them. Thinking aloud, I said, "but Matt would have noticed that these were made out to the wrong payee…" The staff account interrupted and say, "no, he gave his signature stamp to Lori." Brilliant.

I had my laptop with me – I Googled the payee name and the Walmart in which the checks had been cashed (the information was on the back of the check). There were several results for the individual who lived in that area. With a few more keystrokes, I was able to determine that this individual was Linda's sister who was married and had taken her husband's last name. I asked the accountants if they felt like they had identified all of these fraudulent transactions – Jill said, "God no. We need to go through every canceled check because the information in our payables system shows that the checks went to the vendor." So, we had no idea how much had been stolen from us and how long this had been going on. I was already looking at about fifty thousand dollars worth of checks in front of me. My blood was boiling.

I left the two women in the conference room and went to find Murray and Devlin – after all this had happened under their nose and was a direct result of their inadequate of controls and processes, not to mention, they slack culture. Neither was in the office. Devlin's assistant told me they were at Starbucks – of course they were. I then went down to one of the staff members I trusted and asked him to Google Linda's name and Portland, Maine as well as the neighboring towns and bring me anything he found as soon as possible. I returned to the conference room and asked if either of the accountants knew when Lori would be in again. They said she was in the ladies' room. "Right now, she is in the office? Oh, great," I said, "could one of you please get her, and bring her to the bigger conference room?" I went in and waited.

The three women came in with her shortly thereafter. Linda had her head down and sat across from me. I said hello but she didn't respond or even look up. I said, "Linda, are you ok?" She mumbled something incoherent, still looking down. All I could see was her mop of bleached blond hair. I asked her to look at me. When she looked up, I was startled to say the least. Her eyes were red; like a demon or the devil. No joke. Without thinking, I said, "oh my God, your eyes." She calmly said, "they are contact lenses", stared at me for a moment and then put her head down again. I couldn't believe what I had seen – call me old fashioned, but I feel like this could have also been a red flag, pun intended, that maybe she shouldn't have had access to our blank checks, accounts payable system, signature stamps and the ability to come into the office whenever she liked. Did anyone in this company have any common sense?

I handed her one of the canceled checks and asked her if she had seen it before. She mumbled, "I don't know." I handed her another one and got the same response. I said, "OK, let's try this another way. Linda, you handle accounts payable for the company, right?" She mumbled, "I guess so." I said, "you guess so? Do you, or don't you?" She still had her head down and didn't answer. I raised my voice slightly and told her to look at me. She looked at me and, although it was hard to tell through the blood red contact lenses, she looked impaired. I asked if she was OK and she started to cry and talk in fragmented sentences. She said things like, "I can't do this…I've been through too much… my poor kids…I don't know where to go…". The senior accountant put her arm around Linda and was trying to calm her. I stood up and motioned for Jill to step out of the room with me.

Once in the hallway, I asked Jill if this was Linda's normal behavior, not the crying, but the head down, contact lenses, mumbling, etc. She said, "for the most part yes." I said, "and people thought this was normal and acceptable behavior?" She just shook her head. We went back in the room. I walked Linda, step-by-step, through what I believed she had done. With her head still down, she didn't interrupt or deny my allegations. The door opened to the conference room and the young man I had asked to do some research walked in – seeing the women at the table, particularly, Linda, startled him. He apologized, handed me some papers and left. I scanned through the print outs and saw Linda's name, a driving under the influence charge, picked up walking late at night on the highway, etc. Clearly, this woman had issues and needed help.

I took a deep breath and asked Linda about her children. She mumbled that she had two young sons and started to cry again. I told her that she needed help and that we would get her the help. I assured her that we would figure this out, but that she had stolen from the company and this was a serious matter. I told her that I needed her cooperation. I asked, "are you willing to help us get our arms around this?" She nodded yes. Ok, now we may be making some progress, I thought. I asked her how long she had been doing this. She paused a while, like an entire minute. It was uncomfortable, but I was not going to speak. She tilted her head side to side a few times, then said, "only a couple of months." I asked her when she did this for the first time – she said, "two months ago." She was lying – I had a canceled check in the folder that went back over six months. I said, "I'll be right back."

I left the room, called the Portland police and explained the circumstances. They told us to keep her in the building until they arrived. As I was on the phone, in walked Murray and Devlin from their Starbucks run. They nodded hello to me as they passed and then looked in the conference room which had a glass wall. They could tell something serious was going on – they both went into Devlin's office which was only a few doors down. When I hung up with the

Police, Devlin, who already looked beat up, simply sighed and said, "Oh Jesus." I told them that the police were en route and that I needed to get back in the conference room to keep Linda from leaving. They had the nerve to ask me why I called the police? I said, "why do you think I called the police? She has stolen *at least* fifty thousand dollars from us."

I returned to the conference room and Murray followed me in – I'm not sure why. He said hello to Linda and started asking more questions about what she had done. Quite frankly, it wasn't helpful. I interjected a couple times saying things like, "Don, we agreed earlier that we will get Linda the help she needs" – I felt like I needed to keep her calm. At one point, it occurred to me that this woman had stolen a substantial amount of money from the company, appeared to be impaired and desperate. For all I knew, she could have a weapon in her bag. The two accountants were talking to Linda about her kids to try to distract her and keep her in the room – it was working. At one point, there was a long silence. I was fine just letting it happen. Murray, apparently, wasn't as comfortable. He got up and said, "Linda, I will be right back." Moments later he returned, handed her five twenty-dollar bills and said, "here, take these, I want to help you out." I had witnessed some bizarre behavior in this company, but this took the cake. The former CFO just gave one hundred dollars in cash to one of his staff who just admitted to embezzling thousands of dollars from the company. I felt like these people were out of their minds.

The police arrived and I walked them through her scheme. They took Linda away. I met with the two accountants as they were already designing an audit plan to determine the extent of the embezzlement.

It was Friday and I needed to drive back to Rhode Island – I spent the two-hour plus ride providing our outside counsel, insurance carrier and board members with a summary of what had transpired.

Whenever I got home from Epic, I had nothing left for my family. I was finding that I was never mentally present at home, my mind was elsewhere. I wasn't the same husband and father that I had been before. I knew it, but I dismissed it as being so busy with work and

159

that it wouldn't last forever. I felt a duty to clean this place up, I had no other choice but to put my head down and get through it. I didn't realize how detrimental this was to my personal relationships and my health.

CHAPTER 12

In early November 2018, the board of directors came to the conclusion that Devlin needed to be terminated. Between the company's poor financial performance; the lack of processes and controls; his decision-making; accounting misrepresentations; unwillingness to allow unfettered access to company information; the continued efforts to manipulate financial reporting; undisclosed related party transactions and potentially competitive activities, he needed to go. It was pretty apparent that all confident and trust in him was gone. There was one issue that needed to be addressed - the timing and process of his termination. Devlin had scheduled a company summit the week before Thanksgiving. The summit was to be held, in of all places, a casino. When I originally heard that he had chosen this location, I suggested any venue other than a casino since we were a youth sports company - it just felt so inappropriate. He said that the casino had given the company a great deal and BBFC had held meetings there in the past and enjoyed the facility. He wasn't going to consider making a change.

The board members wanted to wait until after the summit. Immediately after the summit. I disagreed. Devlin thrived on company meetings. He loved to serve as the master of ceremonies, placing himself on stage most of the time and between sessions, he tried to create a pep rally-like setting. In addition, he was planning on communicating *his* 2019 vision to the company's employees. To allow him to host the event and engage with the employees in such a manner, only to terminate him immediately afterwards (the week before Thanksgiving) would make the board look heartless and clueless. I suggested that we either terminate him right away or wait until after the New Year. If we terminated him immediately, we could use the summit to announce the new CEO and his vision - a way of gathering the troops in person, explaining the change in leadership, soothing concerns, demonstrating that the company would be fine, answering any questions the employees may have had, etc. If executed properly, folks would breathe easier, have a break for Thanksgiving, allowing for some time and space from the termination of their CEO. If he wasn't terminated in advance of the summit, I felt we would need to leave him in place through the holidays. The CFC guys said they would make the call - one of the senior partners said, he "would handle it." He said, "I've had to terminate CEO's a number of times. It will be surgical." I was skeptical.

One of the partners at CFC called me about a week before the summit and told me that the non-executive members of the board had decided to terminate Devlin the day after the summit. We had already scheduled the board members to attend the summit and we were planning to hold a board meeting, at the casino, the morning after the summit wrapped up. He told me that we would go forward with the board meeting, adjourn into executive committee and two CFC partners, along with Tom Gates, would meet with Devlin and terminate him. I thought the entire plan sounded like a disaster. I tried to push back, but to no avail. He then told me that I would be named the new CEO. He didn't ask me if I wanted the job, instead, he told me that no one knew this industry better than me, that I was the "right man" for the job and that I "needed to clean this place up." I felt a certain responsibility to step in and try to fix things. I accepted. He told me the board would present a new compensation package, including an increased base salary, bonus and equity plans before the board meeting. That never happened.

Over the next two weeks, Devlin and others were working on the final details for the summit, including travel arrangements, hotel accommodations, a guest speaker, sales training, break-out sessions, cocktail hours, dinners, team building exercises, etc. At the same time, we were pulling together the board package which had changed

161

dramatically since the first board meeting in July. During this time, I sensed that Devlin knew something was coming. He looked tired and far less engaged than in the past. In hindsight, I believe he had to be constantly wondering what else we had found or were going to find.

I stayed at home in Providence the night before the summit. The next morning, I pulled out of my driveway and headed down college hill to get on Route 95 south. About a half a mile from my house, before I got on the highway, I noticed a black Mercedes SUV two cars behind me - at first glance, I thought it was a friend of mine who drove the same car and had an office just down the street from my house. I was going to call him, then I took another look and realized the SUV didn't have the roof rack that my friend keeps on his. I got on the on-ramp and headed south. Only moments later did I notice that the Mercedes was still behind me. About thirty-five minutes later, I took the exit to the casino and noticed the black SUV was still behind me, just far enough back that I couldn't get a good look at the driver. I thought I may have been paranoid, but I had a feeling it was Devlin - he drove the same car. I sped up to create some distance on the long exit ramp, took a right and immediately pulled into a parking lot just off the ramp. I quickly turned my car into a parking space that faced the road. Moments later, the Mercedes passed with Devlin at the wheel. He had been in my neighborhood - this guy lived in Maine, about two hours north of Providence. What was he doing in my neighborhood at 6:30am? My mind raced, this was no coincidence, I don't live just off the highway - you have to make an effort to get into my neighborhood. He and this entire company were starting to creep me out.

I arrived at the casino, parked in the main garage and found my way to the hotel check-in desk. There were a few other Epic and BBFC folks there as well, but no sign of Devlin. I checked into my room and set up to do some work. I was a bit early. No sooner did I settle into my emails and I received a call from one of the CFC partners. He told me they would be arriving around dinner time. He also proceeded to layout the plan for how they intended to terminate Devlin. The partner told me that he was "like a navy seal" in circumstances like this and that the termination would "go off without a hitch." What the hell was he talking about? According to

162

him, we were going to hold our board meeting, then I would leave so they could go into executive session. The majority of the board would approve a pre-prepared resolution to terminate Devlin and remove him from the board. They would then ask Devlin to come back into the meeting room to terminate him. The CFC partners and Gates would deliver the news to him along with a separation agreement that included a severance package.

The plan was for me to leave the casino immediately following the official board meeting and start driving north to Maine. I was to wait for confirmation from the board members that Devlin had been terminated, at which time I was going to make a number of calls from my car. I would call and deliver the news of Devlin's departure to the leaders of each divisions, our bankers, outside counsel (CFC has been getting advice from Perkins & Black rather than Epic's counsel who was based in Portland, Maine), audit firm, insurance agent, head of HR, CFO, VP of finance, marketing manager, the company's IT consultant, and Devlin's assistant. In all, I had a list of about fifteen people I would need to call - I had planned on ten minutes for each call which would consume most of the drive to Portland. I would also schedule an office-wide meeting at HQ in the morning for the staff in Portland, then head out to meet with the tours staff. I disagreed with the strategy, but they had made up their mind.

The summit covered about a day and a half and included speakers, meetings, seminars, break-out sessions, a team building exercise and social activities at night. Devlin kicked off the summit during lunch with a walkthrough of the agenda, a reminder to everyone to behave, and an explanation of how the "drink tickets" would be distributed later in the day.... I thought to myself, "give me a break." He then tried delivering one of his bastardized Tony Robbins speeches about how we all have the ability to be great and to be leaders, but it lacked the same salesmanship I saw from him in the past. Was I the only one seeing him differently because of what I knew, or had he lost his touch? I think it was a little of both - I think he knew the end was near and he couldn't keep up the charade much longer. He then introduced the guest speaker and handed over the microphone. In advance of the summit, everyone took a personality test with the results sent to the guest speaker. The speaker was a Myers-Briggs evaluator and management "guru." Only later did I learn that we paid him a handsome speaking fee and that he was a friend and former work colleague of Devlin's. We listened for nearly two hours to the guru explain personality types and how we need to adjust our behavior and communication style to suit our colleagues.

We all dispersed and went to our assigned meetings and seminars for the balance of the day. The sessions wrapped up around 5:30pm and cocktails started at 6:00pm. During the sessions, I had put my phone on vibrate. Walking to my room, I noticed that I had several text messages from Tom Gates and Jake Maddox from RevCap. They had arrived and wanted to know if I could meet with them before dinner. We met in a bar just off the casino floor. They told me that they disagreed with the plan to terminate Devlin the next day. They agreed that he needed to go, but that this wasn't the place to do it. They, too, agreed with my recommendation that we should have done it before the summit or waited until after the New Year. Gates knew Devlin better than any of us. He said that if the termination wasn't handled properly, Devlin would be disruptive to the business. He said that Devlin would be vindictive, would likely pursue a scorched earth plan - destroy the company from the outside if he couldn't lead it. While we were talking, I received a text from one of the CFC guys that they had arrived. I told them that I was with Gates and Maddox - they joined us. Gates brought up the topic with the CFC guys and tried to make his case for punting the termination out a few weeks. The CFC guys would hear nothing of it - they were fully committed to their plan.

The cocktail hour and dinner were almost overwhelming - because so many of the company's staff worked in remote locations, this was one of the few times over the course of a year when you could catch up with people in a casual setting. The next day was more seminars and breakout sessions culminating in a team building exercise in which people had been assigned to a team that had to work together to formulate and present a "wild ass" new idea, as Devlin coined it. The presentations would be delivered on a small stage in a restaurant during cocktail hour. When I arrived for cocktail hour, Devlin was seated alone at the bar having a drink. He motioned to me and I headed over. Before I could say a word, he asked if I would MC the presentations. I found this very strange - this was the stuff he loved; on stage with his staff, microphone in hand. I believe he had been tipped off that he was getting fired the next day. He wasn't humble or self-aware enough to hand off the baton this way, he simply wasn't up for the task. He looked awful. I played the role of MC for the presentations. Dinner was uneventful.

The next morning, the board meeting started at 8:00am sharp, breakfast in the meeting room at 7:30am. Three long tables, covered with white tablecloths, were assembled in a "U" formation with a projector on a separate table in the open end of the "U". The cover slide to the board package was projected on a large screen. We called the meeting to order and approved the prior meeting's minutes without any changes. I kept the board minutes. Danny Finch, interim CFO, presented the financial statements. Despite continued unfavorable variances against budget, there were no questions. This was unusual; normally, there would have been a fair amount of back-and-forth between board members and Devlin. I assume the board members didn't engage with him or ask any questions since they knew he would be fired in a couple of hours.

I had been asked to present updated findings of the forensic work and analysis we were conducting on the historical BBFC financials. The board had asked Patrick Baldwin to attend this portion of the board meeting and he was seated directly across from me, alongside Devlin. I stood alongside the large screen and walked through about ten slides that covered the rationale for the work and analysis, the methodology, key findings, financial impact, and next steps. This was an uncomfortable topic, but one that I was entirely comfortable discussing since we had put in so much work and finally understood the BBFC accounting.

We had learned that Epic, going back as far as late 2016, had been recognizing BBFC revenues based on assumptions that weren't accurate and the revenue recognition timing was inappropriate. They were using targets for the number of players registered for each team they operated instead of using the actual number of players who registered and paid or were making payments. This resulted in overstated revenues. We also believe they understated the discounts issued to families to provide incentive to register with BBFC. Again, this, too, resulted in overstated revenues. Regarding the timing of revenue recognition, revenue can only be recognized when it is actually earned; in this case, when BBFC operates the event or delivers the coaching services. Epic's accounting staff had recognized revenue before it was actually earned, particularly in late 2017. As a result, 2017 revenues had been overstated. In addition, Epic had also implemented an accounting policy of capitalizing certain BBFC expenses as prepaid assets. These included some items that made sense like field rental costs for future events, but others like legal, travel, car rental and visa (immigration) expenses, were not appropriate. As a result, we believed BBFC's 2017 expenses were understated and its profitability was materially overstated. Our outside audit firm agreed. As a result, we were going to have to restate the 2017 financial statements. This is a big deal - having to restate financial statements is an embarrassment and has an impact on tax filings, shareholders, bankers and auditors. Neither Devlin nor Baldwin said a word during the presentation.

The implications here were significant: 1) the valuation of Epic for the April 2018 RevCap and CFC financing was based on 2017 profitability; and 2) a significant portion of the purchase price of Epic's interest in BBFC, and Baldwin's proceeds, was based on 2017 profitability. I was becoming convinced that Baldwin and Devlin knew that the 2017 numbers were overstated. They both had reason to benefit from this - Baldwin would receive greater proceeds and Devlin: 1) was under pressure from the board at that time to deliver results and 2) a higher valuation for the April 2018 financing meant less dilution to him as a shareholder.

The beauty of accounting, assuming there are appropriate controls in place, is that any misrepresentations will eventually catch up to you. For example, if you accelerate 2018 revenue into 2017, 2018 revenues will suffer. If you capitalize certain expenses to the balance sheet in 2017 and have to expense them in 2018, 2018 will suffer. Even a cursory review of a balance sheet or cash flow statement would reveal unusual increases in prepaid expenses or decreases in deferred (unearned) revenue - but alas, management almost never

166

included balance sheets or cash flow statements in its financial packages provided to the board.

My analysis showed that there was unusual activity and accounting entries in 2018. I continue to maintain the practice of always "ticking and tying" interim (monthly or quarterly) financial statements to prior financials statements, both actual and budget. What does this mean? Let's start with "actual." As an example, when I receive February financial statements, they include the month of February as well as year-to-date February. I then take the January financials that I was provided a month earlier, add them to the February financials that I was just provided to make sure that they "rolled." This proves to me that the year-to-date February financials are accurate and reflect the January performance I had already been provided.

I do a similar exercise for the budgeted numbers that are included in any internal reporting package. I had performed this exercise, as I always do, when I received the June 2018 Epic financial package. But something didn't make sense - the year-to-date actuals rolled, but the budget didn't. I dug deeper and found that the BBFC June budgeted revenue and expenses had changed. Both the budgeted revenue and operating expenses had gone down about $1.0 million from the original budget that had been approved by the board and shared with Epic's lender. I had a couple of issues with this: 1) you can't change the budget mid-year and not let the board know; 2) the company had provided the budget to its senior lender with interim financial packages, surely they would have questions about this; and 3) BBFC was a relatively fixed cost model - how could operating expenses decrease dollar-for-dollar with revenue?

When I found this, I first went to Devlin, but he had no answers. I then went to the CFO... as usual, no answers. I went to the VP of Finance, Matt Jackson. I liked Matt, he seemed like a nice guy. The problem was that he was over his head from an accounting perspective and he suffered from Stockholm Syndrome - he worshipped the ground Devlin walked on. There had been moments when I thought he was about to come clean, but he would also appear to get nervous and stop short. I walked him through the June board package, compared it to the original board-approved budget, and asked how it could have changed and how expenses could have decreased about $1.0M in June alone. His eyes darted from number to number, he scratched his head, he looked out towards accounting staff and said, "I'm late for a meeting with my team, can I get back to you on this?" I said, "sure," took my papers and returned to my office. Digging in further, I was able to find the BBFC monthly closing work papers on the Google drive. I was able to get the detail that comprised the BBFC income statement. Something stood out like a sore thumb, team revenue for the month was negative... negative! I went back to the original budget, which had detailed tabs supporting it, and found that BBFC June team sales were budgeted to be just over $1.0M. Bingo! Revenue came in below budget and rather than tell the truth, a couple of months after taking in a sizable investment, they changed the budget hoping no one would notice.

But, hang on - the team revenue didn't just come in under budget, it was negative. This meant they had recognized too much revenue in prior months too. My attention turned to the expense side, $1.0 million less than originally budgeted. Again, the company's operating model had a pretty predictable and fixed expense side. It was comprised of management salaries, rent, utilities, insurance, coaches, referees and field rentals. There was no way you could possible turn down the expenses by $1.0 million in such a short amount of time. The expense details in the closing worksheets didn't provide me with any insight. However, I found a tab labeled prepaid expenses. This worksheet included a lengthy detail of line items that were clearly specific expenditures made by the company through June that the accounting team had decided related to future periods. As I wrote earlier, these included payments for things like field rentals and such for later in the year. These should be capitalized under the "matching principle" (match revenues and related expenses) of accounting. I reviewed the tab in detail and agreed with most of the items. However, at the very bottom of the tab was a single item with no description for $1.0 million. Here we go again.

Later in the day, just before 5:00pm, I went back to Matt's office to follow-up, but his lights were turned off and the door closed. I turned and walked back to my office - as I did, one of the staff accountants, Jill, made eye contact and said, "I think Matt left for the day." I said, "no problem, I'll catch him tomorrow, thanks." Back in my office, with my door shut, I stood at my whiteboard mapping out the inter-period impact on the BBFC financial statements of this $1.0 million entry. I photographed the whiteboard. Next, I sketched out the different BBFC revenue streams, where the respective supporting data resided, who controlled it, and the methods by which the revenue was recognized. I was deep in thought when someone knocked on the frame to my office door. It was Jill, the staff accountant. She said, "I'm taking off for the night, did you need me or have any questions?". I looked at my watch and realized it was almost 7:00pm. I said, "no, I think I am fine, it can wait until Matt gets in tomorrow." She looked at the complicated diagram on my whiteboard and said, "are you sure, I don't have to be anywhere." I looked at the whiteboard too and said, "would you mind helping me out?" She stepped into the office and took a seat.

We worked until after midnight. Jill had brought her laptop into my office and we toggled between the general ledger, accounting workpapers on Google Drive, a spreadsheet I was constructing on my laptop, and the whiteboard. Over the next several months she proved to be invaluable to me. She was one of only a few people I felt I could trust, she was my point of access to the general ledger (I didn't want to ask for access since it would have raised a red flag and I was concerned data would be destroyed), and she hadn't been with the company long enough to drink the Kool-Aid. She had been there just long enough to have concerns about the accounting function. Jill found the journal entry for exactly $1.0 million booked at the end of June to reduce operating expenses and increase prepaid assets on the balance sheet. The general ledger had an audit function that identified the user who recorded all entries. Matt Jackson had booked the entry.

Back at the board meeting, I walked everyone through what I had found... the changed budget, the negative revenue, the arbitrary $1.0 million entry, inappropriate revenue recognition, the audit firm's plan to restate the 2017 financials, and the impact this would have on the 2018 audit - significantly more substantive test work since the internal control environment was deemed inadequate. Gates, Maddox and the CFC guys asked questions. Not a word from Devlin or Baldwin. Baldwin, the CEO of the soccer division that was getting a proctology exam, seemed unfazed and unconcerned about it all. At one point during my presentation, he rose from his chair, walked over to the coffee station and asked a waitress, who was bringing in fresh coffee, if he could get a cup of English tea. Devlin, on the other hand, looked exhausted.

After I presented, we had our leaders from the hotel bookings and tours divisions, respectively, come in and present their preliminary 2019 strategic plans. The hotel division leaders presented first. I had worked with them in advance of the board meeting and, while their strategic plan wasn't fully complete yet, I felt they had a strong understanding of their industry / market, and good relationships with their customers. We were focused on refining their processes but needed help with marketing and sales strategies. Overall, they did a nice job presenting to the board, particularly, after the bomb I had just dropped on everyone.

Next was the leader of the tours division, Scott Boyle. Boyle was visibly nervous presenting to the board. He was overweight and sweating like a pig. You could also tell he had dry mouth, frequently sipping from a bottle of water he placed on the table in front of him. I would have assumed that Devlin had helped him with his presentation but, regardless, it was terrible. He touted himself as "knowing more about Epic than anyone, because I have been involved in so many aspects of the business." He said that the "tours division was the most profitable and best run division in the company." He even criticized the accounting department. His strategic plan for 2019 was no better. Instead of presenting a plan that expanded and grew our hockey and soccer tours, which had only scratched the surface of the market opportunity, he talked about entering new sports like baseball, basketball, team handball, tennis and golf. If I didn't know any better, I would have expected him to suddenly stop and say, "I'm just kidding, we are going to stick with what we know and do best." But no, he stumbled and stammered his way through an unsupported strategy to launch tours in sports that either didn't lend themselves to international tours, were sports in which Epic didn't have any domain expertise or were individual sports that provided far fewer travelers. He literally couldn't have chosen a worse strategy. Again, there were few, if any, questions - it seemed the board just wanted to wrap up the meeting. We covered a few remaining items and adjourned. The CFC guys said the non-management board members were going to meet for a bit and asked that the remaining board members step out but wait nearby in case they had any additional questions. That was my cue to leave. I had already put my travel bag in my car earlier that morning, so I headed around the corner with just my messenger bag in hand and walked to the parking garage.

I drove north on Route 95 for about forty-five minutes and still hadn't heard from CFC that their meeting with Devlin was over. I couldn't wait any longer, so I called one of the CFC guys who had been in the board meeting but wouldn't have been in executive session and asked if he knew if his colleagues were still meeting with Devlin. He said they had wrapped up and were heading back to New York. You have to be kidding me! I hung up and called the CFC partner who was "like a navy seal." He answered right away and acted like the plan hadn't been for him to call me as soon as they were done with Devlin.

I asked, "are you guys done, can I start making the calls?" He said, "it was great to see you; I wanted to let you know that you did a great job last night and today in the board meeting." I thanked him and tried to get him back on topic - I asked again if I could make the calls. He proceeded to tell me that they met with Devlin and "discussed" his termination. He said that they brought him back into the meeting room and he sat across from the two CFC partners and Tom Gates. The CFC partners explained the board's rationale for his termination and then gave him the separation agreement. Devlin just listened, but he refused to accept the envelope; literally wouldn't touch it. Instead of the CFC guys getting up and leaving the room, they engaged in further conversation with Devlin. Devlin seemed to manipulate them - he suggested that the real reason for their termination of him was that the new CEO must have wanted him out of the company. Instead of reiterating the actual, and justified, reasons for his termination, they simply said, "no, that's not the case." He then asked who was replacing him. They told him that I was going to be the new CEO. He said, "oh, so Steve doesn't think I add value to the Company and wants me out." Again, they said "no." I couldn't believe what I was hearing. They couldn't have botched this more if they tried. At that point, one of the CFC partners reached across the table, took back the envelope that contained the separation agreement and said to Devlin, "why don't you meet with Steve and let him decide if there is a role for you in the company." I almost drove off the road.

I was speechless. The CFC partner said, "are you still there?" I didn't answer and he hung up. It hit me, they either fucked this up, which was bad enough, or they wanted me to terminate Devlin - I don't know which was worse. The phone rang. I answered, "yup." It was the CFC partner; he said "so we told him that you would give him a call tonight and get together with him tomorrow and see if you want to keep him around, you know, if there is a role for him that makes sense... it's your call. We told him that it was ultimately your decision." He went on to say that *I* had to terminate Devlin. They wanted him out immediately. I said, "so, you didn't let him go? Do I make these calls or not?" The CFC partner put me on speaker phone and no one on the call could give me a straight answer. They tried to explain that Devlin was terminated but that I needed to finish the job tomorrow - it made no sense.

While I was listening, Devlin was calling me. What a shit show. I told them that I wasn't comfortable calling anyone until I wrapped things up with Devlin. They told me it was my call and hung up. I called Devlin back - he sounded calm and rational - he said, "I'm fine, look, don't worry about me, this is business. These things happen. I just spoke to my wife and she is upset, but we will get through this." I suggested that we meet first thing in the morning. He asked where we should meet. I wasn't going to meet the guy offsite, in some coffee shop. I suggested we meet at the office at 8:00am.

I went straight to the office in Portland, gathered my thoughts, and organized my plan for the next day. I checked into Hotel Portland around 11:00pm - it had been a long few days and I knew the next few wouldn't be any different.

I was the first one in the office the next day, it was a Thursday. I set up in the main conference room thinking we would need some privacy when Jamie and I met. I wasn't sure I wanted to meet in his office, under the circumstances, and my office looked out onto the accounting cubicles - there wouldn't be much privacy and, despite his calm demeanor on our call, I wasn't sure what to expect today.

Jamie's assistant arrived before he did - about five minutes earlier. She walked directly by the conference without looking in - I am sure she had spoken to Jamie about what transpired at the casino. Jamie arrived at 8:00am on the dot. He came into the conference room which was next to the main entrance. He seemed fine and greeted me with a "good morning" as he normally would. He was wearing an Epic baseball hat and an Epic-branded backpack over his shoulder. As he was asking where we should meet, his assistant came in and said that she and others had already reserved the conference room for the morning. She literally never looked at me. She turned and walked away. He suggested that we meet in his office and I agreed. As I was following him to his office, I wished I had met him at Starbucks. This felt strange.

I closed the door behind me as he sat behind his desk. He plugged his laptop in and said, "sorry, give me a minute." He wasn't acting like a guy who had been terminated yesterday - oh, wait, they didn't terminate him, they punted to me. I could tell he wasn't going to leave without a fight. I sat there while he appeared to be looking at emails, clearly an attempt to control the setting. Finally, he closed the laptop, looked at me with hand folded and said, "sorry, so how would you like to handle this?" I replied, "how would I like to handle what?" He said that the board had told him that I was going to take over the CEO role and it was up to me to determine the right role for him going forward. Before I could respond, he said, "I don't want this to be uncomfortable. I am good with this. I love this company, love the people, they are like family. I don't care about titles or compensation, call me the janitor if you want, I just want to be around these people, I need to be part of the company." I felt less anxious - he didn't seem confrontational. I asked, "were you able to get some sleep last night?" I was expecting him to say, "yes, slept great"; instead, he told me how he had an "awful" night dealing with

173

his wife. He said that he was on the phone with her most of the way back from Connecticut. He went on to say that when he got home, he and his wife had to meet in the basement to talk about the "situation" because she was yelling at him and he didn't want the kids to hear it from their bedrooms. This put me on my heels - it seemed polar opposite to what he had just told me. He kept talking, saying that his wife kept saying, "how many times did I tell you that you were trying to grow too fast?" He stopped talking and looked out the window to his left.

I took the opportunity to explain that it was time for him to move on; that I wasn't aware of the details of what had happened after I left Connecticut, but I *did* know that the board had resolved to terminate him. He just stared at me. I asked him for his personal email address, and he provided it to me. I told him that I would have the attorneys send him an electronic copy of the separation agreement that he left behind at the casino. He pushed back immediately. He asked me if I thought that he didn't provide any value to the company. I told him that was irrelevant at this point - the board had made the decision to replace him and we needed a graceful and smooth transition. He told me that would be very difficult if he didn't have a role, even as a consultant or advisor. He said that we would lose the tours and hockey staff if he wasn't involved - he said they had built this company together. He also said that the BBFC guys would be "really spooked" if he was gone - he claimed that the BBFC guys had agreed to the acquisition because they wanted to work with Devlin. He was hanging on tight.

This went on for a while, I had lost track of time, wasn't wearing a watch and didn't want to pick up my phone to check the time. Finally, I said that I had a meeting coming up with our outside accountants who were performing financial diligence on an acquisition target. I looked at my phone and realized I had been stuck in his trap for over two hours. I told him that I had to take a break, he immediately turned angry saying, "what the fuck am I supposed to do?" I was shocked at his language and tone. I paused and said, "go get a coffee or something and come back in an hour and a half. We can pick up where we left off." He was aggravated - I left his office and went to my meeting.

I cleared my head and focused on my diligence meeting. It was actually refreshing to be interacting with a couple of rational people and covering topics that made sense. We were walking through what we called a "cash proof" - basically reconciling the target company's historical income statements and profitability to its cash receipts and disbursements. For small companies, particularly in the event and team management space, this may be the most important diligence exercise. We were almost done with our meeting when I noticed, out of the corner of my eye, someone standing outside the conference room's glass wall. My first instinct was that someone else had the room booked. Then, I saw a confused look in my guests' eyes - I looked to my right and saw Devlin standing outside of the conference room, looking at me with both arms outstretched. When his eyes met mine, he said, loud enough for us to hear through the glass wall, "I thought we were meeting?" He had a crazed look in his eyes. He turned and walked toward his office.

I apologized to our diligence guys, wrapped up the meeting and walked down to Devlin's office. He was behind his desk looking at his monitors. I shut the door and apologized for being a couple minutes late. He didn't say anything. He closed his laptop and asked what my meeting was all about. I gave him a quick update; I couldn't believe I was doing this. I quickly changed the subject and said, "Jamie, I really think it is better that we make a clean cut here." He looked at me and said, "I disagree. I need to be involved. I have been thinking. I need to retain my board seat, need a title like President and COO, and my salary can stay where it is, but my bonus opportunity needs to be increased. RevCap has been promising me an increase in my salary and bonus for the last two years." I was dumbfounded. This is the same guy who two hours earlier said he didn't care about titles or compensation, he said he would be the janitor, he just wanted to be part of the company. This was bizarre behavior. I stopped him and took control. I told him that the board was fed up - the accounting issues, undisclosed related party transactions, the performance of football and apparel, etc. I said, "Jamie, it is time to move on." He literally started to cry, like real tears. He was also making a strange sobbing sound, then he mumbled, "I can't believe this is happening, I am sorry... I didn't

175

want to get people involved in this; I didn't mean to pull you into this…". He was looking out the window to his left and wiping his eyes. He stopped mumbling and looked at me briefly. I must have looked shocked. He looked back out the window and then, without any warning, he clapped his hands together once and grunted "stop it!" Almost instantly, he stopped sobbing and gathered himself.

I was almost frightened. No joke. I have never seen anything like this. He took about thirty seconds of wiping his eyes and then apologized for "getting emotional." He said it had been a rough night, that he didn't sleep well, and that things were not good between him and his wife. He even went on to say that his wife had just retired (which I found as an odd term considering her young age) from her job and that him leaving Epic couldn't come at a worse time. He then suggested several ways he could be helpful going forward. I listened. If I was going to even consider having him involved in the business in some form, it would be in a very limited, consulting manner, with no authority whatsoever - in fact, it would only be for optics so that those staff members and customers with whom he had relationships would view our treatment of him favorably since we couldn't, nor would we want to, disclose what a mess this place really was.

I suggested an advisory role working with hockey and hockey tours - these were both the roots of the company and the divisions in which his closest friends worked. He said he liked the idea, then immediately began talking through the role. In a matter of minutes, he had expanded its scope and his expected authority. He had everyone in those divisions reporting to him. Before I knew it, he was trying to convince me that he needed to have involvement in virtually all aspects of the business since everything was so "intertwined," as he called it. This guy was relentless.

I kept trying to reel back his expectations of an ongoing role. Every time I did, he would try to convince me otherwise. This was a useless exercise. I was getting more aggravated that the CFC guys botched terminating him yesterday and dumped it on me - this should not have been my responsibility. I could also see what would come of this; Devlin would tell the staff that I wanted his job, convinced the board he needed to go, and did the deed myself. The board should have been a buffer for me in this process. Finally, I said that I had a call with the board at 5:00pm. On that call, I would present what a role could look like for him, if any, going forward. He said, "OK, let me help you think through how to sell it to the board". Now, I wasn't just aggravated, I was offended. I said, "Jamie, I am not planning on 'selling' anything and I don't need your coaching." He must have realized by my tone that he was pushing too hard.

He backed off and said, "OK, one more thing." I had thought we were done and said, "hang on." I picked up my phone off his desk to check the time. I had just wasted another two hours of my life. I said, "this has to be quick; I have a call coming up." He said, "well, I am still a shareholder and board member of this company, so I would like to interview my *potential* replacement." This was the cherry on top - in what universe did this guy live? I didn't even know how to respond. I shook my head and started to get up to leave. He said, "no, wait" and took his wallet out of his back pocket. He removed a small piece of paper from it. He unfolded the paper - it was a normal sized sheet of copy paper. I couldn't help but think, who the hell folds a piece of paper that small and jams it in their wallet? I could see from the light coming through the window that there were handwritten notes on the paper.

He said that he had spoken to his mentor between our meetings today and that he had provided Devlin with some great insights. He told me he was going to ask me a question and that I had to answer immediately, I couldn't think about my answer. He then read directly from the paper, "if you were to become CEO of Epic, what sort of culture would you like to build?" I paused a second or two and looked to my right out the window. In that instant, I was deciding whether I should just get up and leave. He startled me with a raised voice by saying, "I told you that you can't think about the question." I said, "dude, you have to calm down." I remember it vividly because I never use the word "dude." I stood up, picked up my phone from the desk, and said, "I would love to see a culture in which customers always come first, our team loves their work, feels inspired, respected and challenged. A culture in which people know that there is upward mobility and effort, teamwork and integrity is

177

rewarded." The words just came out without me thinking about it. He stared at me for about three counts and then delivered a sarcastic, wise-ass laugh followed by, "oh, you were serious? Do you actually think *you* are capable of building a culture like that?" I wanted to slap the smirk off his face. Instead, I said, "ok, I'm done. I will call you after my 5:00pm board call" and started to leave his office. I was almost out the door and he said, "don't forget your folder." I didn't have a folder - but there was one on the corner of his desk. I told him it wasn't mine and he said, "it is now." I took it with me. I opened it about halfway to my office - it contained several formal-looking documents typed in Swedish. I later learned that this was a notice from the Swedish tax authorities advising Epic that it hadn't filed tax returns for several years. Moreover, there was a substantial unrecorded tax liability that Epic management had known about.

CHAPTER 13

I dialed into the 5:00pm board call and provided a summary of my meetings with Devlin. I hadn't even finished when Atwater, from CFC, interrupted and said, "I've heard enough - you gave him more time then he deserved." Both Maddox and Gates agreed - one of the CFC guys said he was going to send an electronic copy of the separation agreement to Devlin. I voiced my concerns about him being disruptive to both employees and customers and that we would be better off spending the dollars on a consulting agreement than a severance agreement and see if he behaved. I then spelled out what I would propose for his engagement. They preferred that we simply terminate him, but they understood the risks I had identified and agreed with my approach.

I called Devlin immediately after the board call and was firm in my proposed advisory terms. He said he was on the ice with his son's hockey team and would like to sleep on the proposal. He seemed calm and rational and thanked me. Before we hung up, I told him that I needed his Google GSuite administrative password right away. Devlin had what he and his assistant called *super admin rights* for Epic's Google account - this provided him with access and controls over everything in the company's GSuite, including email, Google Docs, file storage, even something called Google Vault. He said he would send me the password as soon as he got off the ice. I followed up the call with an email to Devlin laying out my proposal, reminding him to send over the password and asking if we could connect before 9:00am the next day. He said he would call me around 8:00am the next morning.

I waited an hour or so, no password. I called him and left a voicemail. I emailed him and texted him, no reply. I hardly slept that night. I checked my phone constantly expecting to see an email or text with the GSuite password.

The next morning, the Friday before Thanksgiving, I was in the office at an ungodly hour, around 4:45am. I have always had a habit of keeping lists - I was updating my list for the day, the weekend and longer-term tasks that I needed to tackle. One list, in particular, was still in my messenger bag - the list of people I needed to call to let them know that Jamie was no longer with the company and that I was his replacement. We were stuck in a state of limbo. I eased my anxiety by knowing, or hoping, this would all be resolved this morning. 8:00am came and went with no call from Devlin. I talked myself into waiting until 9:00am until I called him again. Just before 9:00am, I walked by his office hoping he may have come into the office, even though I had suggested that he stay away until we reach an agreement on a new role. His door was closed, and lights were out.

I called him, texted him or emailed him starting at 9:00am and every hour thereafter until 3:00pm. No response and my mind was going to very dark places concerning the deletion of emails and other files. A number of people were out of the office, either taking a personal day

179

or working from home after being at the summit the last couple of days. Murray was one of them - it didn't surprise me since he had a lengthy commute from his home down near Boston. Any chance to avoid Friday afternoon traffic would make sense for him. I knew he was close to Devlin, so I called him. Voicemail. Fortunately, he called me back about thirty minutes later. I didn't make small talk. Instead, I asked if he had heard from Devlin. He said, "why?" What a strange answer. "Because I need to talk to him - it's urgent, that's why." He'd paused and said that he had seen him earlier in the day - they had worked out at a local gym and then had coffee at Starbucks. Pretty good, I thought. The CFO can't commute to the office, but he commutes to the gym and Starbucks right around the corner from the office. He went on to say that Devlin was not "in a good place." I asked what that meant. He said he was upset about being fired and was "poisoning the waters." Again, I asked what that meant. He said he was calling a bunch of staff and telling them that "you and the board are screwing him." Great. I then told him that he needed to call Devlin and tell him to call me immediately. He said he would.

I walked down the hall and spoke with one of the few people I trusted in the office – I asked him if he had heard from Devlin today. He told me he hadn't, but he had just heard from several other staff that Devlin had called them and said that he was being pushed out of the company. He said Devlin was spreading "toxic rumors" about the board and me.

Murray called me back about ten minutes later and told me that Jamie needed some time to "clear his head" and didn't want to talk to me right now. I told Murray that if Devlin didn't contact me in the next five minutes with the GSuite password, I would have the Maine State Police go to his house. Murray said, "let me try him again." Within five minutes, my phone rang - it was Devlin. He was sugary sweet - "hey man, what's going on? Don called me and said you were trying to get ahold of me about something urgent?". I told him I had been trying to get ahold of him all day – that we agreed that we would connect this morning. I needed the password for GSuite. He said, "oh man, I'm sorry. I thought I told you last night that I was going to be off the grid for most of today. I turned off my phone for the day and needed to clear my head – I have been thinking a lot about our

180

conversation yesterday and your proposal." He was lying to me. I said, "Oh, sorry, I didn't realize that – so you have been offline all day?" He said, "yea, I even took a long walk on the beach and prayed for guidance. I decided to accept your offer and stay on as an advisor." I said, "great, can you send me the password for GSuite?" He said, "hang on, I'll send it now." He was quiet for about a minute and then I could hear him typing. Then, he said, "I just sent it." I hit send / receive repeatedly until his email with the password arrived. I told him I needed to call him right back because my wife was on the other line. I logged in and changed the password.

I called him back and told him that I knew he had been with Murray at the gym and at Starbucks. I also told him that I knew he had been calling Epic employees during the day spreading malicious rumors. Silence. I then let him know that the board had terminated him effective immediately and there wouldn't be a consulting role for him going forward. I told him his separation agreement would be sent to his personal email address shortly and that he was not to have any contact with our employees.

I hung up and emailed the board that we needed to have a board call immediately. While I waited for a response from the board members, I logged into GSuite and Devlin's email account specifically. I restored all deleted emails. A dial-in number came through from CFC. We all dialed in – I told the board about what had transpired today and that I now had control of GSuite. They were pleased that I had revoked Devlin's offer. I also let them know that I would be making the calls that were originally planned for yesterday over the weekend and then holding a company-wide call and Portland office in-person meeting Monday morning. They agreed with the plan and were both relieved and pleased that we were moving forward. Before we wrapped up the call, the most senior CFC partner said, "Steve, one more thing. Terminate five more people." I said, "sorry, what?" He said, "you heard me. Pick five more people and terminate them. I'm sure there are at least five other bad actors and you probably have a good sense of who they are – it will also send a clear message to the rest of the company that we are not going to put up with any bullshit going forward." I wasn't comfortable with this advice and didn't act on it. In hindsight, I should have listened.

I had been away all week and hadn't even spoken to my wife or kids, only the good morning and good night, "I love you" texts. I packed my messenger bag and left the office to drive the two-hour ride home, it was around 7:00pm so the Boston traffic would have been long gone by the time I crossed Route 93 north of the city. I was only in the car for about fifteen minutes and the phone rang. The caller's number wasn't in my contacts, but I answered it anyway. It was April Nash, the founder of TBA – She greeted me with her typical, overly-flamboyant "hey you!". She must think I am an idiot. I had spoken to this woman only a handful of times and she just happened to be calling me after 7:00pm on a Friday, the day we terminated Devlin. She didn't waste any time, "Can I ask you a question?" I replied, "sure, what is it?" She says, "is Jamie still with the company?" I said, "why would you ask that question?" She said she had heard rumors that he was no longer with the company. I told her that he had been in the office most of the day yesterday and asked why she was calling me about him. She went back to her bubbly self, saying, "You seem to know everything that goes on the business. OK, well, you have a great weekend and, as always, if there is anything I can do, don't ever hesitate to reach out." I thanked her and hung up.

OK... let's all take a deep breath and get our bearing straight.

At this point, I had now been involved with Epic for a little over a year.

Our board had determined that the company's financial performance was materially different than had been represented to us.

We had also uncovered a number of questionable accounting matters, undisclosed related party transactions and executives engaged in competitive activities.

We terminated the founder and CEO. I was now the CEO and was pulling on a few strings that would start to unravel everything very quickly.

Hang on tight, things are about to get really messy.

I worked all weekend… sending emails, scheduling calls and making the calls that should have been made days earlier during my ride north from the casino. I spoke with our bankers, attorneys, auditors, divisional leaders, certain key staff at HQ, even acquisition targets as I didn't want word to filter out without the message being delivered by me. Each of these conversations had their own nuances. I could be completely open with counsel as they represented the company and they needed to know what had gone on. Without withholding pertinent information, I had to be careful with our lender and audit firm – I didn't want to scare either of them to the point that they wanted to end their relationship with Epic. The staff seemed to breakdown into three categories, like a bell curve. On the left side of the curve, the tail, was comprised of those who had longstanding relationships with Devlin and / or were blindly loyal to him; the belly of the curve, which represented most of the staff, had loyalties to the company, their customers and colleagues – they were going to see how things progressed; the right tail of the curve were the select few who welcomed the change – there weren't many, but I knew exactly who they were.

When not on calls over the weekend, I was learning how to use GSuite and, more specifically, Google Vault. Vault provides administrative users with the ability to search all Gmail and Google Chat activity across an account – in our case, Epic staff, except for BBFC and the hotel bookings division, were on Gmail. I was also learning how to navigate around certain users' Google Drives. I quickly realized this was going to take an enormous amount of time and effort. The unfiltered access would now, hopefully, allow me to understand the accounting issues better, begin to get a clearer picture of the company's actual financial performance, get our arms around related party transactions and potentially competitive activities of certain current and former employees; and understand the previous acquisitions. I mapped out a strategy and tactical plan to get through the Gmail, Chats and Drives.

Late Sunday afternoon, I drove back to Portland and checked into my usual hotel. I wanted to be in the office early as I had scheduled a 9:00am office-wide meeting to discuss the departure of Devlin and my new role. I had already scripted out my meeting for tomorrow and decided to take a walk and grab a late dinner. It was a clear and cold night, but the fresh air felt good. About a half a mile down on the left was a great restaurant called Fore Street – it has received high accolades over the years. I looked in the front window and saw a seat available at the bar. I grabbed the seat and ordered a glass of wine. To my left was a couple deep in conversation, the gentleman's back was virtually turned to me – that was fine, I wasn't looking to engage in conversation. However, the gentleman to my right was looking to chat. He broke the ice by recommending a certain dish and we made small talk. He was an older gentleman, drinking a Manhattan and the bartender knew him by name – I gathered he was a regular. He asked where I was from, what brought me to Portland and so on. I engaged, even though I just wanted to eat a good meal and watch the Bruins game.

I proceeded to tell him that I worked for a company based here in Portland and, of course, he asked which one. When I reflect back on that conversation, I realize that I didn't want to answer the question. That was a terrible sign, an indication that I didn't want to be associated with the company. I didn't want to be associated with the company at which I just became the CEO – think about how irrational that seems. In hindsight, I was so exhausted, stressed and uncertain about all of things we had started to uncover that I was reluctant to talk about the company. I did, however, tell him that I worked for Epic, but I didn't tell him my role. He repeated the name back to me and said, "oh my, I attended a presentation not too long ago and saw your CEO speak – what a company! He was fantastic. I had no idea we had such great business on our backyard. That company is huge." I was quickly starting to lose my appetite.

For the most part, the office-wide meeting the next morning went as expected – daggers thrown at me from some, crossed-arm silent stares from others and a few that greeted me privately afterwards with handshakes and support. I was getting constant pressure from Atwater to terminate five more people. He told me that I needed to do it right away if it was going to have the intended impact – that I was now in charge and the former, corrupt regime had been defeated. I told him that I disagreed, that I needed time to objectively evaluate people without Devlin's influence over them. I refused to terminate anyone else until I had reason to. I couldn't fathom firing someone for "effect" – this was their livelihood. I was going to give everyone a chance. He was not happy with my decision.

The interim CFO from CFC, Danny Finch, was helping me aggregate and synthesize the additional information we were pulling together regarding the related party matters and acquisition accounting, particularly, the TBA transaction. I scheduled a call with the hotel bookings team to discuss Devlin's departure and a call with April Nash immediately after to walk through the TBA transaction. Finch was on both calls. The hotel bookings call went fine with very few questions and no apparent hostility. I had already had one-on-one calls with the two leaders, Mike Leishman and Tim Richter, over the weekend. This call was more for their staff to hear my voice, receive the news directly from me, get a sense of my style and vision for the company and, hopefully, ease their concerns about the change.

The next call with Nash started with her telling us how excited she was to be working at Epic, how I was the smartest person she had ever met, she couldn't wait to learn from me... blah, blah, blah. She was high energy and full of compliments and optimism about the future. I had learned enough to not trust her. To be clear, I believe I had been in April's company three times; a brief introduction in the office about a year ago, at a company summit in Florida about eleven months ago, and a week or so ago at the summit in Connecticut. She was artificial and I found talking to her very difficult. She commandeered the conversation and her communication style was a meandering stream of consciousness and random thoughts. Couple that with a loud, bubbly delivery and she made my head hurt. In addition, Devlin had arbitrarily promoted her to a vice president role at Epic with no job description or clear directive. I was going to have to provide her with some direction and guardrails for sure. But this call was about the transaction.

185

Danny and I asked her to explain the transaction structure, particularly, the repayment of funds weeks after the closing. She dodged the question repeatedly, saying things like she "didn't remember that" and that she "wasn't a numbers person." In no way was the conversation hostile. In fact, Danny and I muted the phone at one point and agreed that the call wasn't going to be productive, so we just let her ramble on. Either she really didn't understand the transaction, or she simply wasn't going to tell us what she knew. I began to wrap up the call by suggesting that if she remembered anything else about the transaction to simply give either one of us a call. At that point, she said, "I want you to know that I don't do sketchy" – she said it a couple of times for emphasis. I told her that I wasn't familiar with the expression and she explained that it meant that she does everything above board. "Got it," I told her. The call wrapped up.

The next day, April called me, and I asked if I could get Danny – she agreed. He was in the next office, so I pulled him into the call. She made the usual small talk for a bit, then said she remembered a couple of things about the transaction. She told us that it was Devlin's idea to increase the purchase price and add language to have her return the funds later on. She said she didn't understand why he was doing it and she asked him to explain it. She remembered him saying that his "board of directors was up his ass and he needed her earnings." She said, "that's all I remember." We told her we appreciated the call – she pressed for when we could schedule a time to talk through her role going forward. I told her that I would send a calendar invite shortly.

After the call ended, Danny and I discussed it further – both what we had just heard and the accounting entries that inappropriately created revenue and profits. I also raised a new issue – I told him that I couldn't understand why she would agree to change the purchase agreement and put herself at risk, if there wasn't a quid pro quo. There had to be something in it for her. Also, if she had integrity and ethics, she would have walked away from the transaction at that point. Why would she want to work for a company or CEO who operated like that? We decided to call her back. She answered and I told her that we had one more question. I had no issue asking the question. This company had made me quite comfortable being uncomfortable.

I told her that Devlin must have given her something in return for changing the terms of the transaction. She was calm, but immediately reminded us that she "doesn't do sketchy." Danny had pulled up her photo and bio on the TBA website and was pointing it out to me while I was talking to her – it was distracting, but he kept pointing at it like it was relevant to the conversation. I looked more closely and realized she had actually included the quote, "I don't do sketchy" in her bio. Wow, what a professional and compelling tag line.

While I was reading the bio, she continued with a lengthy explanation of how she had built her company, that she didn't need to sell her company, but wanted to be part of something bigger. She sounded like she was getting frustrated as she spoke. Neither Danny nor I interrupted her. She then said that Devlin "sold her a bill of goods and that she didn't realize that he was such a 'scumbag'." She was rambling on and on. She then said, "you know, he told me that I shouldn't talk to you." I said, "I'm sorry – what?" She explained that about a week ago, Devlin called her and told her that she shouldn't talk to me. He told her that I thought she was "stupid," that I was asking questions about the TBA transaction, and that I would twist her words." I told her that I didn't think that of her and that I had no intention of twisting her words. I told her that we were simply trying to understand why the transaction was structured the way it was. She went silent for a moment. I couldn't help myself – I said, "April, there had to be something in it for you to agree to those changes." She raised her voice and said, "OK, OK. I needed to show my bank that I had extra money in my account because I was getting a mortgage for a condo. But that was it."

I was shocked. I said, "thank you." She said, "you're welcome, now can we just move on?" I said "of course, but I am amazed that in one small transaction, someone could efficiently manipulate financial accounting, mislead a commercial lender and, perhaps, inappropriately secure a personal mortgage... all in one transaction – pretty impressive." She did not find the humor in it. The call wrapped up. The next day I received another call from Nash – one that would prove to be another massive distraction.

It was mid-morning when she called – I picked up hoping that she had more information. Instead, she immediately told me that she was the victim of sexual harassment and a hostile work environment. I almost fell out of my chair. I told her that this was a serious matter and that I would like to have Danny and her on the call as well. She agreed. I got Danny from his office and told him to "hold onto your hat." Of course, our HR manager wasn't in the office. April proceeded to tell us that earlier in the year, approximately eight months earlier, she had experienced a couple of uncomfortable moments while traveling with a couple of male co-workers. She claimed that the three of them had been out at a bar together, after which they took a taxi back to their hotel. While in the taxi, one of the co-workers, in the back seat with Nash, made an inappropriate comment. She said she didn't feel threatened, but the comment was not appropriate in a workplace. Upon returning to the hotel, the three co-workers of them went to the bar for another drink.

I had been CEO for all of a week, now this. I asked if she reported the incident earlier. She said that she reported it to Devlin immediately after it happened and that he told her this was a "great growth opportunity for her. An opportunity to develop her leadership skills and resolve this directly with her colleagues." I was speechless - a female employee claimed she was subject to inappropriate behavior in the workplace and the CEO told her that it was a *growth opportunity*? - oh boy. Before I could ask another question, she said it didn't end there. She said that some of her male work colleagues, including the one who allegedly made the inappropriate comment in the taxi, "frequented strip clubs while at industry conferences and while entertaining clients and that it made her uncomfortable."

I told her that we took matters like these very seriously and that we would need to conduct an internal investigation immediately. She said she appreciated us taking action. I told her that we were calling outside counsel immediately and would get back to her as soon as possible. I also told her to avoid any interaction with any individuals in the company that made her feel uncomfortable. We hung up and called one of our attorneys at Perkins & Black. In the months that followed, we spent hundreds of thousands of dollars on attorneys providing the company with advice and attorneys conducting an independent investigation, including traveling to conduct interviews with all parties involved. This should have been handled appropriately eight months ago.

Epic's human resource manager claimed that she knew nothing about the complaint raised to Devlin in April. Our attorneys reviewed the personnel files of all parties involved and found no record of the complaint. Only months later, did the human resource manager remember that Devlin maintained a separate human resource folder that contained complaints. In that file was a record of Nash's complaint among others.

From time to time, we had follow-up questions for Nash regarding the TBA transaction, including the company's historical financial statements. Along with the other prior acquisitions, we were trying to assemble diligence materials to understand the transactions, the respective valuations and set realistic expectations of what these businesses or events should be generating for revenues and profits under Epic's ownership. We were particularly careful and professional with Nash in light of her complaint. She quickly became defiant and refused to provide financial statements, even though the TBA books and records legally belonged to Epic since the acquisition was for substantially all assets of TBA. Danny and I were both interacting with Nash during this time - it was painful.

Then, out of nowhere, Nash filed a complaint against me. A rambling complaint with human resources that claimed that I was hostile towards her, preventing her from doing her job and that I had made sexual comments about her to others (unnamed) in the company. I was furious, these were absolutely false. I could see what was going on – she was fearful that we were going to terminate her because of her participation in the TBA transaction. So, she decided to lob a false complaint against me knowing that the company could not take action against her for fear of a discrimination and retaliation claims. I had never dealt with anything like this before and it was frustrating to say the least. Next, she filed a

189

complaint against Finch who had become her primary point of contact. Then, she filed a complaint with the State of Maine detailing false allegations against me – these were in the public domain. Finally, she started sending letters to the board of directors demanding my termination and a meeting with the board. Only months later would we learn that Nash had another job while working for Epic. We also learned that she was trying to peddle socks, yes socks, that *cured autism* while working for us.

All of this was distracting to say the least. But what frustrated me the most was that I took the appropriate action to engage counsel to investigate her complaints that Devlin buried while he was CEO and, yet, she was attacking me. Just when I thought it couldn't get worse, I received an email from Steve Lomax, Epic's project manager. He forwarded me an email with the subject line "Whistleblower" and wrote in the body of the email, "did you receive this?" I hadn't received it. The email went to dozens of Epic employees. It was an attack on me, strewn with false allegations, and sang the praises of Jamie Devlin. It was calling for people to file their own complaints against me or to leave the company. It provided links to Nash's public complaint as well as copies of letters she had sent to human resources and the company's board of directors. You can imagine the noise this created. I had literally flown from office to office, meeting with our staff so they would get to know me, talking about our company's values and our vision. I was trying to get everyone to focus on what we should be doing everyday - delivering great experiences for our customers, caring about our athletes and providing the most value to parents. Instead, I was trying to show everyone that the figurative mugshot of me in the whistleblower email was not the real me.

In GSuite, we blocked the Gmail address that sent the whistleblower email. Unfortunately, we missed one group of our staff's email addresses and a second email came through – even more toxic than the first. The scorched earth strategy had begun.

I felt like the "bell curve" was shifting to the left – more people were skeptical of me. How could they not be – people always say, "where there is smoke there is fire." But in this case, the allegations against

190

me were all false. It was so frustrating. On top of it all, Nash was now claiming that I was leaking information about her complaints which supposedly resulted in the anonymous whistleblower emails. She was claiming that these emails were damaging her. She claimed that neither she nor anyone associated with her was sending the anonymous emails. What a circus.

We had retained an additional law firm in Boston – Powell, Sutton and Murphy. Ben Powell was our attorney – he had been a prosecutor in the U.S. Attorneys' office prior to establishing his own firm with partners here in Boston. He was a litigator at heart. Ben came highly recommended, was known to be very bright, a great legal strategist and tough. In fact, he could often be tough on me and I was his client. We had brought him in to look into the accounting irregularities and related party matters, but now I needed his help with Nash and the whistleblower emails. I had been working closely with Ben and one of his colleagues Paul Mooney, providing them with emails, chats and files we had sourced from GSuite related to the accounting irregularities and related party matters. We had developed a good working relationship and, I believe, mutual respect and trust. When Ben read the allegations against me in the context of everything else that went on in this company, I knew he believed me and knew that the allegations were false. I had never been in a position like this before and it was remarkably comforting to have someone like him on your side. For fear of sounding sappy, I will always consider Ben a friend for being there for me and being supportive at such a difficult time.

Sitting in Ben's office one evening, he, Paul and I were reading through the whistleblower emails trying to find indications of common writing style, language, formatting, anything that would provide us with a hint as to who was sending these. These emails were intended to be destructive to the company, we needed them stop and we needed to know who was sending them. Paul suggested we subpoena Google for the user information related to the Gmail account from which the anonymous emails were sent. It was brilliant. Ben agreed but expressed concerns about whether the subpoena would be granted, whether Google would fight it and how long it would take. We understood the risk and had nothing to lose. Paul filed with the federal court in Boston the next morning.

That evening, I went through a five-hour interview with the attorney and her paralegal who were conducting the independent investigation into Nash's complaints, which now included me as a defendant. The interview was conducted at Perkins & Black's Boston offices. We started around 5:00pm and I left shortly after 10:00pm, a nice way to wrap up a busy Thursday. It was the first time I went through an interview like this. I was surprisingly comfortable with the process and never took a thing out of my messenger bag, not a note, nothing. The attorney was professional and well prepared, with stacks of folders containing individual documents and emails. It was refreshing to answer the questions and address the false allegations. I had handled the original complaint appropriately and never did any of the things that were alleged about me.

Over the weekend, I had finally moved into Devlin's former office – I had been reluctant to, but certain board members forced me to. I had two whiteboards in my office that I used frequently – one large one facing my desk and a smaller one to the right. The larger one often included graphics about the industry, our divisions, accounting and systems, and the like… nothing I was concerned about other employees seeing while this white board was visible through the glass door to my office. The smaller whiteboard was not visible through the door – this one often included information about litigation or other sensitive matters.

The door to my office was always locked. I kept the passive RFID key fob that provided access to the main entrance, and the key to my office on the same ring. After unlocking my office door each morning, I would put the ring in my front pocket. If I was in my office, not on a call or meeting with someone, my door was open. I was a creature of habit. However, I had noticed on several occasions that my door was unlocked when I arrived in the morning. It wasn't the cleaning crew, because we had to leave our trash and recycling outside of our office doors since the crew didn't have a master key. And since I never unlocked the door from the inside, I was certain someone was coming into my office. This was disturbing not only because I often had legal strategy on my whiteboard, but my desk was always covered with files that contained documents related to other sensitive matters. I was convinced that certain people now knew what I knew and they were going to do everything in their power to damage or destroy Epic – I knew they had moved on to a scorched earth strategy hoping that the business would fail before the truth would come out.

FORENSICS

"You got good and bad people everywhere."

Suge Knight

CHAPTER 14

We were continuing with our acquisition strategy despite all the other turmoil we were trying to manage. We had sent a message to the marketplace that we were going to be the consolidator of the high quality, elite youth sports space and we had a healthy pipeline of deals. Every week, we were seeing new opportunities. Our board was asking why it was taking me so long to get deals over the finish line; they wanted to put money to work faster.

I held a weekly update call with the board and provided pretty granular detail of all of the issues and initiatives we were managing, plus updates on our acquisition pipeline. They seemed to understand the challenges – however, I don't think they fully comprehended the toxicity of the situation. Most of the board lacked operating experience - it was hard for them to put themselves in our team's shoes. One consequence of this was that I wanted to be very careful about who else I brought into this company - particularly, acquisitions. I was consistent in my position that I was going to be prudent and selective when pulling the trigger on transactions. I also was concerned about our ability to on-board and integrate acquisitions. Neither the processes nor the right people were in place yet. I did not want to repeat Epic's mistakes of the past, nor disappoint sellers who would be joining our team.

Nonetheless, I made the decision to keep the acquisition pipeline alive, but to be deliberate, while making some organizational changes. The first change was to open an office in Boston. In order to attract talent for Marketing, Human Resources, Information Technology and Finance & Accounting, we needed to be closer to, or actually in, Boston. Second, we were in active negotiations with Nike, adidas and others for a global partnership and sponsorship - whichever partner we went with would have team members and outside agencies engaged with us frequently; we needed to have a location close to Logan Airport. The city of Boston and State of Massachusetts were also offering us certain assistance and incentives to have a presence in the city and my quality of life would certainly improve if I could take the commuter rail every day and sleep in my own bed at night. We would initially take a small, flexible space in Boston.

I was actively recruiting, with the assistance of a head-hunting firm, a high-quality Chief People Officer to be based in Boston. I viewed this role as one of the most critical to the business and this hire would be my business partner – Epic would only be successful sourcing and retaining the best team members up and down the organization if we had a great CPO. This would require a professional who shared my vision, could be brutally transparent and challenge me, and was comfortable designing and implementing an HR organization, processes and tools. I met with a number of candidates, but one clearly stood out – Laura McNamara.

Laura was already located in Boston, worked in the hospitality industry earlier in her career and was currently with a global insurance company. The headhunter knew of Laura, but also knew that she wasn't actively looking for a new gig. She reached out to her nonetheless and Laura decided to come in for an interview. During the interview process, Laura came across as friendly and approachable, but also confident and assertive. It was abundantly clear that she was proficient in all areas of Human Resources, but there was something unique about Laura. I don't always adhere to traditional interview techniques, but instead, I end up having a conversation with a candidate, and in the case of Epic, found myself sharing more about the company than asking questions of the candidate. I also believe that a candidate deserves the right to get to know what they may be getting themselves into.

I said there was something unique about Laura - in my interviews with her, I shared what a strange and challenging ride Epic had been for me. I didn't hold back, I put it all on the table. In fact, there was a moment when she asked me how I was holding up. No one had asked me that other than my wife. Not even my board members. She told me that Epic sounded like a great opportunity to "clean up the mess and build something really special." She also saw an opportunity to reshape the business, to really focus on the athletes and families and find ways to impact the local communities in which we operated. She told me that the absence of an HR staff, established processes or integrated applications sounded like a clean slate. She viewed this as something she could build. She told me that she "wasn't afraid to get her hands dirty." She was the right person for Epic and fortunately, she took the position. In case I forget to say it later, she outperformed my expectations.

Next, I would have recruited my CFO; however, I was still waiting on an accounting & finance organizational and staffing plan from my interim CFO. He also lobbied to stay in the role longer to finish some other initiatives – it was difficult to push back as he was a partner at CFC. Also, I knew that moving the accounting & finance staff from Portland to Boston would be impossible during our financial statement audit, which had just kicked off. It would disrupt the entire process. Plus, we still had some time on our lease in Portland. My thought was to keep accounting & finance in Maine and move the tours team into the office with them to take advantage of available space and eliminate the frat house. Then, ultimately, consolidate all corporate functions in Boston.

Next, I prioritized our director of IT recruiting efforts. The company did not have anyone in this position as Devlin had played the role along with outsourcing certain technology functions to one of his friends. Recently, we had been relying on a consultant recommended by CFC – she was doing her best but was not based in the area and had been dealing with some health issues. It simply wasn't working. The company utilized so many different applications, lacked data security processes and a formal disaster recovery plan, and employees were using their own devices. Consequently, the company had no way of securing the hardware - we couldn't definitively control who or what was getting into our company's systems through those devices. Technology would play such a critical role in this company that we needed a competent director of IT as soon as possible. Fortunately, we found her, Emily Woods. She was awesome – brilliant, dedicated and a real character. She had served in the military and was currently head of technology for a company based in Boston. We were lucky to get her. As they say in sports, she had a *great motor*. She was smart as hell, energetic, kind and funny. She was a great addition to the team.

Steve Lomax, who had interned for Epic while in college getting his MBA, joined full time and later would take on a number of miserable projects under prior management, agreed to move to Boston. He was honest, dedicated, driven, polite… you name it. He was our next great addition to our Boston office. He focused on acquisitions but provided support in other areas whenever necessary. He was a great set of hands.

We took a small, open space at the WeWork in the Seaport. We felt like a start-up with everything that needed to be built and implemented, but had revenues, divisional teams and traction in the

196

market. Our small group had decided that we were going to rebuild the culture and the vision for Epic our way. No more spin, no more bullshit, no more self-serving behavior.

Next, we started the planned move of tours into the Portland office. I wanted Boyle's buy-in. In hindsight, I shouldn't have cared, but I was holding out hope that people would come around. I sent him an email, explaining my rationale. I told him that we had individual offices with privacy for each member of the tours' staff. The main office was larger, cleaner, virtually brand new compared to the frat house and the tours team would be co-located with finance and accounting. This would facilitate more interaction between the two groups and, hopefully, resolve some of the challenges about which Boyle had been so vocal.

He replied to my email, basically telling me it was a bad idea. He said that he preferred the current office. He copied a number of his staff on his reply - not a good move. Almost immediately, I was hit with several other emails from his staff members. They were all aligned. They *told* me they weren't moving to Portland. The excuses included: "we just put a lot of work in renovating our office (I assumed they meant building the bar); "there is no privacy in Portland and, you don't understand, we are on the phone with customers all day – WE NEED PRIVACY"; "we have a special culture here at tours, not like the Portland office; and "we don't need people watching us all day."

Instead of simply issuing the mandate to move the office, I tried including Boyle in the process – it had totally backfired. Now, he was using it to rally his troops against me. I called him and asked him to get his guys on board. He told me that he couldn't, that they were not interested in moving to the Portland office. I said, "I don't want to sound like a jerk, but I really don't care if they are interested or not, we can't keep your office when we have plenty of space in Portland." He said, "why don't you forget about opening the Boston office?" This was useless. I called his most vocal staff member who liked using all CAPITAL LETTERS in his emails to emphasize his point. This practice was a shame because his emails reminded me of John Irving's *A Prayer for Owen Meany*; in which Owen's dialogue is always in CAPITAL LETTERS. I love that book but couldn't stand the staff member who was sending me the emails. Hopefully, the day will come when I can read something in all capital letters and *not* think of that jerk.

The call went just about as I would have expected. He was rude – he wanted to debate my rationale for making the move. Finally, I asked him how long he had been with the company. He told me. Then I asked what he did before he joined Epic. He said, "none of your business." I was shocked. I couldn't imagine speaking like this to anyone, let alone the CEO of your company. I asked why it was none of my business and he said that I had no right to ask him these questions – I'm not sure why he felt that way. I told him that I was just curious what his background was and continued, "let me give you some advice. I have heard from others in the company that you know your stuff and do a really good job with the tours. That's great. But your attitude and the way you are talking to me doesn't seem so great. I think you need to take a deep breath and realize that moving the office to Portland is the right thing for the company, the tours division and the staff." Without a pause, he said, "I don't need to take a deep breath and I'm not moving to Portland." He hung up. Houston, we have a problem.

Laura and I discussed the tours situation and decided to bring the tours staff together at the Portland office to have a meeting. The goal was to hear why the staff was so defiant, ease their concerns, give them a walk-through of the office and show them that the space was a significant upgrade. In hindsight, I probably should have shoved the decision down their throats, but I was trying to be inclusive and win people over in light of the all that was going on. Keep in mind, I didn't know that the tours staff was also being lied to at the same time – told that I was planning to eliminate their bonuses and cut their pay.

I picked up Laura when I drove through Boston and we headed to Portland – we reviewed our plan for the meeting one more time during the drive. The intent was to have a town meeting of sorts and listen to their concerns. This wasn't an act, I genuinely wanted to know why they were against the move and so hostile. It was snowing that morning. When we arrived at the office, there was a couple of inches of light powder on the ground. We walked around the office and chatted with the accounting staff and a few marketing folks who were still located in Portland, then we set up in the main conference room. The tours staff started to trickle in shortly thereafter. Observing their body language was so interesting – although, the conference room was immediately adjacent to the reception area and I was seated where they could see me when they arrived, they stood awkwardly in the reception area like they *wanted* to be visitors. They refused to accept this space as their own. Even when I welcomed them and said, "hey guys, come on in," one of them replied, "we are waiting for a few more of *our* people" and stood their ground. I thought to myself, "this will be a fun meeting."

When the entire tours team arrived, about a dozen of them, they came into the conference room. Laura and I stood up and tried to shake hands and greet them all as normal human beings would – instead, most just took their seats, a few pushing their chairs back from the conference table, and avoided eye contact. Once everyone appeared settled, I thanked them all for coming to the meeting. I then suggested that we go around the room and introduce ourselves, tell us how long you have been the company and describe our respective roles - I did this for Laura since she hadn't met everyone yet. There was an awkward moment when no one would start, so I had to intervene and ask the person to my left to begin and direct them to go around the room clockwise. It felt like this group was incapable of self-organizing. About halfway around the room, one guy introduced himself and said that he "wasn't sure how long he had been with the company," which drew laughter from his colleagues. He seemed like a real clown. I took a closer look at him and realized he was wearing shorts and was barefoot. Again, it was snowing outside, the temperature was below freezing, and this guy was wearing a t-shirt, shorts and no shoes. Not to mention how inappropriate it was to attend a company meeting with the CEO and CPO in that attire.

I asked him why he was dressed like that – he said, "it's comfortable" and a few of his colleagues all giggled. I'm sure there were a few in the group who were good people, but the majority were a problem. I replied, "well, for one, you are going to catch pneumonia wearing shorts and walking around barefoot in a snowstorm and two, that is not appropriate attire for the workplace. I will expect that you dress appropriately going forward." He didn't respond, instead he gave me a blank stare. The staff member who liked to email in CAPS then spoke up – he said, "see, this an example of how our culture is different than yours – we don't care how people dress as long as they get their work done. This is one of the reasons it doesn't make sense to try to move us to this office, it won't work." Thankfully, Laura responded. She gave a very calm and professional response about the need for consistency of workplace attire and other policies across an organization. They just listened and remained silent when she finished.

I then walked everyone through the reasons and benefits for relocating their office. When I was done, I told them that we could go around the room and hear their concerns. I did, however, tell them that the decision had been made and this forum was an opportunity for us to ease their concerns and find solutions to any valid operational issues that could arise from the relocation. This was met with a couple of sighs and groans. Shoeless Joe Jackson spoke up and said, "then why are we here?" I replied, "I just told you – to hear your concerns and find solutions to your concerns so you feel good about the move and you can do your jobs efficiently and effectively." He said, "that all sounds good, but we don't want to move." Another individual spoke up and said, "yea, we are going to stay in our office – we like it there." Laura was very helpful – she responded in her typical calm and polite manner, sticking to the facts that justified the relocation. Unfortunately, this group would not buy in – it was obvious. To this day, I am amazed at how defiant they were when their rationale was so flawed. Clearly, they were simply digging in to be disruptive.

When it appeared that the group may have been done pushing back, their ringleader spoke up again. In an aggressive tone, he said, "I don't think you even understand what we do. We work our asses off all year, and we are away from our families all the time. When we are in town, we want to work in our office, the way we want to work – we don't want people to tell us what time we have to come in in the morning and what time we have to stay until at night." I was glad he said it. I told him that I understood the hyper-seasonality of their business, the long hours leading up to the tour, the time away from home and the time required to wrap up the tour, organize expenses, etc. I said, "I am the least parochial person you have ever worked with – meaning, I don't care when you arrive and when you leave the office as long as the job gets done. I have over five hundred employees; do you really think I have the time to watch you? You will each have your own office here – you don't have that now. You will have two tours-dedicated conference rooms – you only have one now. Privacy for calls is not an issue here. What am I missing?" He shook his head, looked at one of his colleagues and said, "he doesn't get it." I asked what it was that I "didn't get?" He wouldn't answer. He just kept shaking his head.

There was an uncomfortable silence that made me feel like the meeting should end. I was waiting to see if anyone had anything else to add or any additional questions. I let the silence sit for a minute or so. Directly across from me, a gentleman finally spoke up. He said, "I don't think you understand the sacrifices these people make for the company." This character wasn't even an employee. Instead, he was a former employee who had left the company and negotiated a half-baked consulting agreement under which he sold soccer tours for a commission. Only later would I learn that he was one of Devlin's college roommates. He also was helping recruit international hockey players to attend Devlin and Boyle's hockey academy and had a son who played in their program.

I told him that I understood the sacrifices they made. He told me the amount of time away from home made it tough on these people and they needed their own space when they returned. I told him he was overstating the sacrifice. I said, "no offense, but these people aren't returning from war; they are coming back from places like France, Italy, Switzerland and so on." He said, "yea, but they are away all of the time." I said, "you are speaking in hyperbole – they are not away 'all of the time.' How many weeks a year do you travel?". He took a moment and said, "eight to ten." I said, "there are fifty-two weeks in the year, that's not all the time. And, it's part of the job. I travel a lot more than eight weeks a year. I bet I'm on the road for portions of twenty-five plus weeks a year." He said, "ok, but you make a lot more money than we do." I could feel my temperature rise. I said, "you don't know what I make. Would any of you like my job? Seriously, anyone?" No one said a word. I asked if anyone had any more questions. No response. I thanked everyone for their time and told them that Laura and I would get back to them with next steps.

I received a call the next day from Shoeless Joe during which he told me that if we still planned to move the office, then most of the tours staff was going to quit. He told me that this would *ruin* the tours that were coming up in six to ten weeks. I simply said, "great, thanks for the feedback." This group was toxic. At the same time this was going on, we also had learned that, during work hours, some of the tours staff were drinking alcohol and gambling on European soccer games using offshore betting sites. When I learned this, I was furious. I decided to let them think they had won, get through the upcoming tours and then make some major changes.

I had a west coast trip scheduled with two days in Colorado and two days in California for in-person meetings with potential acquisitions. With everything going on, making this trip was the last thing I wanted to do, but I had to keep the acquisitions alive. I decided I could also use the in-flight time to review Google Vault and Drive information that I hadn't had the time to get to – there were emails, chats and files that I needed to review and provide to our attorneys. We were still dealing with the accounting irregularities, related party matters, non-compete issues and the harassment claims. I needed to go through a number of folders and files for the attorneys. Ten to twelve hours in the air of uninterrupted time should get it done.

I was about thirty minutes in the air from Logan to Denver when I started using Vault to review Devlin's Epic email – I used key word searches to focus on the related party matters, accounting irregularities and the acquisitions. I was working backwards chronologically when one particular Google Chat jumped out at me because of the date, it was my birthday and wedding anniversary. I opened the Chat and found it was between Devlin and Murray. Murray was in Puerto Rico at the time and Devlin was trying to get Murray to accept an invite to join a video call. Murray was having difficulty getting on the call, either due to poor bandwidth at the factory or his own incompetence. Either way, after trying repeatedly, Devlin gave in and said, "let's just chat." He then said, "Griffin just left my office. He figured out the TBA thing. He is saying that the accounting isn't consistent with GAAP (which means generally accepted accounting principles)." Murray's reply indicated he was concerned. Devlin proceeded to tell Murray that this could be a problem and that Murray needed to put something in the TBA acquisition folder that indicated that the outside accountants had reviewed and signed off on the accounting treatment. Murray agreed.

I then changed my Vault search criteria to focus on communications between Devlin and Murray with the key word TBA. I read through several emails that were benign, but then found one with the subject line "Weekly Thoughts." It was sent by Devlin to Murray and Jackson. I couldn't believe what I was reading. It was sent during the same time when CFC and others were considering investing in Epic; hell, they were actively engaged in their due diligence. The confidential information memorandum had already been distributed to potential investors. The "Weekly Thoughts" email raised a number of operational and financial concerns Devlin had about the company – it indicated that the company was not going to achieve its budget for 2017 and that they would need to get "aggressive with revenue recognition," "take all of TBA's profits for the year," and a few other incriminating recommendations. He even acknowledged that BBFC was not going to hit its targets and that "we may have to get aggressive with revenue and expense management. We need to hit these numbers and so does Patrick for his earn-out." He basically spelled out the game plan to cook the books. At thirty thousand feet, sitting alone, I stared out the window in shock.

I saved the email as a pdf and forwarded one to Powell and another to Danny Finch, our interim CFO. In the body of the email to Powell, I wrote "you are not going to believe what I found – see the attachment. I am in the air and land in about five hours, I will call you as soon as I land." To Finch, who I knew was in the Portland office, I wrote, "terminate Murray immediately, see the attached. Do not let him let him touch his computer before you get his GSuite and Platform passwords. Please provide those passwords to Steve Lomax and he will change them immediately."

Danny and I had asked Murray, on several occasions, about the TBA transaction, accounting irregularities and other questionable matters. In every case, he played Mickey the Dunce. Yet, here was evidence that he knew exactly what had gone on, helped execute it and hide it from us. Danny replied almost immediately, "Great, heading to his office now."

I spent the next five hours using Google Vault. There was an abundance of incriminating information. I was able to locate the emails between outside counsel and Devlin leading up to the TBA closing. In the days leading up to the closing of the transaction, Epic's outside counsel advised Devlin that he would have the closing documents uploaded to DocuSign, a digital signature application that Epic had been using for executing other legal documents, including recent acquisitions. This would allow for an efficient closing, the seller wouldn't have to come to the office, or respective counsels scan documents and FedEx packages. DocuSign had become a pretty ubiquitous tool.

The closing for an acquisition isn't much different than closing on a house. If done in person or electronically, both parties review the documents with their attorneys; the respective attorneys walk the seller or buyer through each document, explain the substance of the document, call out key elements of it, and you sign. Wire instructions would have been set up in advance with funds going to one of the attorneys or an escrow agent. Once all documents were executed and both sides' attorneys were good with the executed documents, the funds would be released.

Instead of closing the transaction using DocuSign as he had done with previous acquisitions, Devlin advised counsel that they were going to do a "wet ink" closing. In an email, he told outside counsel that Nash was "old fashioned" and wanted to come to Epic's office to sign the documents. Simultaneously, he told Nash that she needed to attend the closing. We did not find any communications from Nash indicating that she requested to come to Portland for the "wet ink" closing. Outside counsel also offered to come to Portland for the closing and manage the documents and closing process. Devlin told him not to bother, he could handle it. Outside counsel even told him that it wasn't an inconvenience, he was looking forward to a ping pong rematch with Matt Jackson. Devlin told him to stay put.

Outside counsel sent the closing documents in Microsoft Word format. Devlin then changed the wording to increase the purchase price and include the language for the seller to return the excess funds post-closing. This was the document that was executed and notarized. In reviewing other emails, we found that the bank had earlier received the "clean" draft closing documents from outside counsel – I would assume the bank approved those documents and that structure and didn't perform a detailed review of the final documents that had been changed by Devlin.

One of the undisclosed related party matters involved Devlin and his family participating in international hockey tours and taking discounts and applying unusual credits. As you may recall, these discounts and credits resulted in the company actually owing Devlin a payment for his and his family to travel to Europe for a couple of weeks. During our investigation of the related party matters, I had met with Devlin and walked through the discounts and credits. He was cool and calm during the meeting and confidently explained each item. He told me that the company had a written policy that supported each of these items. I asked him if I could get a copy of the policy for the file and to close this out with the board. He said he would email it to me shortly. The next day, I received an email from Devlin with a pdf attachment that was the tours division's employee discount and credit policy – it supported each of Devlin's line items perfectly.

In reviewing Devlin's emails and chats during the flight, I found a communication from Devlin to Boyle in which he told him he needed a written employee discount and credit policy for tours. He then spelled out exactly what the policies needed to be. He told him he needed it in the morning. There was a reply the next day from Boyle to Devlin with a Google Drive link to the policy. Devlin thanked him. I clicked on the link and it shows the date and time the document was created – the day after I interviewed Devlin. Another lie.

205

The football joint ventures came up often in Devlin's emails. Every time I had offered to help with the JV, Devlin declined my offer. Based on his behavior in other areas and the cast of characters associated with the JV partner, I had grown skeptical of that partnership. At the end of 2017, the auditors had identified an unusual journal entry in Epic's general ledger. It was a revenue item for nearly three-quarters of a million dollars with an offsetting receivable due from an affiliate of the JV. Keep in mind that I had only been with the company for a short period of time at the end of 2017 and was pigeon-holed in strategy and M&A – I was getting blocked from seeing financial statements or having any involvement in finance and accounting.

However, I recall walking into Devlin's office late in 2017. He was with Murray – Devlin told me to come in and answer an accounting question. He told me that he had a discussion with one of the developers of the proposed JV sports complex. Devlin said that the discussion involved the JV partner acquiring a 50% interest in Epic's football division. He then asked, "how would you account for that?" Before I could answer, he said, "it's revenue, right?" I laughed and said, "no, it's not revenue." I thought for a moment and said, "it would be treated as a sale of an interest in a subsidiary, we would have to determine what our carrying value of our investment was in the subsidiary and then calculate a gain or loss on the sale. It wouldn't be in operating income; it would be below the line as a non-recurring item." He pushed back aggressively and said, "why do you always have to make it so complicated?" I reminded him that the Financial Accounting Standards Board set accounting standards and GAAP, not me. He went on to try to justify that this transaction would result in revenue, making up his own accounting guidance as he went along. It was a complete joke and his CFO just sat there nodding along. I couldn't help myself, I said, "guys, I'm the only one in the room who passed the CPA exam, I think I know what I'm talking about. What you're describing is not GAAP. When is this transaction being contemplated?" Devlin said, "now." I asked what he meant, and he said that he had a commitment from the developer, and it was a "done deal." I said, "whoa, slow down. It's not a done deal. It needs to be papered, board approved and closed. The developer doesn't have the authority to bind the Hall to a contract. You can't book this based on conversations." Devlin ended the conversation at that point with his usual, "I have to hop on a call."

At this point during my flight, I was reviewing emails between Devlin and Murray in which they decided to book the revenue despite being told it wasn't allowed under generally accepted accounting principles. Fortunately, the auditors forced them to reverse the transaction. Devlin also referenced booking this transaction in his infamous "Weekly Thoughts" email in order to show better financial performance in 2017.

I also saw email activity between Boyle, Jackson and Devlin related to Boyle and Devlin's hockey programs' use of Epic's registration system and the company's accounting staff to process their customers' payments and transfer funds form Epic to the programs. There was one particular exchange that was concerning – in the string, Boyle was pressing Jackson for a fifty thousand dollars transfer of funds from Epic to the hockey programs (keep in mind that the hockey programs are not affiliated with Epic, but instead owned by Boyle and Devlin). Jackson advised Boyle that Epic did not owe the hockey programs the money; in fact, the programs owed Epic funds at that time for apparel it had purchased from the Epic's Puerto Rico facility. Boyle pushed back in his usual aggressive manner and advised Jackson that the programs were experiencing a short-term cash crunch. Devlin, who was copied on the string, then intervened and asked Jackson to come down to his office. A short time later (the same day), fifty thousand dollars was transferred from Epic to the programs. It appeared that Epic was providing bridge financing to the hockey programs without Epic's board's knowledge and at a time when Epic was experiencing its own liquidity challenges.

There were so many hits of key word searches in Google Vault that I couldn't get through them all on the flight to Denver. I flagged those that needed to be reviewed later. I spent two days in Denver meeting with two acquisition targets. These were long days of touring the companies' offices, meeting with management teams, performing preliminary due diligence, and then ending each day with a dinner with the owners. Usually, you are exhausted by the end of the day, but you need to rally and treat the owners with respect and get to know them in a more social environment over dinner. I crashed both nights in Denver after dinner. I had decided that I would get back to the Google Vault work on my flight to San Diego in the morning.

I had just gotten in bed when my phone rang just before 10:00pm mountain time. It was my wife. She would never call me this late unless it was important – I had a pit in my stomach. I answered and she immediately said, "everything is ok." I was somewhat relieved, but I knew she was about to tell me something else that wasn't going to be great news. She said that something had happened at our house a few hours earlier. She had been in the kitchen and had let our dog out back, which is fenced in. A few minutes later, Christine heard a noise out back. She assumed it was the dog at the door wanting to come back in. As she opened the door, there was a man at the door. She was startled and let out a scream - the sound brought our dog up from the lower terrace which startled the intruder. He turned, climbed over the fence and ran off. My wife ran to each door to make sure they were locked and then called the police.

The police arrived and checked around the exterior of the house and the cars in the driveway and didn't find any damage or indication that he had tried to gain access to the house through a window or door. Christine assured me that she was fine, but I was worried. I called the police and asked if one of the officers, who had come to the house, could call me at their convenience. I didn't get much sleep. I had also been informed earlier in the week that there were several posts on social media by current and former employees that, while not naming me, implied threats towards me. There was one with a cartoon of employee #1 pointing a gun at employee # 2 with an associated post saying something along the lines that people always get what's coming to them. There was another one calling me trash and saying that the trash will eventually get kicked to the curb.

I texted Christine on the way to the airport in the morning to make sure she and my daughter were fine – she texted back, "all good, have a safe flight - luvya." I also spoke to one of the police officers and he asked if I had someone upset with me. After telling him about the social media posts and work matters, he thought someone may have sent the unwanted visitor to our house to scare us. About a week later, someone broke into my car in my driveway. Nothing was stolen, instead, the contents of the glovebox and center console were thrown all over the driveway and street.

On the flight to California, I resumed my review of the Google Vault key word hits. There was information about a real estate development project adjacent to and including the hockey rink owned by Devlin and Boyle. This wasn't the first I heard of the project. I had heard about a proposed expansion of a hockey academy at the rink, but when I asked Devlin, he denied it. He told me that there were a few kids studying online at the rink, but that was just a "beta test." But based on the volume and dates of the emails we reviewed, it appeared that this was a current priority for Devlin and Boyle and more than a beta test. There were renderings, emails from architects and developers, PowerPoint presentations emailed to potential investors, ongoing discussions with banks, and even letters of support for the project from Maine State officials.

According to the presentations and emails, the project was going to include residential academies for hockey, soccer and lacrosse. The facilities would also be used for tournaments and showcase events. Other potential tenants would include retailers, restaurants, and sports medicine and therapy providers. This was a significant undertaking and one that, in my opinion, was going to be competing with several of Epic's current product offerings not to mention they were benefitting from the due diligence I was conducting on a hockey academy business, at Devlin's direction.

There were other email communications indicating that Devlin was serving as an advisor to another proposed sports development in Massachusetts that would also house a residential academy. He had signed a non-disclosure agreement with that developer only to then provide their presentations to Boyle via Epic's email accounts, telling him that "there could be some good stuff in here that we can use." He clearly was violating the non-disclosure agreement and doing all of this using Epic's email with his signature indicating he was the President and CEO of Epic.

209

Not only did these activities appear in conflict with his duties as an officer and director of Epic, but he blurred the lines between the two companies. Based on the content of the email traffic, one could see that third parties could think that the development included and leveraged Epic's strong position in the market. This alone would provide investors and other potential stakeholder with more comfort. The biographies of Devlin and Boyle referenced their current roles at Epic and touted the size and reach of Epic's events. They also referenced BBFC in their fundraising documents. There was industry data and strategy language that clearly came from other proprietary Epic materials. There were even images and graphics included in the proposed development materials that belonged to Epic.

Every time I found a relevant piece of information, it was forwarded to Powell's firm. Our weekly board update calls now included a legal section presented by Powell. Based on the information we had gathered and rumors that Devlin was talking to employees and being disruptive, the board decided to file a complaint against Devlin for the competitive practices while serving as an officer and director of Epic. He filed a counter suit alleging, among other things, wrongful termination. I was instructed by Powell to send a litigation hold email to all employees. If staff was starting to settle in under my leadership, this would reignite the feeling of uncertainty. I was basically telling the entire company that we had filed a suit against Devlin and that all staff were to preserve their emails and all other files. The necessary legal language in the email was lengthy and sterile although it wreaked of drama.

The meetings in California were productive. In addition to meeting with management of the target company, we visited two of their facilities – massive open fields on which they hosted soccer tournaments. We walked the facilities, of which they were extremely proud, and I couldn't help but notice that it was difficult for me to keep up with the others. I didn't think I was out of shape, but it felt like everyone was walking much quicker than me. I felt like I was shuffling. It was strange; I felt like I was walking in slow motion. Maybe it was just all the toll of the flights and poor sleep in hotels.

On the flight back to Boston, I was catching up on emails and filling time slots on my calendar for the next week. I paused for a moment to think about something and noticed the ring finger and pinky on my right hand were shaking. Shaking uncontrollably. I made a fist a couple of times to try to control it, but it continued. I drank a bottle of water, assuming I was dehydrated. It didn't stop. My fingers moved uncontrollably the entire six-hour flight. I was concerned, but I didn't want to deal with it.

The weekend at home was just another typical, couple of days - trying to stay on top of normal business operations, answering questions from the auditors, re-building the 2019 budget from the ground up with the divisional leaders and so on. In addition, one of the board members maintained a summer house in Rhode Island – often, when he was there, he would drive to Providence and meet with me. Add conversations with the attorneys about each email and file I had sent while traveling and my weekend was consistently shot. I could not get a break.

I returned to my office early Monday morning and noticed that my door was unlocked. I knew for certain that I had locked it before I left the week before knowing that I would be traveling. After I walked in, I reached around and locked the handle again from the inside. I settled into my desk and noticed that I had left some legal notes on my small whiteboard. I really hoped someone wasn't getting into my office – I was less concerned with the information they were accessing since I took my laptop with me every night, but more concerned that there was a faction inside the company acting in the best interest of former employees instead of their current employer.

I made my rounds, chatting with a few of the accounting staff and then I sat with Matt Jackson – it was the first time I had seen him since Murray was terminated. He was still visibly upset a full week later. He said he felt bad for Murray – Finch had provided Jackson with some of details for Murray' termination, but not all. I provided more. Even when he heard about the emails and chats, he didn't take a firm position, meaning he neither condemned nor defended Devlin or Murray. Instead, he quickly transitioned into a "what's going to

211

happen to me mode." I told him that he would be fine if he had done nothing wrong and was honest with us. Jackson was copied on many of the incriminating emails, so I realized he was playing it right down the middle. He wasn't sure what I knew so he thought he may slip through the cracks. But in the end, he was the one who booked the journal entries. He would have to come clean as to whether he took instructions from someone or made those entries on his own. By the way, in his capacity, you don't book a $1.0 million entry with no underlying support without being told to do so.

I went back to my office and closed the door behind me. I wasn't in my seat for more than thirty seconds when I noticed someone standing at my door, it was Ashley, Devlin's former assistant. Despite continued pressure from my board, I had defended keeping Ashley with the company. I told the board that I had no evidence of any wrongdoing on her part, that she always seemed to act in the company's best interest. In addition, much of our staff respected her – she was a go-to person in the Portland office. She was particularly active with the hockey and tours staffs in a customer service role, helping enhance the events and tours. She wasn't my assistant and I didn't feel like I needed one. I knew that she was upset by Devlin's termination and I discussed that with her. I had told her that we should take six months, she should continue to do what she had done before when Devlin was her boss, and let's revisit her role and her appetite to be with the company then.

I looked at Ashley and she put her hand up near her ear imitating someone holding a phone and mouthed "are you on a call?" I shook my head and motioned for her to come on in. She tried to open the door, but I had locked it moments earlier. As I rose from my seat to unlock it, she jiggled the handle aggressively. I opened the door and she immediately reached around and unlocked the handle. In a pissed off tone, she said, "why do you always lock your door?" I said, "because I have sensitive materials in here." She then said, and I quote, "I would like to punch you in the face." Just like that... " I want to punch you in the face." She turned and went back into her office. I didn't know what to say. I was shocked. A moment later, she left the office for the day. It was about 10:00am. I was trying to process what had just happened - I looked down and realized my fingers were trembling again.

The next morning, Ashley arrived in the office, stood in my doorway and said, "my husband told me I should apologize for what I said yesterday." That was it, she didn't actually apologize or explain why she was so mad at me. She turned and went back in her office. This place was an absolute nightmare.

Later that day, Powell, our attorney, came to our office. He, along with a private investigator, met with Jackson for about an hour and a half in the main conference room. This interview had been scheduled for a day or so - in light of the emails we had uncovered, as well as the Devlin and Murray terminations, it was imperative that company counsel speak with Matt.

I was in my office the entire time they met in the conference room. After about an hour, Powell poked his head in my office and asked if I could print something for him if he emailed it to me. I told him, "of course." He asked for two copies. A few minutes later, I received an email with an attachment. I didn't look at the documents. I printed the copies and brought them into the conference room. Jackson was still in the room with Powell and the investigator. Shortly thereafter, I saw Jackson walk by heading down to his office. Powell and the investigator came into my office and closed the door behind them.

Powell handed me a document - it was a two-page affidavit, in bullet point format, signed by Jackson. Not only had he signed it, but he had initialed each individual bullet point. He confirmed most of what we thought and had uncovered in emails and files. I had met with Matt on several occasions asking him to tell me what he knew, what he had heard, what he had been told to do. He was always careful to not implicate himself or others. Now, because the interview was conducted by Powell, he finally decided to tell the truth. He was terminated shortly thereafter.

My oldest son, Riley, was in his junior year at Dartmouth College. Two and a half years had gone by since we first moved him in and we had only visited him a couple of times. When we moved him in, I thought we would make the three-hour drive more frequently to watch his golf matches and spend a little time getting to know his friends, teammates and fraternity brothers. The rest of our life got in the way, work being the most significant factor.

We went up for a weekend in late February to see Riley and watch a production of *Into the Woods* at the Hopkins Center for the Arts. Hanover, is a beautiful college town located along the Connecticut River, bordering Vermont; the Appalachian Trail actually runs right through the center of town. We stayed at the Hanover Inn which is literally next door to the theater and just around the corner from Riley's fraternity. We love the Hanover Inn and its restaurant, Pine; they overlook the green (the grass covered field and common space in the center of the college) and Baker Library beyond.

Christine drove from Providence to Hanover, I worked in the passenger's seat the entire way. Cell service is poor the last forty-five minutes or so leading to Hanover. Once we arrived, I had missed calls, texts and emails - it just never stopped. Christine checked us into the Inn while I took a call in the living room off the main lobby. I didn't mind the work, but I was starting to finally realize that this wasn't normal. I was never present for my family.

During the play, my mind was elsewhere. To be honest, I don't remember anything about the play. Afterwards, we grabbed a drink and a bite to eat at Pine with Riley and some friends. He seemed great - happy, keeping up with his academics, but also enjoying himself. He filled us in about his golf team's upcoming southern trip and the activities at TDX (his frat). He offered to have us come by and see his friends at the fraternity, but I took a pass - my back and legs were bothering me, and I was exhausted. Instead, I went back to our room and did emails.

We met Riley in the morning for a quick breakfast at Lou's on Main Street - gave him a hug afterwards and we were back on the road. It was becoming abundantly clear that I needed to find more time for family and to learn to live in the moment. I just couldn't break away from the mess at work. Deep down, I knew this wasn't sustainable.

CHAPTER 15

We were starting to make progress – I felt like we were winning more than we were losing. I now had a small, core team in Boston that was aligned and had taken some burdens off my plate; I had developed a strong and trusting relationship with Ben Powell, our litigator; we changed outside counsel to George Petit and Jonathan Witt at Nunn & King – they had stepped up and proven to be great counsel in a very short period of time. The hockey, hotel bookings and lacrosse divisions were operating pretty autonomously on a daily basis while embracing our guidance and support from Boston. Don't get me wrong, things popped up periodically with these divisions that required our involvement, but they were manageable issues compared to the dumpster fire with which we had been dealing.

We had exited the apparel business, which simultaneously stopped the cash bleed and brain drain that it had become. Similarly, we had sold Epic's football business (and accounted for the transaction appropriately) and were in the process of selling our interest in the joint venture. Our partners in the JV, the characters involved and their attempt to develop a destination sports complex could fill another book. I couldn't get away from that joint venture fast enough.

Tours and Soccer (BBFC) were on my mind constantly. I had decided that I was going to blow up the tours organization and start over. After the upcoming tours were completed, I was going to make a significant change. Having learned more about the culture of the tours business, the inappropriate activities that went on in their office and the tours' leadership's consistent insubordination, I decided we needed to start over. Moving the office to Portland wasn't going to cut it – we were moving the tours operation to Boston and restructuring the way the division would function.

I trusted our hockey leadership team and hockey families represented the majority of our tours business. It made perfect sense that hockey tours should simply be another product line within the hockey division. I discussed the concept with the hockey leadership, and they agreed wholeheartedly – one of the leaders said he had been pushing this strategy for years. He thought that a separate tours division was only created to provide Boyle with a position that kept him away from the rest of the team. One of the hockey leaders, volunteered to lead the tours business. He was the right guy for this job and I really appreciated him stepping up. Steve Lomax also stepped up and said he could take on a role supporting the tours division in year one to make sure we didn't stub our toe. Laura was putting together a detailed human resource plan. We had prepared a detailed financial model, operating plan, and it all felt good.

BBFC was another issue. Whatever question I asked or attempt I made to help the soccer business; I was stiff-armed. Our accounting and finance staff were receiving similar treatment. I just kept poking the bear, hoping they would accept our help or finally snap. I knew in my heart that something wasn't right with BBFC, particularly when I read the "Weekly Thoughts" email but I was trying to keep hope alive. I was rebuilding the 2019 budget (during Q1 of 2019, not ideal), which required collaboration with Patrick Baldwin, Jack Cahill and others. Cahill was engaged and appeared to be giving the process his best effort. He wasn't an accountant or educated in finance, so he was limited to a degree. He did, however, understand every detail of the BBFC organization and how it operated. He was Baldwin's right-hand man, his COO.

During the budgeting process, we met often at BBFC's Dedham offices, west of Boston, always at a small conference table in Baldwin's office. I had noticed a consistent trend – Baldwin would start at the conference table with us at the beginning of the meetings, we would discuss what we were there to accomplish, and he would try to influence the agenda. Once he felt comfortable with what Cahill and I were going to cover, he would slide over to his desk and work on his laptop - more odd behavior. However, he would also maintain some degree of attention to our conversations, because he would interject or correct Cahill from time to time. When a particularly sensitive topic, like an under-performing region, would arise, he would return to the conference table and override Cahill and provide his opinions, propose corrective actions and attempt to justify a more optimistic 2019 forecast. The more I was getting to know him, the more I found him to be an overbearing bully.

During one of these budget meetings, I stood up and began writing on a small whiteboard in Baldwin's office. I wrote 2015, 2016, 2017, 2018 and 2019B across the top of the whiteboard. The "B" in 2019 meant budget. From memory, I wrote the reported revenue and profit numbers below each of the prior years. I then wrote the current budgeted numbers for 2019. I had left space between each of the year's columns. I turned, looked at Baldwin and Cahill and said, "agree?" They just nodded. I wrote the year-over-year revenue growth amounts and calculated the percentage growth for each year compared to the prior year. Next, I did the same for reported profit figures. I put the marker down and returned to my seat at the table.

There was a long uncomfortable silence as Baldwin and Cahill stared at the board. Cahill didn't comment. Baldwin did. He said, "ok, what's your point?" I told him that the trends didn't make any sense. He said, "sure they do. 2015 we were cash-based and in 2016 we were forced by Epic to convert to accrual-based accounting. The Epic accountants fucked up the numbers all the way through today. We can't even pay our vendors on time....". He went on and on. It was a filibuster. I patiently let him air it out. When he calmed down, I went back to the whiteboard. I said, "forget the year-to-year fluctuations. Let's just look at the big picture. How does a company double its revenue in five years and have its profits decline?" Baldwin said, "I just told you." I said, "no you didn't, you talked about timeliness of financial reporting, vendor payments and the conversion from cash to accrual-based accounting." I explained my issue again and then answered my own question. I said, "I don't believe your company ever achieved these profits" and then circled the 2016 and 2017 profit figures.

I knew this was a tipping point. This was the moment when the bully gets punched in the face and either cowers away or beats the living shit out of the kid he has been bullying. He didn't cower away. Instead, he asked if I was calling him a liar. I said, "no, I'm not calling you a liar, I just don't see how those profits could have ever been achieved. Also, the due diligence materials that we have are a disaster. There was no support for the numbers." He pushed back again, "then you are calling me a liar." I calmly said, "I'm not calling you a liar. I am trying to figure out two things: 1) how this company actually had performed in the past and 2) what I can reasonably expect for the future." I went on to explain that the questions I was asking Baldwin and Cahill were also going to be asked of me by our board of directors. I could not present a budget with revenue growth and declining profits.

I could not get a straight answer or even an attempt from Baldwin or Cahill to help construct a bridge from prior years to the currently contemplated budget. I was simply looking for guidance on which expense items were significantly outpacing our revenue growth. I already knew the answer, but I wanted to see them get to the same place. There weren't individual expense line items that were growing enough to eat up the revenue growth and operating leverage. The 2016 financial statements, the year of the transaction, were inaccurate, as were the 2017 financial statements, the first full year under Epic's ownership. I believed revenues had been overstated and expenses had been understated in the financial statements in the years leading up to the transaction.

I certainly didn't agree with it, but I could understand why 2016 would be misrepresented. The seller always wants to present its best performance when the valuation of their business is based on profitability. That doesn't mean committing fraud, but you can certainly defer discretionary expenses and the like to boost profits. It was 2017 that had me baffled. A significant portion of the BBFC purchase price was driven by 2017 EBITDA (earnings before interest, taxes, and depreciation, basically the common measure of a business profitability and cash flow). But, in 2017, BBFC was under Epic's control, both operationally and financially. Why would Epic allow BBFC's 2017 EBITDA to be overstated if it meant paying an

218

inappropriately high purchase price to the BBFC shareholders? I believe I had found the answer in the "Weekly Thoughts" email as well as another one he had only sent to Murray.

In late 2017, Murray and Devlin knew that Epic was not going to hit its budget. The "Weekly Thoughts" email acknowledged that and laid out the steps to artificially inflate the company's profits. There was also a second email that Devlin sent to Murray that laid out his thoughts for a call that he was about to have with Baldwin. He wanted Murray' opinion on the planned call. In the email, Devlin stated that he knew that BBFC's 2015 and 2016 financials were a mess and likely inaccurate. He also acknowledged that the 2017 year-to-date performance was below expectations. He planned to stress to Baldwin that if the numbers were off plan, Baldwin would receive less proceeds from the sale and Devlin would feel the wrath of his board of directors and lender. Keep in mind that Devlin was already on probation, of sorts, with his board. We had also learned that he had a strained relationship with the company's lender.

In the BBFC purchase agreement, Epic had the right to bring in an independent accounting firm to review the BBFC 2017 financial statements and determine the appropriate final purchase price. Devlin raised this right in the email and planned to tell Baldwin that it wouldn't be in either his or Baldwin's best interest to have the independent accounting firm perform their review. He wrote that if the accounting firm came in, "we would have to live with their findings." He also wrote that he planned to tell Baldwin that they "needed to protect each other."

There you have it. Baldwin had a personal, financial interest in overstating the profits and Devlin, likewise, needed BBFC to appear to be hitting its budget, even if it meant overpaying for the company. He would rather preserve his job and the inflated valuation of the company than accurately present BBFC's financial performance. They were taking a corrupt and myopic approach that would eventually catch up to both of them. They likely believed that BBFC would grow into its earnings in 2019.

Early one morning, I was on the commuter rail heading to South Station like any other day when my phone rang. It was Epic's controller, Heather Howard - I was surprised to see her contact come up one my phone since it was so early in the morning. Heather typically had a very calm demeanor, but not on this call. She told me that all of our bank accounts had been frozen. She was in a panic, particularly because we had a payroll that was to be processed the next day; which meant the funds needed to be withdrawn by our payroll provider that afternoon. If our funds were frozen, we would risk missing payroll. That would be a disaster. She said she hadn't been able to speak with anyone at the bank yet as it was still early. I told her I would call our banker on his cell phone and get right back to her.

I had inherited Epic's banking relationship – a small, regional bank, based north of Boston. They were not the right lender for a private equity-backed company that planned to execute a consolidation strategy via acquisitions. The lender was simply too small and lacked the experience of working with private equity, or family office, investors. We knew this but were hoping that we could move to a larger, commercial bank once our 2018 audited financial statements were ready. Most lenders would require audited financials. I thought we were about a month or so away from having the audit opinion in hand. I called the banker, Brian. He took my call.

We exchanged pleasantries and then I asked if he knew that our accounts were frozen. He calmly said he did as if it was no big deal. I said, "Brian, what the hell is going on?" He said that because he hadn't received debt covenant calculations, compliance certificates and cash flow forecasts from our interim CFO, he had no choice but to freeze our accounts. We had approximately $6.0 million in deposits at the bank and owed them about $4.5 million on our working capital line of credit. The bank certainly didn't have any real exposure, but he was taking drastic action, nonetheless. I made my case to have him release the funds, but he said he wouldn't do so until he received, at a minimum, the cash flow forecast, and he wanted to meet with me in-person that day. He also unloaded on our interim CFO – he said he had been asking for the information repeatedly over the last month and had no other choice but to freeze

220

the accounts to get our attention. This was the first I heard about Finch not getting the bank the requested information.

I told him I was on my way to the office and would get the cash flow forecast to him as soon as I arrived. He told me he wanted to meet me at his Boston office at noon. I agreed. I called, emailed and texted our interim CFO – he had become difficult to track down. He was splitting his time between Boston and the CFC office in New York – this wasn't working for me. He called me back and I told him what the bank had done. Instead of admitting that he hadn't provided the bank with the requested materials, he went off on the banker. I finally interrupted him and asked if he had an updated cash flow forecast. He said he did, and I asked him to email it to me. I also asked him not to call the banker, that I would handle this.

I received the cash flow forecast – it was a disaster. Columns didn't total accurately, there were formula errors and the previous week's cash activity hadn't been updated from a forecast to the actual amounts. I took care of it - I fixed the formula errors, updated the actual cash flow amounts and cleaned up the sloppy formatting. I also did a relatively detailed review of the forward thirteen weeks' projected cash activity to ensure it was reasonable and so I could speak to it. I emailed it to the banker, and he confirmed receiving it almost immediately. I replied, "can you unfreeze our accounts now?" He wrote back, "not until after I see you at noon – I want to make sure you understand our position."

At 11:30am, I packed my messenger bag and left the office, headed west on Seaport Boulevard towards the financial district. Brian's calendar invite included a location of 225 Franklin Street - I knew the building; it was across from the Langham Hotel around the corner from Post Office Square. It was a short walk from my office. I checked in at security and headed up to the office. When I got off the elevator, I realized I was not in the bank's office, but rather a shared workspace. I checked in with the receptionist and waited – Brian came out, greeted me with a handshake and took me into a large conference room that looked east towards Boston Harbor. "Nice set-up, huh?", he said motioning towards the windows. I said, "yea, nice view." Did he think that I didn't know this was a shared office and conference room? I wasn't particularly impressed. I hadn't had much interaction with this guy, but my impression was that he was a bit insecure and didn't have the best bedside manner. He was wearing a pair of Topsiders, jeans, a dress shirt and a wrinkled blazer that probably fit him a little better when he wore it in college twenty years ago. I had a bad feeling about this meeting.

He sat at the head of the conference table and I sat to his right, facing the view. He didn't have anything in front of him. I took out my iPad and two printed copies of the cash flow forecast that I had emailed him earlier hoping we could review the materials. He crossed his legs, leaned back in the chair and turned towards the windows... with his back pretty much to me. "Steve, Steve, Steve, what are we going to do?" I didn't answer him. He continued (while still looking out the window), "I don't think you or your friends in New York understand how this works. It seems like none of you know what you are doing. Do any of you know what you are doing?" He turned and faced me. I told him that we knew what we were doing - I apologized for our finance folks not getting him the information he had requested, and that it wouldn't happen again. I started to tell him that the audit was taking longer than expected when he interrupted, "you don't get it. You don't understand that I can shut this company down if I want to – we are the senior secured lender, your friends in New York better wake up and realize they are below us in the cap table." I assumed my friends in New York were CFC.

He pulled in closer to the table and to me simultaneously. He leaned in and looked me in the eye. It took every fiber in me to keep my mouth shut – I just needed him to release our cash accounts. He said, "Let me help you. You are going to send an email to me and copy my colleagues from the bank, as well as your friends in New York, and you are going to admit that you guys fucked up. That you understand why I froze your funds and that you will engage a consultant to monitor the company's cash activity. Got it?" I told him that I had no problem with the email, but I didn't see the need for the consultant. I would personally take on the cash flow reporting and we would not miss a beat with the bank again. I told him that the added expense was not necessary. "Nope, deal breaker," he said, as he sat back in his chair. "Tell me you are engaging a consultant and I will release the freeze on your accounts, otherwise, you guys are fucked with payroll." I knew that, under normal circumstances, a lender would not want to be responsible for a company missing its payroll, particularly when our cash balances far exceeded the outstanding bank debt – however, this guy seemed "off." I chose to not call his bluff.

I told him I would engage the consultant. He said, "there you go, good decision" and sent me the consultant's contact information by email. He then told me to call the guy on the spot. This was absolutely ridiculous. I looked at my watch and realized we were bumping up against the payroll withdrawal deadline. I said, "you call and have the accounts released and I will call your friend." He smiled and said, "attaboy, now you are getting it." He stood up, had his phone in hand and walked towards the windows. He called a colleague and told her to release our accounts while he was admiring the view of the harbor. I texted Heather, our controller, and asked her to check the availability of the accounts. My text showed that it was delivered. Then I saw the little dots that told me she was typing. She typed, "checking now…". Brian hung up, turned to me and said, "make the call." I said I was opening up the contact he sent me. I was actually just playing with the phone hoping Heather would text me back. She did – the accounts were released. I called his consultant friend on speakerphone and left him a friendly voicemail introducing myself and telling him we were looking forward to working with him.

Brian then told me, "it doesn't have to be like this. Let's agree that you will be my point of contact going forward. I am not working with Finch." "Sure," I said. He went on to explain to me that we should try to connect every day and if that didn't work for either of us occasionally, we shouldn't let two days go by without talking. I had never heard anything like this. He seemed like a psycho. I couldn't help myself, now that I knew the payroll was safe and I had two weeks before the next one – I said, "do you really want to be in this credit?", meaning be our lender. He didn't hesitate and said, "no, not really." There, I got my answer. He then went on and told me that he knew he had been lied to repeatedly by Devlin and Murray. He had

223

no faith in the company and his recent experience with our finance department demonstrated that we were really good at consistently missing deadlines and delivering inaccurate information. Putting aside his odd behavior and theatrics, the guy wasn't completely wrong. I told him we should start the process of paying off the outstanding line of credit and move on. He agreed.

I walked back to the office and didn't make a single call – I couldn't talk to anyone. I, literally, was mumbling to myself a profanity-laced tirade the entire walk back. Every day in this company felt like a boxing match.

In the days and weeks that followed, tensions continued to rise between Epic and its lender. The bank wanted to get paid off and Epic's board wanted a new lender; a "more reasonable and flexible" lender in the words of one of the board members. I saw it both ways – a lender doesn't have any upside, only the opportunity to earn a spread on interest. But banks have a fair amount of downside, particularly in a business such as Epic that doesn't have any tangible assets and its intangible assets (brands, customer lists and the like) are difficult to value and, perhaps, difficult to monetize in times of trouble. Our banker had just told me that he felt like he had been lied to by previous management, that Epic always missed its budgets and, now, the interim CFO wasn't playing by the rules – providing accurate information in a timely manner. Why *would* they want to lend to us?

I also saw it from Epic's perspective. I had taken over and inherited a complete shitshow. When I took on this role, I had been completely transparent with our lender, walking through industry data, internal strategy documents, even board packages. Our banker had told me that he had learned more about our business and had more conversations with me in a couple of months than they had with prior management in years. The least they could do was allow me some time to put numbers on the board and demonstrate that the business was improving. I thought the lender should have been more patient and I certainly disagreed with his tactic of freezing our funds.

A few days before the next payroll, he did it again! He restricted access to our cash. We engaged his consultant friend, although as soon as we engaged him and paid his retainer, he went on vacation. And, we were providing the weekly cash flow forecasts as requested. Now, he was demanding a guarantee from our lead investors. Trust me, that wasn't going to happen – they already had about $20 million invested in the business and were second in line to the bank, why would they guarantee the company's debt. We got our lawyers involved, the bank got theirs involved… now we were paying lawyers and the businesspeople weren't even talking. Good stuff.

We quickly assembled an updated information memo on Epic and shared it with several "specialty" lenders. These were lenders that weren't banks and, therefore, not subject to certain regulatory constraints or traditionally conservative credit committees. They could be more aggressive and lend to companies that had unusual characteristics like recently discontinued operations (the Puerto Rico facility), or were in the process of exiting a cash burning division, or had recently terminated its CEO and CFO, or had uncovered accounting irregularities, or was struggling to complete its first year's financial statement audit. On second thought, this was not going to be easy.

The prospective lenders reviewed the memo and all expressed interest – why wouldn't they, these memos always paint a rosier picture of a company than reality, including recast EBITDA. Recast EBITDA involves taking your actual profit or loss and adding back as many *non-recurring* expenses as possible. This is intended to show a company's cash flow in a normal environment without non-recurring items. The lenders wanted to dig in deeper, so we subjected ourselves to due diligence. At a time when my plate was already more than full, we added this new project with a side dish of hyper-urgency.

All but one of the prospective lenders were kind enough to come to Boston to meet, so I didn't have to travel at least. I was pretty certain that anyone who looked at this deal would say the same things, "We like you, we like the industry, we like your strategy, but this company has a lot of 'hair' on it. There are also has a lot of add-backs. You can't pay interest and principal with add-backs. Why don't you get the financial statement audit completed, show some profitability this year and let's talk again then?"

Sure enough, the responses we were getting, after spending significant time with the lenders and providing answers to diligence questions, were very similar to what I expected. They were all starting to "take a pass" as they liked to say – meaning, they would not lend to us. There was one firm, however, that seemed sincerely interested. The firm was based in Los Angeles and they wanted me to go there to meet with them. Most of the communications with this lender were handled by one of our board members who had worked . with them in the past. Based on his experience with them, as well as a longstanding relationship with the CEO of the lender, he thought it was highly likely that they would provide us with credit. We were able to get our existing lender to release our cash to make payroll based on the supposed progress we were making to secure their replacement.

My schedule was stacked and adding another trip to the west coast was the last thing I wanted to do. I scheduled an evening flight west and a redeye return about twenty-four hours later. A couple of days before the trip, I was told that the CEO of lender wanted to meet over golf - the foursome would include two of our other board members. I thought to myself, "you have to be kidding me." I am a single digit golfer and I enjoy the game. I enjoy it with my family or close friends. I can only enjoy it when my mind is clear and feel like work is in a good place. If work isn't in a good place, I don't want to play golf. There was no way I was going to enjoy this considering everything that was going on back at the office. I had my clubs shipped to Bel Air Country Club. I arrived in L.A. and took an Uber to my hotel. The other two board members were arriving after me. It was about 9:00pm local time when I checked into my room, but I was so tired, I turned in right away. I woke up around 3:30am, still on east coast time, and responded to a text I had missed the night before from my board members about meeting for breakfast around 6:00am in the lobby. I worked for a few hours and then headed down to the lobby.

It was raining sideways, absolutely pouring. Being pre-dawn, with the air conditioning on in my room and the shades down, I didn't know it was raining until I passed through the lobby. I walked out to the main entrance and watched one of the valets trying to sweep the water away from the entrance. His eyes met mine and he said, "it never rains like this." I asked, "what's the forecast?" He said it would clear up later in the afternoon. Great, I thought, we won't have to golf and, instead, we can go the lender's office, have a productive session and try to get a deal done. I couldn't continue to worry about liquidity every two weeks. I met the two board members in the restaurant for breakfast – as I was walking to the table, I could see them both looking at their phones. When I sat down, I realized they were both looking at weather apps trying to convince themselves that the monsoon outside was just a light drizzle. They *really* wanted to golf. We made small talk about the weather, our respective flights and the quality of our hotel rooms. All three of us had healthy breakfasts, I had a green smoothie; one guy had granola and yogurt; and the other had an egg white omelet, with a side of fruit, no meat and no bread.

One of the board members provided more background on the gentleman with whom we would be golfing. One of them had worked with him for years at, what was at the time, one of the largest private equity firms in the world. They had history and were friends. He now managed alternative investments for a family office of the founder of a large restaurant chain. I was told that he was a "quick study" and "could move fast in terms of closing the transaction and taking out our current lender." We finished breakfast and headed out to the lobby – our host would pick us up and take us to Bel Air.

He arrived in an extended cab pickup truck, not what I would have expected. He made light of the truck and said he enjoyed "slumming it from time to time." Both of my colleagues brought their clubs with them so they had to put them in the back of the truck; fortunately, the truck had a cover over the bed so the clubs wouldn't get soaked on the ride over to the course. Our host, Tony, seemed like a nice enough guy, but certainly not someone I would call "warm." On the ride over, he mostly caught up with his former colleague. When we pulled into the club, he pulled up to the bag drop area and we got out of the truck. He opened the tailgate to allow the golf staff to grab the clubs. We were directed to the clubhouse entrance while he pulled around and parked the truck – it was still pouring.

I didn't grow up in a golf family and certainly wasn't a member at a country club. I grew up playing baseball and a few other sports. In my early teens, I, along with a few buddies, started playing golf at a local, nine-hole public course. We would carpool, with one of our parents dropping us off and another doing the pickup. I remember times when a parent wasn't available, and we would actually ride our bikes with golf clubs on our backs. I guess we were hooked.

I had pretty good hand-eye coordination and the baseball swing transitioned nicely to golf. I enjoyed the game and understood the physics of the swing so I could "work on my game" even without professional instruction. I continued to play the game into my early twenties and could score in the high seventies pretty consistently.

But it was during my first year in public accounting that I realized that the ability to hit a golf ball could have a meaningful impact on one's career. I was working in a cubicle surrounded by other young staff accountants when a senior partner came into the large open space one afternoon – he asked for everyone's attention. He then asked if anyone golfed. I hesitated momentarily, but then raised my hand. Mine was the only hand raised. He came over to me and asked if I was working on a client engagement. I told him I was doing accounts receivable test work for an audit client, but nothing pressing. He said, "that can wait. Tomorrow 11:00am at Charles River Country Club – I have two clients and I need a fourth – see you there."

The clients were the CEO and CFO of a large public company, and client, in the Boston area – they both loved golf but sucked. The partner who invited me was a decent golfer, but not great. We were playing in an outing – what they call a *member-three*. For a member-three, a member of the host club brings three guests, you have lunch, the golf staff organizes a best ball tournament, drinks and dinner follow with prizes (usually pro shop credits) to the gross, net, long drive and closest to the pin winners. I played particularly well that

228

day – we won the net tournament and I won the long drive. The guys were thrilled; they bought shirts in the pro shop with their credits. More importantly, they liked me. I knew when to speak up and when to keep my mouth shut. I was usually pretty self-deprecating, particularly if I hit a good shot – I would downplay it. I would also, authentically, compliment the other members of my foursome. I liked how the whole day had felt. The manicured greens, the pristine practice facility (unlike my public driving range), clients laughing, drinks and appetizers, the exclusivity of the club, the whole thing felt good. The partner who had invited me thanked me at the end of the day and told me he appreciated me playing. Afterwards, my relationship with that partner had changed – he would say hello and use my first name when we passed in the hallway. On occasion, he would ask if I watched the PGA event that previous weekend and we would chat about it. On multiple occasions, he would stop me and tell another partner, "you should see this guy hit a golf ball."

Eventually, I worked more for that partner than any other. I was invited to golf outings and gained access to clients, including private equity firms, while my non-golfing colleagues were left behind in their cubicles. So, why do I share this story? Because, I get it – these guys all like to golf (even though most of them can't break a 100). They want to hang around with other golfers, particularly good golfers. They like to tell stories… the drive they "bombed" … "on in two on that long part 5" … "I thought that seven iron was going in the hole, it never left the pin" …. all of that bullshit. Don't get me wrong, I enjoy the game of golf. It is the rest of the nonsense that I can do without. So, I figured that day at Bel Air would be no different.

Still raining like a bastard, these guys decided they wanted to play. I hate playing in the rain. I normally refuse to play in the rain. But, instead, I donned my rain gear, put on my bucket hat and pulled out my Foot Joy rain gloves. I was already sweating because it was warm and humid. We went to the driving range and I hit a few wedges just to find some tempo while the others worked through their entire bags hoping to find some kind of magic. Tony was a short, stocky guy with an even shorter backswing. I heard him say, "everything going right, why the hell is everything going right?" I wanted to say, "because your stance is wide-open, you are coming across the ball, and you're standing up at impact… it *has to* go right!". Instead, I remained silent.

We walked with caddies and the rain had stopped after a few holes. Bel Air is a nice track and it was in perfect condition. Surprisingly, there was very little business conversation on the course. I was able to talk about Epic with Tony while walking down a couple of fairways, but I couldn't get him to engage deeply in the conversation. I was concerned by that. We finished the round, showered, changed and then had lunch in the men's grill room.

Tony talked about his wife and kids, his minority stake in an NHL team, a deal he did with CFC a couple of years earlier, and a few other high-level topics about things going on at his firm. Really nothing of substance about Epic. As we wrapped up lunch, he told us he would take us to his office, meet his colleagues and sit down to "try to get a deal done." I thought, OK, now we are getting somewhere. The two board members told Tony that they were going to grab something in the pro shop – Tony pointed them in the direction of the shop and said he would bring the truck around. I walked out with Tony, I had enough golf hats and shirts at home.

Back at the potential lender's office, we met for about two hours in Tony's main conference room – their offices were in Century City. His small team of five, all young men, joined us. I provided a high-level overview of our industry and our business; our product lines; the customers we serve; average revenue per customer, the key characteristics of our financial model, today and at scale; the competitive landscape; accretive acquisition opportunities; and even the challenges we were managing through. I had asked that they feel free to ask questions or push back along the way – some did, and the questions were relevant and appropriate. They had done their homework. The meeting seemed to go very well; Tony jumped straight to what the terms would look like for them to be a lender. They were a bit aggressive on their proposed interest rate, but not unreasonable considering the risk profile of the business. There was some back and forth with the board members about the interest rate as well as the term (number of years) of the debt, but otherwise, it felt like a very positive meeting. They agreed to provide us with a term sheet in the next twenty-four hours. As we were leaving, two members of their team told me they were looking forward to working with me.

On the way to the airport, the two board members and I rehashed the meeting – we were all in agreement that it went well. We would be so relieved to move on from our current lender; one of the board members said that Tony had taken him aside and told him that he "wanted to get this done" and that they had plenty of capital to provide financing for our future acquisitions. I bursted their bubble when I said, "I just don't know how they get this done without a clean audit opinion." The quick response from a board member was, "I don't think they care about the audit." There was no more back-and-forth. I think it hit them that the audit would be a problem. There was silence until we arrived at the airport and went our separate ways.

The next day, one of the CFC partners called me and asked when I thought the audit would be completed. I told him, based on what I knew, that we were at least thirty days out from having an audit opinion. I had yet to see draft financial statements with a full set of footnotes and the auditors were still performing substantive test work because they couldn't rely on our internal control environment. This meant that the processes and controls were so poor during 2017 and 2018 that the auditors had to test a statistically significant number of transactions and trace those transactions all the way through to the financial statements in order to complete their audit and issue an opinion. This work was still ongoing, and I understood that the auditors were not pleased with the effort of our accounting staff.

The CFC partner then told me that he had received the term sheet from the lender in L.A. and the completion of the 2018 audit and an unqualified audit opinion was a requirement to close the transaction. I told him that we didn't have that much time with our current lender, and I did not believe the company would receive a clean opinion.

On our next board call, we all agreed that our current lender needed to be paid off in full and we couldn't wait for a new lender. CFC and

RevCap committed to investing additional capital to pay off the bank and provide the company with additional cash on hand. In the end, CFC and RevCap basically stepped into the bank's senior secured position. The company negotiated the terms of the investment with the assistance of Nunn & King and complied with the company's operating agreement which provide preemptive rights to all shareholders – meaning every shareholder had the right to invest alongside CFC and RevCap on a pro rata basis. I did not participate, nor did any of the other shareholders. There were rumors swirling, and being spread by certain former employees, that the new round of financing was designed to cram down the other investors and take control of the company. Further, people were suggesting that I was a "plant" from CFC, and I was acting in their best interest. This was absolutely false. I had never worked with or done business with CFC or any of its employees before Epic. I chose not to participate in the financing so that I could always defend myself that I acted in the best interest of the company, its shareholders and employees. I found it particularly interesting that none of the founders participated in the financing.

The bank was paid in full and we had cash on hand – dealing with our lender had been significant distraction and time suck. Now I was freed up a bit, or so I thought.

IS THAT A LIGHT AT THE END OF THE TUNNEL?

"We know that we cannot live together without rules which tell us what is right and what is wrong. We know that it is law which enables men to live together, that creates order out of chaos. We know that law is the glue that holds civilization together."

Robert F. Kennedy, May 1961

232

CHAPTER 16

A new culture was forming in the Boston office. Laura, Emily, Steve Lomax, our new CFO, Peter Saunders, and others were bringing energy, professionalism, and optimism to the business.

Peter had everything we needed in a CFO - he was technically strong from a finance perspective, had the right education pedigree and had come from a multi-national retail business that was going through its own transformation. He worked for a billionaire hedge funder who had acquired the retailer; so, Peter knew what it was like to work in a private equity environment and under very dynamic circumstances - a time when retail was reinventing itself via e-commerce and brands going direct-to-consumer. More importantly, Peter was an honest, hardworking gentleman. Based on our conversations, I knew that he was a great husband and dad. I felt like I finally had partners with me - each much smarter than me in their respective areas. This is what it should have been. In addition to their competence and commitment, they were really good people - the kind of people you wanted to be around every day.

Decision making was changing for the better as well - we were able to make decisions as a leadership team. We trusted each other and were comfortable seeking other opinions and being challenged. No more defensiveness. Finance and accounting hadn't transitioned fully from the Portland office yet and we still had the tours team up there as well. I needed to address this - since the international tours had just wrapped up, now was the perfect time to reorganize the tours group.

Their original leader, Scott Boyle, had quit a few months earlier. Thank God and good riddance. After telling me that he "didn't trust me or like me," he resigned and told our human resource manager in Portland that I had harassed him and created a hostile work environment. The tours office was toxic - a nice mix of anger, laziness, alcohol and gambling - just lovely for a youth sports business. We had made the final decision to move the tours business to Boston. We would outsource the soccer tours to a global tours company, WorldTours, and merge the hockey tours into the hockey division.

The decision to outsource the soccer tours seemed like a no-brainer. WorldTours was the largest educational travel business in the world - they served over 100 countries and almost 500,000 travelers a year. They had significant resources, risk mitigation practices and purchasing power that we could never realize. In the event something ever happened that resulted in our customers being stranded in a foreign country or a child becoming ill, WorldTours had the processes in place to take care of our customers appropriately. God forbid something horrible happened, WorldTours carried insurance that we never could afford... and, as an outsourced partner, they indemnified us. On top of it all, the gentleman that ran point for WorldTours was a professional and a pleasure with whom to work. We structured a partnership in which we could actually generate more profits from a soccer tour without lifting a finger *and* our customers would have a much better experience. Done!

With WorldTours in place and a plan for our hockey tours, Laura, Emily, Steve and I planned every detail necessary to close the Tours office immediately and announce the closure of Portland as well. We would hold the meetings back-to-back so that we could control the messaging, both, internally and outside of the company. We had some concerns about a couple of staff in the Tours office, so we decided to have a security guard on the property in case the meeting went sideways. If things heated up, Laura would text the security guard to come into the building. As soon as we started the meeting, Emily's IT folks would lock down all of the staff's access to email and other company systems.

To be clear, the thought of terminating anyone makes me sick to my stomach. I think about that person hearing the news, processing that they are out of work, having to tell their loved ones, worrying about bills, and so on. I hate it. Even in the case of staff that disliked me, I still find no pleasure in letting people go.

We entered the tours office and most of the staff was already in the frat room seated around the large conference table. A couple of others were still in their offices. We greeted everyone at the table and waited for the others to join. Laura texted Emily to lock down the tours staff's email accounts and access to other systems. I sat at the table with everyone and thanked them for meeting. I told them "we had made the difficult decision of closing the office, outsourcing the soccer tours and merging the hockey tours into the hockey division - this would mean that this office and the current roles here would no longer be required. Consequently, we were forced to terminate everyone effective today. You all may apply for any open positions with the hockey division and I would encourage you do so. Please note that those roles will be based in either Michigan or Boston. Any questions?"

One gentleman got up, left the room without saying a word and went to his office. I kept an eye in his direction, but he didn't seem like the violent type. A young lady asked a couple of reasonable questions about gathering things in her office and downloading some personal items from her laptop. The guy who had attended the earlier meeting in shorts and barefoot (during a snowstorm) didn't seem to understand the news right away. Then he looked around the table and back at me - he said, "that's it? You mean, that's it? I'm fired?" I told him that he was terminated immediately and had thirty minutes to gather his personal belongings. He pushed his chair away from the table aggressively. He remained seated and took a couple of deep breaths while looking around the table. Then, he got up and went to his office. His behavior concerned me - we texted the security guard who quickly came up stairs and stood outside of Shoeless Joe's office while he packed his personal belongings.

The gentleman who had left the room first, returned after only a couple of minutes with his laptop and power cord. I stood up and

235

stepped away from the table. Laura stepped forward, passed around folders and proceeded to brief everyone on their severance, accrued vacation time and COBRA benefits rights. There was no doubt that she provided a much-needed sense of calm and structure that stifled any thoughts of aggressive behavior. While Laura was doing her thing, I walked around the office. It was disorganized and dirty - and yet they had known that we were coming for today's meeting. Either they didn't have enough self-respect to clean their office or they had cleaned, and it must have been a real pigsty beforehand. The bar had dirty glasses and mugs on it. The kitchen had a pile of dirty dishes and glasses on the counter that appeared to be a few days old.

Over the next thirty minutes, the staff turned in their laptops and keys, packed their beer mugs, dog beds, dart boards and hockey jerseys and left the building. After all of the staff had left, we quickly gathered external hard drives, physical files and other potentially critical items and headed to the Portland office. We would be back later to clean out the rest of the office. We repeated the exercise in Portland without incident. We were officially out of the two offices in Maine.

While to restructure the business, setting up shop in Boston, bringing on new talent, and implementing processes and systems, we had, simultaneously, gotten to the bottom of most of the shenanigans that went on at Epic before my arrival. We understood and gathered documentation that proved the accounting misrepresentations, undisclosed related party transactions, conflicts of interests, competitive activities, inappropriate use of corporate resources, and so on. We were also able to identify the so-called whistleblower.

Google responded to the subpoena requesting information about the Gmail account that had sent the two anonymous emails. We were provided an IP address – an internet protocol address. This is an identifying number that is associated with a specific computer. When connected to the internet, it is the IP address that allows a computer to send and receive information.

The nice thing about IP addresses is that you can often geolocate them. The geolocation data isn't precise, but it can certainly put you in a general proximity of where the device is located. Because the IP address is used for sending and receiving data, the IP address owner's internet service provider often shares this anonymous data with geolocation application service providers. The IP address is like a fingerprint - for example, every time a user signs into their email or company network, the IP address is recorded.

Once we had the IP address, we ran the geolocation of the device and, bingo, it hit within a very short distance (a few hundred yards) of the home address of one of our employees. We were not aware of any other employees who lived in that state, let alone that neighborhood. Interestingly, the employee had claimed that they had been harmed by the anonymous emails. The employee had even filed a complaint against Epic and me claiming that management had leaked information that the whistleblower used to disparage the employee. Now we knew this employee *was* the so-called whistleblower. Despite the geolocation data virtually pinpointing the whistleblower's home, our attorneys advised us that the geolocation data, in and of itself, wasn't sufficient evidence to prove who was sending these intentionally destructive and misleading emails. I was frustrated to say the least. We were confident that we knew who was doing this, but we couldn't take action and stop them.

That night, I woke up sweating as usual – however, this time, an idea had come to me in my sleep. If this individual's IP address was static, then it would reveal itself and be logged every time this person signed onto our network. Every time they checked email, submitted an expense in our accounting system, and so on. That morning, our IT people checked our company-wide systems activities and found that the IP address was, indeed, tied to the specific employee's accounts. We finally had them.

I cannot emphasize enough how destructive this individual's emails were. During a time when so many employees were confused about the changes made within the company, this individual provided people with damaging lies about me and others. This person was clearly participating in the "scorched earth" strategy to destroy the company before we could find everything. The attorneys would put a stop to it

From time-to-time, the YHI acquisition would come to mind. This was the acquisition of the small hockey events business in Minnesota. I had been dealing with so many other issues, that I hadn't prioritized getting to the bottom of this one. You may recall that there was a significant reduction of the purchase price months after the closing and I hadn't been able to get any real explanation from Murray or Jackson. With everything else we had uncovered, I was confident there was something fishy with this deal, but I couldn't pinpoint it. On an overnight flight to London, I had read through the closing documents again, something wasn't right. I Googled the sellers' names and was able to locate a phone number for one of them.

I called the former YHI owner later that day - she answered my call. I explained who I was, and she said, "thank God, you called." Her name was Maggie. Even though this transaction had occurred two years earlier, the wound was still raw. I asked why she was so glad to hear from me. She proceeded to explain to me that she and her partner had been taken advantage of, lied to, threatened, and forced to spend money on attorneys to try to collect money that was rightfully theirs. Over the next hour with Maggie, and several subsequent calls, including her business partner, they explained the details to me.

They claimed that after they sold their company to Epic, they were notified by Devlin that certain accounts receivable were not collectible and, therefore, the purchase price would have to be reduced. He told them that they had no choice but to accept the reduction in proceeds. He even told them that if they chose to pursue legal action, that was fine with him – he said his company had far more resources than they did, and he was prepared to pursue litigation.

The purchase price adjustment was no small amount to the sellers. But the thought of spending money on attorneys was not particularly appealing. Maggie and her partner were confused. The only receivables outstanding were rebates due from their hotel bookings provider. In all of the years of operating their business, their rebates had always been collected. In fact, they had always used the same hotel bookings company, so they were certain there was simply a mix up.

They reached out to their hotel bookings' company point of contact, who had always been responsive, but not this time. They tried a number of times but couldn't get a response. When they finally did, the tone from the CEO of the hotel bookings company was markedly different than it had ever been in the past. It was polar opposite to the usual cheerful, upbeat, artificial, sugary-sweet tone they had always heard in the past. Instead, they were threatened again with potential legal action. The hotel bookings company was TBA and the person on the other end of the phone was none other than April Nash.

We were able to determine that Devlin and Nash had known each other for years, long before the YHI acquisition. We also learned that Devlin was in negotiations with Nash to acquire TBA when the YHI transaction closed. This was never disclosed to Maggie and her partner. There were even emails in which Devlin and Nash discussed the YHI receivable and the fact that Nash was not only willing, but pleased, to not have to pay the receivable to Epic. In the end, this benefited Nash, as she kept the funds, *and* Epic, as the purchase price adjustment reduced the note payable to the sellers. It also appeared that the purchase price adjustment was recorded in the year following to the transaction and was recorded as income. It certainly looked like another dirty deal.

From time to time, I continued to hear about social media posts by former employees and their family members targeting me. Most of them were immature and annoying (as I discussed earlier), but not particularly threatening. Nonetheless, these types of attacks started to take their toll. I didn't particularly care what they wrote about me, but instead I was concerned that one of these nuts could get violent at some point. We needed to find ways to bring an end to this type of behavior.

Around this time, Ben Powell and I decided to use mediation as a means to end the settle the sexual harassment claims. The other side accepted the offer to mediate. I am pretty sure, they thought we were willing to do so out of weakness, that we were going to write a check. This was not the case at all.

The mediation was held at the law offices of a former judge, the mediator. It went exactly as I expected. The mediator had the benefit of reading about the case and each side's position in advance. At the opening of the mediation hearing, each side presented their respective positions again to the mediator. Then the mediator would meet, privately, with each side in their own conference rooms. The mediator then provides guidance to each side in an attempt to find a resolution or settlement. I could tell right away that the mediator thought, "where there is smoke there must be fire."

After the mediator met with the other side, he returned to our conference room. He provided Ben and me with his thoughts about the allegations, the likely time and costs associated with going to trial and his estimated range of what he thought a settlement amount would look like today. The range was ridiculous, and I told him so. Ben reigned me in. The mediator professionally reiterated that he was simply providing guidance and certainly not giving an opinion as to the validity of the other side's claims.

Ben provided the mediator with a more thorough background of what had gone on at Epic and the mediator seemed to be absorbing it all – no easy task. He would look at me from time to time, particularly when Ben mentioned one of the more bizarre highlights. Hearing the story of Epic told to a third party was eye opening, even to me. What a sequence of events - a real shitshow. I felt like the mediator was beginning to realize the other side's claims could actually be all smoke. I asked if I could add something, Ben looked at me like he wanted to gag me.

I provided the mediator with my background, my family life, how I came to Epic and why I was now the CEO. I also told him, emphatically, that these sexual harassment claims were 100% false. I told him that I would not settle for *any* amount – this was my reputation and that I would continue to incur legal costs if necessary, to clear my name. Oh, and one more thing, we had additional facts and evidence that proved that the other side was lying. We knew that the claims were part of the scorched earth strategy and had evidence to provide it.

Once the facts were presented and shared with the other side; the claims were dropped. It was without question, one of the most satisfying moments in my career. Even with all of the bullshit we were forced to deal with, this still felt like a victory. We were slowly cleaning the place up.

It seemed like every time I thought we were making progress, something else would pop up. Shortly after the mediation victory, I was pulling information from Epic's Google Drive for our attorneys. They had requested a copy of a document that I had provided earlier in PDF format, but they needed it in the original PowerPoint format. I knew exactly what folder the file was in, but I couldn't locate the folder. Odd. I typed the name of the folder several times but didn't receive a hit.

I typed in the specific name of the file and it came up but showed that it had been deleted about a week earlier. Fortunately, Google Drive tracks the entire history of a file, so I could retrieve the original document. But I was really concerned – how could this have been deleted? Everyone in the company knew we were under a litigation hold. I looked at the history and realized that Devlin's wife (yes, his wife) had accessed the folder and deleted the file along with a number of other files (most of which were evidence of competitive activities). She never worked for the company, nor did she have an Epic email address. But, apparently, she had been provided access to certain folders on the company's Google Drive. We were unaware of this.

I couldn't fathom the nerve or ignorance of this woman. Her husband was terminated by the company and was in the midst of a messy legal battle; yet she thought it was appropriate to access the company's Google Drive and delete files? Give me a break. I notified the attorneys right away. As I was recovering the deleted files, I noticed something else. I hadn't been able to locate the file folder, (which was now empty) not because it had been deleted like the files, but rather because it had been renamed by Mrs. Devlin. Not only had the folder been renamed, but she had shared it with the entire company. Oh, by the way, she renamed the folder, "Steve Griffin is a Douchebag." What a classy lady.

BETTER GET YOUR REST

"A wise man should consider that health is the greatest of human blessings and learn how, by his own thought, to derive benefit from his illnesses."

Hippocrates, 400BC

CHAPTER 17

I had known for some time that something was wrong with me – the back pain, numbness, tremors, and the way I was walking. I was moving slower; my posture had changed, and I constantly felt fatigued. I finally called a friend of mine, Gary L'Europa, who is a well-respected Neurologist. Gary and I played golf together and he had watched my children grow up at Rhode Island Country Club - he was a good guy and a real character. In fact, he had introduced Malcolm Gladwell's ten thousand hours rule concept to my nine-year-old son on the driving range one day, explaining to him that he needed to put in more hours if he wanted to be a great golfer. It apparently paid off as my son ended up golfing in college.

I told Gary about my symptoms and that they seemed to be getting worse. He asked if I could come in the next day. It was unlike me to clear my schedule, but I did. That alone, told me that I knew, deep down, it was probably serious.

His office was only about twenty minutes from my home. When I arrived at his office, the receptionist brought me to an examination room. Gary came in a few minutes later. We talked about our families for a bit then I shared my symptoms with him. He proceeded to put me through a series of tests and observed of my movements. Dr. L'Europa left the room and came back with a colleague. She repeated several of the same tests that had been performed earlier and we discussed my symptoms. They then took me into another room and had another colleague perform a series of tests on me in which she inserted a small needle into my hand, arms, feet and legs while applying an electrical charge. Apparently, it was measuring nerve activity. While she was performing the tests, my right hand was trembling. I could tell they were all watching it, but no one mentioned it.

When we finished the nerve testing, we returned to the examination room. We discussed the internal tremors I had been experiencing; their location and frequency. They asked about my dreams, sleep patterns, muscle cramping and a few other things. Many of the things they asked about, I was experiencing. Then, they left me alone in the room for a while. Eventually, Dr. L'Europa returned alone. He sat across from me and didn't mince words (which I appreciated from a friend). He said, "we think you have Parkinson's Disease, I'm sorry buddy." I had hoped it was stress, lack of exercise, not eating right, dehydration… or a combination of all of these things, perhaps. However, the diagnosis made sense. Like I said earlier, I felt like I was in someone else's body.

Gary explained the characteristics of the disease to me but all I really remember were the words, "it's not a death sentence." He told me how different the symptoms and progression can be for every patient. He told me about a great "movement disorder" (apparently, a nice alternative name for Parkinson's) doctor affiliated with Brown University, Dr. Joseph Friedman. L'Europa had done his residency under Friedman. He called Friedman from his cell phone and left a detailed message about me. He then texted me Friedman's contact information. He told me to call Friedman the next day if I didn't hear from him by then. I stayed calm, nodded along and said, "I've got it, thanks." He said, "are you sure?" "Yup, all good," I told him. I could tell that he felt awful, but I wasn't fully processing the news. I was tapped out - I had nothing left. I stood up, we shook hands and agreed to talk in a couple of days. I picked up my phone and car keys off the table next to me and headed out.

I sat in the parking lot for a bit and let it sink in. To be honest, I didn't know how to feel or what to think. I knew a little bit about the disease, mostly because of Muhammed Ali and Michael J. Fox, but not much. Listening to L'Europa and how the disease manifested itself, and progressed, in so many different ways, the diagnosis felt uncertain or ambiguous in a way. However, I also knew how I felt – that I didn't feel like myself. I told myself, not to be a martyr or anything, but thank God it was me and not something terrible happening to my wife or kids. I thought, I'll take it, I'll deal with it.

244

Without really thinking, I drove to my golf club instead of home, changed in the locker room and went straight to the practice facilities. I hit balls casually for a while, I'm not sure how long, then went into the bar. There were a few guys in there, fortunately not close friends. I didn't want to have to make small talk. I proceeded to have a couple of drinks alone. I then went home and told Christine the bad news. There were some tears, but my wife, ever the eternal optimist, transitioned pretty quickly into "we are going beat this" mode. We decided to hold off telling the kids until we have a clear game plan.

That night I had a dream – I was in the ocean alone, treading water. No boats nearby, no land in sight. The water was warm and clear. I vividly remember the taste of salt on my lips. The waves were light. I felt completely at peace. The dream felt like it lasted only a few moments, but it was so vivid and clear. I had never had a dream like that before.

In the weeks that followed, usually on the train, I would listen to podcasts produced by the Michael J. Fox Foundation. I wouldn't discuss the topics with anyone, but I would listen. The more I listened to the podcast and read about the Foundation, the more I had come to realize how remarkable it was. Fox founded it in 2000, a couple of years after going public with his own diagnosis - the Foundation is committed to research, education and awareness. It has provided almost $1.0 billion to facilitate early diagnosis and, ultimately, find a cure. The Foundation also produces content to help patients and their loved ones understand the disease and how to live with it. I found the podcasts educational, but I was steadfast in my view that I was going to deal with this my way - I would let those closest to me know, but that was going to be it. I didn't see myself hanging out with a bunch of other Parkinson's patients. To be honest, I didn't want it looking back at me. I thought I had accepted my diagnosis, but I clearly hadn't.

CHAPTER 18

The summer and early fall of 2019 were heavily weighted towards soccer division. We had hired a financial planning and analysis person dedicated solely to BBFC – his name was Mike. He was terrific. He had come from one of the big four firms, was extremely organized, diligent and committed to making BBFC more profitable by working with both its senior management team and each of the regional managers. He was a no-nonsense kind of guy. He designed a very specific, structured strategy and executed on it every day. I was particularly impressed with how he had quickly gained the trust and respect of the regional managers.

Mike was quickly providing insights into the regions that we never had before – not just financial information. He provided insights into each BBFC regional manager's operating style, focus (or lack thereof) on budget compliance, who managed their cash flow efficiently, who over-staffed, and so on. He also had learned how to access data and where it resided. He was also beginning to automate the key metrics reporting function - we would finally have the ability to track the performance of this division in real time. Without necessarily knowing it, Mike was playing another critical role – he was actively integrating BBFC's staff, culturally, into Epic. They were communicating non-stop, sharing information and best practices and Mike was that point of contact. I really believed this was a good thing to erase the perception of BBFC and Epic being two separate companies.

Then something strange happened – shocker, right? Periodically, BBFC would bring their regional managers to the Boston area for meetings and training. Patrick Baldwin had scheduled one of these sessions and hadn't invited me to it or even told me about it. Here we are constantly talking about alignment, breaking down silos, getting people to work together, and he doesn't involve his CEO in these meetings.

When I heard about the meetings, I emailed Baldwin and told him that I wanted to participate in the sessions and have thirty minutes or so to address his team. He pushed back that the agenda was pretty tight, forcing me to be more assertive. He finally gave me a thirty-minute time slot during the first morning of the meetings. "Great, thanks much," I replied.

In advance of the session, I sent over a PowerPoint presentation to Baldwin and his marketing director, Gordon Kerrigan. Kerrigan was always the point of contact for presentation materials at BBFC events and meetings and he usually sat adjacent to the presentation area, operating the laptop and projector.

The morning of the session and I arrived at BBFC's offices about thirty minutes early. The BBFC office was on the second floor of a nondescript office building on a side street in Dedham. There was a lot of activity in the office with about twenty-five people on-hand from out of town, plus much of the Massachusetts soccer staff. I chatted with several of the guys who I knew, met a few others and gave Patrick a wave when I saw him. I was hoping to talk to him in advance of the session just to give him a heads up regarding what I planned to discuss. Unfortunately, he was in perpetual motion and I couldn't get any time with him. As people were taking their seats, Baldwin came out of his office to the main open area. He raised his voice to get everyone's attention. He stood at the front of the room rubbing his hands together with a large screen behind him with the BBFC logo projected on it. As I expected, Gordon was seated to Patrick's right controlling the laptop and presentation.

Patrick welcomed everyone in a loud voice and strong brogue for a guy who had been in the U.S. for twenty-five years. It may have been my imagination, but it seemed the brogue got stronger when he was on stage or had a few pints in him. He referenced the slides on the screen behind him as he walked through the agenda for the next two days – this was the first I had actually seen of it. It involved meetings during the day, dinners both nights and a guest speaker, on

247

the second night, who came from the private equity world - interesting that I wasn't invited. He called out a couple of agenda items and sessions that he wanted to emphasize, including one called Project Conquer, his code name for his strategy to takeover youth soccer around the world. He had pitched me on this strategy a couple of times and I still didn't understand it. I continued looking at the agenda and couldn't believe that I hadn't been invited to any of this. He ended his short speech with his typical reminders to his lads, including "don't be late in the morning and don't get arrested tonight." He then introduced me – he said that I had asked to say a few words. Not a particularly warm and inclusive intro.

I stood and thanked Patrick as I was walking to the front of the room. I casually thanked Gordon for running the presentation and turned behind me to see the same slide that was there for Patrick. I looked back at Gordon and he was looking at the audience, not me. I said, "Gordon, can you pull up my slides?" He acted like he had no idea what I was talking about. It was uncomfortable. I reminded him that I emailed the slides the night before. I turned back to the audience, just blank stares. I said, "OK, while Gordon is pulling up the slides, let me introduce myself for those of you who don't know me."

I provided my background, reminded everyone that I had been the CEO of Epic for about nine months or so and began talking about my vision for our company. I turned and saw a blank screen behind me, and Gordon was now looking at his phone. I had been sabotaged. That's fine, I thought, I don't need the slides. I told the audience that we were going to operate as one company going forward, that our sole focus was on our customers and exceeding their expectations. Our culture would be one of teamwork, picking each other up, striving to be our best, mutual respect and trust. I wanted this to be a company that people wanted to be part of – a unique place that provided growth opportunities for everyone.

I provided some background on our investors and why I thought they were good for our company. I gave everyone a quick overview of what the divisions of Epic did and the relative size of each; praising BBFC for being our largest division. I continued to talk about the shared services that we provided at headquarters, including strategy, marketing, finance & accounting, acquisitions, human resources, information technology and so on. I wanted this group to know that our goal was to make their lives easier, to allow them to do what they do best, coach and teach the children. I told them I was aware that a lot of promises had been made to BBFC by Epic over the past few years, that many had not been fulfilled and I was here to change that. I wrapped up by telling them all that I looked forward to working with them and they could reach out to me any time if I could be of assistance. I told them that the number on my email signature was my cell phone. I wanted each and every one of them to know that I was on their team. There was a light applause. I started back to my seat and Baldwin stood up asking if there were any questions. I backed up to the front of the room in case anyone would speak up.

A gentleman in the front row raised his hand. "Yes sir", I said pointing in his direction. I recognized him; he was the general manager in the Carolinas. I had met him last year at the company-wide summit and had a conversation with him. I'm sure he knew soccer, but he was not the sharpest tool in the shed. I noticed that he had a piece of paper folded in half in his hand. Glancing down at it, he asked his question, "I have a two-part question - we have been waiting for almost three years for BBFC's accounting to be integrated into Epic's systems. When will that finally happen? And, uh, my, uh, second question is… (looking down at the paper), we don't think the financial information we are getting from HQ is accurate, we are more profitable than accounting tells us – when are you going to get this squared away?" Great, I thought – they sabotaged my presentation, now they have planted questions in the audience intended to make me look bad. Beautiful.

I answered his questions and others that followed - most were clearly provided to staff by Baldwin. All of the questions had a negative tone to them. If Baldwin thought the questions were going to fluster me, he was wrong. In fact, I immediately recognized what was happening and felt all of the eyes on me, evaluating my demeanor. I forced myself to stay calm and, in each case, thanked the questioner for his question. In most cases, I also acknowledged that Epic hadn't done everything it could have to support BBFC since the acquisition, but I reiterated our plans and told them it was a new day, a new beginning. There were no more questions. I felt like I had dodged the bullet with my name on it.

I returned to my seat and Baldwin stood up. He appeared annoyed. I honestly think he was pissed that his little plan to embarrass me had failed. So he took it into his own hands. As he walked to the front of the room, he was rubbing his hands together and looking down at the floor, as if searching for words. He then lifted his head, surveyed his team and said, "there you have it lads – you just heard directly from the big man that everything that is fucked up in this company will be fixed. So, Steve, when will we actually start seeing some results?" He looked at me with a smirk. I stood up and said that Mike, our dedicated BBFC financial analyst (who was sitting in the back of the room), had already been a great addition to the team. I continued to say that he was working with everyone in the room and that Mike had told me that the staff had been terrific to work with. I was confident that we would all be seeing significant improvements in financial reporting and key metrics dashboards over the next month.

I could see a number of guys in the audience nodding along. One of them seated in front of me actually said quietly, "that is great." I could tell that they liked that I had complimented them in front of Baldwin. Baldwin, paced back and forth for a moment, looked up at the audience, then directly at me and said in his brogue, "fantastic…so if we don't see results by the end of September, we will plan to crucify you…". He turned and pointed at the wall on which the screen was hanging, held his point for effect, and said, "we will hang you right there and I will let the lads throw rotten vegetables at you." A few guys laughed, a few more actually let out a mob-like cheer and others remained silent, looking at me for my reaction. I shook my head in disbelief and didn't respond. Baldwin then handed over the stage to Kerrigan to talk through some marketing initiatives. I stayed for Kerrigan's presentation, but to be honest, I didn't hear a word. As soon as he finished, I snuck out the back of the room and returned to my office in the Seaport.

I was really struggling with BBFC and, Baldwin, in particular. I had originally assessed him as good guy; passionate about soccer and coaching kids; and an entrepreneur at heart who likely wasn't accustomed to processes and controls. As time had passed, I had come to realize that he had big ego. It was not uncommon for a founder to sell one's company and later regret it, regardless of the size of their bank account. After they relinquish control, they often realize they can't make decisions alone, they suddenly report to a board, and view someone like me as nothing more than a "suit." I was aware of these potential challenges and was trying to be patient with Baldwin. I had wanted to give him as much autonomy as possible, but BBFC wasn't performing well, and he was now disrespecting and undermining me in front of his team. My patience was running out.

I was also beginning to have concerns about Baldwin and his role in our partnerships. BBFC had an existing partnership with adidas, but the contract was nearing the end of its term. By most accounts, as well as my own interactions with the adidas representatives, it had been a good partnership and there were a number of healthy, working relationships between our two teams. I liked and respected BBFC's point of contact at adidas. He was Scottish, married with kids, had a warm, friendly demeanor and a certain style about him. He always dressed business casual, but in a way that somehow walked the line between our age and the generation behind us. For example, he would wear a nicely tailored blazer with a high-quality t-shirt and a pair of trousers that were tapered just enough at the ankle to display his latest released Yeezys. He was also remarkably knowledgeable and insightful about our target demographic and the shift from bricks and mortar retail to direct-to-consumer e-commerce.

I viewed adidas as having the incumbent advantage if they could meet, or even come close to our financial expectations. The marketplace had changed since BBFC had signed the current partnership agreement with adidas. BBFC had grown, outfitting and interacting with significantly more athletes around the country; brands were finally making the shift to direct-to-consumer (not as fearful of retailer threats since Sports Authority had vaporized); we knew the value of our reach to the athletes, the key influencers; and competitors, like Nike, were knocking on our door.

I am not a big believer in the new age negotiation tactics you see in books on the newsstands in airports. I simply don't buy it – if you have two companies and two representatives who are relatively sophisticated, have the same data and are looking to work together, they need to find terms that satisfy both of their objectives. One side can't win, while the other side loses – it won't work. Can one side squeeze out a bit more than the other? Sure, but there shouldn't be a lopsided victory. If, by chance there is, the losing side will quickly realize it, lose interest and fail to uphold its end of the partnership. The spirit of the partnership will be gone.

I also have strong feelings about extending existing partnerships, assuming they are working well. Terms of the partnership can be adjusted and enhanced if factors have changed – like, the volume of our customers, our social media reach and influence, and so on. You simply need to provide your partner with the data to support your expectations of enhancing the economic value of the partnership going forward – it's not magic. Remaining with an incumbent partner mitigates a number of risks - your team has been working with the partners' team, they know each other, their operating and communication styles; your customers recognize that the brands are aligned and a change may raise eyebrows or confuse them; there are likely processes in place, like monthly reporting, product sourcing, shared marketing tactics and so on that would need to be redefined with a new partner.

Consequently, I was a proponent of staying with adidas, but I was not averse to making the switch if it made sense. In fact, I had worked with Nike in the past, had a very positive experience, know and respect a number of their people, and recognize the power of their brand.

Unfortunately, I learned from a friend in the industry that Baldwin had been in conversations with representatives of other brands about partnering with BBFC, replacing adidas, without my knowledge. Rather than call him out on it and create a stir, I simply sent an email suggesting that we get together to discuss the expiring adidas contract. We met about a few days later. As usual, Baldwin didn't prepare or provide anything in advance. Instead, it was a

252

conversation and, once again, he was trying to dominate it. He seemed like he had already made up his mind. He wanted BBFC to partner with Puma. He said that he had been in conversations with them for some time and that the economics of their deal were much better than anything adidas could provide. I told him that this was going to be a long-term contract, something we would have to live with for a while, that impacted our customers, would affect our marketing strategies, and we would need to consider affiliate revenue opportunities in light of the shift towards direct-to-consumer brand strategies, and so on. I also told him that I would prefer a single brand strategy across all of Epic's sports and Puma didn't have a presence or product offerings in hockey and lacrosse. I told him that I needed to be involved in the process and, ultimately, this was the kind of thing our board would need to bless.

He responded like a child – he complained about the board getting involved and said that I knew nothing about soccer. Before I could respond, he claimed that his leadership team was sold on Puma and that if we undermined him, he would *lose his locker room*. I asked what that meant – he told me that his team would think that he wasn't running BBFC anymore. He said if that if he lost their respect, they would lose their passion and the business would fail. I thought, wow, this is all very dramatic. There was something else going on. I told him that we needed to do a thorough analysis of the brand strengths of Puma, Nike and adidas, including their social media reach, respective scale in each of our sports, their sponsorships in soccer (youth, college, MLS and Europe), and so on. Of course, we would need formal proposals from each. I told him that we would put together a pitch book on the BBFC opportunity, share it with the brands and run a bid process. He was not pleased.

Several weeks later, after a series of calls and meetings with the brands, we received all of the bids. The financial and qualitative elements of the bids were pretty similar. There were minor differences among them, things like the rebate percentage on uniform purchases, up-front dollars versus annual payments, five year versus seven-year terms, and so on. But, in the end, they were not materially different. We had also gathered all of the brand and consumer reach data. Taking the bid details and brand data, we created a matrix that

253

assigned scores to each element of the proposals. In the end, Nike and adidas were neck and neck... In my opinion, Puma shouldn't have even been in the same analysis. I emailed it to Baldwin, and he said he wanted to have a call as soon as possible. On the call, he was angry and told me the information was slanted. However, he couldn't tell me what specifically was slanted. He said that going with Nike or adidas was not acceptable to him. He told me he wanted to meet in person the following day at my office to discuss this and he was going to bring a few of his colleagues with him.

To this day, my memory of the meeting is remarkably vivid. I'm not sure why, but it may have been the room in which we met. Because our Seaport office was located in a WeWork, we would have to reserve conference rooms for larger gatherings. My assistant, Carolyn, reserved the only available conference room – one that accommodated about six people comfortably with a stand-up table and stools. Patrick had not told us who he was bringing with him, but I doubted more than four colleagues. Carolyn received a notification from the front desk that Baldwin had arrived – I was finishing up a call, so she slid a note in front of me letting me know that she was going to get him set up in the conference room.

A few moments later, she returned while I was gathering my things to head to the conference room. She looked a little flustered as she walked towards me – I asked, "all good?" She said, emphatically, "NO, it's not all good!". I laughed – I had become numb because of what seemed to happen in this company on a daily basis. I said, "what now?" She then told me that Baldwin had brought about ten guys with him. She told me that the room only held about six people and that she had asked him several times to send over an attendee list, but he never responded. I told her not to worry about it, that people could stand up in the meeting. I grabbed my notebook. She told me she was printing more copies of the brand matrix and would bring them down shortly.

On the way to the conference room, I cut through the lobby to grab a water when I noticed one of Baldwin's lieutenants pouring a beer from the tap into a WeWork stainless steel cup. It was 10:00am.

This was before WeWork had changed their policy to activate the taps only after 5:00pm. My impressions of this guy were negative from the start, this just sealed my opinion of him. He was a fast-talking, bullshit artist. I watched him from a distance. He finished pouring the beer, took a big swig out of it and then topped it off again. Unbelievable. I followed him towards the lobby exit so I could catch up to him and make him feel uncomfortable. He opened the door and realized someone was right behind him – he held the door awkwardly with his foot and realized it was me and said, "hey man." I said hello, motioned towards his beverage and said, "you all set? Need anything else?" He said, "no, I'm good thanks." He was either really stupid or arrogant… probably both.

I walked into the conference room and you could cut the tension, and body odor, with a knife. As I tried to get to the conference table, I said, "good morning everyone, wow, we have a full house." No response from Baldwin. All of his guys, except for him, were wearing BBFC co-branded gear head-to-toe. He was dressed like he was the head coach of Manchester United. I always found it odd that he demanded his staff wear only BBFC gear, but he didn't. Perhaps, it was just one more tangible way of demonstrating his consistent hypocritical behavior.

Carolyn tried to squeeze herself into the room. The guys made little or no effort to accommodate her, so she finally handed the papers to one of the BBFC guys and asked him to pass them over to me. She made eye contact with me and raised her eyebrow. I smiled. She knew this was going to be quite a meeting. She left the room. Baldwin started to get everyone's attention. I handed the stack of papers to the guy to my right and asked him to "take one and pass them around." By the time the stack had made it about halfway around the room, Baldwin took notice. He asked, "what is that?" I told him that it was the analysis we had put together. He said, "no, no, no" and told his guys to pass all of the papers to him. I looked at him and he said to me, "you will see... I want these guys to participate in the decision." In hindsight, I should have pushed back, been more assertive.

Baldwin whistled to get everyone's attention as he stood alongside the whiteboard with a marker already in hand. He said, "lads, listen up. You are here today because you guys know our families better than anyone – this is a big decision and we want your input. So, we are down to Puma, Nike and adidas....". He tried to write on the board, but the marker was dry. He was annoyed. He put the cap on the marker, placed it on the tray, and grabbed another one. That one was dry too – he looked at me and said, "Jesus, you can't even get a marker that works in your fancy office?" He tossed the marker at me. I had my arms crossed, made no effort to catch it, let it hit me in the chest and drop to the floor. There were a couple of uncomfortable chuckles in the room.

Baldwin found a marker that worked and proceeded to write the names of the three brands across the top of the whiteboard. He then wrote some categories down the left side. When I tried to add a category he had missed, he ignored me. I knew this meeting was a ruse, an absolute joke. He listed the elements of each brand's bid while talking through them. His guys were commenting along the way with each comment being their personal, uninformed opinion, a silly joke or a childish jab at one of their colleagues. This was a complete waste of time.

After about forty-five minutes of nonsense, he wrote the name of each BBFC attendee on the board. He took a vote. What a shock, a unanimous vote for Puma. "There you have it," he said to me. "So, we are going with Puma," he continued. I sucked the oxygen out of the room when I told everyone that I appreciated their input, but that there were other factors that also needed to be considered, and that this ultimately would be the board of directors' decision. Baldwin told me that it would be a big mistake to not make the right decision, the decision his lads wanted – Puma. I told him I understood his position, that we had a board meeting the following week and that this would be a top priority. The meeting adjourned and everyone left, except for Patrick and his brother, Sean.

Baldwin told me that I made him look bad in front of his guys. He reiterated that they were starting to question his authority. His brother didn't say much other than occasionally repeating the last few words of Patrick's sentences, like, "yea, starting to question his authority." He told me that if we didn't go with Puma, it was going to be an issue. He told me that he already told his guys that Puma was going to be our new partner. I told him that he shouldn't have done that, but I really didn't care. He could tell them we changed our collective mind or, even better, he could tell them that he changed *his* mind. I told him that he could make his case for Puma directly to the board if he liked. He said, "oh, I'll make my case." He put on his scarf, coat and hat and he and his brother left.

Our finance guys were spending a lot of time on BBFC, struggling to find clear solutions to right-sizing the operating expenses and getting back to pre-transaction operating margins. We were now contemplating shuttering certain markets that simply looked like they were incapable to turning a profit and were a drag on the business. I was also beginning to question Baldwin on this *franchise* model. Several years earlier, BBFC rolled out the franchise model, which was built on a questionable strategic plan and unsustainable economics. It was part of Patrick's strategy to conquer the youth soccer world and become the biggest soccer club in the world strategy. The model allowed other clubs around the country to use the BBFC brand, wear their uniforms and promote themselves as affiliates of BBFC – why would an independent club do this? Because BBFC had an affiliation with a European professional club. The youth soccer market had shifted towards clubs having affiliations with professional teams; the storyline was that the professional teams would provide their coaching style and teaching curriculum to the local club. Therefore, American coaches would have the benefit of European soccer expertise. Many independent clubs who couldn't afford or attract a professional affiliation looked to BBFC as a partner who could bring the professional appeal.

Under the franchise model, BBFC would receive from the franchisee a nominal fee per player and a percentage of the uniform sales. The problem was that the independent clubs expected more in return. They actually wanted coaching curricula and support from BBFC. Consequently, BBFC had to invest in some personnel, incur travel expenses and host the clubs at periodic summits to keep them feeling connected. Even so, the clubs were not satisfied and there was

257

significant churn. I had come to believe that when we fully burdened the franchise model, it was losing money and probably damaging the BBFC brand at the same time. I felt like there must have been some other reason Baldwin wanted to gather up all of these franchisees. I kept asking questions about this model and challenging its merits. I couldn't get a straight answer.

I was frustrated that it was taking so long to get the BBFC model refined. It wasn't our finance team's fault; we were getting stonewalled. I felt like an idiot that I couldn't get all the answers I needed. With my quarterly board meeting in about a week, I scheduled a meeting that would include my finance guys, Patrick & Sean Baldwin, Cahill and one of Baldwin's other top guys, Paul Cross. I was convinced that several factors were causing the "underperformance" and I was simply going to walk through those factors in order to get to the bottom of it once and for all. I believed there were five drivers of the poor performance: 1) new markets that were marginally profitable or incurring losses (this was an easy one); 2) the franchise model I discussed before; 3) increasing facility costs; 4) labor costs (something didn't make sense to me with this whole visa / immigration thing); and 5) I didn't believe the company was ever as profitable as portrayed.

In the meeting, I didn't hold back. I shared my views in a calm, professional manner, but I didn't sugarcoat anything. No one pushed back. I let people at the table discuss the topics for just short of an hour. Everyone was cordial, except the Baldwins, who barely participated. No one from BBFC commented. Their body language was terrible. Patrick spent most of the time looking at his phone, appearing disinterested in the meeting. Sean didn't engage either, but instead, sat with his arms and legs crossed. Our finance guys agreed to finalize their analyses and action plans for my first four bullets that I had shared. They would come back to all of us by end of business the next day. This plan would be shared with our board the following week. The fifth bullet, that I didn't believe BBFC was ever as profitable as portrayed, simply hung in the air.

Before we wrapped up, I asked everyone to hang on for a moment while I reviewed my notes to make sure I hadn't missed anything.

Written in the margin next to my notes about labor costs were the words, "BBFC Student Placement Limited." For whatever reason, stress, fatigue, etc., I couldn't recall why I wrote it or what it even meant. So, I said, while still scanning my notes, "remind me, what is BBFC Student Placement Limited?" I kept looking through my notes and realized no one answered my question. The table was silent. I said, "sorry, did someone answer?" No one replied. I asked again. Cahill gave the impression that he didn't know what it was, yet he didn't turn and ask Cross or the Baldwins. I could tell that he didn't want to put them on the spot and that they weren't going to volunteer the answer. He told me he would get back to me. I was on to something.

The following week, our quarterly board meeting was held in Boston. Since we didn't have a conference room large enough to accommodate everyone in the Seaport office, we rented a meeting room for the day at the Intercontinental Hotel just over the bridge from our offices. This was the second time we held a board meeting here - it had worked out well before. Carolyn coordinated everything, including breakfast, lunch and the board dinner. She had everything nailed down. She distributed the board packages and detailed agendas days in advance via email and told the members that hard copies would be provided at the meeting as well. She had the board packages printed, bound and placed at each member's seat along with pads and pens. The screen and projector had been tested before we arrived. She even knew diet restrictions and preferences for certain board members and set the menus accordingly. Board members could stay right at the hotel and South Station was only a block away for those riding the Amtrak Acela.

The board package was over a hundred pages long - the meeting started at 7:30am and wouldn't wrap up until after 4:00pm, including a working lunch. There was a lot going on with the business and I wanted the board fully informed and engaged. We had our audit firm participate to present an update on the 2018 audit including their assessment of our processes and the control environment; Nunn & King provided an update on all of the legal matters they were working on including the open pre-emptive rights offering, ensuring all of our legal entities were current with the respective Secretaries of

259

State, and the Lund Sports tax filing debacle; Powell provided an update on litigation matters; and Perkins & Black provided a final update on the workplace complaint independent investigation.

I also scheduled Laura McNamara and Emily Woods to present their assessments, observations and plans for human resources and information technology, respectively. They both did a great job. The board was blown away by them. I am a firm believer that your leadership team deserves the opportunity to present to the board of directors and demonstrate the value they bring to the company. So many times, CEO's gather information and slides from their team and present it as if they, exclusively, are driving the critical thinking and strategy. That's simply not fair to your team or the board, for that matter.

During these board meetings, we would hold a shorter, BBFC-only board meeting and then the longer, more comprehensive Epic meeting; Patrick Baldwin was a board member of BBFC, so he was in attendance for the former. Our finance guys presented the current financial outlook for BBFC, as best they could with some questions still unanswered by the BBFC management team. We walked the board through those expense items that were dragging down profits and planned corrective actions. Baldwin was quiet during this section of the meeting. He looked like he didn't want to be in the room. Board members had questions that were mostly answered by the finance guys and me. I knew the senior partner from CFC, Atwater, was not pleased that Baldwin was so passive and quiet.

Then, an interesting thing happened. The Epic board package disclosed that the auditors had another identified a control breakdown within BBFC. Prior to me becoming CEO of Epic, BBFC entered into a debt agreement related to the renovation of a soccer field in Mexico. BBFC management didn't have the authority to enter into such an agreement, there was no evidence that even Devlin was aware of the loan. Taking on this debt without bank approval meant that Epic had violated its credit agreement with its senior lender. On top of all of that, our accounting department was unaware of the obligation and hadn't booked the liability. Just when the accounting and finance section of the BBFC meeting was concluding, Atwater

260

asked for more detail about the loan. He was acting like he didn't fully understand what the auditors had found and explained earlier.

Since Baldwin had entered into the agreement, everyone in the room expected him to address it; instead he remained silent. I probably should have let the silence linger a bit longer, but instead, I spoke up. I explained in simple terms what appeared to have happened and why it showed a material flaw in our control environment - unauthorized people committing the company to debt obligations. Atwater looked in Baldwin's direction several times during my explanation, but Baldwin never made eye contact, nor spoke up and took responsibility. Again, this transaction occurred before I was CEO. When I finished my explanation, Atwater said, "Does the person responsible for this understand that if anything like this ever happens again, he or she will be terminated on the spot?" I said, "I believe he understands." The whole exchange and lack of participation from Baldwin was strange and uncomfortable.

The timing of the Mexico debt discussion couldn't have been worse for Baldwin. We immediately transitioned into a discussion about brand partners - Nike, adidas and Puma. We had several slides on the topic. We had slides about brand status, scale, social media reach, professional athlete and club affiliations, television rights valuations, and so on. Each slide quantified these elements and ranked the brands respectively. There was no debate, the statistics pointed to either Nike or adidas. Puma shouldn't even have been in the discussion. Baldwin then presented his slides. There were only a couple and the main slide was a list of his top staff members and their "vote" for our brand partner - unanimous to Puma.

Board members asked how his team members came to their individual decisions about Puma. Baldwin's answers were vague and rested heavily on a potential partnership with a new European professional club that Puma was helping to facilitate. One board member asked if we had surveyed families - Baldwin explained that the families' opinion didn't matter. Eyebrows were raised around the room. He claimed that the coaches' opinions mattered more. Finally, Atwater interrupted, looked directly at Baldwin and said, "we are talking about a multi-year, multi-million-dollar decision. A decision that impacts more than BBFC, it impacts all of Epic. I am not going to let you make a decision based on anecdotal information." Baldwin responded with, "anecdotal information? Well, I guess I built a successful business over the last twenty years on anecdotal information." The partner didn't hold back, "based on the financials we just walked through, I wouldn't call your business successful."

That was it - that was the moment Baldwin was done with the company and the moment our board was done with Baldwin. In the days that followed, I tried to mediate between the two - one minute, telling Baldwin to take a deep breath and realize that private equity guys rely heavily on data to make decisions. The next minute, I was explaining that Baldwin is passionate about what he does but doesn't understand the importance of analysis in making sound decisions. It was fruitless, they hated each other. I was trying to keep the peace, but it didn't last long.

MURPHY'S LAW

In the 1974 comedy, *Young Frankenstein*, there is a scene in the movie in which Gene Wilder and Marty Feldman are in a cemetery exhuming a body.

Wilder, playing Dr. Frankenstein, spits and says, "what a filthy job."

Feldman, playing his hunchbacked companion Igor, responds, "Could be worse..."

Dr. Frankenstein - "how?"

Igor - "It could be raining," as thunderclaps, lightning flashes and rain pours down on them.

CHAPTER 19

The past couple of days actually had a nice cadence. The board meeting was behind me, I was in the office (not traveling), most of my team was there and I could feel the progress and momentum of people working together. Perhaps, we were finally hitting our stride.

I returned to my desk at 3:30pm from a meeting in a nearby conference room. Carolyn greeted me and let me know that my next commitment was at 4:00pm, a catch-up call with Dan Atwater. She suggested that I take a half hour for myself before the call. My back was killing me, and I was still getting accustomed to an increased dosage of Carbidopa-Levodopa, my Parkinson's prescription. I felt particularly slow. I took her advice and headed out to the lobby to sit on a comfortable couch and flip through my emails on my phone. Even if it was just a 30-minute change of scenery away from my desk, it would feel like a break from the routine.

About fifteen minutes into reading my emails, I sensed someone standing about 10 - 20 feet to my right at the top of the stairs (our lobby was on the second floor of the building). I glanced to my right and realized it was Patrick Baldwin. He was wearing a black mid-thigh length coat; a scarf, neatly tied around his neck and tucked into the coat; a *Peaky Blinders*-style cap and dark glasses. He appeared to be looking directly at me although I couldn't see his eyes. I also noted he was holding papers in his left hand.

"Patrick, what are you doing here?", I asked.

He took off his glasses and hat, paused a moment and said, "Hey... you know how you and I haven't exactly been getting along?" He seemed like he was in a fog.

I interrupted and said, "Patrick, we are getting on fine, we will get through this, what's up?"

He continued, "well, we may have bigger issues to sort out now" and held up the papers in his left hand as a reference. I stood up, walked towards him and said, "c'mon, let's sit down and take a look." I had no idea what the papers were or what he was referencing. Quite frankly, those few moments and the interaction are a bit of a blur. I don't know if it was because I was taken off guard by him, his mere presence, his demeanor, the fact that he seemed "off" in some manner, or if what I was about to learn blurred everything.

We walked into a small conference room inside our main office. As Patrick entered the main area, he confidently greeted everyone as he normally would. At that moment, this actually relaxed me a bit as he seemed more like himself. I closed the door to the conference room behind me and sat down at the small round table. Patrick dropped the papers on the table as if he couldn't get them out of his hands fast enough. I looked at Patrick expecting he would provide me with some color and context. Instead, he just looked at me. After a moment, he proceeded to place his hat on the table, took off his coat, placed his scarf inside the sleeve of his coat, and wrapped the coat over the back of his chair. He didn't say a word. He then turned his back to me and looked out the window. WTF?

I turned over the stapled papers, about ten pages worth, and immediately realized that they were legal in nature. Even a quick glance revealed an official letterhead like from a court or government body. The letterhead was from the United States Federal Court, District of Massachusetts. Below it was a heading, *Search and Seizure Warrant*. I couldn't breathe. I continued to scan the document as quickly as I could. In short, a grand jury had been convened and a federal judge had found sufficient evidence of alleged criminal acts perpetrated by individuals associated with BBFC. The allegations included conspiracy, identify theft, visa fraud and perjury. The warrant had been signed by a federal judge. I mumbled, "Jesus Christ." Cell phone numbers, the address of BBFC's headquarters in Dedham, and a list of employees' names were included in the warrant. The remaining pages listed other

BBFC information, records, files and emails to which the feds were seeking access.

Patrick remained silent. I flipped back to the first page and scanned it again to make sure I understood what this was. It was dated about a week earlier. I asked Baldwin when he received the papers. He turned around, looked at me and said, "today."

"When?", I replied.

He paused, rubbed his eyes and said, "about 10am."

I held up the papers and asked, "how did you receive these?"

"A federal agent gave them to me," he said.

"What? Where did he give you these?", I asked.

Baldwin calmly said, "the feds raided my office this morning, probably thirty or so agents. They are still there." He paused, then his tone immediately became aggressive, "What a bunch of fucking assholes. This is what *your* government does, they fuck with people trying to make a living, they do this all the time."

"Whoa Patrick, hold on - what is this all about? What are they alleging here?", I asked.

He said, "it's all bullshit. They do this every couple of years to soccer organizations who bring coaches in on visas. It's total bullshit, probably started by some pissed off former coach. It's all nonsense." I asked, "so, you haven't done anything wrong with work visas?" I will never forget his response - he said, "did we cut some corners or bend some rules? Sure, but we didn't murder anyone, and we weren't selling drugs. Why are they busting our balls?" He had a different look in eyes, one of intense anger. I processed what he had just said and decided I didn't want to push him any further, I let it go.

I sat back in my chair, put my hands behind by head, closed my eyes and took a deep breath to try to calm myself. I then realized that I was in a glass conference room - I opened my eyes and looked to my right. A number of my team had been watching the exchange and, based on my body language and Baldwin standing and pacing, realized something serious was happening. I quickly returned to a normal seated position.

"Patrick, I need to call counsel right away. Have you spoken to an attorney?", I asked.

He said, "Yea, I called Beacon & Lynch and our immigration attorney."

I flipped through the warrant again and realized that the information request was addressed to BBFC's *custodian of record*. I asked Patrick who was the company's custodian of record and who was going to pull all of the requested information.

He said, "not me - you are going to have to handle this." I didn't even respond.

At the very bottom of the first page was a cell phone number the judge had approved federal agents to access, I presume tap. It was printed partially over the footer of the letterhead. I read the number aloud and asked Patrick if he knew who it belonged to. He seemed shocked and said, "that's my cell number, where do you see that?" I handed the papers to him and pointed to it - he must have missed it when he read the document because of where it was printed.

He asked me what it meant - his cell number being included in the warrant. I told him that I presumed it meant they could take the phone, access the call records and maybe even listen to calls since the court issued this about a week ago. He went pale.

I think I may have been in shock during the entire exchange. We had been through so much over the last year and now this. I couldn't even process what was happening. There were about ten seconds of silence and Baldwin picked up his hat and put it on his head. The scarf and coat followed. He then said, "I have to get back to the office" and left.

I simply said, "I will call you shortly."

He turned and said, "don't bother, the feds took my phone" and left the conference room. On the way out, he gave the team a loud "have a great day everyone" like nothing was wrong and left.

I remained at the conference room table, with the door open, reading the document in more detail. I can assure you that I had zero self-awareness at this point. I couldn't believe what I was reading. This investigation was being led by the U.S. Attorney in Boston - the same U.S. Attorney who was prosecuting the college admissions scandal. Because our office was literally across the street from the federal courthouse, we had a front row seat to the media frenzy that was happening every day. Celebrities, wealthy parents, and coaches were being paraded into the courthouse for their arraignments. What would this mean to BBFC or to Epic? Were these allegations true? Baldwin seemed so confident that he had done nothing wrong. But his comments about *cutting corners, bending rules, not murdering anyone or selling drugs* kept echoing in my head. WTF? I realized I had a lot of work ahead of me - I was going to have to quickly get educated on work visas and get access to BBFC employee records.

I flipped through the warrant one more time, then went to my desk to get a notepad. I returned to the conference room and went through the search and seizure warrant in detail, outlining and summarizing its key elements. With any complicated matter, I always find it best to break it down to its basic elements, write them down, put your own words on paper. Only then, do you have a preliminary understanding of the situation and can begin to prioritize the critical steps or tasks to get through it. The process doesn't take long, but it is critical. As I was doing so, Laura McNamara, with her laptop in hand, stood in the doorway to the conference room, "are you ok?", she asked.

I took a deep breath and told her, "nope, have a seat." She closed the door behind her and sat down. She certainly knew the challenges that we had with BBFC and Patrick in particular. Also, she was not a big fan of Patrick's. She had privately confided in me that she viewed him as a male chauvinist, bully. I couldn't disagree. Based on this, she likely thought I was just dealing with another minor personality conflict with Patrick - she certainly wasn't expecting what I was about to share with her.

I dropped the bomb on her - certain BBFC employees were under criminal investigation by the U.S. Department of Justice. I couldn't believe I was even saying these words. I told her about the raid, walked her through the elements of the search warrant, gave my opinion of what we had ahead of us in terms of gathering information and satisfying the DOJ requests and likely additional subpoenas. She just stared at me while I walked through it all. I then handed her the search and seizure warrant.

She took her time and read through the warrant. She asked a couple of questions as she reviewed it. Then paused, looked at me and simply said, "oh boy." We both sat in silence and then she opened her laptop and said, "ok, let's layout what we need to do." I walked her through my notes which she transcribed into her laptop and added her own additional thoughts. We covered everything from getting our outside counsel involved, planning for any potential public relations fall-out, internal communications (if any for now), getting our director of IT involved to lock down email accounts and all file storage applications, contacting and interviewing BBFC's HR staff members, identifying any third party vendors who could be involved in sourcing visas, and we even compiled a list of those on BBFC's leadership team who we thought could be involved in the alleged activities.

We called Ben Powell on his cell phone. It went directly to his voicemail. I called his office and spoke to his assistant. She said he was in his office, but on another call. I asked her to have him call me as soon as possible. I hung up and texted him, "call me asap - VERY serious matter." Within a minute, he called me. I answered and put him on speaker phone so Laura could participate in the call.

Ben said that my text got his attention. He said with everything we had been through, I had never written a word in all capital letters, nor called something a "very serious matter." I explained what had transpired. He just listened. When I finished, he said "holy shit,

268

what is wrong with this company?" He then went right into counsel mode and told us to send him and one of his colleagues a digital copy of the warrant and my notes from my conversation with Baldwin. He said that he was leaving his office immediately to drive to the BBFC office to meet with the federal agents. I asked if he needed me to meet him there - he told me to stay at my office and he would call me with an update as soon as he had one. Before he hung up, he said, "plan for a long night."

While looking through the warrant again, Laura asked me, "do you think they did any of these things?" I said, "unfortunately, based on my conversation with Patrick and his behavior lately, yes, I do."

Laura went back to her desk to contact the BBFC HR staff. I needed her to gain access to all current and former BBFC employee personnel files immediately.

I called in Emily, our head of IT, and explained to her that I needed a memo right away outlining all BBFC's active and archived email accounts; administrative access to those accounts; an immediate plan to preserve, safeguard, and back-up everything; and a similar summary for BBFC's file storage. One of the challenges we faced here was that Epic, under Devlin, never fully integrated BBFC onto the Epic email platform. We were in the midst of migrating BBFC to Microsoft Outlook, so I was confident Emily had all the email information and controls at her fingertips. She confirmed that she did. Unfortunately, she had no idea where BBFC was maintaining their other electronic records and files. Our company-wide integration plan had a couple of phases - email first, then migrate all other files and data storage needs to Microsoft One Drive. Her team was still mapping out all existing storage methods and had learned that BBFC let their employees maintain records where they chose; some on Google Drive (BBFC or personal), others on DropBox, others simply on their devices. Ugh, this was going to be a nightmare. I set Emily off with her tasks. She was unfazed, as usual.

Carolyn scanned the warrant and sent it to Ben and his colleague - when she handed me back the original, she looked at me like she wanted to give me a hug and offer her condolences. She said, "tell me what I can do." I asked her to "email my wife that I won't be home tonight, that something came up at work, but everything is ok." She said, "will do" and told me she would book me a room across the street at the Envoy Hotel so I could shower and clean up at some point - she knew we had a lot of work ahead of us.

I was starting to get emails, calls and texts from BBFC staff that were in the building when the raid occurred as well as others who were not there but were hearing rumors. I didn't want to answer any questions piecemeal, I preferred to put out one statement to all employees. But I needed some additional facts first and guidance from counsel. I called and texted BBFC's COO, Jack Cahill, right after Baldwin had left our office, but he still hadn't responded. I found this concerning.

I started drafting an internal communication that would disclose the Department of Justice's visit to BBFC's office and its allegations. I would advise everyone that we would be cooperating fully with the DOJ investigation, that we would conduct our own internal investigation, and that all employees were to adhere to a litigation hold (do not delete emails or any other files or records). Not exactly a motivating communication to send to your staff. This would be the third such litigation hold email I would have to send since I took over as CEO.

Ben called and said that the BBFC's offices were locked up and no one was there. He put a call into the U.S. Attorney's office but hadn't heard back. Apparently, the DOJ had finished up for the day. Ben was on his way to my office. As soon as I hung up, my phone rang again - it was Jack Cahill.

Cahill sounded exhausted and rattled. I asked him what had happened earlier. He said he was in his office when the search and seizure warrant was executed. He claimed there were twenty-five to thirty agents from several agencies who arrived at the office around 10:00am. They came into the office "aggressively" shouting for everyone to move away from their desks, put down their phones and to get in the central hallway that ran down the middle of the second-floor office space. He said that people were rattled by the way the agents came in - he was quickly separated from the rest of the staff

270

and brought back into his office by two agents. They gathered his laptop and other files from his office, took him out the back stairway and brought him to the federal courthouse across from my office. The federal courthouse also houses the U.S. Attorney's office and other agencies. He told me that he was questioned there until about 5:00pm, at which time, they returned his cell phone, told him to refrain from communicating with Baldwin, and said they would be in touch in a day or so.

He sounded like he was on the verge of tears. He said things like, "I can't believe this is happening... am I going to jail.... what am I going to tell my wife?" I tried to calm him down and tell him that no one was going to jail. He replied, "that's not what they told me. And, they gave me a letter that said I am a target of the investigation." I was at my desk and quickly Googled "DOJ target letter." Just as it sounds, this was a lovely letter from the Department of Justice to let you know that you are under criminal investigation. I was simultaneously trying to keep him calm while reading the search results when I heard him say, "I was just doing what Patrick told me to do."

I asked, "Jack, where are you?" "Driving home," he replied. I told him to take a deep breath and to remember that if he hadn't done anything wrong, then this would all work out. I reminded him that he needed to gather himself before he walked in his house, that his wife and daughters couldn't see him upset. I tried my best to assure him that everything would be fine. He seemed to appreciate it. I asked him to send me a photo of the target letter when he got home. He agreed to. I also asked that he come to my office first thing in the morning so we could get to the bottom of this. He appreciated it and said he would see me in the morning.

I had decided to set up in the conference room for more privacy knowing that Ben was on his way and I would likely have to start a new forensic investigation that night. This investigation would prove, by orders of magnitude, to be more consuming and stressful than our prior internal investigations. Emily walked into the conference room and said she just sent me an email. I asked her to take a seat. I pulled up the email on the large flat screen on the wall -

271

her email was thorough. It explained the BBFC email platform and that it was a tool used by other soccer clubs and the data was maintained by Rackspace, a large data center and storage company. Rackspace had the ability to restore any deleted emails for 14 days - that should help us from a records preservation and litigation hold perspective. One problem, the email provider did not provide an administrative function whereby one could access all email accounts and conduct key word searches, like we had done using Google Vault. Instead, the administrator would have to set a new password for a given account in order to access and view emails. This would mean that if we needed to investigate email activity, we would have to lock out the user and they would know that we were accessing their email. Ugh.

First, let me be clear - I have a strict policy of never accessing or reading employee emails in the ordinary course of business. It is a violation of trust, even though the email accounts are company property. If you are working for my company, it is implied that we trust and respect each other. You can't be snooping around and reading people's emails, it simply isn't right. Second, everyone has a bad day. Everyone has a day when they don't particularly like their boss or a colleague. Sometimes on those days, you vent by emailing a friend or co-worker. Reading an email like that can tarnish one's view of a co-worker. You simply shouldn't go there. However, there are exceptions and two of those are alleged fraud or criminal activity. If the DOJ had convened a grand jury and a federal judge had found sufficient evidence for prosecution, I knew I had just cause to access email accounts. Oh yea, one small detail - we were subject to federal subpoenas.

Emily and I came up with a plan - I would select the email accounts for which I needed temporary access. These would be those accounts that the DOJ wanted to see and those that I needed to access for our internal investigation. I would prioritize the accounts I needed to access, and she would change the passwords for those accounts late at night, typically around midnight. I would then access the accounts, perform key word searches, read and save emails until 5:00am or 6:00am; at which time Emily would return the email account to the previous user's password. When this simply wasn't possible because of an urgent need on my part or a request from DOJ, we would hide under the veil of the Microsoft Outlook migration.

I gave her four names of BBFC employees I would need access to right away, knowing that these individuals had their phones and laptops taken in the raid. I gave her another four to be changed to our new password at midnight. "You've got it," she said. She told me she was heading home for the night, but that she would be available 24/7 and to not hesitate to call. Emily was great. I thanked her and she left.

Ben arrived and walked into the conference room with Laura. After five minutes of "can you believe this shit?", and a quick update from Ben about his visit to BBFC HQ, he gave us a download of a call he had with one of the Assistant U.S. Attorneys ("AUSA"). What little insight the AUSA was willing to provide seemed to indicate that their investigation was focused, for now, solely on individuals and not the company. This was good news, I thought, until Ben was kind enough to remind me that the DOJ always reserves the right to change its mind whenever it chooses.

Laura and I walked Ben through what we had put together as an action plan. He added a few items to it. He and I also agreed that responding to the DOJ information requests included in the warrant needed to be done as soon as possible and the information needed to be complete. He asked me how long I thought it would take. I had no idea, since I didn't even know where all of the information resided. Without thinking too much about it, I told him I would have it out all done by the end of the week. Remember, this is Tuesday night. With pausing, he said, "I will tell them they will have it Monday - that gives you some breathing room." Generous of him, I thought.

We moved on to reviewing and revising my draft of the internal communication that was intended to simultaneously keep everyone informed about the raid, provide some level of calm, and let everyone know that we were, again, under a litigation hold. My draft was less formal than Ben liked and lacked the full page of detailed legal language explaining what a litigation hold means and the various ways you could violate it and put yourself directly in the crosshairs of a civil suit or, worse, the Justice Department. I respect Ben, he is a great lawyer, and I now consider him a friend, but when working together on a draft document, there wasn't much collaboration. Needless to say, he got his way and my comprehensive company-wide communication went out around 9:00pm.

Ben and Laura headed out and I returned to my office to start working on the forensic email review. I have had a number of people ask me why I didn't assign this task to someone else on our team or bring in an outside firm. Once and for all, here are the answers: 1) Internally: at the time, I couldn't afford to allow anyone else to access employee emails - remember, no one at BBFC had been indicted of the alleged crimes. I had to presume their innocence, protect their privacy in this matter and in their emails, and lead such a sensitive investigation myself. 2) Externally: the company had spent a small fortune on attorneys and consultants over the past year or so. We were not swimming in cash, we were still in the midst of a pre-emptive rights offering, the financial reporting was still far from optimized so I didn't have great visibility into the company's performance - the last thing I was going to do was incur more costs with an outside firm. 3) I had learned through the Devlin matter that conducting an internal investigation about potential accounting misrepresentations was complicated and the more forensic work you performed, the more you learned. However, a baseline knowledge of the individuals involved, their respective roles, behaviors, friendships within the company were also critical data points that needed to be considered in the investigation. BBFC was a complicated entity with a close-knit cast of characters - I was going to need to lead the internal investigation, gather and review all of the information in order to get to the bottom of this. Further, in all likelihood, I was going to have to support the DOJ. I was going to have a front row seat to a federal criminal investigation.

CHAPTER 20

I took off my shoes and settled into my desk. My laptop was connected to two screens - studies have shown how much more efficient a multi-screen configuration is, but I think the benefits are actually understated. I can't tell you the last time I printed something since I moved to two screens. I find it remarkably efficient when doing this type of forensics work, not that I am an expert.

I set up a new folder called "BBFC Investigation" on my desktop, then set up several sub-folders named for the individuals whose emails accounts I would be reviewing overnight. On my left screen, I opened the BBFC web-based email application and logged into Patrick Baldwin's account using the password Emily had provided me. Success. I had not used this application before, but it seemed pretty intuitive. Down the left side were the typical folders, inbox, sent, drafts, deleted, with any sub-folders or rules-based folders created by the user below the standard ones.

Patrick's inbox had twenty-eight messages, of which seventeen were unopened. How could this be? I opened his sent folder - nothing. Drafts - nothing. Deleted / trash - nothing. Was it possible that there was a setting that automatically deleted all emails, regardless of their specific characteristics (in, sent, draft, deleted, etc.), once he downloaded them to his laptop? I opened the settings in his account and found nothing of the sort. The email application was pretty rudimentary. I sent an email to Emily asking her to review his account and the settings to make sure I wasn't missing something. While I awaited her response, I moved on to the Jack Cahill's (the COO) account.

Same process, logged-in using the same password, success. Much different outcome. Tens of thousands of emails and a neatly organized *tree* of subfolders populated by rules. Something to dig into, to say the least. In the upper right-hand corner of the application was a search pull down menu; I opened it. It provided fundamental query functionality, but good enough for me - date ranges, sender, recipient, key words, etc.

The next six hours, from about 11:00pm to 5:00am, was spent searching key words, senders and other recipients copied on the emails. Key words like visa, passport, embassy, immigration, fraud, lie, P1, H1B, H2B, J1, and an ever-growing list of other BBFC employee names and third parties - I hit the jackpot. Every time I read a relevant or potentially incriminating email, I opened it as a separate file, saved it as a pdf and gave it a name using my own standard nomenclature that would quickly remind me who was copied and the main subject. I would save that file in the *Cahill folder*, so I knew where it originated. We are talking about hundreds upon hundreds, if not thousands of emails. Most emails revealed something or someone new - so I maintained a separate word document opened on my right screen where I would catalog each email and keep detailed notes. Oh... and I also realized that while Patrick may have deleted all of his emails, those who sent emails to him, received from him or were copied on emails to him, often didn't delete theirs.

Approaching 6:00am, I emailed Emily and let her know that she could reset the passwords for the emails accounts to which she had provided me access. I also let her know that I had only gotten through the two accounts, Patrick Baldwin and Jack Cahill. She quickly wrote back that she had reset the passwords and that her review of the Baldwin account confirmed my findings - virtually no emails on the account and no functionality within the email application that automatically deleted emails once downloaded. We later learned that Baldwin didn't download his emails, but rather used the web browser and, at some point, had initiated the habit of deleting all emails multiple times a day. We were only able to recover about fourteen days of emails. The only emails of substance were his confirmations for flights he took to and from Europe in the days leading up to the raid.

Around 6:15am, I walked across the street to the Envoy Hotel. It was pre-sunrise, cool, damp with a light rain. The previous day had been a partly sunny, mild fall day - in the mid-60's, so I was not dressed for rain. Fortunately, the hotel was literally across the street. I proceeded to check in.

"Good morning and welcome to the Envoy," the receptionist said. "Good morning, Griffin, Steve Griffin checking in," I responded as I took out my wallet. She looked confused; she says, "I had you checking in for last night - is that right?" I explained to her, probably providing too much information, that I worked across the street and had a late night and I just needed the room to freshen up. She looked even more confused, handed me my pass key and told me my room number. I asked for a toothbrush, toothpaste, razor, etc. She said she would have it sent right up.

I got into my room, dropped my wallet and cell phone on the table and lied down on the bed. I had stayed here before - the Envoy was a hip, Seaport hotel with a roof deck bar that is popular with the young professionals because of its one-of-a-kind view of the harbor and financial district. Even in the colder months, the rooftop is open with these heated, igloo-type domes that cover the tables. Whoever designed the rooms here, however, may have been trying a bit too hard - for example, a bicycle had been modified to be the TV stand in my room. I sat on the edge of the bed for a moment, then laid down. Almost immediately, I fell asleep.

I had the dream again – I was alone in the ocean, treading water. But this time, it wasn't peaceful. I was getting tired of treading water and was beginning to panic. The ocean was dark, and the waves were getting higher. I was struggling to catch my breath - I had cramps forming in my feet and calves. The cramps were getting worse and I was beginning to give up. Then, there was a pounding sound like a boat's hull beating against the waves. But I couldn't see it.... I sat up and swung my legs out of bed and pressed my feet flat against the floor to stop the cramps. I was soaking wet with sweat and out of breath. How could these dreams affect me so much?

277

The banging was someone knocking at the door. It was a hotel staff member with my makeshift dob kit. I was sweating profusely, and I couldn't get my feet to stop cramping. I looked at my phone, it was 6:40am. Do I sleep or keep moving? I decide I better keep moving; I cleaned up and headed back to the office.

I spent the next hour and a half on my computer digging into the various Google Drive and DropBox accounts to which Emily provided me access the previous night. I was trying to understand the lay of the land. To which accounts I had access, which accounts had significant numbers of files, which appeared to be well organized, etc. There were so many accounts and most of the files were disorganized. I kept detailed notes in a Word file on the screen to my right so that I could prioritize the accounts for forensic work later.

I waited until 8:30am, at which time I texted Cahill and asked him if he had a separate Google Drive or DropBox account - he replied almost immediately. He told me that he had one. It was his personal account, not a BBFC account, but it contained all of his BBFC files. I asked if he could please provide me with access. I hit send and wondered how he would respond. He didn't respond immediately - while I didn't want to read into this, I couldn't help but wonder if this was a true tipping point for him. After a couple of minutes, he wrote back, "sure - the password is…". I thanked him and logged into the account. It prompted me, asking for a code that had been sent to the account holder's mobile phone. Bloody two-factor authentication! I texted Jack asking for the code and he provided it. I input the code and I was in his Google Drive. I did a few key word searches and could immediately see that there was some good information here. I also could see the activity on the account down the right-hand side, so I would know if anything has been modified or deleted. Google Drive also tracks who else has access to a file - this would prove helpful in determining who else had accounts and was involved in any alleged schemes.

I left the browser window open to Cahill's Google Drive account, opened another tab and continued to search the other accounts and information Emily had provided me. A couple of our IT folks, plus Steve Lomax, and Laura arrived in the office. Steve said good morning politely as usual and settled into his desk nearby. He was working with me on three lacrosse acquisitions set to close sequentially in the next 30-45 days. He had a lot on his plate.

Laura sat two desks to my left. She greeted me as well and settled in. I looked in her direction a few moments later, made eye contact and she asked if I had been up all night. I nodded. A few minutes later, I sent her a calendar invite for 9:30am in the small, glass conference room and she accepted immediately. In the interim, I continued to reply to "normal" work emails that I didn't get to yesterday afternoon or overnight. Carolyn had also arrived, made eye contact and asked if I was ok - I must have looked like shit. I said, "yes, I'm great, why?" She said, "please don't take this the wrong way, but you look awful. What can I do to help?" I asked if she could clear anything that wasn't absolutely critical for the next two days.

Carolyn, in a very short period of time, became someone that I trusted and valued tremendously. She is caring, conscientious and selfless. I was reluctant to bring on an assistant, but the board had been pushing for it, and it took Laura to convince me that it was the right thing to do for the company. The first time I met her, I knew she was perfect for the job. Thankfully, for my psyche, Carolyn supported a lot of people in the office, not just me, so I could rationalize having someone on the payroll helping me. She managed my calendar, scheduled all of my appointments, reminded me of critical items that I needed to tend to, told me when I needed to eat something and even helped me stay on top of my medication. She also had her finger on the pulse of the staff - who needed some time with me, who was feeling down, etc. For me to let her get that close so quickly said a lot about her.

Laura and I met in the conference room - she briefed me on her findings from overnight - what she learned from her conversations with the BBFC HR staff and I reciprocated with what I had found, or didn't find, in the Baldwin and Cahill email accounts. I also let her know that I had access to a bunch of Google Drive and DropBox accounts but hadn't dug into them yet. We agreed that we needed to be protective of the file storage accounts because they likely included personnel files and sensitive information like passports, visas, dates

279

of birth, social security numbers, etc. Consequently, we decided that only Laura and I would review these folders. Regarding email accounts, we decided that I would do a first pass and then have Steve Lomax help with organizing and cataloging the relevant emails. I also knew that I would need a second set of eyes to review these accounts in case I missed something. Laura had a plan to pull together all of the employee information requested by the DOJ. I told her that I would send her links to Cahill's Google Drive since it appeared to contain a lot of folders including employee information like visa applications; copies of passports and visas; signed employee handbooks, etc. She suggested that the BBFC HR staff (there were only two, one whom was based in the U.K.) could pull the information. I was reluctant to include them in the process yet - I needed to know whose hands were dirty first.

Cahill arrived at the office - the night before was such a blur, I forgot he was coming in. He looked awful. No joke, he looked like he had just been crying. His eyes were red, hair unkept and he hadn't shaved. We sat alone in one of our break-out rooms that included a couch and two chairs with a coffee table separating us. I asked how he was doing? He told me that he didn't sleep at all - he couldn't believe what was happing. There were long pauses, his head was down, rarely did he make any extended eye contact with me. I tried to tell him that he would get through this, that his wife and daughters were the most important thing and that he couldn't let this eat him up. He didn't know what I had read overnight in the emails.

I asked him what this was all about. He stumbled through his initial explanation, starting with "we've done nothing wrong; we were taking our immigration attorney's advice." He provided me with an explanation similar to Baldwin's - that the federal government was "just busting their balls." He didn't mention yesterday's raid and his one-on-one meeting with the DOJ - which I found odd. I would have thought that those would have been such traumatic experiences that they would have been top of mind. I pressed for more details about the immigration advice and played dumb. He went on to explain that as the company was growing so quickly, from about 2014 through 2017, they couldn't find enough local coaches to work for BBFC, so they started bringing coaches over on work visas. They also believed that Europeans were the most qualified coaches. Cahill laughed and said that parents also thought the Irish or British accents meant they knew the game of soccer better than American coaches. The problem was that the visa process was complicated and getting more and more restrictive. He explained that the company's immigration attorney came up with a couple of different strategies to help bring in more coaches. He would stop at times, shake his head and mumble, "I can't believe this is happening."

I asked questions along the way like, "who was your immigration attorney; who worked with him on BBFC's behalf; who found these coaching candidates in the U.K.?", etc. Jack answered all of the questions - he told me that the attorney also provided similar services for other soccer clubs around the country as well as with some of the professional teams. He said the attorney also worked with hotels and resort communities bringing in seasonal workers on visas. He told me that Patrick worked closely with the attorney and that the two had a falling-out in 2017. I asked what caused the falling-out. Jack claimed he didn't know the details, but that Patrick had indicated that the attorney billed for some visa-related work that hadn't resulted in securing visas for coaches. Baldwin got angry and moved to another attorney. The more questions I asked, the more it seemed that Baldwin was leading the visa schemes and Jack was his task master. From what I read overnight, however; Jack's fingerprints were all over this as well. After all, he was the COO and Baldwin fancied himself as a high level, strategic CEO, not one to get in the weeds and certainly not process paperwork.

The more we discussed the details of the visa process; the more upset and emotional Jack became. He broke down and cried a couple of times. When he did, I just sat in silence and let him go. He explained to me that there were several BBFC people in the U.K. who identified potential coaching candidates and managed the recruitment process over there. He said a couple of names, I recognized the names and had even met a couple of them earlier this year when I was in the U.K.

I felt like I had gotten enough from him for now but had so many more questions. I also felt like he may stop talking all together if I pressed too hard on the immigration details. Instead, I asked "what happened yesterday?" He told me that it all started around 10:00am. He was in his office, which shares a wall with the stairwell. He heard a lot of people coming up the stairs, then shouting. He came out of his office to see federal agents instructing staff to get away from their desks and move into the central hallway. He said it was a scene right out of the movies, the classic blue nylon jackets, firearms visible in their holsters, badges in hand, etc. As he began to move out to the hallway, one of the agents stopped him and asked his name. He told him his name and the agent turned to another and said, "I have him." The two agents then guided him back into his office and closed the door.

He could hear commotion outside of his office, but the shouting ended pretty quickly. Then, he could only hear draws of desks and filing cabinets opening and closing, and the occasional mumbled conversation outside of his office. He also heard people consistently moving up and down the stairway. The agents told him that they "knew everything" and that he would only have one chance to come clean. He said he was nervous, scared as hell, but he knew what they were talking about. I found that odd - Jack had just told me that their immigration strategy was driven by their outside counsel - if that was the case, I would expect that he thought their strategy was legal and the last thing you would expect is a DOJ raid. Only months later would I learn that Jack and his colleagues at BBFC had known that they were under criminal investigation for at least ten months prior to the raid.

The agents provided Cahill with a summary of the allegations, including some of the details of how the visa fraud was perpetrated. They then asked him to drive, in his own car, to the U.S Attorney's office in the Seaport (across from my office). They took his laptop and files from his office and followed him to the federal building. Once there, he was brought into a conference room where he said he was interviewed for about five or six hours. He told me that he was shown copies of emails, read transcripts of phone conversations, and provided other documentation that showed extensive investigative work had been conducted. He was told that a grand jury had already been convened, presented evidence and that a federal judge had determined that the evidence was sufficient to proceed with the search and seizure. They handed him a target letter and suggested he engage an attorney. They also told him to not have any contact with Baldwin or any other BBFC executives. He had sent me a copy of the target letter the night before, but I figured I should grab a photocopy of the original while he was there.

When I returned to the room, Jack was in tears again. I returned the original letter to him and allowed him the get himself together. I had never been through anything like this before and my head was spinning. I liked Jack, always found him to be professional and likable. I knew he was a hard worker and I had found him trustworthy. But, at that moment, I couldn't help but think that these could have been crocodile tears. He had his head down while he was crying, but would look up at me occasionally and make eye contact - it felt like he was checking to see how I was taking it all in. It was a very strange feeling. I asked if he had an attorney - he said, "not yet." He said he had a friend with whom he had spoken on the way in this morning who was going to refer him to an attorney. I told him head home, get some rest, spend the day with his family and do not speak to Patrick. We agreed that we would talk again at the end of the day.

Baldwin returned to my office without warning around midday. Two days in a row - great. This is a guy whose office was about ten miles away, but almost never would come here before this all unfolded. He too looked tired, but not nearly as bad as Cahill. Just like yesterday, he walked in confidently and delivered a loud greeting to the staff. I made eye contact with him from my desk and he said "coach, got a minute?" "Sure, Patrick," I replied with a sigh. I grabbed my notebook, motioned to the glass conference room and he headed in. I followed and closed the door behind me.

I sat across from him at the table. He leaned in and proceeded to tell me that I shouldn't have sent the company-wide litigation hold email, that I should have run it by him first. I was speechless. What a fucking nerve. His actions had brought a federal criminal investigation into our company, put the company and our staff's

283

livelihoods at risk and he walked in here with zero humility critiquing my email.

"Patrick, seriously?" I asked.

He said, "Look, this investigation is total bullshit, we have done nothing wrong and that email is going to cause more harm than do good. My lads need to know that you have my back and that we are sticking together through this."

I countered with, "Patrick, we are talking about a criminal investigation being conducted by the U.S. Department of Justice. I have to preserve emails and other records, that's why we issued the litigation hold…". He tried to interrupt me. I closed my eyes, tilted my head to the left and put up my right index finger and said, "hold on, I'm still talking." He stopped and I looked at him - I saw something in his eyes I had not seen before. *Intense* anger. He looked like a different person. I said, "I haven't slept, and I probably won't for a few more days because I have to deal with this shit show. I have to deal with the attorneys, the DOJ, and my board. We are going to conduct an internal investigation and get to the bottom of this. You need to stay out of it."

"What does that mean, stay out of it?" he said.

Thinking on the fly, I suggested that he take a couple days and stay home - stay away from the office. "No fucking way. I will lose my locker room, I will look weak to the guys," he said.

I said, "I am telling you to take a couple of days."

He stared at me, then said "do you have my back?"

I said, "Patrick, I hope this is all a big mistake and that the investigation proves that no one did anything wrong, but I don't know enough yet to tell you where I think this all lands."

He said, "Do you realize that I can walk away from this company and have another one up and running in five minutes and all of my guys will follow me? BBFC will go to zero - do you understand that?"

I didn't want him to know it, but I had a pit in my stomach. Scenes in the movies always flow so smoothly with the dialogue between the antagonist and protagonist choreographed like a dance. That's not how moments like this really unfold. In that instant, between the circumstances at hand, his previous behavior, arrogance, his tone and the look in his eye, I realized the relationship was officially over... done. He was a bully. He had done *something* wrong, hell, he admitted yesterday that he "cut some corners, bent the rules..." and, now, he was backed into a corner. I stood my ground.

I took a moment, tried to stay calm and said, "Patrick, I need to remind you that you are still a shareholder of BBFC and as a result you have both a fiduciary duty to the company as well as a non-compete. You also have an employment agreement that includes non-compete and non-solicit language. Let's take a deep breath and trust that we will get through this." I actually couldn't believe the words came out of my mouth - it was like someone else was saying them.

He backed off a bit and said, "OK, but just don't send anymore fucking emails to my guys without me seeing it ahead of time." I said, "sure," just to avoid a fight and try to move on. I changed topics and told him that I had a bunch of questions for him about the whole visa process. I opened my notebook, preparing to make some notes. I said, "tell me how the P1 visa process worked."

He looked surprised that I referenced P1 visas and said, "we don't use P1 visas anymore." I replied, "ok, but you did in the past - how *did* it work?"

"You would have to talk to Cahill about that - he handled the visas," he said.

I nervously laughed and said, "Come on Patrick, you know every detail of your business. How did we obtain P1 visas?"

He said, "talk to Cahill."

I said, "I did, this morning. He told me you and the attorney handled the visas".

He said, "I'm not answering anymore questions until we have a joint defense agreement in place."

I'm no attorney, nor is Patrick, but I know three things: 1) I know what a joint defense agreement is; 2) Patrick wouldn't know what a joint defense agreement is without an attorney planting the seed, so he had already lawyered up; and 3) there was no chance in hell we were going to align with him.

I told him that I needed to understand all of the facts before we could make a decision like that. Further, that would be a board decision, certainly not one I could make on my own. He calmly said, "OK, well, I'm not talking until you get your facts straight and we have an agreement." I tried to get him to stay and talk, but he stood up, put his coat on, and bid a loud and confident farewell to my staff as he left.

The next four days, Thursday through Sunday night, were an absolute grind. I worked around the clock trying to operate the business in the normal course, plus multiple board and legal calls throughout the day. Then I would repeat the forensic exercise of taking over email accounts around midnight and play email voyeur until 6:00am. I was able to get through the top dozen or so of Baldwin's lieutenants' emails and the picture was becoming far too clear. I had also mapped out the files stored on Google Drive and DropBox. I had enough information to determine that the allegations brought forth by the DOJ not only seemed to have merit, but I had uncovered other information that appeared to show that key executives had breached their fiduciary duties to our company and likely misappropriated funds. All of this was intertwined. What a mess.

CHAPTER 21

My routine had become remarkably consistent over the last year - *if* I slept, I was out of bed by 5:00am, no alarm required. I would often wake up between 2:00am and 3:00am, mind racing. Work issues swirling in my head, too many to prioritize and settle in my mind. If it wasn't work that woke me up, it was a family matter or just some twisted dream.

Civil litigation, the DOJ investigation, rebuilding the corporate culture, managing employee morale, still trying to get accurate and timely financial statements, was our board pleased with our progress, would we be able to close these acquisitions and integrate them effectively, was our marketing team delivering... If it wasn't work, I was worrying about my wife, three college-age kids, grandparents, siblings... someone or something.

Nothing ever seems like it will have a positive outcome when you are dealing with it alone in the middle of the night. I have always been a worrier - my mind tends to go to the worst possible outcome, then I work my way up from there, thinking about how to eliminate the biggest risks and mitigate the smaller ones. It is exhausting and can prohibit you from living in the moment. I envy people who can simply roll with the punches or dismiss them and enjoy an idle mind.

Christine told me that she was worried about me, that I wasn't present when I was home and always seemed distracted and on edge. She said the kids were also worried about me. I told her that I just had so much going on at work and that things should settle down soon. I didn't get into the details. I had found that I couldn't relive even portions of my day when I got home at night. In addition, I couldn't talk to anyone about the criminal investigation - I had been instructed to not say a word.

I wasn't taking care of myself. I had put on weight and wasn't exercising. I wasn't eating bad I just wasn't eating great. In hindsight, the level of stress I was under likely slowed my metabolism. But I was also drinking to find an escape - not a good move. It's one thing to have a drink after work with a friend or colleague, or over dinner with your spouse. It's an entirely different thing to have a drink, or two, alone after work at a bar inside South Station while you are waiting for your train. That's called a *problem*.

I had also punted on dealing with my Parkinson's diagnosis. I didn't want to deal with it. Christine had enrolled me in a recurring physical therapy class for Parkinson's patients. I went to a couple of sessions and simply stopped going. I was the youngest person there and I didn't like how it made me feel; like I had Parkinson's. My excuse was that I couldn't fit it into my schedule. I wasn't lying, my schedule was unsustainable, but I should have made time for it. Instead, I joined the Equinox gym in our building in the Seaport - it was literally one floor above our office. Over the next year, I went to the gym once - to take a sauna.

It had been about six months since I was diagnosed, and my symptoms were definitely progressing. While I was experiencing involuntary movements, I was dealing more with rigidity in my arms, shoulders and back; muscle spasms; a changing gait and posture that seemed to be causing my lower back issues, including sciatica. Spasms and cramps in my feet and legs that would wake me up at night and mornings were a real challenge as my medication had run its course while I was sleeping - it would take about fifteen minutes for my meds to kick in after I took my morning dose with coffee before I shaved and showered. I was told to not take my meds on an empty stomach, but I am not good about eating breakfast. Consequently, I suffered through nausea every morning while riding the commuter train from Providence to Boston.

Most days, Christine would drive me down college hill to the train station; if it was unusually early, I would Uber. Once there, my routine continued - a small non-fat skim vanilla latte at Cafe La France in the train station. The staff there had gotten to know my routine so well, that by the time I reached the register, my latte would be waiting. Even if I had wanted to switch it up and order something else, I couldn't do that to them. I was starting to sense that the staff at Cafe La France may have felt sorry for me as they had started to bring my coffee to me instead of letting me wait in line. They also frequently asked *how I was making out*. This meant that my symptoms were more obvious than I had hoped.

The hour-long ride to South Station was easy and went by quickly as I usually scheduled several early calls. Providence was one of the first stops, so I would have my choice of seats - a single right next to the car door. Each stop thereafter, the train would begin to fill until it was standing room only... South Attleboro, Attleboro, Mansfield, Sharon, Canton, Route 128.... About half the passengers would disembark at Back Bay, the rest of us at South Station, the last stop. This is Boston, so people were actually pretty polite exiting the train and moving en mass to the station and out onto Congress Street. My pace had slowed noticeably, but people would politely work their way around me.

The walk from South Station to my office in the Seaport should have been an easy and enjoyable one, about a 1/2 mile or so. Take a right out of South Station onto Congress Street past Fidelity Investments' offices, cross over the bridge, left on a boardwalk that borders Boston Harbor and alongside the Children's Museum - I remember bringing our kids here when they were small. After the Museum, I had been watching the progress on the new playground being built in honor of Martin Richard who was tragically killed in the Marathon bombing. The playground is in a beautiful location and will be a wonderful tribute to Martin and his family. Across Seaport Boulevard is our office, on the corner of Sleeper and Northern Avenue.

Unfortunately, what should have been an enjoyable morning walk, had turned into a painful struggle for me. My balance had gotten worse and my pace had become quite slow. The sciatica was causing not only extreme nerve pain, but my right leg was numb, and I had begun using a cane. I would stop several times along the way and try to stretch my back or lean to one side to try to alleviate the sciatica and reset my balance. I recognize that people have to deal with much worse challenges, so I hate to complain, but this was starting to take a toll on me. I was always physically uncomfortable and experiencing extreme pain at times. I knew things were getting worse and I was starting to become self-conscious. I did my best to never make eye contact with anyone during my morning commute. Using the cane had become essential, but I wanted to throw it in the harbor.

I was usually one of the first couple of people to arrive in the office. I typically settled right into my desk and leaned into the day. On one particularly mild day in late November of 2019, I hadn't grabbed my usual latte in Providence, so I walked around the corner on Northern Avenue to Starbucks. Passing the federal courthouse, I noticed a number of news vans with their transmission dishes set up, journalists milling about with their camera persons, and several black SUVs parked in the area. I asked one of the journalists what was going on. He said that they were expecting some significant indictments that morning. I asked what he thought it was related to - he said he thought they was related to college admissions scandal, but he wasn't certain. I felt a pit in my stomach. After Starbucks, I decided to head back to the office along the harbor, which is on the back side of the courthouse, to avoid the crowd and enjoy the unusually mild weather. Turning the corner, I nearly bumped into Mossimo Giannulli and Lori Loughlin hurrying towards the back entrance of the courthouse in an effort to avoid the press. I made eye contact with both of them and did the uncomfortable "you go this way; no, I'll go this way" shuffle with Mossimo. I paused for a moment, heard shouts from the press corps and decided to turn back and head straight to the office. The pit in my stomach was gone - at least none of our employees would be indicted today.

My typical day had become a mix of meetings and calls with our corporate team, marketing one hour, IT the next, HR, Finance and certain divisions in the afternoon. Sprinkled in would be impromptu calls with Powell or our corporate counsel from Nunn & King. Every day, at least one board member or an employee of CFC would also call and check in. It had become exhausting and, at times, inefficient dealing with board members individually. At night, I continued my forensic work investigating the BBFC visa scheme in order to determine if there was wrongdoing on the part of certain employees and to satisfy DOJ subpoenas.

Based on emails, electronic documents and interviews with certain current and former BBFC employees, we determined that there likely was wrongdoing on the part of several employees. We had assembled a comprehensive, detailed timeline of the visa schemes including footnotes that referenced supporting materials (emails and other documents). When printed and organized in binders, the materials were compelling. We held several informal board calls, including our outside counsel, to review the materials - the majority of the board members wanted to terminate Baldwin and others immediately. I pressed that we should give Baldwin the opportunity to review the findings and defend himself. After all, he hadn't received a Target Letter from the DOJ yet, let alone been indicted. Certain board members thought I was being weak. My position was that he was innocent until proven guilty and he should have an opportunity to refute our findings. Furthermore, I wanted to be prudent about how we handled this to ensure that we didn't violate his employment agreement. Lastly, I knew that when we terminated him, he would rally his troops against the company. There was no doubt in my mind, he too would resort to a scorched earth strategy, even if he still owned a minority interest in the company.

Fortunately, Ben Powell agreed and recommended that I ask Patrick to come back in for an interview so that we could hear his side of the story. He was still an employee, actually an officer and board member of the BBFC entity, so he had certain duties to the company. The plan was that Ben, Laura and I would meet with Patrick and have Ben interview him. We would provide the evidence to him - we needed to protect some elements of the DOJ investigation, according to Powell who had participated in several conversations with the AUSA.

I called Baldwin and left a voicemail about getting together for the interview. He called me back within fifteen minutes and asked that the meeting be limited to just the two of us - I told him that I needed Powell and Laura to be there as well. He asked again if I would have the company enter into a joint defense agreement with him. I told him that we had discussed his request with the board and that the board had determined it was not in the best interest of the company to do so. He told me he needed to check with his attorney and would get back to me.

A couple of hours later, we received an email from Baldwin advising that he had decided to not participate in the interview unless the company entered into a joint defense agreement in advance of the interview. I called Patrick and asked him to reconsider and reminded him that he had certain duties to the company and that I simply wanted him to have a chance to address our findings. He became aggressive with me, saying, "do you know who I am, you are making a big mistake, I will blow this whole thing up...". I remained calm, tried to reason with him, but he wanted none of it. The call ended. I provided the board and outside counsel with a summary. We scheduled another board call for thirty minutes later.

On the board call, which was an Epic (parent company) board meeting, we decided to schedule a BBFC board call for the next day to resolve to place Baldwin on unpaid leave unless he cooperated and until such time as the internal investigation concluded or the DOJ took action, whichever came first. I sent out a formal notice for the board call to all board members, including Patrick Baldwin and two non-voting observers appointed by Patrick, his brother and another BBFC executive. Early the next morning, we received a lengthy email from Baldwin's attorney at Beacon & Lynch (who had also represented BBFC) indicating that Baldwin would not be participating in the board call because he wasn't provided sufficient notice nor was the BBFC board properly formed - neither of which were true. Our counsel responded appropriately.

During the day, counsel drafted the appropriate resolutions for the BBFC board meeting, I reviewed them, provided comments and the final drafts were distributed to the board members in advance of the call. I also prepared a detailed agenda for myself based on the summary agenda provided in the notice the day before. I preferred to be overly prepared for board meetings since I would be the one to take roll call, convene the meeting, provide background, present the resolutions, take the votes, and, ultimately, adjourn the meeting. Fortunately, I had Jonathan Witt or George Petit, from Nunn & King, on all of these calls to ensure that I adhered to some version of Robert's Rules of Order.

We dialed into the board call at 3:00pm. Since I was the host, I was alerted about how many callers were on the line, but I couldn't reconcile the number to the board members because CFC often had several younger guys listening in as well. I waited until 3:02 and proceeded to welcome and thank everyone for joining the call. I took roll call and, to my surprise, Baldwin, both of his observers and two of his attorneys were also on the call. No pleasantries were made. As soon as I called the meeting to order, Baldwin's counsel advised that her client wanted it reflected in the minutes that they disputed the validity of this meeting based on their email from earlier in the day. Jonathan Witt spoke up and refuted their claims. There was no rebuttal from Baldwin's counsel. I then proceeded to provide background to the resolution (i.e., grand jury convened, search and seizure, subpoenas, internal investigation preliminary findings and Baldwin's refusal to be interviewed by the company and counsel). There was some debate back and forth about Baldwin demanding a joint defense agreement. I was then instructed by counsel to ask for a motion to support the resolution to place Baldwin on unpaid leave. The motion was made, seconded and the vote taken - Baldwin was the only dissenting vote. No other matters were discussed and the meeting adjourned. Immediately after the call, Laura provided formal notice to Baldwin regarding his status.

The next day, Baldwin called me - he was surprisingly calm and made his best effort to be friendly. He told me that he never said he wouldn't participate in an interview without a joint defense agreement in place, which was not true. Even his attorney had the same demand. I just listened. He said he was willing to meet for an interview, would need to have his attorney present and did not want to be interviewed by Powell. I told him that Ben was handling the internal investigation and representing us on the DOJ matter, and he would need to be in the meeting. He told me he would get back to me.

I hadn't had any direct contact with the U.S. Attorney's office yet and I didn't like that feeling. You read that correctly - I did not like being in the dark regarding their investigation. I wanted to know what they knew. I wanted to know if they thought the CEO of Epic, me, was somehow complicit with any of these alleged crimes. I never thought I would be asking to meet with the DOJ, but that is exactly what I did at the end of November 2019. I was overtired, stressed, at times paranoid, and suffering from bouts of anxiety. Everything that I encountered at this company was beginning to take its toll on me. I wanted to tell someone what we had been through. I wanted the U.S. Attorney to know that I had inherited an organization built on lies and misrepresentations... and now, we had evidence of a scheme to illegally obtain visas. I wanted them to know that I had nothing to do with any of this. Instead, I was actually the one who had uncovered a number of other fraudulent acts and was doing everything in my power to clean this place up.

I wanted to have this conversation for my own sake, my own sanity, but also for the company and for our good and honest employees. I couldn't help but think that if the U.S. Attorney's office had the same information that I had uncovered, then they would think this entire company was corrupt. I needed them to know that this simply wasn't the case. I was afraid that the company was being viewed as some shadowy, criminal enterprise. I needed to put a human face in front of the DOJ and walk them through the binders that I had put together for my board. I believed that they would view me as credible and honest and begin to think of the company, its employees and investors as victims in this whole mess. I called Powell and left him a detailed voicemail about what I wanted to do.

It seemed like everyday someone was getting paraded into the federal courthouse to be indicted, testify or enter a plea agreement in the college admissions scandal. I could gauge the level of importance or celebrity-status of the defendant based on the amount of media activity outside of my second-floor office window. The more I saw this activity, the more I wanted to get in front of the U.S. Attorney and out in front of the story. I feared that when the media uncovered this, it would extend its current story about wealthy, privileged parents buying their children's admission into elite colleges to the madness of competitive youth sports, the scandal around illegal immigrants coaching their kids and someone financially benefiting from it.

Powell returned my call - he wasn't entirely sold on the idea of me volunteering to meet with the DOJ before they even asked - after all, who in their right mind would do that? Any attorney worth his or her salt would discourage their client from volunteering to meet with the DOJ. But the more we discussed the concept; he began to agree. "Let's demonstrate our commitment to cleaning up this company, ridding it of the bad actors and sharing information we have found during our own internal investigation with the DOJ," I told him. He agreed.

Ben called the AUSA and told him that we had assembled the additional information demanded in the search and seizure warrant and that we also found some additional, relevant information and would like to share it with him. Ben explained to the AUSA that I wanted to be helpful and I needed to understand the DOJ's allegations, the employees implicated, and the strength of its case. The AUSA was open to the meeting and they scheduled to meet with us at the U.S. Attorney's office that Friday, only a few days away, at noon.

In this company, it seemed that every week was insane, but this one in particular was over the top. Shortly after scheduling our meeting with the DOJ, Baldwin's attorney agreed to have her client interviewed. She would attend the interview with him. She also let us know that Baldwin had engaged a criminal defense attorney who would also attend. After some back and forth, the meeting was set for Thursday, the day after tomorrow and the day before my meeting with the DOJ. Ben and I agreed that we would meet the next day to prepare for both meetings.

The next day, I met with Ben and his colleague Paul at their office in Back Bay. Their office is in one of the towers adjacent to the Prudential Center. Below and connected to the Prudential tower, were several office towers and a retail area that included Saks Fifth Ave., Lululemon, Canada Goose and other high-end retailers. I took the "T" from South Station to Back Bay and walked through the retail area. It was humming with Christmas shoppers who appeared to not have a care in the world. I had been so consumed with work that I wasn't even thinking about the holidays. In fact, over the last ninety days, I had dropped the ball on my wife's fiftieth birthday, our wedding anniversary and was a ghost of myself at Thanksgiving.

I walked through the crowds dressed casually with a Barbour coat over a blue sweater, khakis, and a pair of Nikes. I was wearing my laptop bag strapped across my chest and carrying two binders under my left arm that contained hard copies of the evidence that was organized and tabbed with the timeline serving as the graphical table of contents. In my right hand was my cane. In recent days, I noticed that the rubber bottom of my LL Bean cane had worn through and now the sound of the metal tip clicking on the tiled floor of the mall was annoying not only me but drawing looks from others.

I checked in with security and took the elevator to the fifth floor. Ben's receptionist had gotten to know me over the last several months - she gave me a warm greeting and set me up in the main conference room. She told me that Ben would be right in. I put the binders on the table, opened the laptop and connected to Ben's WIFI.

Paul came in first. He was younger and junior to Ben. Even under these bizarre and high stress circumstances, I had enjoyed getting to know Paul and have a great respect for his intelligence, knowledge of the law, work ethic and ability to always stay calm under the most challenging circumstances. He was also very good at handling Ben, which was not always easy. He asked how I was doing with a bit of a laugh as if to acknowledge that he knew it was a bit of a stupid question. I told him that I was "fine" and that I was looking forward to getting through tomorrow and Friday's sessions. He comforted me by telling me to be myself - he said, "stick to the facts... nobody knows this stuff better than you, you will do great." Ben came into the conference room with a slightly less warm demeanor but no less likable. A quick hello and no small talk - he was either really busy or hyper-focused... likely both. He had stacks of manila and accordion folders under his arm - he dropped them on the table. I slid one of the binders over to him and said, "here, I had one made for you." I was proud of the binder - it had taken an enormous amount of work to gather information, let alone organize it and synthesize it into the graphical timeline.

He looked at me and said, "what is this?" I told him that it is my internal investigation materials. He looked back down while organizing his folders and said, without looking at me, "is there anything in there that you haven't already sent to me?"

"No", I said.

"Good, then let's walk through my materials," he replied. He didn't even touch the binder. I reached over and took the binder back. As I placed it on top of my other one, Paul reached over and took the binder and started flipping through it. I wasn't sure if Paul was genuinely interested in its contents or just sympathetic to me and wanted to show me some respect. Either way, I appreciated the gesture.

Ben proceeded to talk through the sequence of events and questionable activities we had identified during the internal investigation. Without a note of paper in front of him, he recalled each individual involved, each critical item, located the specific supporting documentation, reviewed the documents, called out an interesting tidbit or two, then would put the folder in chronological order. He even laughed a few times and said things like, "can you imagine putting this in writing," "the AUSA is not going to believe this one," or "I can't wait to ask Baldwin about this." Paul interjected along the way, reminding Ben of a required change of sequence or a forgotten email. Otherwise, we let Ben do his thing.

I realized that this must have been Ben's process of owning the information and crafting his story. Simultaneously, he was prepping me on what elements were important and which ones likely were not. The session took about two hours and it was one of the most impressive things I had ever seen. However, when we finished up, I told Ben that the contents and sequence of his folders were virtually identical to the binder I handed him at the start of the meeting. It was meant to be a bit of a jab and joke at the same time. Paul laughed.

While gathering his folders to leave the room, Ben said, "good, then we are all on the same page." Meeting over. I took the "T" back to South Station, binders in tow. I would spend the rest of the afternoon and evening working on "normal" business matters. I would get back to Providence just before midnight.

Laura and I met at Ben's office first thing the next morning. I was exhausted but definitely riding the adrenal rush in anticipation of the interview of Baldwin and the meeting next day with the DOJ. I knew I would likely crash this weekend. We settled into a smaller conference room off of the reception area. We agreed to meet about an hour early so Ben could brief Laura on today's plan and provide her with the opportunity to update him on anything relevant from her HR investigation of the visas and information she had gather for the DOJ. In addition, Jonathan Witt from Nunn & King, our outside corporate counsel, was in attendance. Ben gave Jonathan an overview of the interview plan as well.

After everyone was up to speed on the plan for the interview. Ben told us that he would be shocked if Baldwin actually showed up. He said that if he was representing Baldwin, there was no way he would let him participate in this interview while under criminal investigation. He said that there was "absolutely no upside, only downside." We debated this back and forth and finally decided to make some friendly wagers.

Ben bet that Baldwin and the attorneys would arrive but would leave within an hour after realizing the questioning was driven by facts that would hurt his criminal case. Jonathan believed he would stay longer than an hour, but less than two. Laura agreed with Jonathan. I bet that he would stay for over three hours. I know that I could have simply taken the *over two hours*, but I was making a point. I told them that I had come to realize that Patrick was arrogant. He had an innate, indefatigable need to win at all costs. It was in his DNA. Knowing Ben's demeanor and style, Baldwin was not going to like Ben. He was going to view Ben as his opponent. Unless his attorneys dragged him out of the room, he was going to settle in for the fight with Ben and try to convince everyone in the room that he

298

had done nothing wrong. He knew what he had done, but he would never admit it.

Through the glass wall of the conference room, I saw Baldwin arrive with one of his civil attorneys - they were about five minutes early. Ben's receptionist brought them to the large conference room I was in the day before. A couple of minutes later, another gentleman arrived, Baldwin's other attorney. Ben and Jonathan were having a conversation about a separate legal matter and Laura was looking at her phone. I lost myself in thought for a moment. Baldwin was from a working-class family in Belfast, Northern Ireland. He was, by all accounts, a gifted soccer player who leveraged his talents to attend and graduate from an Ivy League school. He started a soccer club, had a family, grew the business and sold it - providing a nice nest egg for his family. And... he was still the CEO of his business, with a nice salary and other perks while also owning a piece of the upside. What an amazing success story.

Instead of enjoying his position in life, he was now sitting in the conference room about to be interviewed about an illegal visa scheme, was probably spending a small fortune on both civil and criminal defense attorneys, waiting to be indicted by the DOJ and about to hear what we have uncovered. What a goddamn nightmare.

I had started to become intrigued by what drove people to slide off course ethically. When they cross the line, ethically or legally, do they realize they are doing it? Do they know they are making unethical decisions, but actually do some internal calculation of risk and return? Or, does the greed and power become so overwhelming that they *have to* do it or simply don't believe they are subject to the same rules as everyone else? At some other time, I would like to research and try to understand the minds of people who make these choices.

It was time, we headed into the main conference room - uncomfortable greetings abound. Patrick was seated between his attorneys and our group sat across from them. As we were getting settled, another gentleman walked into the room. I recognized him right away. He was the former U.S. Postal Inspector who was now a private investigator. Ben engaged him to do some work on the Devlin matters, including attending the Jackson interview. I thought, "why is he here?" Ben greeted him, asked him to sit at the head of the table. We went around the room introducing ourselves. The private investigator introduced himself as a consultant working with Powell, Sutton and Murphy. I later learned that he was in the room to take notes, evaluate Baldwin's answers, demeanor, body language and so on. Ben wanted an independent set of eyes watching Baldwin while he was conducting the interview. The attorneys then went back and forth setting the ground rules for the meeting.

I had my binder in front of me and I noticed Baldwin had glanced at it several times. Ben had his stack of folders in front of him. Baldwin had nothing in front of him, just his hands clasped on the table. Everyone else had notepads. Patrick did not look comfortable but tried to act like he was. He actually seemed to have a smirk on his face. Before Ben started his questioning, one of his attorneys leaned into Baldwin and whispered in his left ear. Baldwin simply nodded.

Ben reminded Patrick that his was not a deposition, but rather we were interviewing him as an employee in conjunction with an internal investigation driven by the search and seizure warrant executed a few weeks ago. Patrick said that he understood. Ben opened the first folder, took his time looking over the documents inside and then handed a copy to Patrick and one of the attorneys - this exercise would be repeated about twenty times over the next three and a half hours - yes, I won the bet!

"Do you recognize this document?", Ben would ask - in each case, Baldwin would review it and then answer. If it was an email that included him, he would usually either say, "yes" or "I assume so, I am copied on it." Ben started with the search and seizure warrant - Patrick confirmed that he had seen it. He said he was the one who received it. Ben then asked him to explain what happened that morning. Patrick said that he was a bit late getting to work that day.

Powell interrupted and asked, "Why?"

Baldwin said that he arrived home late the night before and decided to sleep in.

Powell: "Why were you late the night before?"

Baldwin: "I got in late on a flight."

Powell: "From where?"

Baldwin: "Ireland."

Powell: "What were you doing there?"

Baldwin: "Visiting friends."

Powell: "Oh, nothing to do with work?"

Baldwin: "Nope."

Powell asked Baldwin to describe what happened the morning of the raid. Baldwin explained that he had pulled into the parking lot at the BBFC offices in Dedham and was walking up the flight of stairs when he heard a number of car doors closing. By the time he walked into his office, he looked out his window and saw Massachusetts State Police vehicles blocking the road and other unmarked black cars and SUVs in the street and parking lot. He also heard a number of footsteps coming up the stairwell. Next, he heard shouting and saw, what he quickly learned were, federal agents swarming the office. They were telling everyone to step away from their desks, not to touch their computers, to put their phones down and get into the main hallway. Two agents entered his office told him to step away from his desk and to sit at the small conference table across from his desk.

One agent took his phone and placed it on his desk while the other agent went through his desk draws, filing cabinet, even his small refrigerator behind his desk. The agent who took his phone handed him the search and seizure warrant and explained what was happening. He also asked Patrick for any personal identification.

301

Patrick handed him his driver's license and the agent photographed it with his phone. Another agent entered the room with flat file boxes and assembled a few. They removed everything from the desk and filing cabinet, took the computer, a few thumb drives and his cell phone. They photographed the office from every conceivable angle. After about thirty minutes, he was told by an agent to leave the property and to take nothing with him. He was escorted down the stairs and out of the building. His brother and a few other colleagues were standing in the parking lot while a number of other employees were still on the second floor, in the hallway, being questioned. An agent came over to Baldwin and told him and the others that they had to leave the premises. Patrick, his brother and several others drove around the corner to a local coffee shop and waited.

I had inserted several blank pages in the front of my binder, in which I was taking notes. Laura was doing the same on her notepad as did the private investigator and Jonathan Witt.

Ben asked Baldwin if he knew that the search and seizure was coming or if he was aware of any sort of investigation. He said, "no". Ben asked, "what happened next?"

Baldwin said that some of the other lads came over to the coffee shop and said they had been questioned about their citizenship or visa status. They also told Patrick that the agents had been gathering a lot of items in the office - emptying draws, filing cabinets and such into bags and boxes. Baldwin said that the agents were aggressive. When Ben pressed him on the word aggressive, Baldwin backed off and said that there wasn't any physical aggressiveness, they just "came in like they owned the place." Baldwin said that he remained in the coffee shop for a couple of hours and then drove back to the office. He said that he didn't see any employee cars in the lot, but there were still State Police and unmarked vehicles there. He then drove to the Seaport to tell me what had happened and provide me with the search and seizure warrant.

No one asked Baldwin about this, but his timeline didn't add up. We know the raid happened at 10:00am, but he didn't arrive at my office until after 3:30pm. My office is fifteen to thirty minutes away

302

depending on traffic. I doubt he sat in the coffee shop for four to five hours.

Ben asked Baldwin about the allegations - specifically, were they true. Baldwin said that they were completely false, that neither he nor anyone else at BBFC had obtained work visas illegally. Further, he said that the company had always relied on an immigration attorney to manage the process. He confirmed that the majority of the immigration work was handled by an attorney named Kevin Pulman. Ben asked Baldwin to provide the background and history of working with Pulman; how did he come to engage him, how long had they used his firm, and so on. Baldwin couldn't recall how he was introduced to Pulman, he provided rough date ranges and said that BBFC stopped working with Pulman in 2017 or 2018. Ben asked why. Baldwin said that Pulman had "gotten greedy," had billed for certain services that hadn't resulted in coaching candidates obtaining work visas and Baldwin did not think BBFC should have to pay for those services. So, he switched to another firm. He couldn't recall the name of the new firm.

Whenever Ben felt like he completed his questioning on a given topic, he would ask Patrick and his attorney to return the exhibits he had handed to them. Occasionally, Ben would open a folder, review the documents inside, sometimes making the document somewhat visible to Baldwin, only to return it to the folder, not ask any questions about it, and move on to the next one. He did this, quite dramatically, with one particular folder. The folder contained a two-page document with the BBFC logo centered on the top of the first page - having reviewed thousands of documents and files, this is the only one I had seen with this particular letterhead. It was unforgettable, even if you saw it upside down, like Baldwin would have. This particular document was located on Jack Cahill's Google drive and was shared with a number of BBFC executives, including Patrick Baldwin, and countless visa applicants. Further, there were emails in which Baldwin was a recipient and this document was an attachment. Baldwin actually commented on it, making recommended revisions. This document was distributed to coaching candidates who were applying for P1 visas. The document was, in

303

short, instructions on how to lie to embassy officials when a coach was applying for a visa. I referred to it as the *script*.

The DOJ investigation was initially focused primarily on P1 visas. A P1 visa is intended exclusively for athletes (or other professional entertainers) and their coaches or support staff. Typically, the applicant is an internationally recognized athlete or athletic team seeking to enter the U.S. in order to compete or participate in an event of international standing. BBFC's coaches and staff did not qualify for this type of visa. Patrick Baldwin knew the P1 visa wasn't appropriate, other BBFC executives involved knew, and the applicant should have realized it when they received the script.

I had found the scripts through a rather circuitous forensics route. Using key word searches, we had identified tens of thousands of emails, attachments, folders and files. We scoured through them all, extracting and saving those that related to the allegations or revealed other questionable activities. The final, clean copy of this particular document was stored in only one place. Had we not been provided access to Cahill's Google drive; we would not have located it. It was buried in a series of folders and sub-folders and was pushed to potential candidates via a hyperlink, usually by a member of BBFC's HR staff based in the U.K. In our searches, the link would not trigger the key word. We got lucky - I had read virtually every document and link I could find, but sometimes you create your own luck - we had read so many emails.

The script included language such as the following (bold text is consistent with the bold text in the original script):

> What to take with you to your interview?
> When going to the embassy you will need to take along with you:
> - **A condensed version of your contract** – this will be sent to you from the HR department. This is a generic contract that is relevant to your P1 (**The professional club sponsoring you**) that will be sent to all staff. It will not contain any specific details that were sent to you in your initial BBFC contract

- **DO NOT TAKE YOUR BBFC CONTRACT WITH YOU!**
  - This P1 contract is another form of proof of where you will be working in case asked for at the embassy.

The script instructed visa applicants to tell embassy officials that the applicant would be working for a professional team, in the state where the professional team was located and living with a host family near the professional team's offices. The applicants were coming to the U.S. to work for BBFC, not the professional teams.

This document clearly was instructing applicants to lie. We then identified a number of the specific candidates who received the script and traced their visa history. In every case, we found that the applicant had been granted a P1 visa, the visa listed the individual's employer as the professional club, yet the individual worked full-time for BBFC. The visa workers did not provide any services for the professional clubs, nor did they receive any compensation from them. In most cases, the visa worker didn't even work or reside in the same state where the professional club, who signed the visa application, was located.

We also found that many of these applicants had cycled through a variety of visas before receiving the P1 in order to be in the country working for BBFC.

Ben held the script in his hand as he reviewed it, leaving the other copies exposed in the open folder. I was seated immediately to Ben's right, so I knew right away what he was reviewing. I looked across the table and saw Baldwin looking at the extra copy that was face up in the open folder. He then made eye contact with me and immediately looked away. Ben put the copy he was holding back in the folder, closed the folder and moved it aside. Baldwin said, "what was that?"

Powell: "What was what?"

Baldwin: "That folder - are we going to discuss what you were looking at?"

Powell: "No, not now."

Baldwin looked angry. He was accustomed to controlling meetings, dictating terms, and bullying his staff. His face was red and he leaned in towards one of his attorneys and whispered something. She then said that if we were going to be playing games, then her client was not going to subject himself to this. Ben told her that her client could leave whenever he liked. We continued on.

Ben dug into the type of work visas BBFC had used over the years. He asked when BBFC started using visa workers. Baldwin said that he had found there were very few good youth soccer coaches in the U.S. and, as a result, he had used coaches primarily from Britain and Ireland from the beginning. He said that the European coaches knew the game, loved coaching and were looking for career opportunities that simply didn't exist in the U.K. He went on to say that he and his brother had developed a unique professional development program that involved continuing education for the coaches that no other youth soccer program offered.

Ben asked Baldwin to explain H1B, H2B, J1, and E2 Visas. Baldwin explained, at a high level, the differences between the various visas, but said that Jack Cahill and the immigration attorneys were the real experts in that area. He went on to say that he had no direct involvement with the visas. The conversation was flowing in a more comfortable manner now with Ben nodding along as Baldwin spoke. There was a brief pause and Ben looked directly at him and asked, "Have you ever told a visa applicant to lie?"

So much for a comfortable conversation. Both of Baldwin's attorneys intervened immediately, "whoa, hang on a second... who are you to ask my client... Patrick, you don't have to answer that question." Baldwin didn't flinch and said to the attorneys, "no, it's fine." He looked at Ben and said, "no, I have never told anyone to lie."

Powell: "You have never directed anyone to make misleading statements about the nature of their visa?"

Baldwin: "No."

Powell: "Are you aware of anyone at BBFC telling applicants to lie?"

Baldwin: "No."

Powell: "Thank you."

Powell proceeded to jump ahead a few folders, while doing so, he asked a couple of benign questions. No doubt, this was simply a way to pass the time and let Baldwin think he was winning while he waited to hit him with another body shot.

He opened a folder, gave Baldwin and his attorney a copy of the documents inside and asked, "have you seen this before?"

Baldwin read the two-page document and says, "I think so."

Powell: "You think so?"

Baldwin's attorney: "This isn't a deposition, he just said he thinks he has seen it, give me a break."

Powell: "Patrick, can you describe what that document is all about?"

Baldwin: "It's a scouting agreement between BBFC and a professional club."

Powell: "What kind of professional club?"

Baldwin: "A professional soccer club."

Powell: "A men's professional soccer club?"

Baldwin: "No, women's."

Powell: "So this agreement requires that BBFC employees will perform scouting services for a professional women's club, correct?"

Baldwin: "Yes."

Powell: "In exchange for what?"

Baldwin took a long pause. He did not want to answer the questions. Finally, he said, "I believe they provided us with staff who would coach for us."

Powell: "Sorry, this is very confusing. A women's professional soccer team would provide your company with *twenty-five* coaches who would in turn scout players for the professional team?"

Baldwin: "Yes."

Powell paused and slid the open folder to his right - I had to move my binder out of his way. This will be the last time I bring this binder to Ben's office. He opened the next folder, immediately handed Baldwin and his attorney the contents and said, "do you recognize *this* document?"

Same, routine... Baldwin said he thought he recognized it and Powell asked him to describe it. He said it was a sponsorship agreement between BBFC and the same professional women's soccer club. Ben asked him to describe the terms. He said it included BBFC paying the club $50,000 per year in exchange for some tickets and signage at their stadium. Ben asked if this agreement and the previous scouting agreement were connected in any way. Baldwin said, "no." On to the next folder.

Ben then provided copies of a contract to Baldwin and his attorney - both attorneys leaned in for the first time to take a closer look at the document in front of Baldwin. It was a single agreement that outlined terms under which BBFC was required to pay the professional club $50,000 for twenty-five P1 visas. Ahh, the simple elegance of Google Docs.

The BBFC lads had drafted the agreement in Google Docs and saved it on Google Drive, consequently, the entire version history was saved; including who made the changes and who viewed the document. They had realized that this agreement, and several others like it with other professional clubs, was a contract to, likely, commit visa fraud, so they broke it into two separate agreements in an attempt to conceal the act. In short, they were buying visas and trying to hide the substance of the transactions through these phony agreements. By the way, call me old fashioned, but I don't think the DOJ, Homeland Security and other federal agencies are big fans of people selling illegal access and entry to the U.S.

Baldwin denied that was the substance of the transaction. He was clearly rattled but was steadfast in his position that the BBFC coaches here on P1 visas were scouting for the professional teams. His description of how they were scouting lacked any depth. To me, it didn't matter if they were scouting or not - it was this simple, the professional teams signed visa applications as petitioners attesting that they were going to be the employers of these visa candidates. None of these visa workers were ever employed by the professional teams, they were employees of BBFC. The professional teams knew this when they executed the applications. In addition, the professional teams listed the visa workers intended work address as the professional teams' headquarters and stadiums, further proclaiming that the worker would reside within a certain radius of the facilities. This was not the case.

The visa workers never actually worked at the professional teams' facilities. In fact, many of the visa workers actually worked in different states than where the professional teams were located. In my simple mind, the DOJ, Homeland Security, and Immigration needed to know what visa workers were doing for work and where they were doing it - BBFC and the professional teams had conspired to mislead the U.S. government.

So, who benefited from this scheme? BBFC, its shareholders, and the professional clubs. Baldwin believed he was getting low wage labor for BBFC; keep in mind that this scheme was perpetrated in the years leading up to the sale of BBFC to Epic, thereby inflating its profits through the use of low-cost labor. In addition, the visa workers were inappropriately gaining access to the U.S. and the professional teams were being paid by BBFC to secure the P1 visas. We were convinced others were benefiting from this scheme as well, but we hadn't figured out who yet. Others were being damaged by these acts as well. Domestic coaches were losing coaching opportunities to illegal immigrants and BBFC's competitors were at a competitive disadvantage. Not to mention, Epic had likely over-paid for its ownership stake in BBFC and we had this entire mess dumped in our laps.

Powell continued to press Baldwin on how the BBFC scouting function worked. When and where did coaches who predominantly coached boys' teams scout girls' teams? Were scouting reports consistently prepared and who at BBFC managed that function? Could he provide copies of scouting reports that were provided to the professional clubs? Over the years, how many players scouted and identified by BBFC actually signed professional contracts to play for these professional teams? Baldwin was getting frustrated but said that his coaches did indeed perform scouting services, but he was not well versed on the details. He said he was certain that scouting reports were prepared on a consistent basis. Ben asked if Baldwin could circle back and provide us with examples of those reports as well as a detailed overview of how the scouting services worked. Baldwin said he would do so. I never saw a single scouting report provided to a professional club.

Powell took back the agreements from Baldwin and the attorney, placed them in their appropriate folders and put the folders face down on the pile he had been through. He opened the next folder, did not distribute the documents in it and asked Baldwin, "did you enter into similar sponsorship and scouting agreements with other professional clubs?". Baldwin looked down and off to the side as if trying to remember. I couldn't help but think how ridiculous this was. I had read the emails, some of which included detailed back and forth negotiating between Baldwin, Cahill and representatives from the professional clubs. Hell, I had reviewed the multiple drafts of agreements and executed agreements that had Baldwin's fingerprints all over them. I found it ridiculous that he was acting like he couldn't remember.

He finally responded with, "I think so."

Powell: "Do you recall the names of the other professional clubs?"

Baldwin: "I can't recall. I wasn't that involved, Cahill handled most of those."

Before Ben could respond, Baldwin's attorney asked if we could take a bathroom break. We all agreed.

CHAPTER 22

Let's catch up a bit on how all of the information Ben used in his interview of Baldwin was actually sourced and organized.

Since the raid, we had been through hundreds of thousands of emails and related documents. It was exhausting - like putting together a puzzle when people were doing everything they could to hide the pieces from you and you didn't even know what the puzzle was supposed to look like.

But I had a starting point - the government's allegations. I knew the focus was on visas. Unfortunately, Patrick Baldwin had deleted virtually all of his emails and we could not recover them so I couldn't do key word searches on his email account. At first, this felt like a devastating blow. But I quickly found that very few others at BBFC employed the same practice, despite, being instructed to delete emails or use personal email accounts by BBFC management from time to time. Instead, I found that I could piece together the emails that

Baldwin had sent by sourcing them *from* his staff's inboxes. I also could find emails sent *to* Baldwin as long as another BBFC staff member had been copied. What I couldn't obtain was emails that Baldwin sent to, or received from, a third party and that did not include a BBFC staff member. I had learned, however, that Baldwin tended to delegate and include others in his communications, therefore, I suspected, that most emails would include copying Cahill or one of his other lieutenants who would have to do the actual work.

The forensic workflow first required gathering, organizing and reviewing all of the Patrick Baldwin-related emails sourced from other employee email accounts. Next, I performed the key word searches on these emails and on the BBFC leadership emails accounts - this started at about twenty individuals and expanded significantly as time went on. These key words originally included terms only related to the DOJ's visa-related allegations but expanded as we learned more. Emails that were clearly incriminating or even remotely relevant were extracted and saved as PDFs. The emails were saved in the appropriate folder, named accordingly, and tagged with sender, recipients, date, subject line, topic and content description. By going through this exercise individually, I became intimately knowledgeable of each of the individuals involved. We understood the depth of their involvement (who had a leadership and active role) and who was a follower simply executing assigned tasks. We could see how often people communicated, their tone, language, etc. In other words, we started to develop profiles for each person involved.

Going through this process, other individuals I hadn't even considered or even heard of became relevant because they were copied on an email or their name was mentioned in the body of the email. The scope kept expanding and I would have to investigate their emails and files. I was also finding new names of third parties that I had to research and understand their relationship to BBFC or members of management. This always led to new key words and terms that I would have to use in new queries across all of the relevant email accounts.

Still, I could not hand any of this off because it was so confidential because of both the criminal investigation and need to protect the confidentiality of employee emails. The more I dug, the more I found - it was like going into a cave and finding different branches that led in different directions and kept expanding. As I was exploring, I would place a lantern in each branch to enlighten that particular brand and map my progress. At times, it felt like it would never end, but I knew there were only so many emails - I was getting close. The shadows on the walls of the cave were slowly getting clearer - pardon the Plato's Republic reference.

I felt like I had fully exhausted the emails and files associated with the P1 visas and agreements with the women's professional teams. We had copies of the visa applications and the signed affidavits from the applicants and the professional clubs. We had the actual visas, our payroll records, individual job descriptions, and the script provided to the applicants to mislead the embassies. We even had the bogus agreements between BBFC and the professional clubs and countless emails that indicated the participants knew they were breaking the law. This was a lot of incriminating information that took a lot of work to source, but I couldn't help but think I was still missing something else.

Baldwin had a big ego; he was arrogant and greedy. He would see other ways of making money for himself related to the visas and would pursue it because he thought he was above the law - that is what I had come to think of him. I was riding the commuter rail home late one evening thinking about the DOJ allegations and the information we had gathered. I took out my notebook and made an outline of the categories of key evidence we had found. Below the list, I included several qualitative data points and events that concerned me about Baldwin, besides the personality traits I listed above. He had never wanted me to get deeply involved in his business - I dismissed it as entrepreneurial ego. But now I knew there were other reasons - the P1 visas. But, the P1 visas were not utilized while I was CEO - why would he care if I was digging into his business now to help make it more profitable? Understanding the details of the BBFC business and helping with strategy should have pleased him, not concerned him.

Then I reflected on a couple things. First, I had attended two of the annual soccer coaches' conventions (*the* big event everyone in the industry attends); and at each one, Baldwin behaved like he didn't want me there. He didn't include me in his scheduled meetings or make any effort to introduce me around - I would see him having cocktails with others from the industry or seated in a corner of the hotel lobby meeting with people I didn't recognize. He would make eye contact with me and return to his conversation. He never included me or introduced me to his contacts in the industry. It was odd. Again, I felt like I didn't want to step on his toes, but I was here to help. Was he concerned they may say something about Patrick that he didn't want me to know? Did he think that I would not provide value because I wasn't a soccer "guy"? Nonetheless, I felt like he was overly protective of his industry relationships; many of whom were competitors.

The second series of concerns involved a trip I had made to Europe. I was going to meet Patrick in Belfast and then take a few meetings around Europe at the end of January 2019. I had been the CEO of Epic for all of sixty days and I needed to be in Belfast, London and Barcelona. BBFC was acquiring an elite, youth soccer event in Northern Ireland. The same week, BBFC staff were presenting at a conference sponsored by the U.K.'s equivalent of the NCAA in London and I was meeting with a soccer event acquisition target in Barcelona later that week. It would be a busy week of travel, but I preferred it that way if I was going to make the trip the Europe.

Hours before my flight to Dublin, while en route to Logan Airport, I received an email from Patrick Baldwin - the topic was about annual pay increases for his staff. He had been pressing me to approve his recommended increases, yet I had told him repeatedly that we could not put through any pay increases until we finalized our 2019 consolidated budget, not to mention BBFC was not performing well. Also, our board's compensation committee would have to approve these pay increases, not me. We were obviously late (since we were already at the end of January 2019), but with everything we uncovered from an accounting perspective, I needed to construct a new, detailed budget from the bottom up before we could be comfortable presenting any pay increases or bonus plans to the board. I had told Patrick this more than once over the past month. At the end of his email, he said he wanted the pay increases approved immediately and wanted to let me know that if I didn't, he may have to introduce me to the Shankill Gang when we were in Belfast. I had no idea what he was referencing so I Googled the Shankill Gang. Apparently, this was a now-defunct criminal organization that was based in Northern Ireland known for killing people based on their religion with the preferred method of slitting their victims' throats. *Strike 1.*

When I arrived in Belfast, I felt the same treatment I had felt at the annual soccer conventions. I attended the PR event announcing our acquisition of the Belfast Cup tournament at a castle on the outskirts of Belfast. Patrick was already there when I arrived. He was mingling with other attendees, gave me a nod when our eyes met and then took a seat in the front row with the board members of the event and a celebrity guest, some retired professional footballer.

Not being a soccer historian, I looked him up on Wikipedia. The footballer was born in Belfast, played in a couple of World Cups for Northern Ireland and played professionally for a couple clubs before his career was cut short by a knee injury. He signed with his first pro club when he was only seventeen years old and is still one of the youngest players to ever play in the World Cup. I thought it was pretty cool that they had a hometown hero here for the announcement. I kept reading through the Wiki when I noticed an odd reference in the *personal life* section. It stated that he married his wife despite fears of reprisal from the Shankill Gang, with him being Protestant and his wife being Catholic. I looked up and saw Patrick with his arm around the footballer, leaning in and whispering in his ear. What are the odds?

I was seated in the back of the room alone. Believe me, I wasn't looking for publicity or to be in the spotlight, just a little common courtesy. Baldwin had played in this tournament as a youth player and was from the area, so this made for a great story and he was the right representative from our company. But I couldn't help but feel that he did not want me to get too close. Following the event, we

315

returned to our hotel and agreed to take a couple of hours to freshen up, check emails, return calls and meet for dinner at 7:00pm.

A BBFC staffer based in Ireland, Paul Macklin, had driven me from the airport in Dublin to the event at the Castle. He also drove Patrick and me back to the hotel. The three of us had agreed that we would have dinner that night. Paul and I had a nice conversation on the drive from Dublin, mostly talking about the PR event and the future of the Belfast Cup. I had met Macklin before, and he seemed like a gentleman and a family man. I learned that he was the BBFC point of contact for all activities in Europe, from the Belfast Cup event to our academy affiliations around the continent. He spoke quickly with a thick accent and was not shy about sharing his plans for a broad expansion of the BBFC brand not only throughout Europe but into China as well. I enjoyed his passion, but, quite frankly, my head was spinning. When we had arrived at the Castle earlier, I told him that I would love to continue the conversation and get a better understanding of his vision, perhaps over dinner. He seemed genuinely happy that I offered.

At about 5:30pm, I had caught up on my critical emails and I thought about the conversation I had with Macklin earlier. I thought I may not have the opportunity to spend time with him in person, one-on-one without Baldwin's participation, for a while. So, I texted Macklin to see if he wanted to grab a beer before dinner. He responded immediately and told me that he was parked outside of the hotel - apparently, he lived far enough from Belfast proper that it made more sense to sit tight rather than drive back and forth. I felt bad he was sitting in his car - I met him in the lobby immediately. I ordered a Guinness and he order a Diet Coke. We chatted a bit more about the PR event and he filled me in on the history and prestigious nature of the Belfast Cup. He told me that it wasn't likely to be a profitable event for us, but one that carried a lot of history and respect - I wasn't so sure I liked the sound of that. Believe me, I understand the value of prestige and aspiration, but there is no reason all of our events can't at least break even.

I asked him to walk me through his European growth strategy again. I would like to think that I am a pretty quick study, but this was absolutely impossible to follow. He would move from one country to another in the same sentence, mentioning people I had never heard of, referencing our current professional club relationship one moment, then the likes of Manchester City, Manchester United and Valencia in the next breath. I had no idea what he was talking about. It was making me anxious. He was passionate about it all but based on the structure (or lack thereof) of his thinking and how he communicated, I was concerned about BBFC's international strategy and whether we had the right leadership. From what I could gather, his strategy was a blend of BBFC owning and operating academies in certain markets and, separately, licensing deals by which local operators would manage a soccer academy using the BBFC brand and we would simply collect a licensing fee. I needed to see the respective financial models, understand the demand in each target marketplace, the incumbent competitors, and the quality of our operators before I could sign off on such an aggressive international strategy when BBFC still hadn't optimized its domestic business.

I wrapped up the conversation with Macklin at about 6:15pm and suggested we text Patrick and grab dinner a little early since it was just going to be the three of us. Paul said, "I don't think that will work, Patrick specifically said 7:00pm." I thought, ok, so why can't we meet forty-five minutes earlier? I pressed politely but could tell that Macklin didn't feel comfortable trying to move the dinner up - he seemed like he didn't want to inconvenience Baldwin. This made no sense to me - I don't want to sound like a jerk, but I was the CEO of the company, these two guys worked for me and we couldn't have dinner forty-five minutes early, at my request? I told him that I would text Baldwin - he looked nervous. I sent the text, suggesting that we meet early. No response. After a few minutes of uncomfortable silence of Paul and I looking at our phones, I said, "where is Patrick?" Paul hesitated, clearly not wanting to answer and said, "he has another meeting now. He said he would meet us at Bert's at 7:00pm." I just stared at him. I then said, "well take me to Bert's then, I would rather wait there than here, maybe he will be early." I got up and walked toward the exit. Paul followed.

We got in Paul's car and started driving. I pressed again on where Patrick was. He said he didn't know who he was meeting with, but he said he was meeting at the Merchant Hotel. He asked if I had ever been there. I said, "no." I thought to myself, how the hell could I have ever been there when I have told you three times that this is my first visit to Belfast? He proceeded to give me a history lesson on the Merchant Hotel as we drove. I asked where the hotel was located, and he said it is only a couple of blocks ahead. He said that we would be having dinner right around the corner from the hotel. The traffic stopped and he pointed ahead and to the left and said, "see that building with the dome, that's the Merchant." Without thinking, I released my seatbelt and opened the door. He asked, "what are you doing?" While getting out of the car, I said, "I'm going to meet someone at the Merchant Hotel," and I closed the door behind me.

It was cold and damp, just a nasty night. I hustled across the sidewalk and up the steps of the hotel. It was grand, to say the least. The main lobby was beautiful, with brass handrails leading up a short flight of stairs to the concierge and reception desks, detailed wood carvings with gold trim and a domed ceiling that must have risen fifty feet above the massive lobby. I looked around, saw a bar to the right and headed in that direction. As I entered, I noticed it was rather quiet, only a couple of people at the bar - to the far right, near the front wall of the building was Patrick Baldwin and two other men seated at a table in the corner. I headed in their direction.

I got about ten feet from the table before he looked at me - it was the first time in my life I can say someone looked like they saw a ghost. He was shocked to see me. "What are you doing here?", he said without hesitating. "Meeting you for a drink, what's up?", I said. Before he could respond, I introduced myself to his two companions. The gentleman closest to me was massive - I would say 6'3", 300 pounds plus, with a huge, shaved head and tattoos covering both arms. I could also see a tattoo creeping up his neck from under his collar. He stood up and shook my hand - his hand was massive and cold. He didn't smile but grunted his name. His brogue was so thick I couldn't understand him. He sat back down. The other gentleman, more human-sized, didn't stand up, but simply nodded and said, "nice to meet you." No brogue. He didn't say his name. He looked like a miserable bastard but also looked familiar to me. I looked back at Patrick - he didn't say a word. It was uncomfortable. I scanned the table and noted that they were about halfway through their beers. I asked, "can I grab you guys another round?" Patrick immediately said, "no - can you give us a few minutes to wrap up here?"

Talk about uncomfortable. I nervously laughed for a moment and then realized he was serious. I said, "sure" and walked away. I moved to the furthest end of the bar. I couldn't believe what just happened. I was fuming. Who were these guys and how rude could someone be? I flew over here for this kind of treatment? Jesus, he reported to me and he treated me like that? *Strike 2.*

I ordered a Guinness and made small talk with the bartender but couldn't help but look over at Baldwin's table from time to time. They were leaning into the table having a serious conversation. No one was smiling, this was not three buddies who grew up together catching up when their pal, Patrick, was back in town. I thought about how I could get myself back over there, so I asked the bartender to bring their table another round, he said, "sure thing." I watched him pour their beers, place them on a tray and headed over to their table. He placed the drinks down and motioned that the beers were on me. I didn't get a thank you, a raise of the glass, not even a goddamn nod of appreciation. That was it, I was pissed. I took my beer and headed over the to table. I grabbed a chair from the next table and seated myself.

Patrick tried to diffuse the tension of me joining them without an invitation by saying, "good timing, we were just wrapping up." "Great, so how do you guys know each other?", I asked. Patrick answered for them - said he grew up with the big guy and the other guy is a friend. I nodded along smiling looking at the two friends when I realized again that the smaller guy definitely looked familiar. I said, "God, you look so familiar, I feel like I know you." He immediately replied, "no, I don't think so." Who says that? Normally, you would say something like, "really, where are you from?" Not this jerk. I wanted to tell him that he seemed like a miserable bastard, but instead I said, "I really do feel like I know you from somewhere." Patrick interrupted with, "no, you don't know him." I found it odd that Patrick felt the need to opine that I didn't know this guy. How would he know?

I asked where the miserable bastard where he was from and he told me "Boston." OK, something I can work with - "me too", I said. "What do you do in Boston?", I asked. He told me that he owned bars in Boston, Chicago, Ireland and Thailand. I found the Thailand reference really strange. I asked him if he knew the Glynn family from Boston who own a bunch of restaurants and Irish bars in and around city - he coldly said, "no." In my mind, I called bullshit on this guy. Anyone in the food and beverage business in Boston knows the Glynns. Something didn't add up here.

Patrick said, "well guys, I have to get to a dinner, great to see you both," as he slid his chair back, stood up, walked around the table and gave each guy a handshake and man-hug. I had never seen Baldwin do anything remotely so personal. I shook their hands again, first with the monster who grunted something unintelligible, then the Boston guy. As I shook his hand, I realized how I knew him. He was on my overnight flight from Boston to Dublin, literally only about twelve hours earlier. I held his hand a second longer and told him he sat across the aisle from me on Aer Lingus. He seemed shocked, but almost aggravated by the fact that I recognized him and was on the same flight. I then said, "Oh my God, what a small world, you sat right across from me. That is crazy, what are the odds?", as I looked back and forth between him and Patrick. Neither the guy nor Patrick responded as any other human being would. It was like they were disappointed that I had even met him, let alone knew what flight he was on. I found it very strange. He literally did not respond. He and the monster turned and left. Patrick and I sat back down. I said to him, "wasn't that bizarre that he sat right across from me on the flight?" He had the nerve to say, "what are you doing here?" I could tell he was aggravated. I told him that I was early and didn't feel like sitting in the hotel lobby alone with Macklin. He didn't even reply; he was acting like a brat. After a few moments, he asked, "where is Paul?" I told him, "out in the car, I guess." He called for the check. It was abundantly clear that he had not wanted me to see him with those characters.

The three of us had dinner around the corner - I was tired and aggravated. I also couldn't stop my mind from wandering back to those two guys - what was Patrick up to? Why was he meeting with them? The whole thing seemed suspect to me. Paul and Patrick talked about the European strategy the entire dinner. Paul's scattered and incomplete thoughts coupled with Patrick's incessant Braveheart and Game of Thrones references gave me a headache and killed my appetite. It was all soft, qualitative hyperbole about how BBFC would be the biggest soccer club in the world.

We were eating in a restaurant that had a jazz bar feel to it, not something I would have expected in Belfast. The food was fine, but I didn't want to be there. As we finished dinner and Patrick ordered an English tea, a keyboard player started playing in the far corner of the room. A young woman came out and began singing while leaning against the keyboard. Patrick became completely distracted, watching the singer. The waiter put his tea in front of him and Patrick didn't thank or even acknowledge the waiter. He seemed consumed by the woman. Another pet peeve of mine - people who treat service providers, like wait staff, as irrelevant servants and men who blatantly leer at women. I cannot stand that type of behavior. After a moment, out of nowhere, Patrick made a few inappropriate remarks about the woman singing. I knew that Patrick was married with two young children and I now knew, for certain, that he was a real asshole.

The next morning, Patrick and I flew to London to meet several of his staff at a sports education conference. During the flight, he explained to me that one of his guys would be presenting at the conference. He would be presenting a strategy to bring U.K. college students, concentrating in sports management careers, to the U.S. on apprenticeship programs. He was calling it "Pathways" - he said it was going to be a win-win. BBFC would get access to young, passionate coaches and these students would get practical experience and bring these newfound skills back to the U.K. When their apprenticeship was completed. He also said that BBFC was sharing a booth at the conference that a few other members of his staff would be working. I asked who our target audience was at this conference? He didn't seem to have an answer. Rather than press further, I decided I would figure it out once we arrived.

We arrived in London and went straight to the conference center hotel. In the lobby of the hotel, we met the BBFC staff. There were four gentleman and one woman, all between mid-twenties to late thirties, wearing BBFC gear head-to-toe. I had met two of them before in the States. They all seemed genuinely happy to see me. Patrick asked one of them if he was ready for his presentation and what time it was scheduled to start. The presenter, Nick Hammond, said he was all set and that he would be going on at 1:00pm, in about three hours. I asked if I could see his presentation ahead of time. Hammond said, "sure, let me grab my laptop." He and I sat at a table off to the side while Patrick met with the others. While Hammond was getting his laptop ready, I asked what message he was looking to communicate to the audience today. I received another scrambled run-on of thoughts that confused me more than enlightened me. This guy made Paul Macklin sound like Bill Gates. When he finished his answer, I said, "OK, let's walk through the PowerPoint." The presentation provided some clarity but needed a lot of work. I didn't want to come across as a micro-manager or rattle him a couple of hours before his presentation, but I also wanted him to succeed. I was selective and gave him a few recommendations for the slides and reminded him that people can only remember three to five things from a presentation - nail down those themes and stick to them. He seemed appreciative.

From what I could tell, BBFC was trying to partner with a number of public colleges in the U.K. as a preferred apprenticeship provider in the U.S. for sports management majors. The problem I saw with the presentation was that BBFC was touting its ability to provide additional curriculum and training to these students as well as supporting career development - I had yet to see those as resident skills at BBFC. I would need to get a better understanding of the proposed commitment and the resources BBFC was planning to put towards this. I wanted to make sure we weren't making promises we couldn't keep and if we were going to do it, it would have to make sense financially. It was becoming clear that BBFC often put the cart before the horse and cut corners. In my experience, that never ends well.

Baldwin and I walked into the conference center, checked in, picked up our credentials and the usual gift bag full of unnecessary corporate specialty items, like pens, mugs, and stress balls. I kept the event brochure and put my bag down on the first table I passed. We walked the trade show floor and found the booth that BBFC would be sharing with a soccer video service provider. Based on the other exhibitors that included online education software providers, curriculum developers, recruiting firms that specialized in placing professors and college administrators, I couldn't get my head around where BBFC fit here. Patrick was talking to the gentleman staffing the video booth, so I excused myself and explored on my own. I found the main conference room where Nick would be presenting at 1:00pm. There was a presentation going on, so I closed the door gently behind me and took a seat in the back row.

I realized from the slide on the screen that the gentleman presenting was the head of the association that put on this conference. I was a bit surprised by his appearance - he was wearing a crazy-looking, maroon colored suit, flashy black and white shoes, a flowery tie and a hat. No joke, a hat, like a fedora. This character is the president of an association of colleges and he was wearing a hat on stage. I couldn't believe what I was watching. He looked like he should have been doing magic tricks. However, the audience seemed to love him; he was actually a pretty engaging speaker; and his message was pretty clear - he wanted to elevate the education experience and opportunities for young people in the U.K. He provided a cross-functional framework for the audience challenging them to *break the mold*. When he finished, the audience applauded authentically, not the typical polite, OK, let's get on to the next speaker type of applause you typically hear at these conferences. A woman took the microphone, thanks the guy in the fedora and said there would a thirty-minute networking break before they would resume again at 1:00pm. The audience began to exit the room.

I stayed in my seat looking at the conference brochure when the woman who just spoke stopped at the end of the aisle and asked if she could help me. I looked up and realized that everyone else had already left the room. I stood up and introduced myself - I could tell she had no idea who our company was, so I told her that BBFC was one of our divisions and one of our team members was presenting next. She had heard of BBFC. I asked what the previous speaker was referencing when he said it was time make changes and break the mold. She explained to me that the public college network in the U.K. was funded primarily by the government and that the colleges, effectively, were competing with each other for those funds. Those colleges that could attract students through innovative curricula and clear *pathways* to a job post-graduation, would not only survive, but thrive. I asked who the typical attendee at this conference was. She said that the audience members were primarily administrators looking for ways to differentiate their colleges. "Got it, thank you that is very helpful," I said. She smiled and walked away. *Pathways*, I thought. I was starting to understand why BBFC was here.

I stayed in my seat, reading through the brochure and Googling some of the presenters to better understand the conference. As people began to return to the room, I moved to the second row, on the right. Baldwin came in and sat next to me. Hammond presented with another gentleman who introduced himself as some sort of dean from a local college. When we met earlier to review his presentation, Nick failed to tell me that he had a co-presenter. We had reviewed each slide, I provided comments, recommended content and formatting changes, even how I thought he should present each slide, yet he didn't tell me that someone else would be presenting some of the slides - odd.

The dean wasn't dressed like an academic - I expected khakis and a tweed blazer. Instead, he was wearing a silvery blue, shiny suit with a matching vest, pointy loafers, a light blue dress shirt with a white collar and French cuffs and a bright geometric print tie. He had bleached blond hair and long sideburns. He looked like he should be in the cast of the Hunger Games. Standing next to Hammond, who was wearing a BBFC adidas sweat suit, the Dean looked even more ridiculous.

Hammond was uncomfortable presenting - his cheeks red and stumbling over his words. He split his time looking at the screen behind him and the note cards in his hand; he rarely looked at this audience. He was stiff as a board. The dean, on the other hand, was *too* comfortable in front of an audience. He never looked at the screen, no notes required, and he moved around the front of the room casually as he spoke. He was like a southern Baptist minister with a cockney accent. Instead of selling Jesus, he was selling the success of a *beta test* the college had just completed with our Back Bay Football Club. He spent a lot of time explaining a graphic on the screen behind him that looked like a subway map - it represented a cradle-to-grave strategy designed to take children just learning how to kick a soccer ball for the first time through a series of steps that ultimately would lead them to a career in soccer. My takeaway from the forty-five-minute presentation was that I found the dean to be artificial, annoying and untrustworthy. Immediately following the presentation, Patrick and I had to head to the airport to fly to Barcelona. We complimented Nick on the way out, I met the dean briefly, only to shake his hand and promise to schedule a call to get to know him better, and we said goodbye to the rest of the team.

On the flight to Barcelona, I was making notes of my time in Belfast and London and thinking about the presentation I had just witnessed. I asked Patrick about the so-called beta test. He simply reinforced the thesis that Nick and the dean had presented. I told him that I didn't know we had even been conducting such a test. He acted surprised, like it was my fault that I hadn't been aware of it. I asked about BBFC having proprietary sports management curricula and he seemed offended that I would even ask - he said, "I can't believe you don't even know what we have created, that's what my brother works on every day." I backed off on that topic. I asked about the financial model - he said that "eventually, we will receive, from the college, a revenue share of the tuition for each student using our curriculum." I thought for a moment; OK, if we have attractive and compelling sports management and soccer coaching curriculum as well as apprenticeship capabilities, then I could see how colleges would find this attractive. But I was skeptical that we actually had a compelling curriculum.

I had a second question that was of equal importance to me. I asked Patrick if the program that we beta tested with the local college went well, wouldn't we want to roll that out with other colleges? He said, "Of course, that's the whole point of it." I thought aloud, "then why would the dean be promoting it to all of the public colleges in attendance at the conference?" At first, Baldwin acted like he didn't understand the question, forcing me to explain it again. Then, he responded that the dean is a *great guy* and wanted to help BBFC. He went on to say that the dean was proud of the program. I told him that didn't make any sense. I told him about the woman I had spoken with before Nick and the dean's presentation. If the colleges were competing with each other for enrollments in order to secure a larger share of public funding and unique curricula and programs were the differentiators, then why would the dean promote our program to competing schools. Baldwin seemed frustrated with the conversation and asked why I had to be so skeptical all the time. I told him that I wasn't skeptical, I was simply trying to understand how this all worked. There was a long silence while I continue to try to understand both the curriculum and partnership model - Patrick was looking out the window of the plane. I then said, "there must be something else in this for the dean." He looked at me, shook his head as if disgusted with me and said, "you are unbelievable." There was something not right about this dean and his motives. Not another word was exchanged between us until we arrived in Barcelona.

We arrived in Barcelona and passed immigration quickly since we were coming in from London. We were picked up at the airport by a representative of the target company we were going visit. A young man named Rico was our driver - thankfully his English was excellent as I don't speak Spanish. He greeted us like an old friend. He was kind enough to provide us with a running commentary of the area as we drove from Barcelona to La Pineda, where the company was located. I had communicated a number of times before with Rico via email and had always found him to be helpful translating between me and the owners of the company we were visiting. During the drive to La Pineda, Rico explained his role with his employer - he seemed to touch every aspect of the business and was quite knowledgeable in all areas. If we acquired this company, he would be a valuable member of the local team. I also learned that Rico was a part-time singer and had competed in Spain's version of American Idol. The cast of characters was expanding.

Upon arriving in La Pineda, we checked into our hotel and then met with the owners of the target company in the lobby of the hotel. I had met them once before in person in our offices in Maine and had since maintained a lengthy, email dialogue with them, a couple of their financial and legal advisors, and Rico as their translator. Things had dragged on too long. The courtship and diligence had been challenging due to the language barrier, distance, their lack of financial sophistication (their books and records were messy), and the risk associated with a single event business. They operated one event per year, a large youth soccer event that attracted teams and family members from all over the world. I needed to fully understand this event (e.g., where it fit in the competitive landscape, it's attractiveness to teams, the quality and availability of local hospitality to meet customer expectations, it's true financial performance and operating risks); I would only get one chance per year to correct any mistakes. If my diligence was off and I grossly overpaid, it would take a couple of years to recover. I was trying to be prudent, but I felt like the owners were getting "deal fatigue"; thus, my trip to get some face time with them and bring this to a conclusion, one way or another.

It was evening when we met, and the owners acknowledged that we must be tired from our travels. As a result, we met only briefly to layout the agenda for the next thirty-six hours that we would be together. After doing so, they left for the night. Patrick and I decided to grab a quick bite to eat. The hotel receptionist pointed us to a restaurant within walking distance. Most of the town appeared to be closed down as it was the end of January and La Pineda was primarily a summer resort town. The restaurant was small, seating less than fifty people at most. There was only one other table occupied when we arrived. Patrick and I reviewed the menu and ordered our food from our waiter who had a thick Russian accent. We discussed our agenda for the next day - topics we both wanted to cover with the target company. Baldwin was particularly bullish on this event and wanted it in his BBFC portfolio, but he seemed to be aligned with me about the risks. We delved into a fair amount of detail about how we could ensure that our time with the owners was efficient and productive so that we could leave Barcelona prepared to move forward and present an investment memo to our board or cut bait. We had a plan and were on the same page.

We finished dinner and the waiter asked if he could get us anything else. The restaurant was now empty, the waiter had been setting tables for the next day (which made me think he wanted to head home), and I was exhausted. Patrick ordered a cup of tea and I said I was all set. While waiting for his tea, Patrick leaned in and said, "can I ask you something?" "Sure", I replied. He said, "can you cut the shit with all of this accounting investigation nonsense and start looking forward instead of backwards?" I was taken aback not only by the question and topic, but how it was delivered. Although there was no explicitly stated threat, I actually felt threatened. His body language, the way he leaned in towards me, the way he folded his hands on the table - it was all very theatrical, like something he had seen in a movie. It felt very deliberate. I said, "what are you talking about, I am not investigating BBFC's accounting. I didn't want any of this." I reminded him what a nightmare I had been dealing with regarding Epic - the accounting misrepresentations, litigation, sexual harassment claims, threats, etc. I told him that I inherited all of this crap.

He seemed unfazed and said he wanted to know if I was going to start looking into BBFC the way I had done so with Epic. I asked him if there was any reason for me to do so. He sat back from the table and said, "you really are unbelievable." I replied, "why am I unbelievable? Patrick, we have to restate the last two years of financial statements because of accounting irregularities at Epic. Do you understand how serious that is?" He said, "that's not my fault - I just want us to put everything in the rear-view mirror and move forward." I was tired and frustrated. I said, "Me too. Why do you think I am flying all over Europe this week - I am trying move the business forward. Do you really think I want to deal with all of this other bullshit that I inherited?" His response was, "I want to be clear with you. It's not in your best interest to start digging into BBFC." Before I could respond, he then said, "...and approve my fucking pay raises." He then held his stare for a moment, looked away and took the final sip from his pint glass. I was speechless. The waiter returned and placed Baldwin's tea in front of him. *Strike 3*.

CHAPTER 23

Back at Powell's office, we returned to the large conference room from our restroom and email break. Everyone settled back into their respective seats. Ben opened the last folder he had been looking at, reviewed its contents and returned it to the pile. He then took the next folder, placed it in front of him, looked directly at Baldwin and said, "are we ready to resume?" Everyone responded, "yes."

Ben asked, "can you explain to us what BBFC UK Student Placement is?" Baldwin looked down towards the table, then up and around, like he was searching for the answer. He said, "I think I do, but don't hold me to this, that entity is our company in the U.K."

Powell: "Who's company?"

Baldwin: "BBFC."

Powell: "So, you are saying that BBFC owns BBFC UK Student Placement Limited?"

Baldwin says, "I think so," then looked directly at me and said, "right?" Ben told me not to answer.

Powell: "I didn't ask Steve, I asked you."

Baldwin: "Well, I'm not sure."

Powell: "You don't know what that entity is and who owns it?"

Baldwin said, "give me a second" and he looked down at the table in front of him again, clearly thinking. He then said, "actually, I think that is the entity that handles the payroll for our visa workers." Powell asked who owned the entity. Baldwin explained that if it was the entity that "handles the payroll", then it was owned by Nick Hammond and his brother.

While asking these questions, Ben was looking at documents I located that had been filed with the U.K. Companies House (the U.K. equivalent of combining the U.S. Securities and Exchange Commission and individual Secretaries of States' databases) that showed that the entity was owned by Hammond, Hammond's wife and Hammond's brother. I still couldn't believe what I was hearing and my mind drifted back to what transpired only a couple months ago.

In the months leading up to the DOJ raid, I, along with members of our accounting and finance team, had been spending a fair amount of time trying to understand the BBFC financial model and why the company was performing well below expectations. The poor performance was driven by increasing expenses. Facility costs, insurance, car rentals had all increased, but we couldn't seem to get-it collective heads around labor costs. While this normally would be easy to analyze with most companies, the challenge here was the absence of consistent historical data - BBFC had been a cash-based accounting company until recently and had maintained its accounting records on QuickBooks until we migrated them to Epic's accounting system. Consequently, the chart of accounts had changed, and the way employees were coding expenses differed year-over-year. As a result, I tried another approach - I had a member of our accounting staff prepare a multi-year vendor analysis for me. A simple analysis that included all vendors for each of the last three years and the amount BBFC paid each vendor. After the vendor name and before the amount, we included the expense category. I could sort this any number of ways. I started by looking at the vendors to whom we had paid the most money in 2018 and 2019 - one of the top vendors was BBFC UK Student Placement. I asked what this entity was only about a month ago and no one could provide a clear answer. Later, I followed-up and asked both Patrick Baldwin and Jack Cahill who this vendor was, and both told me it was an inter-company account; that it simply was the account we used to record our payroll paid to our visa coaches. I took their answers at face value, but shortly thereafter, learned during a conversation with our outside auditors that it was not an inter-company account, but rather a separate legal entity. No one seemed to know or wanted to share with me what this entity was.

Based on its name and wiring instructions included in its vendor file, it appeared to be a U.K.-based entity. I search the U.K. Companies House database and found the filing that included the formation documents and ownership information. This was all happening about thirty days or so before the DOJ raid. When I read the filing, I grew concerned that Neil Hammond, a BBFC employee, was listed as an owner of the U.K. Company. I sent an email to Hammond asking what the entity was and what it did for BBFC. While waiting for his reply, I reasoned that this entity must be associated with the *Pathways* initiative he presented at the London conference. However, I still didn't understand why he, his wife and brother would own this entity. I also questioned why a guy responsible for a U.S. region and living here would be leading an initiative with operations in the U.K. I searched the address of the registered company and found that it was a used car dealership. A search of the used car dealership's name in the U.K. Companies House database indicated it was owned by Hammond's brother.

While I awaited Hammond's reply, I returned to the vendor analysis and decided to sort the records based on name. I found another vendor with BBFC in its name - BBFC UK Football Academy Limited. Another U.K. Companies House search yielded immediate results. This entity was also owned by Nick Hammond and a gentleman named Russ Crenshaw. I had met Crenshaw as well during the conference in London back in January. I was told he was a member of BBFC's U.K. staff. I asked Laura to pull his employee information and she told me that he wasn't in our employee database nor in our payroll files. Hmm. I performed a Google search and found him - he was a former amateur / semi-pro soccer player in the U.K. The only article specifically about him involved his arrest outside of London a few years ago for an alleged racially motivated assault on a taxi driver. Ugh.

BBFC UK Football Academy also listed another director of the company - I Google searched that individual and found that he was also an owner of a payroll processing company in the U.K. A Google search of the listed address for BBFC UK Football Academy came up as the address for the payroll company as well. Odd.

Back to the vendor file. No hits on the payroll company, it had never been paid as a vendor. But, knowing that Russ Crenshaw was not in our employee records, I searched and found that he was being paid as a vendor. I also searched the BBFC email accounts and found that Crenshaw had an active company email address - only after the DOJ raid would we run all of the necessary key word searches on his account. I then searched our vendor management system and reviewed all payments that had been to Crenshaw, as well as supporting documentation for each. I found something odd. Several of his invoices provided no detail of the services rendered, but instead, referenced an "agreement per Jack Cahill."

The invoices did not include any detail of hours or an hourly rate, but rather a flat, consistent dollar amount captioned *consulting services*. At the bottom of one of the invoices was another company's name in the footer - it looked like it had been left there in error. The company name was Active-Youth Training Limited. I followed the process as I had with the others and sure enough Active-Youth Training was a registered U.K. company owned by Russ Crenshaw with the same mailing address at BBFC UK Academy and the payroll provider. Active-Youth was also in our vendor file and payments to it had been made in the last twelve months. The same invoice was attached to each payment. I reviewed the invoices and noted that it also made reference to an "agreement per Jack Cahill." I was quickly becoming concerned that I had uncovered more questionable practices. Just when I was beginning to feel like most of the deceptive behavior was behind us... now this.

I hadn't heard back from Hammond about what the U.K. entity did, and it had been more than twenty-four hours, my personal tolerance for waiting for an email response. I sent a follow-up email and also asked about the BBFC UK Football Academy entity and what Russ

Crenshaw's role was with the company. Within a half hour or so of this email, Patrick Baldwin called me. He didn't waste any time. He said, "why are you contacting Nick Hammond?" He sounded angry. I replied, "Patrick, I am simply trying to understand what all of these companies are, what they do, who owns them and so on." He tried interrupting me, but I said assertively, "hang on, let me finish - you asked me a question, let me answer it." He went silent.

I said, "we are in the midst of our first financial statement audit, the outside accounting firm can't even rely on our processes and controls because of the shit that went on here in the past. I am not going to allow undisclosed related party transactions on my watch, so I am trying to understand these different companies. Patrick, I am the CEO of this company, I have every right to ask these questions." He didn't back off, instead he said, "are you done?" I didn't answer. He proceeded to tell me that going around him to his "guys" undermined him and caused them to lose respect in him. He went on and on about how if he loses their respect, they lose their motivation and they won't perform. This was the same story he was spinning when he wanted to get his way with our sponsor selection. I just listened, I was tired and didn't feel like arguing. I had resigned myself to the fact that he couldn't be trusted and wasn't our guy long term, so why bother fighting him.

I let him finish and said, "so, Patrick, can you explain to me these companies and their relationships to BBFC?" He told me that BBFC UK Student Placement was a company set up simply to pay U.K. residents who were here on temporary work visas. That U.K. law required that a U.K. company employ them and that a U.K. citizen must own the entity, consequently, he had asked Hammond to form the company. I thought to myself, if this was the case, why are Hammond's brother and wife also owners? Further, it sounded like a sham of a company. I hoped we weren't creating a tax issue the way they structured this. I specifically asked if Hammond was making any money off the entity, he quickly said, "no, absolutely not. It is just a pass through."

I also asked about BBFC UK Academy. Baldwin told me that BBFC had licensed the academy rights in the U.K. to Hammond and

Crenshaw - this was news to me, and I told him so. He claimed Devlin was well aware of it and that there was a licensing agreement that had been in place for some time. I asked him to send the executed copy to me. I was getting aggravated; it was starting to feel like a recurring nightmare. I would ask a question, get one answer. Find some new information, ask the same question and get another answer. Only when I presented the facts, would I get the truth.

He thought the call was ending, when I said, "hang on, I have more questions." I asked about Active-Youth Training. He claimed he had never heard of it. I told him it was an entity owned by Russ Crenshaw and that it was a vendor of ours. I waited. Again, he said he had never heard of it. I asked if he could check with Cahill and ask what Active-Youth does for BBFC and he said he would. Patrick never got back to me on the topics of Crenshaw or Active-Youth despite the fact that we were in contact multiple times per week by email, phone and in person. Before the call ended, I said, "Patrick, are there any other related party transactions, affiliated companies, potential conflicts of interest of which I need to be aware? Seriously, I need to know now so we can deal with them and disclose them in the audited financials." I even provided examples and continued, "If we don't disclose them now and they come out later, our investors will lose their minds." Again, he claimed that there was nothing else that needed to be disclosed.

Our finance team and BBFC management were working still actively to develop a detailed plan to get the company back where it needed to be from a profitability perspective. This was their main project at this point, besides trying to put together accurate and timely financial reporting (which had always been a challenge for this company). On a weekly basis, the BBFC senior management team, three or four guys, would come to our Seaport office and meet in person. Patrick and his brother, Sean, would often attend. A couple of weeks before the DOJ raid, one such meeting took place and I was in attendance as well. Our CFO had prepared a presentation that detailed our finance teams' analyses, findings, and recommendations to finally optimize BBFC's financial performance. A heavy emphasis of the presentation was on the true cost of immigrant workers when factoring in the legal costs associated with obtaining their visas, international travel, local room & board, the use of rental cars and the related insurance costs (particularly since BBFC staff, in the aggregate, had a terrible driving track record and premiums had skyrocketed). Patrick debated every point with no quantifiable support. He was growing frustrated. He eventually became apathetic and stopped participating in the meeting. I'm sure his guys had witnessed this type of behavior before and knew that was a sign to wrap up the meeting. My CFO said he would take the lead with Laura to develop a 2020 staffing plan focused on sourcing domestic coaches instead of visa workers. One of the BBFC guys said he would participate. They went through the other proposed initiatives, forming small teams and agreeing to put together target timelines and milestones. The meeting wrapped up. The Baldwins asked to meet with me privately.

In the conference room, Patrick told me that he was *done*. That he was either going to quit and move on or we could sell him his business back. I played dumb and asked what was driving this. He said that we weren't aligned, that I didn't trust him and that he did not want to work for our board any longer. Keep in mind that the DOJ raid hadn't occurred yet.

Epic still owed the BBFC minority shareholders a portion of their original notes from when they sold the ownership interest to Epic. We had not made the current payment when it was due for several reasons: 1) our senior lender prohibited us from making payments to subordinate lenders while Epic was in technical default; 2) we were waiting for the 2018 audit to be completed to make sure there weren't any additional skeletons in the closet (it was starting to look like there were more); and 3) our board believed that BBFC shareholders had misrepresented the financial performance of the company and violated the representations and warranties included in the purchase agreement. The Baldwins said that if they could find a partner with whom they could repurchase BBFC, the issue with the outstanding sellers' notes would be resolved. I wasn't particularly concerned about the notes because I was confident that they were not going to be paid due to reason number three above. However, his offer of the BBFC buyback didn't seem like a spontaneous idea. I acted interested and said, "look, we like BBFC, we like the model, we like you and your management team. I don't think the board has any interest in getting out of BBFC. Having said that, I know that our investors are commercial and would listen." Sean asked what I thought it would take from a valuation perspective. I told him I had no idea. I asked if they thought they had access to capital to get it done. They said they did - at this point I knew they were already shopping BBFC, a company in which they, together, were only minority shareholders. Unbelievable.

I heard Ben's voice saying my name and I realized I was deep in thought... distracted. He was trying to show me a document and ask me a question. Everyone in the room, especially Baldwin, was looking at me. I gathered myself, looked at the document and recognized it right away. I looked back at Ben and realized he was simply letting me know that he was about to cover this topic - I nodded affirmatively.

Ben asked Baldwin if he was familiar with an entity called Hub Staffing Enterprises, LLC. He tilted his head side-to-side a few times as if he was contemplating how to answer the question. This was going to be sensitive subject. Baldwin said, "yes, I am familiar with it."

Powell: "Can you explain what the entity does?"

Baldwin: "It's not a real entity, it doesn't do anything. It was an idea we were considering, but we never did anything with it."

Powell handed Baldwin and his attorney a document. "Do you recognize this document?", he asked. Baldwin said, "no." Powell told him that it was a document Baldwin had filed with the Secretary of State of Massachusetts to establish the LLC. Baldwin said, "ok."

Powell: "Do you remember filing the document?"

Baldwin: "I, uh... I think so."

Powell distributed another document and said, "do you recognize that document?"

Baldwin nodded yes. The document was a confirmation from the Internal Revenue Service that provided Hub Staffing Enterprises, LLC with a federal employer identification number. Powell didn't follow-up with any additional questions.

Powell immediately shared another document that included multiple pages - you could feel the momentum and tension building. He said, "can you take a look at this document. Take your time." One of the attorneys leaned in again to review the document in front of Baldwin. After reviewing it, Baldwin said, "I don't recall seeing this document before." He had to be sick knowing that we had this - the document was the operating agreement for Hub Staffing Enterprises. It included a cap table detailing the shareholders of the entity. Ben handed him another page and said, "this is the signature page, is that your signature?" On the page was Baldwin's signature along with four other members of BBFC's management team. Baldwin reviewed it and said, "yea, it looks like my signature." He then shifted in his seat, smiled and said, "look, that was never a real business. We never did anything with it, it was just an idea that never went anywhere." Ben neither acknowledged nor responded to Baldwin's comments.

Ben opened another folder, looked at the document. I could see it and recognized it immediately. I could tell Ben didn't know what it was or why it was relevant. Before I could lean over and explain, he beat me to it. He leaned back and towards me - all I had to say was "HSE expenses" and he nodded and moved back towards the table. He distributed the document and said, "do you recognize this?" Baldwin said, "no." The document was a spreadsheet with individuals' names, vendor names (restaurants, airlines, hotels, etc.), dollar amounts and descriptions. The names on the spreadsheet matched the names on the operating agreement. Ben then handed a copy of the email that accompanied the spreadsheet and said, "this goes with it, take your time." The email was sent by Cahill to Baldwin. The body of the email described the attachment as expenses incurred by a new company, Hub Staffing Enterprises.

Based on this email, others and conversations with certain individuals, it was clear that Baldwin and his colleagues formed a new entity to qualify for new types of immigration visas. One of these visas, was an E-2 - these were intended for foreigners who made a substantial investment in a U.S. company. Under the E-2 program, the individual investor would qualify to bring in foreign workers on visas to work for the company. The shareholders of the entity, all of whom signed the operating agreement, were Patrick and Sean Baldwin, Jack Cahill, Nick Hammond and Russ Crenshaw.

As Ben was preparing to address the next folder, Baldwin spoke up and said, "this is silly. That was not a real business. It never did anything. We never used that to get any visas." Ben looked up and said, "well, it incurred expenses, right?"

Baldwin: "No, those weren't real expenses."
Powell: "What do you mean those weren't 'real expenses'?"

One of Baldwin's attorneys leaned over and told him that he didn't have to answer that question. Baldwin was trying to explain to the attorney, but the attorney said, "not now" and Baldwin stopped talking, sank in his chair a bit, looked in my and Powell's direction and shook his head in frustration.

The next folder yielded a lease agreement for an office under the name of Hub Staffing Enterprises. Baldwin said he had never seen it before. Another folder provided evidence of a bank account in the name of Hub Staffing Enterprises. Baldwin said he was unaware of it. Even another Secretary of State filing for Hub Staffing Enterprises as a foreign company was handed over to Baldwin and his attorney. Again, he said he had never seen it before and not aware of its existence. The way this was going, I was shocked that he was still sitting in the room and, perhaps even more surprising was, that his attorneys were allowing him to participate.

Ben paused and said, "do you recall when Hub Staffing Enterprises was formed?" Baldwin said "no".

Powell: "Does March 20, 2018 sound about right?"

Baldwin: "I don't recall."

Ben shuffled through the folders that he has already been through and pulled out a document - it was the formation document for Hub Staffing Enterprises. He handed it Baldwin and asked him to read the date. Baldwin looked at it and said, "March 20, 2018."

Powell: "Do you know what else happened on that day?"

Baldwin: "No."

Powell: "that was the day that Epic closed on its financing round with RevCap and CFC. The day that new, institutional, professional investors came into the company. Is that a coincidence?"

Baldwin: "I have no idea."

One of Baldwin's attorneys asked if we were almost done. Ben responded, "we are getting there, just a few more minutes if that's ok?" I was shocked when Baldwin didn't take the opportunity to say he was done, or needed to be somewhere, or any other possible excuse to get out of that room. Instead, he said, "I'm ok for a little longer."

Ben returned to his folders and kept the process going.... "do you recognize this document?"

Baldwin: "I'm not sure."

Powell: "Is that your signature on the last page?"
Baldwin: "It looks like it." He then acted like he suddenly remembered the document and proceeded to explain that this was a consulting agreement between BBFC and Russ Crenshaw. That Crenshaw was a consultant in the U.K. He said that Crenshaw was engaged to assist with international operations.

Powell opened another folder and distributed another agreement. This was an agreement between Active-Youth Training and BBFC.

Baldwin took his time reviewing it. This could not have been enjoyable for him. Ben asked if he recognized the agreement.

Baldwin squirmed in his seat and tried to explain that this was not a *real agreement*, but rather part of the Hub Staffing "thing." Ben said that he didn't understand what that meant. Baldwin simply said, "this is not a real agreement, it is meaningless."

Powell then directed him to a paragraph that outlined the terms of the agreement in which Active-Youth Training agreed to invest a certain amount of money in Hub Staffing Enterprises and BBFC, yes BBFC, was to repay the amount invested by Active-Youth plus *interest* over the proceeding several months.

So, not only did they concoct a scheme to qualify for visas for which BBFC didn't really qualify, they also created a separate legal entity for their scheme while they were employed by BBFC. In addition, they funded the new HSE entity through a fraudulent consulting agreement between BBFC and an individual who was already getting paid as a consultant to BBFC. The same individual was also benefiting as an owner of a licensee of the BBFC brand in the academy space in the U.K. A tangled web to say the least…

I also didn't believe Baldwin's claim that this Hub Staffing Enterprises entity never actually operated. Based on the documentary evidence and the timing of the company's formation (the same day as the RevCap and CFC investment in Epic), it appeared that this group believed that they had figured out how to manipulate the visa process and was looking to benefit from it by selling visa workers to companies other than BBFC. Further, based on my interactions with Baldwin, I am confident that he had come to realize that I was principled and relentless - that's why he was concerned that I was going to continue to look in the rear-view mirror.

CHAPTER 24

---

*May the foundation of our new constitution, be justice, truth, and
righteousness. Like the wise man's house, may it be founded upon
those rocks and then neither storms nor tempests will overthrow it.*

- Abigail Adams, 1776

Inscribed on the John Joseph Moakley U.S. Courthouse, Boston, MA

Ben and I continued to add to the binders that contained not only the
information requested by the DOJ in their eight separate subpoenas,
but additional information that we believed was relevant to their
investigation. In an attempt to protect Epic and BBFC, we had made
the easy decision of cooperating with the DOJ. I met Ben at the
Starbucks across from the Moakley Federal Courthouse. During my
short walk to meet him, I noticed several members of the media
setting up their cameras – I assumed there was a hearing today for
one of the defendants in the college admissions scandal; or at least I
hoped there was.

Ben and I talked baseball a bit – he had two young sons and coached
their teams. Although it was November, we were nonetheless talking
about his son's teams and, more specifically, one of his son's 10:1
strikeout-to-walk ratio. We were also talking about exit velocities
and launch angles for twelve-year-old baseball players. Further
evidence that youth sports may have gone too far.

He filled me in on what to expect from today's meeting with the
DOJ; he told me to let him lead the meeting from our side – that was
totally fine with me. "Answer their questions honestly and
succinctly, this isn't the time to elaborate. Just answer their
questions, you don't ask the questions. Understand? They ask the

questions, you don't," he said. I understood. There wasn't much more to discuss, we headed across the street.

The federal building was built in 1999 and is a massive brick and granite building that occupies a full city block. The 675,000 square foot building has ten stories overlooking Boston Harbor and downtown. The construction of the courthouse may have launched the redevelopment of the Seaport from an industrial area to its current rebirth as one of the most desirable areas to live and work in Boston. Breaking up the expanse of the brick exterior of the courthouse are quotes about justice and the constitution engraved in granite rectangles. I often walked by without taking notice, but not today. I read each one I passed. We entered the building and started to approach the security desk – Ben turned to me and asked if I had my phone or laptop. He seemed concerned. I said, "of course I do, I have both." With his back to the security staff and in a hushed voiced, he told me to give him both of my devices. He put them in his briefcase. He identified himself as an attorney, placed his briefcase on the belt leading into the x-ray machine. He told security that I was his client.

The center of the courthouse is a massive, open rotunda that reaches up six or seven stories. While the exterior of the building is somewhat unassuming, the main foyer was the opposite. I couldn't help but think that the architect knew this element of design would symbolize the power of the U.S. justice system and, likely, the gravity of a situation one often faces when entering this space. Even though I had done nothing wrong and wasn't a target, I was sick to my stomach. I felt lightheaded. Walking through the rotunda, Ben asked if I brought a toothbrush. I was so rattled, I said, "no, why?" He said, "in case they take you into custody, it is always nice to have your own toothbrush the first night in jail." Funny.

The reception area for the U.S. Attorney's office was smaller than I would have expected. There were about ten chairs and a check-in window like you would see in a doctor's office. To the left of the window were framed, formal photos of President Trump, Vice President Pence and Attorney General William Barr. This was getting real. We gave the receptionist our drivers licenses. She scanned the bar codes on the back of the licenses, checked her monitor, then returned them to us. In less than a minute, the door opened, and a gentleman said, "Ben, Steve?" It was one of the Assistant U.S. Attorneys leading the investigation. We followed him down a long hallway while he made small talk with Ben. I just followed and tried to keep up with their quick pace.

The AUSA stopped outside of a conference room and motioned for us to head in. We were about to enter a conference room, when the AUSA looked at me and said, "oh, do you have your phone, laptop or a tablet?" I told him that I didn't have them with me – he looked at Ben and smiled. I assume that if I had them in my possession, rather than my attorney's briefcase, they would have taken them and copied the emails, files, contacts, texts, etc. We settled into the windowless conference room and the AUSA said he would be right back. I placed my binder in front of me and Ben took out his folders and a notepad.

The next four hours proved to be oddly enjoyable. The lead AUSA returned with another AUSA and two federal agents. All were polite and extremely professional. This wasn't like some crime show where the feds were trying to intimidate or coerce someone during an interview. Instead, they asked me to tell them about myself and how I got involved with Epic. I did so. Next were questions about how Epic became an owner of BBFC and how BBFC operated. I'm lucky to have a pretty good memory and can usually organize and articulate my thoughts well; I hope to God that doesn't change in light of my diagnosis. That's my worst fear. I can deal with the progression of the physical symptoms, but I worry about cognitive decline.

The feds quickly came to understand that Epic's investors were well respected with good reputations; I believe that I came across as professional and honest. Hearing the backstory, they seemed sympathetic to our situation. They took notes and nodded along. Occasionally, one of them would ask a simple question to clarify the timing of one of the facts or incidents I mentioned.

Then, they asked if I was aware of the subject of their investigation. I told them I was. The lead AUSA asked if I knew anything about how

BBFC sourced visas. I told him that I was still getting up to speed and that I knew a lot more now than I did before their raid. I told them that my access to information was much better since I terminated Patrick Baldwin. One of the agents, a woman seated across from me, said, "you terminated Baldwin?" I told them that we terminated him the previous day. They all looked at each other – I couldn't tell if they were just surprised by the news or if I had done something wrong, so I asked, "is that ok?" The lead AUSA said, "of course, we just didn't know he was gone." They asked about his termination. I told them that Baldwin had originally refused to cooperate with our internal investigation, so the board resolved to put him on leave; he then came in for an interview and we found that he mislead us on several matters. We also found that he had created a separate company, in which he and other employees were owners, and diverted BBFC funds to that entity.

The lead AUSA asked what I knew about BBFC's use of P1 visas. I told them that I had never heard of a P1 visa prior to the raid. I then explained to them my understanding of when BBFC used P1 visas and how they sourced them; I named professional clubs and individuals who were involved based on emails I had read. Again, I noticed they were looking at each other often when I said a professional club or individual's name. Ben was helpful during this portion of the interview – he must have felt the moment when I had achieved a level of credibility with the feds and they were starting to trust me, because he intervened and said, "we have a number of documents that you may find interesting."

They looked like kids in a candy store. I opened my binder and got started. For each document, I would explain the topic, the context, relevance and, in some cases, who the participants were on an email or a file. I would then read the portion of the communication that was incriminating. They were taking notes feverishly, then Ben would hand them a copy of the email and any attachments. We repeated this process over and over again. Each document would go to the agent directly across from me and work its way around the table until it was in the hands of the lead AUSA. Several times, the first agent would lean towards the second agent and point to something on a document that I had provided. This would prompt either an exaggerated look of surprise or a shake of the head implying disgust. It was clear to me that they were learning new facts.

I had been in the room for several hours at this point and we were making progress in terms of providing helpful information and building a relationship with the DOJ in order to mitigate risk to the company. However, I had forgotten to take my medication and I realized that my hands were shaking, my speech had slowed, and I felt like I was freezing up. I was starting to sweat. Ben noticed it and asked, "are you ok?" Everyone looked up from the documents we had been providing and showed genuine concern. I must have looked awful. I told Ben that my meds were in my bag, he got my bag which was behind me and an agent left the room, returning a few moments later with a glass of water. I mumbled that I had Parkinson's. We took a fifteen-minute break.

The meds kicked in and I felt a bit more like myself – we resumed. I think the feds were relieved that I was feeling better - they didn't want to stop. We continued to provide documents and connect the dots on how these visas had been sourced. I was surprised at how many of the documents we provided, they had not seen before. How could this be? I felt like Ben and I were way ahead of the feds, but how could that possibly be since they executed the raid before I had even heard of a P1 visa. Ben had been pretty clear that I wasn't allowed to ask any questions, but I couldn't help myself. There was a moment when everyone was looking at documents and I asked the lead AUSA if I could ask him a question. I received a cold stare from Ben. Without looking up from the document in front of him, the lead AUSA said, "it depends on the question." I said, how long has this investigation been going on?" He asked why I wanted to know. I replied, "had you guys not raided the BBFC office, I think I would have figured this out in another two weeks." He smiled and asked why – I told him about BBFC's financial performance, the stonewalling, identifying BBFC UK Student Placement and so on. He looked back at the document in front of him and said, "we have been investigating BBFC for about three years."

The lead AUSA then explained to us that they had been very careful throughout the investigation, but even more so since the search and seizure warrant had been executed. They had been particularly careful to not review any documents or communications that would violate the targets' attorney-client privileges. I wasn't sure I understood their concerns. Only later would Ben explain to me that the DOJ hadn't been able to review most of the evidence obtained. Had they inadvertently opened an email between a BBFC employee and an attorney regarding visa activity and read the communication, they could have violated attorney-client privilege and potentially complicated the investigation or disqualified a prosecutor. We later learned that all of the evidence they had obtained during the raid had been sent to attorneys not participating in the investigation who would scrub the information and separate attorney communications on the DOJ's behalf, called a *taint review*. This took time. Consequently, we had accelerated that process and Ben had been diligent about not providing any evidence that included BBFC / attorney communications.

We wrapped up the meeting and the lead AUSA told us how much he appreciated our time and the effort we had put in to pulling together the information we provided. He went on to say that he viewed Epic, BBFC, the investors and, even, me as victims in this case. He actually used the word *victim*. We came into this meeting wanting to do the right thing – the right thing for the investigation and the right thing for the company. I felt like we achieved both. Before we left, the lead AUSA said he had one more question. His colleagues sat back down and seemed particularly interested in their boss' question. I was still putting my binder into my messenger bag when he asked, "based on the information you have seen, who do you have concerns about?" It was a great question. I closed my eyes and named a dozen BBFC employees or consultants. They agreed with all of the names I listed, and they suggested I add one more to the list – they gave me the name. Ben gave them a thumb drive of the files in my binder.

Ben and I walked across the street to my office. It was Friday and after 6:00pm, everyone was gone for the day. We sat and debriefed. He was very pleased with how the meeting went and complimented me – I can't tell you how much that meant to me at that moment. I had come to respect Ben, in a relatively short period of time, for his intelligence, legal mind, integrity and work ethic. He did not distribute compliments haphazardly. He said, "they called the company a victim" several times. He felt like we may have dodged a bullet and that, for now, the DOJ would focus solely on individuals and not BBFC or Epic.

In the subsequent days and weeks, emails from BBFC employees and third parties to BBFC staff, were intercepted that included veiled threats against me. Examples included things like "fuck Steve Griffin and fuck King George" and "don't worry, we will be waiting in the tall grass for Griffin." I was being made out as the villain, yet I had done nothing wrong. The DOJ was investigating BBFC long before I was even involved with Epic. I certainly had nothing to do with their investigation or the raid. The board of directors terminated Baldwin, not me. And, further, people appeared to have broken the law, yet they wanted to blame me for their troubles.

As much as I hated to admit it, it was getting in my head. I couldn't help but think that people get desperate and do crazy things when they lose their job, particularly when their identity is so closely tied to the role, let alone face criminal charges. My late-night walks from the office to South Station made me nervous. There were several times when I would hear footsteps on the boardwalk behind me and I would walk to the railing along the harbor and let the person pass. I would vary my route and even Uber the short distance from time to time. Since I was walking with a cane, I tried to convince myself that I could use it as some sort of a weapon if need be. I even changed where I typically sat on the train ride home. I wasn't concerned about the ride into work in the morning because it was packed with commuters and potential witnesses, but the ride home later at night was light with riders. In the mornings I would sit at the end of a car in a single seat close to the door. It reduced how far I had to walk. However, for evening commute, I sat in the middle of a car, against a window. I kept my cane on the seat next to me and watched each person on the train closely. I had pictured someone about to get off at Ruggles when they quickly leaned in, slit my throat and vanished into the darkness. This was the kind of shit that was getting in my head.

The forensic work continued every day. Ben and I would receive requests from the DOJ, but we also needed to get answers for the

347

company. I couldn't have people working for the company who had committed crimes or misappropriated funds. I also didn't know who was loyal to Baldwin and was either providing him with information or undermining our business from the inside. I had also uncovered information that raised concerns about current staff that were here on visas.

Needless to say, we learned more and more every day. I was trying to understand the BBFC activities and legal entities in Europe but continued to get stonewalled. Finally, through emails and conversations with former visa staff and a colleague in the U.K., I was able to get a basic understanding of what was happening. Hammond formed the BBFC UK Student Placement entity. Through that entity, he and others would then recruit young men and women who wanted to come to the U.S. and their only potential way in was through soccer. Through a network of relationships throughout Europe, Hammond and Paul Macklin would source these coaching candidates. We have since been able to confirm that many of these candidates would then pay a so-called professional development fee to the entity in the U.K. This entity was not owned by BBFC or Epic. These guys appeared to be selling access to the U.S.

In the case of the P1 visas, BBFC staff would have a professional women's club in the U.S. complete the visa application as if the professional club was going to employ the coach, when in fact, the visa worker would actually be employed by BBFC. In exchange for this, BBFC would pay a fee, disguised as a sponsorship, to the professional club. In other cases, we found that BBFC management had provided other consideration to the professional clubs - like the use of rental cars for extended periods of time (a year or longer), all on Epic's dime. It appeared that the professional clubs would then allow their professional players access to the rental cars.

At some point, concerns grew within BBFC about the P1 scheme. Apparently, immigration and / or homeland security agents began asking questions at U.S. youth soccer tournaments and, in at least one instance, following a team practice. At that point, BBFC Leadership shifted its visa strategy towards education-based visas (J1's). Hammond and Crenshaw forged relationships with several U.K.-

based colleges. In order to qualify for a J1 visa, the visa applicant had to prove that they were a full-time student in the field of sports management and that their curriculum included an apprenticeship in the U.S... in this case, with BBFC. Hammond and Crenshaw would direct potential coaches to one of these colleges to enroll.

Student loan agreements were often executed, and, in some cases, promises were made to visa applicants that BBFC would pay the student loan when the loan payments became due, following the student's graduation. There was no formal documentation of such a tuition reimbursement program, nor were any appropriate accruals recorded on the company's books.

We later learned something troubling. Commissions were paid by one or more of the colleges to BBFC UK Student Placement Limited or one of its affiliates. So, BBFC employees were benefiting directly, outside of BBFC, from professional development fees (a fee to secure a work visa) and commissions from U.K. government-funded colleges for BBFC staff coming to the U.S. on visas. Unbelievable.

On multiple occasions, I had asked Hammond and Baldwin if the BBFC U.K. entities made money – each time they acted offended when I asked and repeatedly told me "no."

The J1 visa program was intended to provide foreign students with the opportunity to come to the U.S. to complete their education, not to be cheap labor. During our investigation, we learned that former coaches had filed numerous complaints with BBFC, other third-party student sponsors working with BBFC and U.S. government agencies claiming that the apprenticeships were bogus. The coaches claimed that they had been mistreated and forced to work long hours and insufficiently compensated. These claims had not been brought to our attention by BBFC management. In our subsequent review of emails, we also found disturbing communications from former employees claiming that they had been harassed by certain BBFC managers, had their visas and passports withheld from them on occasion and, in one instance, made assertions that visa workers were *encouraged* to marry in order to remain in the country.

349

If that's not enough, we found a few other interesting things. We found staff that were here on BBFC sponsored visas, but working for non-BBFC clubs, both so-called franchisees and for direct competitors. We also found instances where BBFC had sourced workers on visas procured by competitor clubs. It took me a while to process and understand this. A club that was competitive with BBFC would, effectively, lease a coach to BBFC who was in the U.S. on a visa with the competitive club. What the hell? There appeared to be dark web or black market for these youth soccer coaches here on visas which led us to the entity called Hub Staffing Solutions.

On Cahill's Google Drive, we had found a folder named "HSE." In the folder were corporate formation documents, an operating agreement, a capitalization table that listed the individual owners, federal employer identification number paperwork, a detail of start-up expenses, and so on. While we were able to understand much about the entity from this folder and emails that included the key terms *HSE* or *Hub Staffing*, it was something unusual and fortuitous that really filled in the blanks. In one of the email exchanges between Baldwin, Cahill and others about HSE, Cahill mentioned a name, in a benign, passing reference, that was familiar to me. I couldn't remember where I heard it, but I searched BBFC emails and remembered that he was a web designer based in the U.K. that BBFC used from time to time to create landing pages and the like. I reread the HSE email that mentioned his name but couldn't understand the context in which it was referenced. Days later, likely because my subconscious had been working to connect the dots, I realized that they must have used him to create a website for HSE.

It didn't take long to find it. Much to my disbelief, there was an active Hub Staffing Enterprises website that provided a full description of its services. The website actually referenced that HSE had access to one of the largest youth soccer providers in North America. It also claimed that it could make expedited employment offers for international candidates looking for work in the U.S. Just when I thought this company couldn't show me something new and even more bizarre, it delivered this. The website even included a *Team* section – Crenshaw, Hammond and Cahill were listed as Hub

Staffing Enterprises employees with two of them including their BBFC email addresses in their contact information.

Trying to get honest answers from the people involved became impossible - I was getting completely stonewalled. I knew that people were paying fees in the U.K. to get a visa to come to U.S., but I couldn't get access to the bank accounts that were receiving those funds. I also knew that visa workers in the U.S. were getting "leased" to other entities - likewise, I couldn't track the fees associated with that activity as well. As I mentioned earlier, I did see leased vehicles being traded for access to visa workers.

The more we dug, the more we continued to find. Despite repeatedly asking Baldwin and others if they were involved in any other related party transactions, competitive activities or using company resources for their own personal benefit, their response was always an angry and offended *NO*. However, we later learned that certain executives had a financial interest in the company that provided our athletes and families with their uniforms and other merchandise.

This amounted to millions of dollars of business each year. I couldn't help but think that there was something else going on here. I imagined a number of scenarios in which conflicted individuals could benefit from promoting and selecting one brand partner over another. One may even push for a partnership with a certain brand when Nike or adidas were clearly more appealing partners. Is it possible that one deal presented more margin to the team dealer than Nike and adidas?

I called the team dealer and asked if we could get together - we met for lunch. I knew that he was a longtime friend of several of BBFC's executives. I knew they traveled together. I also learned that the team dealer often paid for the trips, for certain BBFC executives - Hawaii, the Kentucky Derby, and even the U.K. to watch Manchester United play. I knew that he *split* season tickets to the Red Sox with certain executives, but he paid for all of the tickets. He didn't know what I knew. I had very few interactions with him before this lunch.

We met at the Envoy Hotel across from my office. He started off by letting me know that his relationship with BBFC was a business relationship and was separate and distinct from his friendship with any of the executives. He told me that he wanted to keep and, maybe even, expand his relationship with BBFC and Epic. He tried asking me a few questions about the DOJ investigation, but I told him that I wasn't privy to the details. He then pitched me on his company providing all of Epic's apparel needs. I couldn't believe what I was hearing. I played along through lunch.

After we finished lunch, I asked him if there was anything else I needed to know about his business dealings with our employees. He asked what I meant. I explained what the term, *related party transactions* meant. I asked about any joint ownership or financial interest in his businesses with our executives. I also asked about any unusual perks that may have been provided to our staff. He told me that there was *nothing like that*. I asked why some of our guys travelled with him on occasion - he became very uncomfortable. He said that he had lost a couple of bets and the trips were payback. I played dumb and laughed it off.

We wrapped up lunch and he said he would send me a proposal for the rest of our Epic apparel business. Before we went our separate ways (for good, I hoped), he suggested that we meet for dinner at the Capital Grille in Providence and maybe drinks at the Foxy Lady (a strip club) afterward. I said, "I'll check my calendar" and I walked out. I looked to my left at the federal building and wondered how the investigation was going. I couldn't wait to be done with all of this.

We had found a replacement for Baldwin as the CEO of BBFC. We brought in an outsider for two reasons: 1) there wasn't a clear heir apparent already in the business; and 2) even if there had been, we didn't know who we could trust internally. The new person couldn't start until the end of January (more than thirty days out) because he was wrapping up his current position – we would have to wait, but I was itching to get him started. He seemed like an excellent fit, had a good education background, had been a college soccer player and was high energy – exactly what it would take to manage BBFC through the challenges it was facing.

God, I needed someone in that seat as soon as possible. I had enough on my plate, and I couldn't keep my eye on the daily operations of BBFC for much longer. It was a complicated business to begin with but was far more complicated because of the lack of structure and process. Plus, we needed a soccer guy. The new hire would ease some transition concerns of the BBFC team because he came from a soccer background, so he had some *street cred*. Coming from a global consulting firm, we, as a board, expected that he would clean up and refine BBFC's processes so we could scale the business and operate it as a business, not like some criminal enterprise.

At this time, my daughter, Georgia, was in her first semester at Boston College. Georgia is bright, hard-working, quick-witted and incredibly caring. She loves her friends and her family, but she worries more than she lets on - I knew that she was worried about me.

Georgia had an assignment to interview a woman in the workforce and asked if she could interview my assistant, Carolyn. Carolyn was happy to accommodate, and they scheduled a time for Georgia to come to our office. The day arrived and I had completely forgotten about it - it wasn't on my calendar; it was on Carolyn's. I was surprised and thrilled when I saw Georgia sitting with Carolyn in our lobby. On the one hand she still looked like my little girl, but on the other hand, seeing Georgia in a different setting, interviewing Carolyn made her look so grown up. Where the hell had the time gone. When I walked over to the table, she stood up and gave me a hug. I loved it. I asked if she could stick around after she finished up and maybe grab dinner. It was only 3:00pm, but she said she would hang out and do homework at the Starbucks around the corner.

We met up again around 6:30pm and grabbed a bite around the corner at the Scorpion Bar, a Mexican restaurant on Seaport Boulevard. It was so nice to be with her, hearing about school, her roommates and social life. But she didn't seem like her usual upbeat, happy self. A couple of times I asked, "OK?", only to get "yea, everything is fine" as a response. Georgia had come home for a few weekends during the semester and I couldn't tell if she was having issues with roommates or was homesick. I didn't push it.

We took the T to Back Bay and Georgia took an Uber to BC from there. I continued on to Providence.

That weekend, Georgia came home again. She had confided in Christine that she was worried about me, my health and my work hours. She had seen, firsthand, the pace of our office when she was with Carolyn. I think Carolyn also shared with her a sense of my schedule. On top of that, Georgia is an avid reader and had been doing her research on Parkinson's. As we all know, the internet can be a wonderful resource, but it can also play to your deepest fears. She probably knew too much. It didn't help that she wouldn't see me for gaps of time and when she did, she would notice the progression of my symptoms.

Christine gently encouraged Georgia to spend more weekends at school, to trust that I was taking care of myself and to enjoy this time of *her* life - her friends, tailgating for football games, playing on the squash team and so on. Over the next few weeks, she seemed better - she even stayed at school for several weekends in a row. It wasn't always going to be smooth, but we could tell she was settling in and trusting that I would be OK. I realized that I needed to be more aware of the impact my diagnosis was having on my family and I needed to communicate more. One good thing that came out of it was the occasional Monday morning commuter rail rides back to Boston with my Georgia.

One night when I got in to bed, I saw a small note on my nightstand. It was on Georgia's personal stationary. It read, "I'm sorry that you're going through this pain. It's not fair, but something good is coming our way, I have faith. Love you. XO G."

CHAPTER 25

A few days before Christmas, I was walking back to my office from a meeting down the hall. Two of our IT guys worked in a shared, glass office along the hallway. As I walked by, I happened to notice that both of them were looking intently at one of their monitors. Dave was seated at his desk leaning into the right-hand monitor and Mike was standing to his right pointing at something on the screen. It didn't strike me as anything significant, but I did notice it.

I had just returned to my desk when Dave came into my office. Now, keep in mind that both of these guys reported directly to Emily, the head of IT, so my interactions in the past had involved getting to know them a bit when they first joined the company; small talk occasionally in the kitchen area and the occasional beer at an office social event. I didn't interact with them directly on a professional level very often, if at all.

Dave asked if I had a moment, I said, "sure, what's up?" He seemed nervous and said he wanted to show me something on his computer. I had a sinking feeling... he wasn't.coming to get me go show me a new screensaver he had found. His workspace was only a short distance down the hall. During that walk, I said, "this can't be good." He said, "no, it's not."

We turned into his office, Mike was in his chair and he stood up immediately, allowing Dave to take his position in front of the monitors. Dave asked Mike, "is it still happening?"

Mike said, "yea, I just kicked them out again."

I asked, "what's going on?"

Dave pointed to the right-hand monitor and explained that we were looking at the administrator's dashboard for the BBFC email system. I knew that we hadn't completed the migration yet to Microsoft Outlook since I was still using the incumbent system to conduct much of our forensic work. Dave continued to explain the layout of the dashboard, account names down the left side, the next column that indicates the respective email accounts' data storage and so on.

"OK, I get it, so what's going on?", I said to Dave to keep him moving. He looked back at me and said, "someone is deleting files."

"Are you fucking serious?", I replied. "How?"

He said he didn't know - Mike seemed horrified that I had just dropped an F-bomb.

Dave continued to explain that he was preparing to prioritize the email accounts for the Outlook migration; that's why he was in the administrative account, when he just happened to notice that the data storage for one of the email accounts was decreasing. As soon as he noticed it, he kicked out the active user by changing the account password - easy to do as he was in the administrative dashboard. As he and Mike were trying to understand how that could possibly happen and while taking the necessary steps to recover any deleted emails, they noticed it started happening again. This cycle played out three of four times until they saw me walk by and decided they needed to get me involved. Both Dave and Mike knew all too well that the company was under a litigation hold. While they were not privy to the details of the DOJ investigation, they certainly knew there had been a raid. They also were taking every measure possible to preserve all records and files and responding to my daily requests for access to different email, Google Drive and DropBox accounts. They knew how serious this was.

While we were trying to understand how this was happening, the user logged in again and began deleting emails. "There," Dave said, "he is in again." Dave quickly reset the password and the user was kicked out. So, here's what was happening. Someone else had administrative access to the account, because, each time we reset the password, this unknown user would reset it again. It was like a ping pong match. I asked Dave who else had administrative access - he told me no one. Emily had been out of the office for another meeting and returned in the middle of our conversation. She was up to speed in a minute - I told them to contact the email provider right away and find out who else had administrative access. I also reminded them how critical it was that this stopped - the DOJ would not be happy if we lost these emails since we hadn't been able to back up all of the files yet due to the limitations of the email platform. I told them to update me every thirty minutes regardless of progress and let me know immediately if anything new developed. I returned to my desk.

Thirty minutes later, Emily told me that they had put in a "support ticket" with the email provider but hadn't heard back yet. She said they were having difficulty making contact with anyone at the provider. She assured me, however, that we would not lose any files since there was a fourteen-day backup and recovery function with Rackspace, the actual email host. I felt a little better.

The next three updates, in thirty-minute increments, were the same - no change. To be clear, this was not Emily's fault. I Googled the email provider, found the main office number and called it - I was panicking thinking about the DOJ. There was an automated greeting and after working my way through the menu of department choices, I finally reached a live human. It was a customer service person. I told them I was calling from Epic and explained the situation. The customer service person advised me that there was already an active support ticket outstanding and that a company representative would be in touch with Dave as soon as the problem was resolved. I tried to provide more color about the situation, but the representative didn't seem to care. I asked if I could be transferred to the CEO. He told me that he couldn't do that, it was not their "normal protocol." I realized then that I wasn't going to get anywhere with this person, who was just trying to do their job. He had no idea how serious this was, nor could he possibly understand what was at risk. So, I decided to ask if he could pass on a message to his supervisor. He agreed to do so. I told him that the U.S. Department of Justice was in the midst of a criminal investigation and that evidence critical to its investigation resided in the email system. Emails were actively being deleted from that system and, as a result, the investigation and potential prosecution of criminals may be compromised. I needed the CEO to call me immediately. About five minutes later, the CEO called me.

I explained the situation to the CEO, and she was attentive, understanding and apologetic that there had been a delay in getting to us. I told her that there was no need for an apology as these were pretty unusual and unexpected circumstances. I asked if she could confirm who else may have administrative access to our email accounts. She took a few moments and patched in one of her colleagues into our call. They logged into our account and told us that there were two additional administrative access points of which we were unaware. The problem was that there wasn't any way of knowing who had access to these. They deleted both accounts immediately. At least we knew they were deactivated. I asked if we could get a history of the administrative activity for both of the users - they confirmed they could and in a matter of minutes, we received two separate Excel files with the requested information. Oddly enough, the account that was being used to repeatedly change the password for one of the email accounts had minimal activity over the prior several months. Unfortunately, that was not the case for the other administrative account.

I was shocked to learn that the more active administrative account had deleted an entire email account, not just certain email files, but an actual user account about twenty days earlier. Twenty days was beyond our fourteen-day recovery window with Rackspace. The email account deleted was one of Baldwin's closest and most trusted lieutenants who had resigned from the company shortly after Patrick's termination. I printed the administrative account history and met with Emily and Dave. I learned that we could not recover the account. This was disappointing to say the least and was going to be a black eye for us with the DOJ. I needed to know who controlled this administrative access and would delete an entire email account under these circumstances.

To commit such a deliberate act knowing that there is an ongoing criminal investigation and a company-wide litigation hold was astounding to me - it also further reinforced my concern that certain individuals knew they were guilty and would do anything to try to cover up their illegal acts.

We reviewed the administrative account activity in detail trying to see some pattern of behavior or activities that would provide a clue to who controlled the account. Neither Emily nor Dave could see anything revealing. Nor could I, at first. Then I noticed that this user had set up several new BBFC email accounts over six months ago - these accounts were what we called "info" accounts; basically, email addresses that potential customers could contact if interested in a particular event or team. This was closely tied to our marketing activities. I then noticed additional activity, deleting emails within accounts related to BBFC social media accounts - more marketing activity. I had a hunch that this administrative account belonged to Gordon Kerrigan, the former BBFC marketing manager who left the company a short while ago.

Kerrigan was about thirty-five years old, married and had originally come to the U.S. on a work visa. He was not only responsible for marketing, but he also coached several BBFC teams in Massachusetts. I had been in Gordon's company a number of times and had been impressed with the quality of his work. Baldwin considered him one of his best employees. Baldwin's accolades for Kerrigan made it even harder for me to understand why he had let Gordon leave the company without making an effort to keep him. A few months back, Baldwin told me that we needed to hire a new marketing manager because Gordon was leaving to take a position with a tech start-up. Knowing how Baldwin felt about Gordon, I asked what we could do to convince him to stay - was it all about compensation? He told me that Gordon had made up his mind and there was no convincing him otherwise. He seemed oddly resigned that Gordon was leaving the company. This struck me as really odd since Baldwin had fought in the past to keep his team together, going as far as pursuing legal action to enforce non-competes against even coaches to keep them with BBFC. I had to ask two or three times where Gordon was going before I was provided the actual name of the company - after some quick Google searches, I realized Gordon was leaving to go work for another BBFC coach who also was the

Director of BBFC's non-profit foundation. I thought, here we go again, another undisclosed affiliate or potential related party transactions.

I explained to Emily and Dave my hunch about Kerrigan and the circumstances under which he had left the company. While I was talking, Emily was still looking over the administrative account's activity log - she then mentioned that the IP address for the user had changed not too long ago. I looked at it and quickly realized that it changed around the time Kerrigan had resigned. Equally as important, the IP address appeared to be static, meaning consistent, since the change. We ran a geo-location of the IP address and were able to pinpoint it to a location just west of Boston. It took about another five minutes, at most, to locate it in the vicinity of Kerrigan's new employer. I took out my phone and called Kerrigan expecting to get his voicemail - I hadn't even planned what I was going to say. Much to my surprise, he answered on the first ring.

I strongly doubt he had my number in his contacts - all the more reason I would have expected him to let an unknown number go to voicemail. He said hello, I did same and told him it was me. I asked him how he was doing and if he had a moment. He said, "I'm good, thanks. Yea, I have a minute, what's going on?" I asked him if he still had administrative access to the BBFC email platform. He paused briefly and told me that he had given his password to the new IT person when he left. I said, "oh, OK, you gave it to Emily?" and he said, "yea, I gave it to Emily." Silence. I waited a moment... then thanked him, told him I hoped his new gig was going well and hung up. I sat for a moment thinking. Emily and Dave were just looking at me waiting for a download. I knew he had lied to me. By me asking "if he *still* had administrative access..." he assumed that I knew he had it at one time and couldn't deny it. So, his only option was to say that he gave his password to Emily. I told Emily what he said - she confirmed that she had never spoken to him about the account, let alone received a password from him.

Only a few minutes following my call with Gordon, I texted him - I told him that we knew he still had access to the administrative account, that he had used it recently to delete an entire email account

360

and that we were able to tie the activity to the IP address of his computer and geo-locate him at the office of his new employer. I was shocked when he replied almost instantly - he admitted that he still had access and had, in fact, deleted the email account in question. He said he did so because the user of the email account had pressured him to do it. With a few keystrokes, Kerrigan had, effectively, admitted to obstruction of justice and willful destruction of evidence related to an ongoing federal criminal investigation. A few months later, Kerrigan was indicted and subsequently entered a guilty plea in federal court and is facing up to twenty years in prison. One bad decision. It was clear to me now that none of these people understood how serious this was.

I cannot emphasize enough how much stress I (and our team) was under. While living it every day, I ignored it as much as I could. I didn't have the luxury of dwelling on it - I believed that if I had complained or even shared the complete Epic story with anyone, I would fold... I would give up. Instead, I kept my head down and kept grinding.

Occasionally (not nearly as often as I would have liked), I would attend Catholic Mass at the Our Lady of Good Voyage Shrine in the Seaport. Known as the Seaport Shrine, it was built in 2017 just around the corner from the where the original church had been located. The original shrine had served the needs of the blue collar, Boston dockworkers years before the Seaport reinvented itself.

The new Shrine was built on a parcel obtained through a land swap with a developer who needed the location of the old church. The Shrine is directly across the street from my office and adjacent to the Martin Richard Playground - together, the shrine and the playground feel sacred. The chapel is a small brick building that incorporates historical features and references to the dock workers of Boston Harbor. The chapel is also unusual in that it was built in an emerging urban neighborhood, where real estate is such a prized commodity, to provide access primarily to the younger generation who lived and worked in the Seaport.

On the occasion that I didn't have a midday work commitment, I would attend Mass. The chapel seats about 250 people, but usually would only have about 25 or so attendees at midday. The priest would celebrate an efficient, 30-minute Mass and provide a brief, but usually, relevant homily. Every time I attended, there was a message I could takeaway - I was looking for some signs of hope.

A few days before Christmas 2019, I attended Mass. There were a few more people in attendance than usual, likely due to Advent, but still less than 50 people. I arrived only a minute or two before Mass began and sat about halfway down to the right at the end of a pew. Almost immediately, I heard someone shout out an odd noise - I didn't know what it was, but it startled me. A moment later, the same type of sound. It echoed a bit in the chapel which made it difficult to determine where it was coming from. I looked around, but no one else seemed to flinch. Heads were down.

A third time... I realized the sounds were coming from the front, left section of the chapel. It was a gentleman in the front row who apparently suffered from Tourette Syndrome. The priest walked onto the alter, we all stood, and Mass began. It took a few minutes for me to become immune to the gentlemen's periodic sounds; a grunt, a few incoherent words or the occasional profanity. I couldn't imagine the strength and faith it took for this gentleman to make the effort to come to Mass.

The Priest's homily focused on a reading from Isaiah that said, "Strengthen all weary hands, steady all trembling knees and say to the faint-hearted, 'Be Strong! Do not be afraid. Here is your God, vengeance is coming, divine retribution; he is coming to save you.'"

I remained in my pew for a few moments after Mass had ended to reflect on the homily, the gentleman in the front row, and my own challenges. When I left the Chapel, the gentleman in the front row was shaking hands with the Priest on the front steps and wishing *him* a Merry Christmas. I felt rejuvenated, blessed and a deep sense of gratitude.

IT'S LIKE A FLU

CHAPTER 26

Before the end of 2019, we had planned on closing on $5.0 million of additional capital from existing investors before the end of 2019. The process, like everything else, was taking longer than expected. However, we had been provided assurances from CFC and RevCap that there were no issues with the funding. I had been working closely with Nunn & King to get the closing documents cleaned up so we could wrap things up as soon as possible - we needed the liquidity. In early January 2020, I received a call from one of our attorneys asking if I knew why the funding amount had changed. I had no idea what he was talking about.

The Nunn & King partner told me that the latest revision of the documents that just came over indicated that the funding would be for $2.0 million instead of $5.0 million. This was going to be a problem - we had been stretching vendors and repeatedly told our divisional leaders that we would have additional capital shortly to get caught up with all of our payables. If I had to go back to our team and let them know that we were short $3.0 million, I would lose credibility with my team but our investors would lose even more.

I called the partner at CFC who was managing the closing documents on their side. When he answered, he acted like everything was fine -

I was polite, made the usual small talk, then asked about the change in the funding amount. He dismissed it as "nothing to worry about." He said that they had determined that it would be easier and quicker to close on the $2.0 million and then follow-up with the additional $3.0 million in a matter of weeks. He said that they were tired of dealing with the preemptive rights in the operating agreement and that after this funding, the board could change the agreement to eliminate the right for others to participate and streamline funding process. I explained to him the urgency for the additional $3.0 million and he told me that he knew all to well. He reassured me that the entire $5.0 million would be funded in a matter of weeks.

I gave a few members of our leadership team a heads up, but chose to hold off on a few others that I knew would be upset with the news. I would deal with it tomorrow. I stayed in the office a bit later than usual, but I realized that if I didn't head out shortly, I would be on a really late train. I packed up quick and headed out. I was walking to South Station while looking at my phone, checking a bunch of emails I had missed while on and off with the attorneys much of the afternoon. On the boardwalk between Seaport Boulevard and Congress Street, I walked by a guy standing along the railing overlooking the the harbor and the financial district beyond. I didn't even notice him until he said, "Are you doing OK?"

He said it to me as I passed him. It caught me off guard. I wasn't sure if he was talking to me, but no one else was nearby and he didn't appear to be wearing headphones. I looked back and he was still leaning against the railing, but, he was now looking casually, over his left shoulder at me. I kept moving and said, "I'm doing OK, you?" He didn't answer, but he left the railing and started to walk behind me - a comfortable distance, but close enough for me to take notice. The boardwalk was empty. He followed me as I approached the Children's Museum on my left - then, I heard him say, in a louder and more aggressive voice, "are you sure you're doing OK?" I didn't answer. I took a right onto Congress.

Halfway across the Congress Street bridge, it felt like he was on my heels. I was walking as fast as I could, my LL Bean cane clicking on the sidewalk and my breath visible in the cold air. A few people passed me heading in the opposite direction, so I wasn't panicking, but each time someone passed, I felt the guy behind me getting closer. My mind was racing - was I paranoid? This was probably just some poor homeless guy. I was telling myself not to worry about it. At the midpoint of the bridge, I stopped directly in front of the Boston Tea Party Ships & Museum, coincidentally called Griffin's Wharf. I turned to my right to step off the sidewalk toward the museum entrance, which was closed. I assumed the guy would walk by.

I acted like I was reading the sign at the the museum entrance with my back to the bridge. While it was only a few seconds, I couldn'thelp but think that this entire setting was bizarre - I was standing in the middle of a bridge, feeling threatened and the speakers outside of the museum were blasting colonial music played on a fife.

Assuming my new friend had passed, I turned around and found that he was standing with his back against one of the trusses of the bridge. He had a smirk on his face. He was only twenty feet or so away from me. I made eye contact, tried to act casual and resumed my walk west on the bridge. He said, "we are good, right?" I didn't answer - it seemed like he was looking to start a fight. I just kept moving. He followed. Then, I heard him say, "do the right thing, man. Do the right thing." He was still behind me. I took a left on Dorchester Avenue and a right on Summer Street, hugging the front of the Fidelity building and, then, into South Station. I felt like he had followed me into South Station, but I convinced myself that I was just paranoid. Nonetheless, I was never so happy to be inside South Station. I looked over my shoulder as I passed the Transit Police office and there was no sign of him.

I couldn't feel my legs and I was sweating even though it was freezing out. I leaned my cane against a table, took a seat in the open area between Starbucks and Au Bon Pain and checked the trains - I had about ten minutes before I could board. I texted my wife to let her know when I would arrive in Providence. She replied almost immediately and let me know that she could pick me up. She asked if

I needed dinner. I told her not to worry about it. I put my phone on the table and took a deep breath.

I looked around and saw the guy who had followed me standing across the lobby, adjacent to the newsstand. He was looking at me. What the hell? He definitely was not homeless. Since he was on the other side of the main lobby, I could take a longer look at him and feel safe. He had on a cap, like an Irish cap; a Barbour-style jacket, jeans and work boots. He appeared clean cut. To this day, I believe he was there to deliver a message. As much as I don't like to admit it, I still think about that walk to South Station. I even dream about it from time-to-time. The anonymous emails, social media posts, intercepted emails threatening me, the Shankill Gang and crucifixion references... all were taking their toll. This wasn't just a job anymore, I literally felt threatened and it was impacting me emotionally and physically.

A couple of days later, another anonymous e-mail was sent to Epic's employees; this time about the mistreatment of BBFC executives who had been terminated. This one, too, was full of misrepresentations intended to paint me and our board in a negative light. We learned from the first couple of whistleblower emails how to quickly block the sender from distributing additional emails and how to communicate with our team about the email. Regardless of what we told the team, these types of emails had an impact on the organization. Any form of negativity puts doubt in one's mind, drives conversations among the staff, and drags down morale and productivity.

The day after the anonymous email, we were contacted by a journalist who wrote for a soccer publication. I was surprised it had taken this long. Now, I could clearly see the plan that the other side was executing. I knew Baldwin well enough to know what he was doing - his constant Braveheart, Game of Thrones and Gladiator references told me he had a series of tactics he was rolling out. I am convinced he thought he was executing a paramilitary operation. The anonymous email was to put doubts in the staff's mind about his termination and remind his people that he wasn't going quietly; a few BBFC people had left to go work with a competitor who happened to have a long friendship with certain BBFC executives (this served to reinforce to Baldwin's former staff that he was still active and in control behind the scenes); follow that with a lawsuit (an indication that he is here to fight); send someone to spook me; and then cap it off with an article in a soccer publication (tell the world *his* story) - the article would surely be about the " greedy suits" stealing the soccer coach / entrepreneur's company.

I wanted to speak to the journalist, but I knew that was not the smartest move. We were not going to fight this matter in the press. I also knew that Powell and Jonathan Witt would never let that happen. Our board also had encouraged us to engage a public relations firm - each call included about six people from their firm, plus me, Laura, our VP of marketing and the new BBFC CEO. In my opinion, these calls were a waste of time and money. This situation was too fluid and complicated for an outside PR firm. Laura and our VP of marketing would provide the most tangible guidance on the calls and then mark-up and revise the planned communications sent over by the PR firm afterwards.

The journalist from the soccer publication told us that he was running his story by the end of business, the next day with or without any comments from Epic. He provided us with a draft of the story. It provided a high-level commentary of the DOJ investigation, Baldwin's proclamation of innocence, and then his wrongful termination case. I felt like if we didn't respond, we looked weak. The attorneys, however, advised that we had to be careful with what we said. Baldwin had the benefit of referencing his wrongful termination complaint which had been filed with the court and, therefore, was already in the public domain.

We had just learned that Baldwin, other BBFC executives, and BBFC's outside counsel (at the time) were aware of the DOJ criminal investigation approximately ten months before the search and seizure warrant was executed. None of these people brought this to the attention of the BBFC board of directors, Epic's management or board of directors. They had a duty to do so. Had we known about the investigation and allegations ten months in advance of the raid, we could have taken a number of actions that would have mitigated the risk to the company legally, operationally and financially. Instead, the raid and events that followed destroyed significant value in the business.

Powell worked all night preparing a complaint against BBFC's former outside counsel - to stop the firm from representing Baldwin, since they were clearly conflicted, and for its failure to notify the board of the criminal investigation. The complaint was filed mid-morning and provided to the journalist hours before his deadline.

The complaint provided details about the DOJ allegations; Baldwin and others' prior knowledge of the investigation; the circumstances leading to his termination and so on. The journalist was provided a much more complete and accurate portrayal of the current circumstances at BBFC. The complaint changed the substance and tone of the article.

Neither Powell nor I spoke with the board about the complaint. Instead, we chose to file it on behalf of the company; I had the authority as CEO. If anyone had responsibility to notify them, it was me, not outside counsel. Quite frankly, we were moving fast and the complaint was justified, in my opinion. It was inappropriate that the law firm who represented BBFC on a variety of matters, including executive employment agreements, was trying to represent Baldwin against the company. In addition, their failure to notify the board of the criminal investigation was unacceptable and seemed potentially negligent on their part. Nonetheless, the board was pissed at me for filing the complaint.

On our Monday informal update call, I provided board members with detailed updates on a variety of topics including the article that was published over the weekend and how our complaint changed it, materially, in our favor. I explained the details of the complaint filed against the law firm as well. The call lasted an hour and also included updated about all of our divisions, not just BBFC. Immediately, following the call, I received a text from a board member asking me to call him. I did. I was greeted with, "what the fuck is wrong with you? Are you out of your mind?" I honestly had no idea what he was talking about or why he was so upset.

He said that I had no right to file a complaint against the law firm without the board's approval. He went on and on about how expensive litigation is, never mind against a law firm. I didn't say a word, but I disagreed - it needed to be filed for a variety of reasons. This board hadn't been shy about flexing its litigious muscles and now I was getting my head handed to me for filing a complaint that may actually yield benefits to the company. I was professional and polite - I simply said, "it had to be filed." He responded with, "did you listen to anything I just told you?" I told him I did, but that I disagreed. I suggested he call Powell and get his perspective as well. The call ended. To this day, I don't understand his position. In fact, there were several instances afterwards where he asked counsel what he thought the potential damages could be as a result of the complaint. When he heard the potential range, he was clearly pleased that the complaint had actually been filed.

Sleep was becoming a rare escape for me. I wasn't working all night, but my brain was always working, and my body never stopped moving. I found that I would fall asleep quickly, but after about 1:00am I would wake up. The internal tremors that had started in my mid-section and hips now extended to the tips of my fingers and toes. I found them far more distracting now, perhaps because the nerves are more sensitive in your extremities - I don't know. The cramps in my feet and calves became intolerable. In bed, I had to lie on my stomach, slide down the bed so that my feet hung off the bed. Then I would pull my toes to the end of the mattress to prevent them from curling under. Not exactly a relaxing way to sleep. To make matters worse, my neck, shoulders and back were in a con state of spasm. I could not get any relief.

As I have said before, everything looks different in the middle of the night when you are alone. The problems at work seem insurmountable and the anxiety and worry about your family is magnified. During these periods, I hadn't dwelled on my own circumstances. I think it was because I had so many other things to manage, both work and family, I simply put it aside. I also didn't want to deal with it. Looking back, I was in denial. I hadn't dealt with my Parkinson's diagnosis at all. I recognized that I would need to... at some point.

It was a cold, rainy, miserable morning in Boston. The train was late and my walk to the office sucked - there was no other way to describe it. For whatever reason, I was having an *off period* - this is when my Parkinson's medication isn't working optimally. For me, *off* means tremors and severe rigidity. I had to stop about ten times between South Station and my office - at one point, I ducked into a Starbucks and just sat there for about five minutes to gather myself. My office was on the second floor and I couldn't even take the stairs anymore. This may have been the bottom for me and the day that I started to move towards acceptance.

Hitting the bottom in the middle of winter in New England isn't good for the soul. I checked all the boxes - I was frustrated, irritated, anxious, overwhelmed, and almost ready to walk away from everything. My mind was starting to go to dark places. I am not proud of that. I couldn't give up, but I really didn't know where to turn.

I walked into my office and was greeted by Carolyn. I smiled and acted like all was good in my world. We talked about her train commute and the challenges she had that morning getting her kids off to school. She reminded me that my calendar was booked solid, literally from 8:30am to 7:00pm - she told me that she would grab lunch for me, and I could eat during a call I had at 12:30pm. She was great. I put my head down and went to work.

Carolyn and I managed my calendar in a manner in which we scheduled any necessary advanced preparation on the calendar in the days leading up to that particular call or meeting. In other words, if I needed to review a presentation that was going to be delivered to me, there would be a time slot the day before for that review. As a result, I could pretty much go from calendar event to calendar event throughout the day efficiently and without worrying about being unprepared. I headed into a small conference room for my 12:30pm call, Carolyn came in with me and brought me a salad from Sweetgreen. I looked at the calendar event and I didn't recognize the person I was supposed to call - Andy O'Brien from a major Wall Street bank. I asked Carolyn what the call was about - she said she wasn't completely sure. She looked at her calendar and said that he was on the board of the Michael J. Fox Foundation.

This was the last thing I needed today. I vaguely recalled a friend introducing me via email to Andy some time ago and a call had subsequently been scheduled. I assumed this was going to be a call during which some board member would ask me to donate to the Foundation because I just became a lifetime member of their *exclusive club*. I told Carolyn to reschedule it - she said, "no, you are taking this call." She told me that I was already late, and it would be rude to cancel. She walked out of the room. I dialed the number, reluctantly.

It was his direct line and he answered after the first ring. I introduced myself and, as I recall, I didn't even allow him to tell me anything about himself. I told him that I had been diagnosed less than a year ago and that I was doing fine, that I was lucky that I didn't really have much in the way of symptoms. I then told him that I would make a donation to the Foundation and that I was pretty sure that my wife would participate in one of their 5K runs in our area. I wanted to get off this call as fast as possible. In hindsight, I must have sounded like a real jerk.

As I was talking, I was looking at Andy's bio - he had a big job and had been with the bank for over 30 years. He went to Holy Cross in Worcester, Massachusetts. Over the years, every person I had met from Holy Cross was solid - the college has a culture and core values similar to my alma mater, Providence College. After I finished speaking, he calmly thanked me for calling him and providing my background. Almost immediately, I noticed something in the way he spoke. Then I realized that he had Parkinson's too. He asked me how old I was - he told me that he was diagnosed around the same age as me. He asked about my family - he too had children about the same age as mine when he was first diagnosed.

This guy didn't know me, but he went on to share very personal experiences with me on our first call... on a day when I needed it most. He talked about worrying about his wife and children and how they had been worrying about him. He told me how he learned to communicate with his family about the disease. He talked about business travel and how difficult it had become. He was an avid golfer, like me, and he shared how Parkinson's had limited his ability to enjoy the game. He asked about my medications. He had gone through the same medication protocol and cycles. He was about five to seven years ahead of me on his journey. He told me what to expect from the medication and the likely need to increase dosage over time.

Then, he told me that he reached a point when he had maxed out the medication and its effectiveness. He then had deep brain stimulation surgery, by which a device was implanted in the brain to send electrical signals to mimic dopamine and influence body movements. He said it was a game changer. Literally, changed his life.

He could now travel more comfortably, sleep better, was actually golfing again and spending quality time with his wife and kids. His insights were so personal and relevant to what I was facing. Equally important was how he delivered them - in a genuine, caring manner. And this guy didn't even know me. Before we wrapped up the call, he told me to call him any time. He also told me that his family and faith provided him with the strength to get through this and encouraged me to focus on those two things. God, I needed that call. I knew there would be tough days ahead and more work to be done, but Andy provided me with visibility towards acceptance.

CHAPTER 27

At the encouragement of the board (and I agreed), we had begun holding monthly leadership meetings in Boston; two-day sessions. With most of our folks in Boston now, we only had to bring in a few people from outside the area. Therefore, travel costs were relatively low and we hosted the sessions in a classroom space in our Seaport office. These sessions were proving to be a great way of bringing people together socially; reinforcing the company's vision and strategy; sharing best practices, finding solutions to challenges; and getting the divisional leaders to leverage and work with each other *and* our corporate resources.

Carolyn coordinated the logistics and Laura spearheaded these sessions - it was no small task. We would solicit preferred topics from the participants a month in advance of the next session. Laura and I would take the ideas, prioritize and group them. We would also engage the participants to lead certain sessions. We were making progress, but we had some work to do.

For a Chief People Officer, Laura had the unique ability to maintain her focus from a human resource perspective (i.e., implementing systems, executing on professional development strategies, encouraging collaboration, improving culture, etc.) while simultaneously evaluating the organization and people from an operations perspective. She was a remarkable judge of character and competence, but she also knew what the company needed across all functional areas. She was using these leadership meetings to evaluate and help people while also shaping and influencing the company's operations in real-time. Very cool.

At our January leadership meeting, several board members participated. Some were more active than others and there were moments when the board members would step out of the meetings to take a call or miss a session all together - this did not make a great impression on certain members of our team. However, the first evening we attended a Boston Bruins game together as a group in the TD Garden's new Rafters section - it was a great way for everyone to mingle and get to know the board members and the board members to put faces to names of our divisional leaders and corporate team. The evening was a success.

The next day, something pretty special happened. Laura had scheduled a time slot during which our leaders could ask questions of the board members in attendance. When she first suggested it to me, I wasn't sure it would fly, but when she explained her rationale and how she envisioned it, I was 100% on board. We put together sample questions of our own and sent them to the board members in advance.

The Q&A with the board members went well. However, there was one sensitive topic in particular. I was thrilled actually that it was raised. The question was about liquidity, the investors / board's commitment to Epic, and the timing of overdue vendor payments. The team member who asked the question emphasized that we had been stretching our vendors for too long and we needed to catch up on our payables and provide our vendors with a commitment that we would be on time going forward. The leader wanted to hear the board's view of this.

One of the board members stood up - when he did, I was surprised since he typically didn't like to speak in public. He proceeded to deliver an impassioned speech about the future of Epic, the quality of our team, and our purpose and mission. He reiterated the board's commitment to the company and acknowledged that we, as a group, had weathered storms together and would not waiver. He also recognized that we had not been good partners to our vendors and that additional capital would be provided to the company in a matter of weeks to catch up on payables. The room was fired up. I had a colleague tell me after the meeting that he had never been more excited about Epic than after listening to that board member.

I thought he did a tremendous job and told him so. I also told Laura immediately after the meeting that the board just put themselves in one hell of a position. They had this team excited and fully committed and that was great. However, if they didn't honor their commitment to us, they would lose the trust of a lot of these people very quickly. If you are going to deliver a speech like that, you better back it up.

In late January, I needed to make another trip to England, Spain and Ireland to meet with some staff and partners in those markets. It was the last thing I wanted to do right now, but time felt like it was passing so quickly, and I needed to show the commitment of meeting in person, having dinner and simply being on our partners 'home turf. The trip would be quick - fly overnight on a Sunday and then back Friday. London was a couple of quick meetings, productive and then off to Spain. My flight was the last flight to land in Valencia before Storm Gloria hit. No joke, I hadn't even checked the weather. The plane felt like a roller coaster - one of the worst flights of my life. My luggage never arrived. It was still in London. I spoke with the airline and they said my bag likely wouldn't be in Valencia for a couple of days due to the storm. I would be in Belfast by then.

I had the taxi driver bring me to a shopping mall near my hotel. I don't speak Spanish, so purchasing a piece of luggage, clothes and personal hygiene products proved to be quite an experience. Nonetheless, within a couple of hours, I had a couple of outfits that made me look like a local even though I had to cuff my pants. By the time I arrived at my hotel the power was out. While I was checking in, water was flooding the lobby. My hotel was one block from the Balearic Sea - winds were approaching 75 miles an hour and the waves were over 25 feet. I felt like I was moving from one storm to another. I hunkered down in my fourth-floor room until the morning. A part of me wanted to hunker down longer.

The next morning, I was picked up by our two partners for BBFC Spain, Diego and Alex. I had met them both before. I liked them both very much - they were hard working young men who seemed to be in the business for the right reasons; they loved coaching and developing young soccer players. We drove a few miles to their academy, trees and power lines were down along the way. The rain had stopped, and you could feel the winds were finally subsiding. I spent the day touring their facilities, meeting with players and a few parents who were in town visiting.

This was my first time visiting this academy and I recognize that the weather conditions weren't the best, however, the facilities were less than impressive. No offense to Diego and Alex, it wasn't their fault, but the quality of these facilities had been grossly exaggerated back in the U.S. I was also benchmarking against New England prep schools which carried a similar price tag. Sure enough, the parents with whom I met had numerous complaints about the facilities. They loved Diego and Alex, but were disappointed with the dormitories, classrooms, fields, gym and social areas. We had some work to do here.

I also met with the local professional football club. Leadership was warm and welcoming, and their facilities were pristine. I understood that we had a partnership with the local clubs as their youth academy partner throughout Europe similar to our U.S. club's partnership with a different European professional team. As we toured their facility, we watched a youth team practicing - they appeared about the same age as the boys I had just met at our academy. I asked how it worked, how we co-existed in the same city. In far better English than my Spanish, the gentleman from the professional club told me that our academy was prohibited from using their name or logos in Spain. I couldn't understand it - so, we had a partnership to provide their official youth academies throughout Europe, except for in their home country, the one market where the brand was the most relevant. Just another poorly conceived and structured agreement. Put it on the list.

On to Belfast. I was picked up at the airport by Paul Macklin, the same gentleman who picked me up in Dublin about a year ago. He seemed genuinely happy to see me and I appreciated him picking me up. We asked about each other's families, he asked how I was holding up. I told him that I was doing fine and kept it very high level. I think he noticed me looking at my phone, so he said, "take a few minutes and catch up on your emails, I'm sure you had a bunch while you were on the flight." I took him up on it.

After a couple of minutes, while I was still head down, typing an email, he asked, "has my name come up with the Department of Justice?" Just like that - boom. I paused and told him "not really." He looked at me nervously and said, "what the hell does 'not really ' mean?" I told him that the investigations, both the DOJ and our own internal one, were confidential. However, I told him that I hadn't been asked specific questions about him from the DOJ. That seemed to ease his nerves a bit. However, he then went into a long explanation of his role in sourcing coaches and how he didn't do anything wrong. I must have nodded and said "I hear you" twenty-five times. What else could I do? We went straight to my hotel - I had been advised, for my own safety, to go to the hotel, hold my meetings there and then go straight back to the airport in the morning. Based on the source of the advice, I was not going to leave the hotel.

Macklin and I met for a while in the lobby of the hotel before our guests arrived. We talked about my trip to Spain, the structure of that partnership and the broader academy model. I told him we had a lot of work to do to ensure quality control and best-in-class offerings to North American families considering sending their children to school in Europe. Regardless of the topic we were covering, he often would find a way to ask about the investigation. I dodged it as best I could.

Our guests arrived for dinner - several members from the board of the Belfast Cup tournament with whom we had partnered about a year earlier. They wanted to know why Baldwin was no longer with BBFC and how his departure may impact our relationship. I explained Baldwin's termination in professionally vague terms - I could tell they were concerned and skeptical about our relationship at first, but by the time we finished dinner, they seemed comfortable with the relationship going forward. They didn't have much choice as the agreement didn't provide any "outs" for them. We also discussed planning and logistics for the event which was scheduled to be held in a matter of months. We wrapped up for the day and Macklin asked if we could meet for breakfast after which he would bring me to the airport.

We had agreed to meet at 8:00am and I would need to be on the road by 10:00am. I was in the lobby early having a cup of coffee and catching up on the news - the lead story was about some sort of flu that was starting to spread across Europe. Macklin didn't arrive until almost 8:30am. As he approached the table, I knew something was wrong. He looked rattled. Standing next to the table he said in a loud voice, "why didn't you tell me? You knew. You were with me for hours yesterday and you didn't tell me?" I told him to quiet down and take a seat - he was making a scene. I told him I had no idea what he was talking about. He reluctantly sat down and wouldn't look at me. He was breathing heavy and shaking his head. I asked him again what he was talking about. He said, "the Department of Justice." I said, "what about it?" He looked at me and said, "you know." I told him that I honestly had no idea what he was talking about. He stared at me, like he was trying to see if he could figure out if I was lying. By the way, I *was* telling the truth, I had no idea what he was talking about.

378

I said, "Paul, I swear on my family - I have no idea what you are talking about." He sighed and said that a federal agent called him that morning, just as he was getting in his car. The agent told him that they would like to meet him next week, in Belfast. Bad timing, I thought.

I had breakfast, he didn't. He was so distracted; it was impossible to talk business. He would look off into the distance, then shake his head, sigh and say something like, "This is terrible." I told him that everything was going to be fine. It didn't seem to ease his fears. At one point, he asked me if he should meet with the DOJ. I couldn't believe the question. I said, "of course you have to meet with them." I told him that if he had nothing to hide, he should meet with them and get it over with. He was visibly shaken by the thought of meeting with them. I told him that I had met with them and it was not what you would think. They were professional, polite and courteous. The more I watched him, the more I realized he was really scared. He seemed overwhelmed with fear. I think he was less concerned about meeting with the DOJ and more concerned about the potential consequences from others if he actually spoke to the agents.

He drove me to the airport - he was quiet the entire ride; it was unlike him, he normally talked non-stop. When we arrived, he opened the trunk and I took out my bag. I thanked him for the ride and, again, told him that everything would be fine. I told him that he should just take the meeting with the DOJ and get it over with. I put out my hand to shake his, but he didn't extend his. He reached up, closed the trunk and said, "God bless you and your family." He turned away without shaking my hand, got in the car and left. Jesus Christ.

I returned to Boston later that day only to learn that Macklin had refused to meet with the DOJ. On Saturday, I was notified by one of my IT people that Macklin had deleted a significant number of his company emails and files stored on Google Drive. We changed his passwords and retrieved the deleted files. He called me that afternoon in an absolute rage about having his email privileges revoked. It was impossible to talk to him - he was completely off the rails. That was the last time we spoke.

CHAPTER 28

For the past few years, I have participated in a winter golf trip with seven good friends. I had never really been a golf trip kind of guy - I have always traveled so much, that I didn't want to be away from my family if it wasn't for business. Now that my children were older and doing their own thing, even my wife had encouraged me to take these trips. This year's trip was scheduled for early February at a resort called Streamsong in Bowling Green, Florida.

In case you haven't heard of Bowling Green, Florida (which I doubt you have), it is located about an hour outside of Tampa. Streamsong was built on 16,000 acres of a former phosphate strip mine owned by the Mosaic Company, a multi-billion dollar, publicly traded company specializing in fertilizer products. The property is remarkable - it feels more like Scotland than Florida because of the contours of the land created by the mining and the creative course designs and agronomy. When you go to Streamsong, you are there to play golf - you stay on property in the hotel and you eat your meals at the hotel, or the restaurants located in the clubhouses that serve the three distinct courses. While I was reluctant to take any time away from work, my wife and others were encouraging me to get away for a few days. I felt like the Department of Justice investigation was in a good place (as good as a DOJ matter can be); our team in Boston was working well together; our tours, hockey and lacrosse numbers were stable; and our new BBFC CEO was getting his footing or, at least, had taken some burden off of me.

I flew back from the Europe trip and had a day or so before I was heading to Streamsong. Keep in mind, this is early February 2020, the dead of New England winter. I was run down physically and mentally. I was exhausted before the Europe trip and came back with a deep cough. However, I convinced myself that a long weekend of golf in warm weather would be the fix I needed.

Streamsong is a *walk-only* course, meaning no golf carts, only caddies. I could no longer walk 100 yards, never mind a 7,000-yard hilly course. As a result, I had to have my doctor send a letter to the Streamsong golf staff confirming that I was now disabled so I could ride in a cart. I'm not going to mislead you, when my friend (and head pro at our club) who organized the trip told me I would need the disability letter, it felt humiliating. I know I shouldn't say that, but it did. Here I was a perfectly fit and capable person a year or so ago, and now I needed a golf cart with a blue flag telling the world that I was disabled. I was pissed. I even considered not going on the trip, but my wife and friends convinced me to go.

We had some good laughs on the flight and in the van ride from the airport to Streamsong. People say that you are lucky if you can count on one hand really good, caring friends - I am fortunate that these seven guys are true friends. We would go to battle for each other. The Streamsong property was beautiful, the hotel was all we needed, and we were scheduled to play eighteen holes that day. Fortunately, there was no cell service on the courses, so I couldn't even think about checking emails. I rode in the passenger's seat of the golf cart with my caddie driving me - he was a nice guy and I enjoyed his company. However, I realized riding in a cart while your three playing partners are strolling down the fairway talking and laughing isn't the same as it was. I was also coughing non-stop, not enjoyable for me and likely worse for my playing partners as they were trying to make five footers to save par. By the end of the round, I felt like I had been hit by a truck.

We had dinner that night together, followed by drinks and cigars on the roof bar of the hotel. I had a couple of drinks, but I don't smoke. I felt like I had the flu - I excused myself and turned in early - we had thirty-six holes scheduled the next day. That night, I sweat through the sheets of my bed. I had awful chills all night. My dreams were darker and more disturbing than ever. In my dreams, I was drowning but was pulling others I loved down with me - it was terrifying.

In the morning, it took me a while to gather myself. I called housekeeping, asked them to change the bed and apologized that I had likely broken a fever. After I hung up, I wondered how many people actually would say that. I convinced myself that I had been dealing with a bug and the fever had subsided. I actually felt a little better, but I was still weak. I didn't have an appetite so I met the guys just in time to hop in the van that would take us to the Red Course. As we played, I realized I couldn't finish the round. I was too weak. I bagged it after about twelve holes and returned to the hotel. I got back in bed. I stayed in bed through the afternoon round, tried to rally for dinner, but that only lasted about an hour before I returned to my room and got back in bed. Another night of sweats and nightmares.

Needless to say, the trip was a disaster. Not only was I unable to get any R&R, I came home in worse shape. When I landed in Providence, my wife took me straight to the walk-in clinic. A couple hours later I was diagnosed with pneumonia. I was relegated to bed rest for a week. About a month later, COVID-19 started to emerge in the state of Washington, California and New York. I am convinced I contracted COVID-19 during my trip to Europe. I had never felt so sick in my life. Shortness of breath, a deep cough, weakness, and it felt like my bones were brittle. It took me a forty-five days or so to begin to feel like myself again. However, I was only able to take a few days out of the office, even then, I worked from bed.

In late February, we were tracking COVID-19 cases around the world and early cases in the U.S. using the Johns Hopkins website. Trump was playing down the virus as a "flu" that would not have an impact on the U.S. and would "disappear quickly." Early on, the Johns Hopkins dashboard wasn't providing trend reporting so we were pulling the raw data, dumping into Excel and doing our own analysis of cases, death rates and so on, by region... around the world. We were using an exponential forecasting curve to set our own expectations in Italy, Spain, France, Germany and the U.S. Why were we so concerned about COVID-19 early on? Because, about

90% of our international tours took place between April and July and our customers were looking forward to visiting Italy, France, Germany and the like. In addition, I had staff in Europe and in some of the U.S. states that were dealing with early cases. On a daily basis, I would come into the office and review the overnight data from Europe that was shocking. Italy, in particular, was out of control. New cases were quickly outpacing our forecasts.

Then, some cases emerged in Boston stemming from a Biogen corporate meeting held a short distance from our Seaport office. Initially, I was criticized by certain board members for my decision to allow staff the option of working from home. They said it was premature and they were concerned about our team's productivity. Only a week or so later, we had to tell people to work from home; stay at home orders were being issued throughout the entire northeast; New York was now the epicenter of the pandemic.

I was in frequent contact (multiple times a day) with board members and we continued to hold formal, weekly update calls. The board did not want to officially cancel any of our events or tours; they were *encouraging* us to only reschedule. If we canceled an event, we would have to issue refunds. There were so many challenges with trying to reschedule events at that time. First, we didn't know when the pandemic would subside; second, we couldn't possibly predict what destinations would be safe and open for business; third, some of our athletes would age out of an event depending on the rescheduled date and deserve refunds; and fourth, the logistics of rescheduling were a nightmare - rebooking airline tickets, reserving hotels and ground transportation, and trying to recover deposits we had paid to our vendors.

Internally, we, in Boston, knew that the tours to Europe would need to be rescheduled or cancelled as would most of our domestic programming. Some of our staff at the divisional level were having a difficult time understanding why we couldn't move forward with scheduled events - they simply didn't understand the severity and exponential growth of the pandemic. Consequently, we were trying to manage our own staff's expectations as well as our customers and board members.

Ah, the customers...they *needed* answers. The customers, on average, were remarkably patient during the first couple of weeks of COVID-19. We had sent out a couple of email communications advising that all of our events, both domestic and international, were being postponed due to the pandemic. We stressed that our primary concerns were for the health of our players, relatives, coaches and company staff. They understood. We all were dealing with something for which we never could have anticipated nor planned. Unfortunately, we did not provide definitive guidance about credits and refunds because we were waiting for direction from our board. However, at some point, customers who had paid substantial deposits would need firm answers.

I recommended to the board of directors that we strongly encourage our customers to be patient and take a credit for a future event (hopefully the event they registered for at a later date) for the amount they had already paid us, *plus* a 20% premium. This would allow them to upgrade their hotel room, add on another local activity, or even bring another family member on a tour. The incremental cost to us would be marginal, but we would simultaneously build goodwill with our customers and avoid issuing millions of dollars of refunds. However, I also recommended that if a customer wanted a full refund instead of the credit, we should issue it. This did not go over well, to say the least.

There was a clear, irreconcilable, philosophical difference between my position on customer refunds and the majority of our board. Interestingly, most of our staff shared my view even more passionately than I did. This drove a wedge between the management team and the board. More on that shortly.

Simultaneously, with Laura and Peter's participation, we prepared a *mothball* strategy and financial model in which we would furlough a significant percentage of our staff and institute salary reductions for those not furloughed who earned over a certain threshold. The mothball plan also involved other stringent uses of cash, meaning the continued stretching of our vendors. There were two vendors in particular, however, that needed to be paid - our attorneys. Certain attorneys at Powell, Sutton and Murphy as well as Nunn & King had been, and would continue to be, critical members of our team. I talked to Powell multiple times a day on litigation and DOJ matters. Nunn & King was our corporate counsel, we were in the process of closing another round of funding to weather the storm and they would need to represent the company's interest in the negotiation of terms and the preparation of closing documents. In addition, one of the Nunn & King partners, Jonathan Witt, was a seasoned, well respected restructuring attorney; exactly what Epic needed when we were stretching vendors and perhaps facing a potential Chapter 11 reorganization depending on how long COVID-19 stuck around. In addition, Jonathan had become a trusted advisor and friend. He is one of the brightest and most honorable people with whom I have ever worked.

I presented my plan to the board - furloughs, pay reductions, only *keep-the-lights-on* vendor payments, and some good faith payments to our two law firms. It wasn't aggressive enough for the board - although I was complimented on the depth of analysis and recommendations. I was told that the board appreciated how difficult it was to make personnel decisions like this. I felt like the call went well overall, but they wanted me to cut deeper. We agreed to reconvene the next morning for another call on which I would make additional recommendations, make some final decisions and work through the logistics of executing the furloughs.

The next day, the tone had completely changed without any explanation. I was told that I needed to cut much deeper and allocate more resources to BBFC and away from the other divisions and corporate. I was confused - of all of our business units, BBFC was the least compelling. Certain members of management of BBFC were under criminal investigation, the DOJ could change their tune at any moment and indict the company, there was litigation between the company and its founders, a significant percentage of the BBFC staff appeared loyal to its exiled founder, and the business model, itself, simply wasn't that compelling. I later learned that the new BBFC CEO had prepared his own mothball model and pitched it to the board. Unfortunately, his assumptions and projections for BBFC were overly optimistic.

On the board call, I pushed back - I told them that I disagreed with the strategy, that BBFC was not our most valuable asset and that we could not take incoming resources from one division and allocate them to another. On the last point, I reminded the board that these divisions were separate legal entities. If they were planning to collect customer deposits for future events in one division and use those deposits to fund the BBFC operating expenses, they were putting the company, its officers, and directors at risk. My worst fear was that the music was going to stop and there wouldn't be enough chairs - the customer would be the ones who suffered.

I also heard a board member raise the possibility of filing a Chapter 11 petition as early as that week. I pushed back again. I reminded the board that our largest creditors were our service providers (attorneys and accounting firm), the sports facilities at which we held our events and programming, and our customers (because they had paid us deposits). I told them that we needed all of these constituents to want to work with us in the future. Going through a bankruptcy would destroy our relationships with all of them and the company would wither and die. The brands would be destroyed. I told them that now was the time to do the right thing. They had committed to providing capital only weeks ago, step up and deliver. If not, there were buyers in the market who would jump at the chance to own certain of our assets. I was confident that we could sell certain assets, offload the related liabilities (like the unearned revenue associated with customer deposits) and avoid a legal proceeding that would kill the remaining brands.

They listened but there was no discussion or response. I was glad that outside counsel was on the call to provide their views on Epic's obligation to meet payroll and a potential bankruptcy process.

I was tired of trying to get people to do the right thing. It seemed like so many people that had been involved in Epic simply couldn't make the right and appropriate decisions. I believed I had a very clear view of what needed to be done. We needed payroll, first and foremost. We also needed to execute the mothball plan, as difficult as that would be - particularly furloughing staff. We needed to make some partial payments to our attorneys as they were critical advisors, particularly while we were furloughing staff and we were engulfed in litigation and cooperating with the DOJ; workout payment plans with vendors; and make our customers whole - those who had paid deposits for future events and tours deserved full refunds.

Certain board members' view of customer refunds was that no one else in the marketplace was issuing refunds, why should we? My position was that some competitors were, in fact, issuing refunds and whether they were or weren't was irrelevant; our customer contracts provided language requiring refunds. It was the right thing to do. The debate got rather heated - I found it interesting that much of the debate was done via email or text. At one point, I was told that I should stop stating my position in writing because the emails could be admissible in future litigation. When I didn't stop, I received an aggressive call, followed by an equally aggressive text, telling me that I was trying to create a *paper trail*. I wasn't trying to create a paper trail, I was trying to articulate my position - if they didn't like it, too bad. The fact that they were concerned about a paper trail, said it all to me. I *was* doing the right thing.

Unfortunately, I wasn't getting anywhere. I needed to find leverage and not be afraid to use it. The only reasonable leverage I had was *me*. I'm sure most CEO's feel this way... that the company needs them, particularly under difficult circumstances. In addition, the board would be in a difficult position if I resigned over their decisions about potentially missing a payroll that was already earned and accrued.

I sent an email to the board advising that if the original mothball plan wasn't approved, guarantees of payroll being met the following week and a payment plan for our two law firms, I would resign from the board and as CEO of the company at 4:00pm the next day. No one from the board responded.

At 3:00pm the next day, I sent a follow-up email to confirm that the board members had received my email. Only one board member responded, indicating that he had, indeed, received it, nothing more. At 4:00pm, I resigned. About thirty minutes later Jake Maddox resigned and shortly thereafter, an independent board member appointed by CFC also resigned. The board was now comprised solely of CFC partners.

Only a few people in the company knew that I had resigned, those closest to me. I wanted to use the resignation to get the commitment we needed from the board. I was surprised they called my bluff. I held out hope that they would reach out to me in an attempt to bring me back, so I was going to give it a couple of days before we made a company-wide announcement. I knew my resignation would have an impact on staff, partners, those we opposed in litigation and, potentially, the DOJ. I assumed some staff wouldn't care that I left, others would be rattled by it. Litigants may see this as a positive for them - they could use this in a variety of ways. Lastly, I was concerned that the DOJ could view this as an indication that I had uncovered something else nefarious in the company that led to my departure - if they thought that, or felt their only known ally in the business was gone, it could change their view that Epic was a victim. My head hurt trying to weigh all of these factors. I assumed the board was weighing these as well. In hindsight, I strongly doubt it.

Twenty-four hours after my resignation, I received a call from a board member. It started with small talk. Here we are in the middle of a global pandemic, our company on the brink of bankruptcy, and he was literally talking about how inconvenient it was working from home. Finally, he gave me the *come-on man, come back to the company - what are you doing?* line. I told him exactly what I was doing and why I was doing it. I asked him if payroll was going to be met and he didn't have a firm answer. I politely wrapped up the call. The next day, a Friday, I received a text from a different board member. He asked if I was available to talk Saturday morning. I agreed to talk at 9:00am.

On that call, I reiterated my positions and requirements. He told me that it was unfair for me to demand that we refund customer deposits. I strongly disagreed. He said that we needed to preserve liquidity and so on. I told him that I understood all of that, but if we didn't do the right thing by our customers, there wouldn't be a business after COVID-19. He didn't want to hear it. His responses included...

people have short memories... no one else is issuing refunds... the world has changed, consumers will understand... where else are they going to go? and... most of our competitors will be out of business.

I held firm on the position that the customers signed our registration contract that included language for refunds, and they were owed their money back. He wouldn't have reached out if he didn't think he needed me. I knew I had some leverage.

Most of the customer deposits were related to the hockey, tours and hotels divisions. Hockey and tours were now combined operationally, so that was one division. I knew that the current board was focused on BBFC - they liked that business, God knows why. I recommended that Epic sell the hockey and hotels divisions. I explained to him that, by doing so, we would rid Epic of almost the entire customer deposits liability and generate net cash proceeds to support BBFC going forward. He said he would do that in a heartbeat. I told him that the management team (and former owners) of the hotels division were deeply frustrated with the board's decision of holding back vendor payments (in the hotel bookings division's case, vendors were actually event owners, their customers) and I was confident they would welcome the opportunity to buy the business back. I then told him that I knew a couple of hockey event businesses who likely would be interested in our hockey division. We had discussions in the past with a few of them about an acquisition, however, I felt that one in particular was in this for the long haul and viewed Epic's hockey division as the target not the other way around.

On the call, he agreed that the accrued payroll would be satisfied, an additional $3.0 million would come into the business to provide liquidity to cover the mothball plan and ride out COVID-19. In addition, payments would be made to the attorneys and we would pursue the sale of the hotels and hockey divisions. Based on these terms, I agreed to come back, but not as CEO nor a board member. One of my most trusted colleagues reminded me that I could do a lot more from inside the company to influence a positive outcome than if I walked away. But I had seen enough. I did not want to be an officer or director of this company. I had seen behaviors that concerned me, and I didn't want the personal risk or exposure. Also,

I wanted my colleagues in the company to know how I felt - that I wasn't aligned with the board's strategy. A short-term consulting agreement was prepared and executed.

I reached out to the hockey event companies that I thought would have interest. One, in particular, made the most sense to me. I had conversations in the past with one of the owners. He seemed like a true gentleman (I remember how he spoke about his family on one of our first calls), very smart, and a former partner of a well-respected private equity firm. I provided him with a high-level overview of the hockey division - he knew the business pretty well already as his company competed with us in certain markets and age groups. He also understood the current circumstances with COVID-19 and our board's desire to simplify the business and focus more on the soccer division. I told him that this was not going to be a fire sale and that, if he was interested, diligence would have to be efficient and the valuation would have to represent the real value of the business in a non-pandemic environment. He understood and was ready to lean in.

I had a similar call with the head of our hotel bookings division. He had sold his business to Epic several years ago. He had spent his entire career in the industry and, by all accounts, had a good reputation with both event and hotel operators. I had warned the board that we were at risk of losing him and, if we did, customers would follow him out the door. While there was a non-compete in place, I doubted that any court would restrict him from providing for his family during a pandemic and while his former employer was threatening bankruptcy. He appreciated the call and told me that he could move fast; he indicated that he had already been speaking with his attorney about putting together an offer to buy the division.

Immediately following the call, the potential buyer of the hockey assets, executed a non-disclosure agreement and we sent over preliminary diligence materials. By end of day, he had asked to have a call to walk through the materials. That evening, I hopped on a call with him. He had been through all of the materials provided. He was asking all of the right questions - his focus was really only on two topics: 1) how our division was staffed; it seemed that he operated a leaner model from a labor perspective; and 2) he wanted to understand the hotels division. His company procured and booked all of the hotel room inventory for their own events. He wanted to understand how the relationship worked between our hockey and hotel bookings divisions. We covered that in about fifteen minutes. He wanted to sleep on it but said that he may be interested in acquiring the hotels division as well. We agreed to talk the next morning.

Over the next week or so, I provided daily updates to the board on the potential sale discussions; the execution of the furloughs, other cost reductions and other initiatives that were in process. The board implemented a daily cash call that included a representative from our lead investor, our CFO, and the BBFC CEO. It took about a week for the process to be refined and the daily deliverable to meet the needs of the everyone on the calls. It was basically a rolling cash analysis - the dates were down the first column with specific cash activity categories across the columns moving to the right. The last column on the right would be the ending cash balance for the day which would then be linked to be the opening cash balance for the next day. It was pretty straight forward.

What wasn't straight forward, however, was the way the process was managed, and decisions were made about cash disbursements. On the first couple of calls, our CFO had slotted in payments to our attorneys. The board members told him to move those payments out a couple of days. However, on the same calls, they were approving payments to BBFC vendors. I also noted that I did not see the $3.0 million inflow of capital reflected in the cash analysis. I decided I would give it a couple of days. After all, I wasn't the CEO anymore, I was just a consultant. But I felt conflicted. Two of the conditions for me to return, even as a consultant, were the $3.0 million commitment and payments to our attorneys.

After about three days of, I decided to raise the issue of payments to the attorneys. I asked, "when can we get some payments out to Powell and Nunn & King?" No answer. I didn't expect our CFO to answer, he was taking his direction regarding disbursements from the board. I then said, "anyone, anyone?", an inappropriate joke and reference to Ben Stein as the economics teacher in *Ferris Bueller's*

Day Off. One of the board members responded, "have you looked at the cash flow analysis? We need to conserve cash for operations, we can't be making payments to attorneys?" I responded, "we agreed that we would make partial payments to them - I told them they would be getting a payment this week. What am I supposed to tell them?" The response I got was, "tell them to fuck off - they can wait."

I nervously laughed and said, "come on guys, let's be serious - they need to get some kind of payment." The board member was clearly angry as he said, "I am serious - they can wait. I guarantee you none of their clients are paying them right now." I told them that we not only owed them a payment, but that we needed them to continue to work with the company on a number of matters. The response was, "if they want to get paid at some point, they will keep doing the work. If not, we will get another firm to take on the work." I pushed back, "I am telling you, if we don't make a payment to both firms, they are going to withdraw." They didn't seem to care. One of the partners asked what I thought it would take to keep Powell actively engaged. I told them the amount and they acted shocked. I had given them an amount that represented a fraction of the total owed. They deliberated how much we could pay Powell, but never discussed Nunn & King. This really pissed me off because it was certain board members who told us to use Nunn & King in the first place. Hell, at one point, they told me that I should have been using Nunn & King more often. How could they screw them like this?

Based on the tone of the call, I knew in my gut that they were not going to issue refunds or make payments to the attorneys or certain vendors. After the call, I spoke with our CFO - he said that he wasn't aware of any planned payments to the attorneys either. He had, however, received draft documents for additional funding for the company, but wasn't sure when the funds would come in. I asked who was representing the company on the financing - he said that the board had directed him to use a new firm, not Nunn & King.

I firmly believe that the board did not like Nunn & King's position and counsel regarding a potential bankruptcy filing - their professional view that a filing would destroy brand value, customer

392

and critical vendor relationships, be time consuming, costly and allow for the formation of a creditors' committee that would only increase costs and disruption to the business. The board seemed like it wanted the company to have counsel that was aligned with its thinking. I believe they wanted the company to file a Chapter 11 petition, credit bid to own BBFC, allow other buyers to pick up the other pieces of the business, flush all unsecured liabilities and keep any additional cash proceeds since they were senior to the common equity and unsecured creditors.

On the next cash call, I asked about the $3.0 million capital commitment. The answer I received was laughable. The board member, the one who negotiated my return on that Saturday morning call, said, "that was a commitment with a lowercase 'c.'" I asked what that meant. He said that meant that they could invest in phases, *up to* $3.0 million. I said, "that's not what we agreed to. You can't fund this in tranches and expect management to feel good about operating this business and making decisions every day when they don't have sufficient capital or a committed board." He said that he never agreed when and how the money would come in. It was so disappointing to hear this.

Meanwhile, Epic's senior management was holding end-of-day calls with its divisional leaders to provide updates regarding COVID-19, the status of customer refund requests, furloughs, and to try to answer any questions. These calls were awkward. Management wasn't receiving any communication from its board at a most critical time. The board seemed frozen and reluctant to have any direct communication with management. Those who believed in the board were growing concerned. Those who had been skeptical of the board, now, fully distrusted them. Those who distrusted them, despised them.

CHAPTER 29

We had verbal offers for both hockey and the hotel bookings divisions. The potential hockey buyer decided to pass on the hotels business because he felt he could service the hotel needs of Epic's domestic hockey business with his existing, internal team. If he had sufficient capacity to service our business and wasn't looking to expand his own hotels business to serve third party clients, then he would realize a nice margin pick-up with our events coming on board. The offer for the hotels division came from one of the leaders of that division.

In my opinion, both offers were reasonable. I delivered the offers to the board via email and simultaneously connected the board directly with the potential buyers. I didn't have any desire to play middleman; there was no upside and I would only be opening myself up to criticism. The board was flip-flopping on a number of critical business decisions at this time - I preferred that they communicate directly with the potential buyers. After all, they were the decision makers.

The offer for the hockey division included the buyer taking all of our hockey employees (including those on furlough) on board; assuming all of our customer and vendor liabilities (they stated that they would provide full refunds to those customers who requested a refund); and paying cash on top of it. In my opinion, those elements provided not only a reasonable valuation for the division but solved the customer deposit and stretched vendor issues. Every day that passed, I was growing more concerned that a couple of creditors would get together and force the company into bankruptcy. It only takes three creditors to work together and petition the court. My fear was that some of our customers and vendors were also competitors - we had customers who brought teams to events and tours who also operated events and tours; we also rented ice from rink owners who operated tournaments and showcases. These people were starting to smell blood in the water, and I could feel the sharks starting to circle. I was also concerned some of our former employees could have been fanning the flames with our vendors. I made this clear to the board and the response was, "those people aren't smart enough to pull that off." I disagreed.

A board member was now negotiating directly with the potential buyer for the hockey division. About four hours after I made the introduction, I received a call from the potential buyer. He said that he had a call with one of the board members who told him that if he couldn't increase his price substantially, then the board would simply put the company in bankruptcy. I was speechless. If you were trying to negotiate higher value for an asset, why would you ever threaten to put the company in bankruptcy.

The potential buyer told me that he much preferred to acquire the division as a going concern (meaning as an operating business, not the assets out of a bankruptcy process); wanted the Epic events and brands to live on; hoped for a smooth transition and soft landing for our staff; and, perhaps most of all, he wanted the customers to be made whole. This was not out of benevolence. He knew that stepping in and doing the right thing for the customers was good business. His company would be the white knight. I got it and I agreed with his strategy. I told him that he should take a closer look at his valuation and see if he could find some common value with the board member - I even reminded him of the pick-up in margin he would realize with our hotel rebates and commissions.

The hotels bookings offer was slightly more complicated. The buyers offered to forgive amounts due to them from Epic as part of the original divisional acquisitions. They would also commit to keeping all employees and assume all liabilities; vendors, customer deposits and rebates. There wouldn't be any cash proceeds from the transaction, but, again, Epic would offload all liabilities. There were mainly two types of customer liabilities with this business: the first were rebates that had been earned and were due to the division's third party event customers; and the second were deposits that consumers (families) had paid to secure hotel rooms for future events - these amounted to tens of thousands of consumers. In my opinion, this could get very messy from a consumer protection perspective.

When I had raised the issue of customer deposits, repeatedly, to the board, the response was, *come on, do you really think people are going to hire attorneys over this? Besides, the courts are going to be tied up with much more pressing matters with all of the bankruptcies that are going to result from COVID-19.* Again, I couldn't understand why we weren't simply making the right decisions, the ethical decisions.

The board had one of the CFC partners handle the negotiations with Tim from the hotels division. The partner was trying to get Tim to add some cash to the purchase price. Tim was keeping me up to date - he seemed to be doing his best to find additional value in the business, but he could only reach so far. He was already taking on substantial liabilities related to the customer commissions and deposits. Customers were already talking about moving their business elsewhere because we were so slow paying them their commissions.

Tim held firm with his offer and the board member dragged his feet. Every day that passed, hotel bookings customers were growing more frustrated; more and more were pulling their business and moving to competitors. Simultaneously, certain staff, both active and on furlough, left the company to join competitors. A few others left to start their own competing businesses. The longer the board waited, the more the hotels business was imploding. Tim expressed this repeatedly to me and to the board member with whom he was negotiating. Again, there was no movement. It was like the board was burying its head in the sand - they didn't know what to do and they wouldn't listen to anyone.

I was amazed that the board was still comprised solely of CFC partners. The board was making all of these decisions, including turning down offers for certain divisions and managing cash on a daily basis, without an independent board member. Then I heard they were adding a new board member. I was told this from a CFC partner. He told me the board member's name and I did a little research and asking around. I learned that he typically dealt with distressed situations and spent most of his time moving around as an independent board member for hire. I also learned that he was a partner in a fund that invested in cannabis companies, a nice tie-in to our youth sports business; what were the other board members thinking?

I did some more research and found that the new independent board member was also on the board of several other companies. Literally as I was reading his bio, one of the CFC partners called me regarding the hotels division offer. At the end of the call, I brought up the new board member. I asked how they had found him. He told me that he was also on the board of a target acquisition. I didn't say a word. He then told me that putting him on the Epic board could only help their chances to win the other deal. I couldn't believe what I heard.

The new board member never contacted me. I also understand from my former colleagues that he had very limited interaction with any members of Epic's management team. I have no idea how he could possibly perform the duties of a board member (particularly, the only independent board member) at such a critical time, without interacting with management.

The daily cash calls had become intolerable. Virtually no discretionary disbursements were being made for anything except BBFC. Payroll, health insurance and directors & officers' insurance were about the only items being paid for Epic corporate and the non-BBFC divisions. Conversely, BBFC expenses and deposits for future field rentals were being paid. I was furious - cash receipts, as much as they had declined due to COVID-19, were still coming in from each of the divisions. The receipts would be from credit cards or checks received at division-specific bank lock boxes. Each night, each bank account balance would be swept into the corporate account, from which accounts payables were processed. On a cash call, that was driven by board members, I reminded everyone that these funds should be segregated, that cash received from customers in a certain division should only be used for that specific division. Not only did I think the company needed to do this from a legal perspective, but it needed to be done to preserve staff morale. The divisional leaders were being told each week that none of their payables were being processed, yet they knew that they had cash receipts - they wanted to know where that money was going. I explained this on the cash call, but it fell on deaf ears. The next day, I noticed that the recurring, daily cash call invite was no longer on my calendar. I had been removed from the call.

The next morning, I was copied on an email from an attorney I didn't recognize asking if I could join a call later that morning along with enter, Epic's CFO. Peter called me and said this was the new firm that the board wanted the company to retain. He would be signing their engagement letter shortly.

We had the call that day. There were two attorneys on the call - they knew virtually nothing about Epic. They only knew that they were replacing Nunn & King as outside counsel and that the board was weighing bankruptcy options. If they went this route, it would be the death of the company. Peter and I provided them with an overview of Epic, the subsidiaries, ownership structure, ongoing litigation, the DOJ investigation, potential sale of the hockey and hotels divisions, recent furloughs, liquidity issues and so on. They had to be overwhelmed. They told us that two board members had provided an overview the day before but not to this level of detail. They went on to say that the board was considering a number of options, including, a Chapter 11 reorganization of the entire company, Chapter 7 liquidation of certain subsidiaries, and even a potential foreclosure on certain assets. It sounded like the board was trying to figure out how to hold on to certain assets and flush as many liabilities as possible. They still didn't understand that the optics, alone, of a bankruptcy would kill this company.

By pure coincidence, shortly after the call with the new attorneys, we received notice from Nunn & King that they had officially withdrawn from representing Epic due to non-payment. The board refused to authorize payment to our attorneys for past services rendered, but instead was instructing our CFO to wire over a retainer to the new firm. By the time this all wrapped up, the amount paid to the new firm would have likely been more than satisfactory to Nunn & King...

and senior management wouldn't have had to spend countless hours bringing the new firm up to speed.

As the weeks passed, our customers were growing more and more frustrated. Management could not provide definitive rescheduled dates and locations for events and tours nor answers to refund requests. The hockey division was feeling the brunt of the customer frustration. The board was not providing any reasonable guidance. Finally, a call including senior management, the hockey divisional leadership and board members was scheduled. The call was meant to allow the board members to hear the frustration of management and bring the groups together to get consensus on the refund / credit policy.

The call proved to be a mistake. Hockey management had prepared a presentation in advance in an attempt to make the call as productive as possible. The materials provided support for their recommendation that the company offer full refunds to those customers who needed the cash, or their child was aging out of the event. As an alternative to a refund, they would offer a credit with a premium attached. Without me influencing them, management had come to a similar position and recommendation that I shared with the board forty-five days earlier; when customers still had faith in the company. They were also stressing the need to make some disbursements to critical vendors. Hockey management was starting to hear rumors of frustrated vendors getting together and engaging an attorney - creditors petitioning Epic into bankruptcy was now a real risk.

Instead of reviewing the materials and allowing management to make their case, a board member kept interrupting. He was critical of their analysis and presentation and his tone was both aggressive and condescending. Words like *stupid* and phrases like, *this doesn't make any sense* were used by the board member. Several times, he even used profanity. During the call, I received several texts from members of management indicating their frustration and disgust with the tone of the call. Look, I get it - everyone was frustrated with the situation. But this call spun out of control very quickly. In short, this was the moment when the board lost their management team for

399

good. And, still no decision on a refund policy or payments to critical vendors had been made. In the days following the call, several employees filed complaints with human resources about the behavior of the board member on the call.

I, along with Laura and Peter, were trying to keep divisional management calm and intact, but we were losing the battle. Some members of the hockey management were now communicating directly with board members and the tone was heated at times. Laura was put in a terrible position. She actually had to inform a board member that he could no longer have direct contact with our employees. She had to do it - if an employee spoke, or sent emails, to another employee in the manner the board member had been communicating, the employee would be reprimanded or terminated. She could not allow for a double standard and put the company at further risk with employee complaints.

Things had turned toxic. The CEO of BBFC was communicating directly with board members and failing to include his colleagues in Epic's finance and human resource departments. BBFC seemed to be operating in a silo to the detriment of the other divisions. The board was enabling this behavior. The board had furloughed more hotel bookings' employees and turned down the offer from management to buy the division. They basically were closing down the division but hadn't formally made that decision nor had a clear plan to wind it down. The hotels division was still under the cloud of a significant customer deposit liability.

Hockey management wanted their division sold so they could move on; they made their point loud and clear, they would never work for this board or ownership group. Lacrosse, the smallest division, was in a terrible state of limbo - unable to commit to coaches or facilities for the upcoming season, because they hadn't been provided confirmation from the board that the funding would be in place. Lastly, as is always the case in situations like this, the smart, marketable people were starting to leave. When employees lose faith in their ownership group or leadership, the best staff recognize and acknowledge the negativity first and they are also the ones who

400

usually have opportunities. As they leave, the death spiral accelerates.

I had the same conversation over and over again - with an attorney, a colleague, my wife, a friend... *Does the board have some plan that we can't figure out, or are they lost, flailing?* My opinion? They were lost. In their defense, this company had faced a series of challenges that few have likely every encountered in a single portfolio company. Because of this, I think the board was suffering from deal fatigue. I honestly believe that they were exhausted. I know I was. But I was still listening to our team and I thought I was still thinking clearly. I recognized that I was living it every day and knew more about the company, its customers, vendors, and our staff than the board did, however, they weren't listening. They underestimated the risk associated with stretched vendors, the frustration of the employees, the viral nature of the youth sports market (everyone knew everyone, and word spread fast), and overestimated their negotiation skills. They thought the hotel division leaders would come back with a better offer; instead they walked away. They kept pushing potential hockey buyer to increase his bid for the hockey division; he too reached his ceiling and moved on.

The board changed their plan multiple times... no bankruptcy; then a Chapter 11 with the lead investor providing debtor-in-possession financing and credit bidding for certain assets; then, a Chapter 7 liquidation of certain subsidiaries, including the hotels division in order to flush the customer deposit liability; then no bankruptcy at all and simply a foreclosure on certain assets as senior, secured lender. Even if you don't know what all of that means, all you need to know is that the strategy was constantly changing. And then... a legal letter was received by the company. Several creditors had finally gotten together and petitioned the company into a Chapter 7 bankruptcy. This was exactly what we, management, were worried about and had been trying to explain to the board.

CHAPTER 30

My daily routine had changed dramatically. Instead of getting on the commuter rail every morning, I would head down to my office in the basement. We were fortunate that the previous owner of our home had built a beautiful home office. Two built-in desks, bookcases, recessed lighting, and plenty of light as that side of the house was above grade. It felt completely separated from the living quarters and we had furnished it and decorated it nicely, so it was a comfortable place to work. I still had my multi-screen set up and my days were occupied with Epic calls and ongoing research for the DOJ and supporting other litigation.

Something else was also changing. About a year earlier, I had ordered a Peloton bike; mostly for my wife, but I hoped the rest of the family would use it as well. Christine is a runner, but also enjoys spin class. I had been to class with her a few times on weekends and I loved the workout; it was just impossible to fit it in my schedule. Perhaps now that I wasn't commuting, this would change.

My middle son, Chase, suggested a competition for the month of April - he said, "let's see who burns the most calories for the month." I liked that he was initiating something like this and knew, that deep down, he was trying to get me to exercise more. I got the message loud and clear. I put together a spreadsheet template to track everyone's workouts and we agreed on the rules - we would be tracking total miles, minutes and calories burned. We were off.

From a business perspective, I had been intrigued by Peloton. When the product had first launched, I thought they were going to over-spend on paid advertising. I couldn't believe the number of television ads and the time slots they were buying. In addition, the production value of the ads was impressive. These were not inexpensive productions. They caught your attention... the young, fit mom riding her Peloton, at her convenience, in her Frank Lloyd Wright designed mid-century modern home. They were certainly presenting an aspirational lifestyle, but not exactly to middle-America. To be honest, I didn't see how the model could possibly succeed. Over time, I would occasionally hear a friend mention that they had bought a Peloton and loved it. I was surprised how many people I knew had bought one. I was hearing nothing but good things.

I went online and checked out their website. A very clean and intuitive user interface and experience. A couple of clicks and you could own it, schedule your white glove delivery for a time slot that met your needs (not theirs, like the cable companies) and they would set it up in your house, connect it to your WIFI, fit you and you were off to the races. I bought one... and, everyone in the family loved it. I loved it, but I was never home enough to use it consistently. Until COVID-19.

I am rather competitive, and I have an addictive personality. I like clean, fresh starts, like starting a competition on the first day of the month. And, I like when my family can be involved in an activity together. I loved that my son came up with the competition.

Chase had dealt with his own challenges and health issues; most recently tearing the labrum in his right shoulder, having surgery and going through a long and difficult rehabilitation. He is a baseball player and the injury set back his start to college and derailed his commitment to play college baseball. Instead, he had to do a post-graduate year, at a prep school north of Boston, in order to get healthy. It hadn't gone as planned. In my opinion, he was somewhere he didn't want to be, it wasn't the right time or place. A big part of his identity, baseball, had been taken from him and he was away from home for the first time. Early in the Spring semester, we made the decision to bring him home. He needed to be home and he needed to know that he was loved.

Little did I know that making the decision to allow Chase to come home early, he would have such a profound impact on *my* life, as well as his. We were both struggling, but at least we were together, and the daily Peloton ride became a consistent focus of our day. We would compare our stats, encourage and drive each other. In addition to the endorphin spike, I could see Chase's energy and self-esteem coming back.

Besides the physical workout, the Peloton instructors provided motivation and inspirational guidance throughout the rides. Alex Toussaint became Chase and Christine's go-to instructor. I was doing rides with Toussaint as well as Emma Lovewell, Hannah Frankson and Jess King. Even the instructor-guided meditation sessions were becoming part of my daily routine.

I was losing weight and I noticed that my body felt more fluid after I rode and meditated. I started riding in the morning *and* at the end of the day. As an FYI, April isn't exactly a motivational month in New England - *April shower bring May flowers ...* it is actually quite depressing. I'm not sure what I would have done during this time if I wasn't able to embrace the Peloton experience. The family competition was the forced commitment to exercise and mindfulness that I needed, so desperately, to create a new habit.

The prior two years had drained me. I was at a point where I couldn't handle much more. I inherited a real mess at Epic, fought through it all, eliminated the bad actors, added incredible people to our team, moved our headquarters to Boston, managed litigation and a federal criminal investigation... Through it all, we were making progress. The business was stabilizing and turning a corner. Then, a global pandemic hit and shut down our company. We were in the live event and travel business and the world simply stopped. Literally, our monthly revenues dried up in a matter of a couple of months.

If my son hadn't cared enough to encourage me to focus on my health, I don't know how things would have turned out. I mean it. This series of events, the constant body punches, are the types of things that can destroy one's psyche. Instead, oddly enough, I felt like I was getting some sort control of my life again. My morning ride followed by a fifteen-minute instructor-guided meditation session rid me of the normal morning stress and provided me with a sense that I had the strength and peace of mind to get through the day. I felt like I was starting to get some small pieces of my life back - time with my family and personal redemption.

On a Saturday in mid-April, my wife came down to my office and handed me some mail. A couple of bills and a small package. The package didn't have a return address and my home address was handwritten in black. I opened it up and inside was a single postcard from the Cooperstown Baseball Hall of Fame. On the front was the image of Joe Cronin's (former Red Sox shortstop, manager and general manager; as well as the president of the American League) plaque at the Hall. On the back of the postcard were the handwritten words, *Joe wants you to exercise more.* I had no idea who had sent it to me. I read it several times - it actually felt creepy because my Peloton was located in my office next to the window. I wondered if someone was watching me workout.

I won't bore you with the details, but I received six more packages over the next three weeks, all of which included something related to the Red Sox... a Bobby Doer Hall of Fame Postcard, stacks of random baseball cards, and a program from a Red Sox game in the 1970's. A couple of the packages included other odd hand-written notes like, *I hope to see you at Fenway soon.*

I asked several friends and colleagues if they were sending the packages to me - all denied it. A couple, in particular, who were Red Sox fans and / or knew that I was Red Sox fan, I asked several times and told them that the packages were starting to make me and my family a little nervous. They, too, denied sending the packages. Having been through the last two years, dealt with threats, and a federal criminal investigation, I felt like I had reason to be nervous. I started to have crazy thoughts. I wondered if someone was sending these to me so that it seemed like a prank, I would get comfortable with receiving them, then the next package would explode when I opened it. It sounds crazy now, but at the time I felt like anything could happen. I notified the U.S. Attorneys' office.

The lead AUSA had told me to contact them if, at any time, I felt threatened. I sent him an email and he responded quickly. I told him about the packages, and he asked if he could call me right back. He called a few minutes later with another AUSA and a federal agent on the phone. They asked me a series of questions about the packages, when they had arrived, their contents, who I had asked if they had sent them to me, and so on. I had to photograph each package and the contents and email the images to them while I was on the call. Two of the packages received most recently had postmarks from a town in New York. They decided they would get the Postal Service involved and they would be able to identify who was sending these. I assumed they could access the Postal Service's security video since the postage for one of the packages had been paid at the counter of a Post Office in New York.

I also let Laura and Peter know about the packages. They agreed that it was bizarre and that I did the right thing contacting the AUSA. Laura was convinced that the packages were coming from one of the CFC partners. One partner, in particular, was a die-hard Red Sox fan. To be clear, I am Red Sox fan, but I'm not nuts about the team. Some years, I don't even attend a single game. So, we felt like the packages were coming from someone who was really into the team, but we couldn't understand why he was sending them to me. Further, I had asked this particular CFC partner on three separate occasions if he sent me the packages - he denied it each time (twice in writing), even after telling him is was causing stress in my household.

The whole situation felt bizarre. I couldn't imagine sending anonymous packages to someone's house.

Around the time of my resignation, I wrote a memo and emailed it to Laura. I asked that she save the memo in my personnel file. In that memo, among other things, I outlined a communication from two board members that I felt was inappropriate and discriminatory.

When I took over as CEO in November of 2018, I was assured by the board that I would be provided an employment agreement *shortly*. One of the board members, who later joined the compensation committee, told me that the agreement would be a multi-year contract to provide me with job security, would include a bonus plan and a stock award. In the end, I never received an employment agreement, bonus plan or stock award. In fact, bonuses were paid out in early 2019 for 2018 performance to a significant number of staff; I did not receive one nor was I provided a performance review from the board. However, I was complimented often by all board members for my effort and performance during my tenure.

In February of 2020, Laura spoke to a board member about the fact that I didn't have an employment agreement. She raised the issue in her capacity as Chief People Officer and in light of the fact that we had just provided, with the board's involvement, and executed a detailed employment agreement to the new BBFC CEO that included a substantial bonus plan, stock grant and other perks.

A short time later Laura raised the issue of my employment agreement (or lack thereof) to the compensation committee. A few weeks later, we received an employment term sheet for me on letterhead that included both the Epic and CFC logos. The document was signed by two board members, both partners at CFC. The proposed terms of employment for me were pretty standard, but vague as it related to the bonus plan. It didn't include measurable targets or milestones. In contrast, the bonus plan provided to the BBFC CEO was extremely detailed and even included an exhibit that explained the sliding scale opportunity of the bonus plan and the amount he would earn based on different levels of achievement.

Laura pointed something else out to me on the second page of the employment term sheet that I hadn't noticed. I had read the key terms on page one and when I flipped to the second page, the balance of the document appeared, at first glance, to be boilerplate stuff, like indemnification, death, disability, and the like. She pointed to the disability section. I read it closely. There was language in that section that specifically said that the board of directors, "at its sole discretion, had the right to deem me disabled and unable to perform the duties of my job." It went on to say that they could terminate me based on my disability.

At first, I wasn't even thinking of the legal implications of this. I was just so disappointed. I had wanted to believe that these people actually cared about our team and me, on a human level. Countless calls, emails, texts, breakfast meetings... all under the most extreme circumstances. I felt like we had been through so much together - aligned and fighting against common enemies, trying to reconstruct the company and build something special. At a minimum, I thought there was mutual respect.

I told the board in the summer of 2019 about my Parkinson's diagnosis. I felt it was the right thing to do. My symptoms were evident, and they deserved to know what was going on. I didn't ask for anything. My condition certainly didn't affect my commitment or work ethic. It had not affected my job performance at all. Yet, they put language in an employment document that would allow the board to determine when I was disabled? I was so disappointed.

At the time, I didn't raise the issue because the last thing the company needed was its CEO and board at odds. I simply wrote back that the offer needed work. The board members never brought up the employment offer again. I guess I got my answer.

In addition to the issue of the board wanting the right to decide when I became disabled, I also outlined my concerns in the memo about the board's behavior and actions - I even included the risks and potential negative consequences associated with those actions. We had started to see some of the consequences resulting from their behavior becoming reality. I also added the details of the packages being sent to my house along with inappropriate text messages from CFC partners and staff over the past eighteen months.

I called Laura and said, "Laura, I never thought it would come to this, but it is time to release the memo to the attorneys."

Why did I do this? First, I want to know who the hell was sending packages to my house. If it was a CFC partner, perhaps they could tell the truth to corporate counsel. I wanted to get to the bottom of it and I wanted it to stop. Second, I wanted company counsel to investigate all of these matters and I wanted to speak to counsel one-on-one. I believed the attorneys would have to interview me and this would be my opportunity to make sure they had all the facts. Third, I wanted to know if the new law firm representing the company was loyal to CFC. If they were, they would call CFC immediately after they spoke with me and disclose detailed of our conversation. I was concerned that they weren't acting in the company's best interests, but rather the investors' best interest.

During this period, I had a recurring dream. I had it over a couple of months, maybe once or twice a week. In the dream, I was seated in the front pew at a church. The church was not familiar to me, nor was the priest on the alter. My wife was seated to my right, she was in tears, but no one else was in the pew with us. I knew that others were seated behind me, I could feel their presence, but I didn't know who it was. I couldn't turn to see who was behind me - it was incredibly frustrating, because I wanted to make sure it was my three children.

As if this dream wasn't unnerving enough, I could feel that my teeth were loose. As I bit down, I could feel my teeth moving. I put my thumb and index finger to my front teeth, and I could have pulled them out with little effort. I closed my mouth and covered it with both hands. I was afraid that my teeth were going to fall out at any moment.

There was a casket to my left. I was sweating... a cold, clammy sweat. I didn't know whose funeral this was, I didn't know where I was, I was so confused and frustrated. Then, I fixed my attention on the priest and heard him say, "... though I walk through the valley of the shadow of death, I will fear no evil; for thou art with me; thy rod and thy staff they comfort me." He was looking directly at me. With his palms open, he asked me to come up to the pulpit and say a few words. My wife put her hand on my knee, I looked at her and she said, "you will be fine, go ahead."

I walked towards the alter and placed my hand on the casket to steady myself - I still didn't know who was in it or what I was going to say. I felt something at my feet and looked down; water, about an inch deep, was covering the marble floor, moving gently like an incoming tide. I took the first step towards the alter but my right foot caught the second step and I fell forward. I put my hands out to catch myself.

Before I hit the floor, I woke up every time... sweating through the sheets and my feet fully cramped.

CHAPTER 31

As expected, I received an email from Epic's new outside counsel asking to set up a call as soon as possible. The attorney was woman, whose name I didn't recognize. She indicated that she had not been performing any work for the company so far, nor had she ever done any work for CFC. She indicated that she was completely *independent* and would be interviewing me and, potentially, others about the contents of my memo. Great - we scheduled a call for the next morning.

I didn't know what to expect, however, I was pleased with the call. It lasted about two hours. The attorney seemed very kind and sympathetic to the complicated circumstance of the company and the series of bizarre events with which I had been dealing. At one point, unexpectedly, she even asked, "how are you holding up?"

Over the course of the call, I came to trust her. She said that she would review her notes, speak with Laura and get back to me in the next day or so with any follow-up questions or next steps. I asked if she would be speaking with any board members and she said, "no, not until I speak with Laura and follow-up with you." She told me that everything I shared with her was confidential. Before we hung up, she said, "oh, one more thing - have you retained an attorney?" I told her that I had spoken to my personal attorney but had not engaged him on this matter. She then paused and said, "well maybe you and I should not be speaking directly if you have already consulted with your attorney…". Before she could finish, I told her that I was fine with speaking with her without an attorney and that I preferred to not get an attorney involved. She said she understood, but if at any point I didn't feel comfortable speaking with her, that was my prerogative.

Within an hour, I received a call from someone associated with the company who I trusted implicitly. He asked me, "what did you do?" I told him that I didn't know what he was talking about. He told me that he just received a call from one of the CFC partners asking how important I was to various company matters, including the DOJ investigation. I got one of my answers - the law firm had called CFC. The so-called confidential investigation of my employee-related matter wasn't so confidential after all.

The next day, I received an email from the attorney conducting the investigation. She simply asked, "can you provide me with your point of contact at the DOJ and his or her information?" I wrote back, "why do you need this information?" Powell continued to serve as Epic's attorney related to the DOJ matter, so I couldn't imagine why would she be looking for this information. She wrote back that she had identified the person sending the packages to my house and wanted to let the DOJ know that there was not an imminent threat against me.

I wrote back, copying Powell, indicating that I would have liked to have known that and I wanted to know who sent me the packages. She confirmed it was the CFC partner. I asked why he was sending packages to my house - she said it was a *silly prank*. Powell advised her that he should be on any call with the AUSA.

Powell later told me that he and the attorney conducting the confidential investigation had a call with the AUSA, during which the AUSA indicated that he was not pleased that someone thought it was a silly prank to send packages to my house. He told her to ensure that it didn't happen again.

A week passed and I hadn't heard back from the attorney. I sent her an email and left her a voicemail looking for an update. I repeated this cycle for the next seven days – no response.

The board was wasting precious time - it seemed unable to settle on a single strategy. The clock was ticking, and people were talking – staff, vendors, customers and competitors. The problem was that the board wasn't talking to the management team and the management team lacked clear direction and an understanding of the board's strategy, if there was one. It was pretty apparent that management had lost confidence and trust in the board. I had repeatedly told the board, our leadership group and our attorneys that there was a potential strategy that would result in a relatively favorable outcome for all constituents:

1) Accept the hotel division management team's offer to acquire their division - the staff would be employed, and the customers and vendors would have been made whole;
2) Sell the hockey division to the third-party buyer - the staff would be employed; the customers and vendors would have been made whole; and Epic would have received additional cash proceeds at closing;
3) Continue to operate BBFC and lacrosse - both entities (according to their respective divisional leaders) would be profitable in 2020 and 2021;
4) Shrink corporate operating expenses substantially to only service the two remaining divisions (lacrosse and soccer); and
5) Pursue the claims related to the DOJ investigation and civil actions associated with securities matter and breach of representations and warranties.

The litigation with the former founders was supposedly nearing a settlement. Legal costs would be coming to an end. Any litigation associated with the BBFC minority shareholders would be favorable to Epic in light of our internal investigation findings coupled with the DOJ criminal investigation. Therefore, there wasn't a likely, long-term legal expense hangover for the company that warranted a bankruptcy filing. By executing the above strategies, the customers would have been made whole in every case - preserving our respective brands' values. The investors would continue to own the BBFC and lacrosse operating entities and, potentially, recover proceeds from the BBFC and former employee legal matters and collect loans due from certain former employees. If the company, instead, pursued *any* bankruptcy strategy, competitors would have seized on the word *bankruptcy* and used it to solicit our employees, customers, and key vendors.

This wasn't difficult to understand. Hell, it was a two-paragraph strategy. Instead, the board played a game of chicken with the buyers for the hotel bookings business and the hockey division and underestimated the risks associated with a potential bankruptcy process. The buyers walked away, a bankruptcy petition was filed by angry creditors and accepting bankruptcy was the only option due to the customer deposit liabilities.

Word leaked out - The BBFC CEO had consistently told his team that the division was not at risk of a bankruptcy, whatsoever. Even though, several of the potential strategies being considered by the board *did* include BBFC being part of a Chapter 11 reorganization. When the BBFC staff began to hear about the creditor-petitioned Chapter 7, the team lost its trust in their CEO. Key staff started to leave... and they left quickly. With BBFC customers already on the edge because of the DOJ investigation, rumors swirling about criminal indictments, and competitors further embellishing the negative circumstances, it wouldn't take much. It only took a few respected regional directors and coaches to depart, to push the division over the edge.

In a matter of days, the BBFC CEO adjusted his forward revenue projections down dramatically. In my opinion, his projections were far too optimistic to begin with in light of the uncertainty of COVID-19. Regardless, his new lack of confidence in a viable, near-term business model caused the board to pull the plug. Their indecisiveness bit them in the ass. They couldn't have played this out more poorly if they tried - they had turned down several offers, allowed creditors to a petition bankruptcy and, as a result, scared away the key staff. The board advised Epic's attorneys to notify the court that the company would accept the Chapter 7 petition in Massachusetts.

All of our employees would be terminated immediately, and our customers would be classified as unsecured creditors.

Unbelievable.

During a global pandemic, when fifty million people were out of work, this company should have survived, hunkered down and emerged stronger when live sporting events could resume. Instead, the residual effects of greed and corruption, coupled with one bad decision after another put a dagger in the company, our customers and our employees.

The company would be managed by a court appointed trustee who would liquidate the assets. Two problems with the process - 1) the assets had lost most of their value and any remaining value was eroding each day that passed; and 2) the trustee was likely overwhelmed with other bankruptcies due to COVID-19, so the process would take months, if not years. It was unlikely there would be any real value leftover for the unsecured creditors. Just like that, it was over.

It had been over 100 days since we all began working from home. We had all been blindsided by the pandemic. We were witnessing unfathomable, rising death tolls everyday with no clear visibility to a healthy and safe future. Our economy was shut down and our country divided. As I wrote this book, much of what I had always thought was safe and predictable in our world was now in question.

Oddly enough, COVID-19 may have *saved* my life. It was the pandemic that forced me to stay home and, ultimately, resign from my position at Epic.

Exercise and meditation had become an essential part of my day - I spent more time with my family, I was learning to be present. While my Parkinson's symptoms continue to progress, my commitment to wellness and time with my family had been renewed. I had also started to reconstruct my life and find acceptance. The past two years taught me more about the human condition than I could have ever imagined.

The morning fog was so thick that I couldn't see the southern tip of Nauset Beach. I could, however, hear the haunting, melancholy moans of the seals.... like children blowing across the tops of soda bottles. I couldn't feel the cold, but the water had to be bone chilling as it was still May.

I allowed myself to go under for a moment, the water filled my ears and numbed my senses.

Then, I surfaced, took a deep a breath and heard the sirens' song again. I stopped treading water, raised my toes to the surface and leaned my head back – I was floating. I felt weightless, no tremors, no pain. Peace.

I decided to trust the current and let it carry me...

EPILOGUE

I never intended to write a book.

In May of 2020, Epic entered bankruptcy and I felt defeated. Our team had dealt with so much adversity, it felt like every day we had taken body punches but had not given in. We had been making progress, turning the corner and then COVID-19 hit.

I felt like a failure, like I let down so many people. Team members stuck with us through extraordinary challenges and other great people had joined the company based on my vision, but we couldn't make it a reality.

I was physically and emotionally exhausted. My Parkinson's was continuing to progress, and my doctor continued to increase my dose of Carbidopa Levodopa to mask the symptoms. I was dealing with side effects like drowsiness and nausea. I was also taking heavy doses of Gabapentin to suppress nerve pain. Even with the medications, I was having difficulty walking more than fifty yards or so. I was struggling with what's called bradykinesia, which manifests itself in symptoms like slowness of movement, diminished fine motor coordination, difficulty walking, episodes of immobility, and difficulty getting up from a bed or chair. It simply takes longer to do everything. It is exhausting and, at times, demoralizing for me.

My Parkinson's was also causing rigidity – my muscles had become stiff and inflexible and I was often dealing with severe muscle cramps. My hands didn't work like they use to – buttoning my shirt and tying my shoes was becoming difficult. I was worried about how my wife and kids were dealing with seeing me like this. Golf had always been one of my primary hobbies and a distraction from work, but I couldn't play anymore. As a result, my social activities had pretty much stopped.

Behind the scenes, I continued to work to support the Department of Justice with its criminal investigation. The work was tiring and stressful – it also created stress on my family. Threats had been made against me in emails and on social media, fabricated allegations of sexual assault levied against me, and, likely not a coincidence, but someone had even tried to break into our home. We had a series of anonymous packages sent to our house that took the stress and tension to another level, only to find out it was a misguided prank by one of the partners with our lead investor.

My oldest son was about to graduate from Dartmouth College – a great accomplishment but also an indicator of how fast life was moving and how much I had missed, bogged down in work. My other two children were living with us and had just finished their semester studying online due to COVID - that wasn't fair to them, they deserved to experience college as it was meant to be. Christine was wrapping up her school year, teaching fifth graders via Zoom meetings.

Not only were we all in the throes of a global pandemic and an economic meltdown, but our federal government had failed to provide a clear and coordinated plan at this most critical time. To the contrary, the President was actually executing a divisive political strategy. Political and social unrest was now the norm. Nothing felt stable or predictable.

As a husband and father, I made the decision that our family needed a change of scenery and time together during this most unusual time. Not exactly an easy decision when your company just went into bankruptcy. We decided to spend the next several months in Chatham, Massachusetts on Cape Cod. We had spent a couple of weeks each summer in Chatham for the over fifteen years or so, but never for such an extended time. Chatham, and the surrounding area, is, without question, my favorite place on earth. It is located at the elbow of Cape Cod with one side of town facing south along Nantucket Sound and the other side facing due east to the Atlantic along the National Seashore.

Our children had grown up looking forward to their time on the Cape each summer - getting breakfast at Chatham Cookware, swimming to the raft at Oyster Pond, and the frequent Candy Manor visits. At night, we would often go to Where the Sidewalk Ends Bookstore and then head down to Lighthouse Beach. The kids would toss around a tennis ball while watch seals gliding in and out of the harbor. The pace was slow and life was simple on the Cape.

Knowing that our summer tradition of spending time in Chatham had created such pure and lasting memories for my family, I thought hunkering down there may stir those memories. I had hoped it would allow all of us to refresh, recharge and find comfort and optimism during a time filled with such uncertainty. We weren't looking to hide, but rather reflect and face these challenges from a beautiful setting and with clearer minds. I am so glad that we did.

We packed a U-Haul with paddle boards, a weight bench, our Peloton, tennis racquets, baseball gear for my middle son, and beach chairs. I drove the van and the rest of the family met me down there in their cars with our two golden retrievers. We set up in North Chatham.

My daily routine became rising early, getting a sweat on the Peloton, ten or fifteen minutes of app-guided meditation, an outside shower and then I would head down to Cotchpinicut, Scatteree or Cow Yard beaches before anyone else was up at home.

In late May, it was still a bit cold and the weather can be unpredictable on the Cape, but I went to the beach regardless of the weather, short of heavy rain. I would go even if it was a light drizzle. Early morning on the beach in Chatham is a borderline religious experience; the sun rising, morning fog burning off, boaters heading out for a day on the water and the cadence of the waves hitting the beach. This was exactly what I was looking for. We had also brought with us about a dozen books. I read a couple of thrillers, some non-fiction ranging from the troubles in Northern Ireland to summer baseball on the Cape, as well as a couple of political pieces. Occasionally, I would throw in my Air Pods and listen to a podcast instead of reading.

As a family, we exercised, swam, walked the dogs, cooked on the grill, did the occasional takeout and played scrabble at night after dinner. I could feel the stress, grind and disappointment of the past couple of years slowly subsiding. I also was starting to feel slightly more energized. It was taking longer than I had expected.

Early one morning I was sitting at Scatteree beach, which is a small neighborhood beach that looks north and east over the backside of the southern tip of Nauset Beach. I could see and hear the high-pitched wailing of the seals laying in large packs on the flats behind Nauset. There was no wind and the sky was deep blue. It was one of those mornings on the Cape that inspire people. Scatteree sits at the top of Pleasant Bay, so the tide rushes out aggressively. The tide was still heading out.

When there was an ebb current, I would walk about fifty yards along the beach to the west, enter the water and let the outbound tide float me back to my chair – I did it a couple times and felt like a child again.

I returned to my chair, toweled off and sat back down. Without thinking, I opened my iPad and decided to outline some of my recent challenges - both personal and professional. I didn't have a plan, I just started writing. Over the next eight weeks, instead of reading every morning, I wrote. I found it therapeutic and, as the book began to take shape, I enjoyed the exercise of weaving together the different episodes and story lines. Perhaps I had found a new hobby. Perhaps I had been given a second chance.

I wanted people interested in business, particularly business ethics, to hear this story and, hopefully, learn from it.

I would also hope that this story encourages people to remain true to their values, live in the moment and, always, have faith.

ACKNOWLEDGMENTS

First and foremost, thank you to everyone who helped me through the most difficult parts of this story. There are too many of you to list here, but I want you to know that I owe each of you more than you can imagine.

Some of you helped by reading drafts and providing edits - I now have a full appreciation for the tedious task of editing.

Some of you checked in from time-to-time, asking how the book was coming along while others called me *just to check in.* I am amazed at how often those impromptu calls came when I needed them the most.

I would also like to express my gratitude to the following individuals: Kathy and Mike Flanagan, Eileen and Phil Griffin, Jane Martellino, Laura McLaughlin, Steve Joyce, Dr. Gary and Ellen L'Europa, Dr. Joseph Friedman, Kate Lentz, Gary Goldberg, Eric Orme and David Macias. All of you provided encouragement in your own way – thank you.

Barry Pollack, Jonathan Young, and Richard Small – at times, it was your counsel and friendship that kept me going.

But, most of all: my family. Christine - thank you for your patience, eternal optimism and love. Riley, Georgia and Chase – you make me proud every day, you are my greatest legacy. Looking forward to the Cape next summer.

CASE STUDY / DISCUSSION TOPICS

- Evaluating an opportunity
  - Ask your questions, get your answers or walk away
  - Optimism, embellishment or outright lies?

- Remaining objective; *If it doesn't make sense...*

- Navigating the investment process
    - Realistic growth strategies
    - Financial, legal and technology due diligence
    - Human capital assessment
        - Management fit
        - Change readiness
        - Organization structure
    - Capital structures & proper corporate governance
        - The value of board diversity

- Corporate culture
    - Human resource strategies
        - Assessing your people
        - Change readiness & aptitudes
        - The role of diversity, equity & inclusion
        - Alignment with stakeholders
        - Communication
    - Striking the right balance – *work hard & do good*
    - Beware of the cult leader
    - Run away from hypocrites

- The *Five Best Friends*
    - Business ethics
    - Strategic decision-making
    - Appropriate organizational structures
    - Financial strength (liquidity and minimal leverage)
    - Timely and accurate reporting

- The almighty financial statement audit
    - The culture must embrace oversight
    - Internal controls
    - Systems and processes
    - Timely and accurate financial reporting
    - Related parties and conflicts of interest

- The importance of legal counsel
  - In good times and in bad

- Internal investigations and forensic accounting
  - Let's hope you don't need these skills

Printed in Great Britain
by Amazon